Visual Basic
The Peter Norton Programming Series

Who This Book Is For

Introductory for intermediate Windows programmers who want to develop and extend their programming expertise and add new performance to their programs.

What's Inside

- More than 100 ready-to-run programs
- Expert hints, tips, and ideas designed to increase program speed and power
- A special learn-by-doing, task-oriented approach to programming that shows code in action in a direct, highly readable style

About the Peter Norton Microcomputer Libraries from Brady Publishing

All of the volumes in the Peter Norton Libraries, written in collaboration with The Peter Norton Computing Group, provide clear, in-depth discussions of the latest developments in computer hardware, operating systems, and programming. Fully tested and rigorously reviewed, these libraries deserve a special place on your bookshelf. These libraries are comprised of two series:

The Peter Norton Hardware Library gives you an insider's grasp of your computer and the way it works. Included are such best-selling classics as *Inside the IBM PC, Inside the Apple Macintosh,* and *The Hard Disk Companion.*

The Peter Norton Programming Library focuses on creating programs that work right away and offers the best tips and techniques in the industry. It includes *Advanced BASIC, Advanced Assembly Language, C++ Programming, QBasic Programming, Advanced DOS,* and more.

Visual Basic

—

Steven Holzner
and
The Peter Norton Computing Group

Brady Publishing

New York   London   Toronto   Sydney   Singapore   Tokyo

Brady Publishing

A Divison of Simon & Schuster, Inc.
15 Columbus Circle
New York, NY 10023

Manufactured in the United States of America
10 9 8 7 6 5 4 3 2

Library of Congress Cataloging-in-Publication Data

Holzner, Steven.
    Visual Basic / Steven Holzner. Peter Norton Computing Group.
       p. cm.
    Includes index.
    1. Visual basic (Computer science)   I. Peter Norton Computing Group.
    II. Title.
QA76.65.H65   1991
006.6'6–dc20   91-224933
                                                   CIP

ISBN 0-13-489295-x

Pages produced by Microtext Publications using Ventura Publisher. Pages
imposed electronically using ImpoStrip. Cover designed using Quark Express.

Contents

CHAPTER 2

Using Buttons and Textboxes   37

CHAPTER 3

Menus   81

CHAPTER 4

Using Dialog Boxes   129

CHAPTER 5

What about Files?

CHAPTER 6

Graphics

CHAPTER 7

The Mouse and a Mouse-driven Paint Program

CHAPTER 8

Advanced Data Handling and Sorting in Visual Basic   307

CHAPTER 9

Error Handling and Debugging   355

CHAPTER 10

Interfacing to Other Windows Applications   399

Limits of Liability and Disclaimer of Warranty

Trademarks

Introduction

Why Visual Basic?

Visual Basic is the stuff of programmers' dreams, especially Windows programmers. If you've done any Windows programming, then you know what it can be like: difficult, time consuming, and hard to debug. Just to get started with the Microsoft Windows Software Development Kit (SDK) takes hours of reading and absorbing. Writing the actual code usually takes many more hours, including time for experimentation and fixing problems. Graphical User Interfaces — GUIs — may definitely be the wave of the future, but they can make life very tough for the programmer.

Even the most elementary Windows application, which might do nothing more than pop an "About" window on the screen, telling you who programmed it, takes about five pages of code and four separate files. The enormous complexity of writing an actual, useful application slows development time down to a snail's pace. To make matters worse, Windows programming tools were (until now) very far from complete — and there are times that the Windows Software Development Kit can be as much a hindrance as a help.

Visual Basic changes this picture entirely. It adds the programming tools that have been lacking for so long in Windows. Working with it for the first time, experienced Windows programmers can hardly believe their eyes. The ideas are simple: If you want a window of a certain size, you simply draw it that size. If you want a text box at a particular point in your window, simply select the correct tool and draw it there. That is, Visual Basic does what programs excel at — it handles the details for you. That's useful because, at last, the aid of the computer itself is being enlisted in the Windows programming process. You can draw just about anything anywhere you need it: list boxes, buttons, combo boxes — whatever you want. When you're done, you write a few (often a very few lines) lines of Basic code to make things work, and Visual Basic creates the working .Exe file for you. From a Windows programmer's point of view, this package is nothing short of astonishing.

Our Approach

This is a book for soon-to-be Windows programmers, so we're going to spend a lot of time seeing Visual Basic at work. In other words, we're going to see what the software is capable of — and to do that, we'll have plenty of examples, which is always the best way to learn about software. We'll start almost at once in Chapter 1, getting a window on the screen and working with it. As the book progresses, we'll see many other examples: an alarm clock, a text editor, a database program, a paint program, calculators, and many others.

In addition, as the name Visual Basic itself implies, we'll spend some time looking at windows on the screen and learning about what makes them tick. This book is unlike other programming books that you might have read in that much of what we'll cover has to do with using Visual Basic to design our software — visually — instead of working through long programs. If you're new to Windows programming, you'll also find that the code we develop is different from what you might expect; in particular, Windows programs are *event driven*, which means that our code will be divided up into many small sections to handle specific events, rather than the linear, continuous programs that you might be used to. This can take some getting used to. But, after a while, thinking in terms of Windows events like mouse clicks or key presses comes naturally. We'll see more about this in Chapter 1.

In a nutshell, then, our approach is the practical approach: task and example oriented, without a great deal of unnecessary theory. In this book, we'll put Visual Basic to work for us.

What's in This Book

Visual Basic is a tremendous toolbox of programming resources. We'll work our way up, from the most basic examples to the most polished. In the beginning of the book, we'll get the essentials down. We'll follow the natural course of Windows programming development — starting with just a blank window, we'll embellish it a little with color and graphics, and we'll start to add buttons and text boxes — what Visual Basic calls controls. When we become comfortable with the idea of controls, we'll add dialog boxes, messages boxes, and then menus. As we work our way through the book, we'll get into the kinds of topics that real Windows applications deal with: the clipboard, bitmaps and icons, and error handling. We'll even have a chapter on debugging and one on dynamic data exchange, which will allow us to communicate with other Windows applications like Microsoft Excel and Word for Windows.

As mentioned above, our orientation will be on seeing our programs work, at getting functioning results. To do that, however, we'll have to understand what we're doing. We'll take the time to understand all the concepts involved in Visual Basic — concepts like forms and methods and projects and modules. And we'll see that Visual Basic is truly object oriented (you may have heard of object-oriented programming already), which means that we'll take the time to understand objects before working with them.

For that reason, part of the first chapter will get us started by exploring the concepts we'll need. We'll begin with fundamental Windows concepts, like windows and buttons, and then we'll work through some Windows programming concepts. Finally, we'll get an introduction to the essential Visual Basic programming concepts as well. This will form the foundation of all we do in the book, so we'll make sure that we get all the basic ideas down before continuing.

From then on, our coverage will be task oriented as much as possible. Most of the successive chapters are purposely designed to cover one specific type of Visual Basic control — for example, buttons, listboxes, combo boxes, dialog boxes, or menus. In this way, we'll build our expertise by building our windows — piece by piece, steadily adding more and more power to our Windows applications. This will allow us to handle the complexities that might arise in a systematic, gradual way.

After we build and design our applications, we'll go behind the scenes, toward adding power to the programming part of our applications (as opposed to the I/O part, which is handled by menus and buttons). We'll investigate how to work with files, as well as passing data in and out of the Windows clipboard. Then, we'll continue with other, more advanced concepts such as using icons, as well as selecting custom mouse cursors.

All this makes for quite an ambitious plan — learning how to design and put to work serious Windows applications with a minimum of trouble. Normally, this would mean a book full of 10- or 20-page programs as well as a great deal of work. However, we'll see that Visual Basic is a whole different story. Getting our Windows programs working — and producing real results — will largely be a matter of simply designing what we want on the screen and then letting Visual Basic handle the details.

What You'll Need

To read this book profitably, you'll need to have some knowledge of Basic. However, you won't need much; the programming here is generally not very advanced, and we'll introduce new Basic constructions as we need them. Even so, you should be familiar with Basic (such as BASICA or QuickBASIC) to the point of being able to write your own simple programs in it. If you find yourself lost in the first chapter, you should probably become familiar with Basic before continuing. The best Basic to review is Microsoft QuickBASIC because, as far as straight programming goes, Visual Basic is a subset of QuickBASIC (however, as we'll see later, Visual Basic does not support a number of QuickBASIC statements).

In addition, you'll need Windows, Version 3.0 or later, since Visual Basic requires it. There's nothing special here, just the normal Win.Exe program — but please note that you should be a Windows *user* before becoming a Windows *programmer*. That is, if you don't know how to use Windows and aren't used to the customary feel of Windows applications, you should take some time to learn before working on programs. Windows users expect their applications to conform to Windows' conventions pretty closely, and the best way to know what's expected is by being a Windows user yourself.

NOTE You'll need a mouse (or other pointing device) for the work we'll do in this book. While Windows applications are supposed to run with either the mouse or the keyboard, it's very difficult to do real work without a mouse — and it's almost certainly impossible to program in Visual Basic without one. That is, casual Windows users may be able to get along without a mouse. But, for the more serious Visual Basic programmer, the mouse is an essential tool.

Also, if you want to follow the examples in Chapter 10, where we link to other Windows applications, you will need Microsoft Excel or Word for Windows. Finally, of course, you'll need Visual Basic itself. Any version will do. If you haven't installed it yet, just run the Setup program under Windows as explained in the Visual Basic documentation. Besides Windows, Visual Basic itself is all the software we need — you'll be able to enter programs directly without the assistance of a word processor or text editor.

That's it. We're ready to begin. Our first task will be to get a simple window on the screen as soon as possible. But, to do that, we'll need to understand a few things about Windows programming and about Visual Basic. Let's dig in immediately with Chapter 1.

Our First Windows

Welcome to Visual Basic, easily one of the most exciting software packages in the PC marketplace, and one of the components of a revolution in Windows programming. This powerful package is one of the new generation of programming tools that are beginning to open up Windows programming as never before. No longer will it take a great deal of patience, experience, and expensive software to produce valuable Windows applications. Under Visual Basic (and programs like it), developing Windows programs will become easier than ever. In this chapter, we'll put together our first Visual Basic programs, and these programs will run under Windows 3.x and above. We'll see that it's easier than you might expect to do this because Visual Basic handles most of the details for us.

You can think of Visual Basic as an immense box of tools and resources waiting for us to use it. To use these tools and resources effectively, however, we'll need to understand them. In other words, we'll have to know what's available — and all about the environment in which it's available — before we can take advantage of what Visual Basic has to offer us.

Accordingly, we'll begin our tour of Visual Basic by examining the environment in which we will work — Windows itself. Next, we'll see how Visual Basic works in this environment and what tools it offers us to manipulate that environment. Then, when we're ready, we'll put Visual Basic to work and get some results. Let's begin now by examining our host operating environment, Windows itself.

About Windows

Many people believe that Graphical User Interfaces — GUIs — are the wave of the future in microcomputing, and they could be right. Certainly Windows 3.0 has been one of the best-selling software packages in history (500,000 copies in its first six weeks; 3,000,000 in its first nine months). In all significant ways, Windows is a full operating environment by itself.

Windows is very different from DOS in many ways. One of the most fundamental differences is that Windows is a Graphical User Interface, which introduces many new concepts. One of the primary ideas here is that most of the available options are presented to the user at once, in the form of objects on the screen, much like tools, ready to be used. The utility of this simple approach is surprising — rather than remembering complex techniques and keywords, a user can simply select the correct tool for the task at hand and begin work. In this way, graphical interfaces fulfill much of the promise of computers as endlessly adaptable tools. Let's take a look at some of the background of this operating environment.

A Brief Windows History

Microsoft actually started working on Windows in 1983, only two years after the PC had appeared. However, the original version, Windows 1.01, didn't actually ship until 1985. This version was supposed to run on the standard machine of that time: an IBM PC with two 360K diskette drives, 256K, and an 8088. The display was automatically tiled; that is, the windows were arranged to cover the whole screen, and it looked less than impressive.

The next major version, Windows 2, came out two years later. For the first time, windows could overlap on the screen. However, Windows 2 could only run in 80x86 real mode, which meant that it was limited to a total of one megabyte of memory. For a while, Windows even split into Windows 286 and Windows 386 to take advantage of the capabilities of the (then new) 80386 chip. Progress had been made, but it was clear that much more was still needed.

Finally, in May of 1990, Microsoft introduced Windows 3.0. The look and feel of Windows 3.0 was a great improvement over its ancestors, and it featured proportional fonts, which made displays look more refined. Version 3.0 also has better support for DOS programs, and many users are starting to use Windows as the primary operating environment for the PC.

The MS-DOS Executive of earlier versions was replaced by a trinity of windows that manage Windows: the *Program Manager*, the *Task List*, and the *File Manager*. Because we're more interested in the programming aspects of Windows, however, we won't review how this user interface works. Instead, let's look behind the scenes.

From a programming point of view, one of the most important features of Windows 3.0 is that it can support extended memory — up to 16 megabytes of RAM. And, in its 386-enhanced mode, Windows uses the built-in virtual memory (that is, storing sections of memory temporarily on disk) capabilities of the 80386 to give programmers access to up to four times the amount of actual installed memory. In a machine that has 16 megabytes, then, Windows can actually provide 64 megabytes. The removal of memory restrictions has always been one of the advantages of OS/2, but now more and more programmers are coming back to Windows. With Windows 3.0, Windows had at last arrived.

The Parts of a Window

A typical Windows 3.0 window appears in Figure 1-1, and you should be familiar with its parts before starting to program Windows applications. In fact, if you are not a Windows user, then you should spend time with Windows before continuing. As we'll see below, it's important to know what the user expects from a Windows application before writing one.

Before starting to program, then, let's spend a little time reviewing Windows terminology ourselves. This will help us later in the book. At the upper left of the window in Figure 1-1 is a system menu box, which, when selected, displays a menu that typically allows the user to move the window, close it, or minimize it. At the top center is the title or caption bar (Visual Basic refers to the text as the window's caption, not its title), and this provides an easy way of labeling an application.

To the right of to the title bar are the minimize and maximize boxes, which allow the user to reduce the window to an icon (called an application's *iconic*

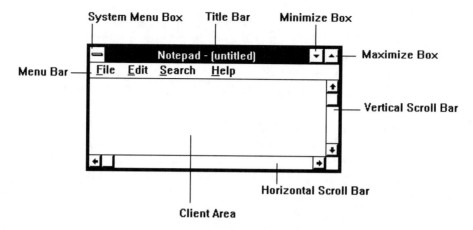

Figure 1-1. A Windows 3.0 Window

state), or expand it fully, usually to the whole screen. Under the title bar is usually a menu bar offering the currently available menu options for the application. In almost every stand-alone application, there will be a menu bar with at least one menu item in it: the File menu. This is the menu that usually offers the Exit item at the bottom, as shown in Figure 1-2.

NOTE The Exit item is the usual way for users to leave an application, so if your application supports file handling, you should include the Exit item at the bottom of your File menu.

Under the menu bar is the *client area*. In fact, the client area makes up the whole of a window under the menu bar except for the borders and scroll bars (it's the area that the window is designed to display). This is our drawing area, the area we will work with directly in Visual Basic; that is, this is the part of the window on which we'll place buttons, list boxes, text boxes, and the other parts of our programs.

To the right to the client area is a vertical scroll bar, which is a common part of a window that displays text. If there is too much text to fit in the window at once, scroll bars let you look at some subsection of the whole, moving around in the document. (By the way, the small square that moves up and down and which you use to manipulate your position in the scroll bar is called a *thumb.*)

On the bottom of the window is another scroll bar, a horizontal scroll bar, which scrolls the text in the client area horizontally. Everything in the window

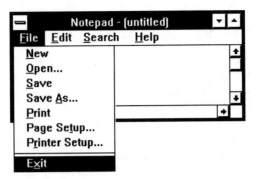

Figure 1-2. A Windows 3.0 Window with Menu

but the client area is called the non-client area; even the border is part of the non-client area. Visual Basic will be responsible for maintaining the non-client area of the window, and we'll be responsible for the client area.

Preserving the Feel of Windows

As mentioned, before programming in Visual Basic, you should be very familiar with the way the user expects Windows programs to work and feel. In particular, you should be at home with the language of mouse clicks and double-clicks, and anticipating what the user might expect from your application.

For example, the fact that the File menu usually has an Exit item, and that item — if present — is always last, is part of the Windows interface you'll be programming in. There are many other aspects of the way users expect Windows applications to work that you should be familiar with before producing applications yourself. In other words, there is a large number of Windows conventions that you should adhere to. Although we'll discuss these conventions as we reach the appropriate topics, there's no substitute for working with existing Windows applications to get the correct feel for the Windows interface.

After a while, these conventions become quite automatic. For instance, in file list boxes (where the program is showing you which files are available to be opened), one click of the mouse should highlight a filename (called *selecting*), and two clicks should open the file (called *choosing*). On the other hand, it is also supposed to be possible to use Windows without a mouse at all — just with the keyboard — so you must provide keyboard support at the same time (in this case, the user would use the tab key to move to the correct box, the arrow keys to highlight a filename, and the <Enter> key to choose it).

> **NOTE** For the purposes of program design in this book, we are assuming that you have a mouse or other pointing device to go along with Visual Basic. Although it is possible to use Windows *applications* without a mouse, Windows *programmers* (or even experienced Windows users) are severely hampered without one, seriously crippling their productivity.

There are other conventions that Windows users expect. If there's some object that can be moved around the screen, users expect to be able to drag it with the mouse. They expect accelerator keys in menus, system menus that let them close a window, and windows that can be moved, resized, or minimized. As mentioned, the best way to know what will be expected of your program is to work with existing Windows applications.

About Windows Programming

Now let's take a look at how one programs applications for Windows, and what makes it different from programming under DOS. To start, DOS programs are written sequentially; that is, one event follows the other. In a DOS program, control goes down the list of statements, more or less in the order that the programmer designed. For example, this is the way an introductory program from a Basic book might look:

```
WHILE INKEY$ = "": WEND
PRINT "Hello from Basic."
```

In the first line, we're simply waiting until the user presses a key. When they do, control goes sequentially to the next line, and the message "Hello from Basic." appears on the screen. If there were more statements, control would continue on with them, looping and progressing in the way that the programmer designed it to work. However, Windows is different.

Windows Events

An application under Windows typically presents all possible options (in the form of visual objects) on the screen for the user to select for themselves. In this way, it represents an entirely new kind of programming — *event*-driven, and object-oriented, programming. That is to say, the programmer is no

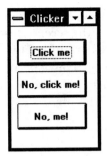

Figure 1-3. Clicker Window

longer completely responsible for the flow of the program. Rather, the user is. The user selects among all the options presented to them, and it is up to the program to respond correctly. For example, there may be three buttons on a window, as shown in Figure 1-3. Clearly, we can't just write our program assuming that the user is going to push them in some sequence.

Instead, we'll have to write separate code for each button. That's going to be the case in general, and it will have significant consequences for us in this book. Instead of monolithic programs that you can read from beginning to end, our code will necessarily be divided up into smaller sections, one such section for one kind of event. For example, we may add a text box to the window, in which we want the message "Hello from Visual Basic." to appear when the user clicks the button marked Click Me. In that case, our program might look like this:

```
Sub ClickMe_Click ()
    Message.text = "Hello from Visual Basic."
End Sub
```

This code is specifically designed to handle one type of event — clicking on the button marked Click Me. Our programs will typically be collections of code sections like this, one after the other. That's how event driven programming works: We'll largely be designing our code around the interface; that is, around the way we've set up the window, at least in the early part of this book. Our programs won't have "modes," the way an editor can have modes (e.g., insert mode, marking mode, and so on); instead, all the options available at one time will be represented on the screen, ready to be used. We'll see how this works soon.

Besides being event driven, Windows programming is also *object oriented.* That is easy enough to see on the screen: Just pick up an object such as an icon or paintbrush and move it around. This corresponds closely to what's called *object-oriented programming.* This type of programming breaks a program up into discrete objects, each of which has its own code and data associated with it. In this way, each of the objects can be somewhat independent from the others.

Using object-oriented programming is a natural for event-driven software because it breaks the program up into discrete, modular objects. It turns out that that's the way we'll be treating our windows and all the buttons, text boxes, and so on that we put in them — as objects. Each of these objects can have both data and code associated with them, as we'll see. You may have heard of object-oriented programming, and you may suspect that it's difficult to implement, but it turns out that Visual Basic takes care of all of the details for us. In fact, let's look into that process in Visual Basic next. Now that we've gotten our background down, we're ready to look at the programming tools we'll be using in this book.

About Visual Basic Programming

Under Windows, the user is king, and, until recently, the programmer paid the price. Programming Windows was often an excruciating task — until now. Now, the programmer is finally benefitting from some of the same ease of application that the user has enjoyed for so long under Windows. Now, the computer itself is being enlisted as an aid for the programmer, not just for the user.

This is a revolutionary step, and a welcome one. If you've programmed for Windows before, you'll love the way this package works. On the other hand, if you've never created actual Windows applications before, then you'll find that this kind of programming is like nothing you've ever seen before. In the same sense that Windows may be thought of as a new operating environment, Visual Basic is the new BASICA or GW-BASIC.

There are three major steps to writing an application in Visual Basic, and we'll follow them throughout this book. Here they are:

- Draw the window(s) you want
- Customize the properties of buttons, text boxes, and so on
- Write the code for the associated events

The first step — drawing the window you want, complete with buttons and menus — is where Visual Basic really shines. Before, it was a tedious process to design the appearance of windows, where the buttons would go, how large they would be and all types of other considerations. Adding or removing features was also very difficult. Under Visual Basic, however, this whole process has become extraordinarily easy. Visual Basic allows us to simply draw — just like a paint program — the window(s) we want, as well as all the buttons, boxes, and labels we want. In other words, we'll see the actual appearance of our application at design-time.

Adding or removing buttons or boxes works just as it would in a paint program, as we'll see; there's no difficult programming involved at all. The next step involves customizing the properties of what we've drawn; for example, we might give a window or button a certain caption, or change its color (or even whether or not it's visible). Finally, we write the code that responds to the events we consider significant. That's how it works in outline; now let's see it in practice.

Our First Window

Let's put together a one-window application that simply has one button and one text box. When the user clicks or chooses the button, the words "Welcome to Visual Basic." should appear in the text box, as shown in Figure 1-4.

Start programming by starting Visual Basic under Windows. The Visual Basic display appears in Figure 1-5. As with any new software, there are new terms and concepts to learn here. (In fact, there are only about 10 major terms to learn in Visual Basic.) Let's work through the parts of the Visual Basic display.

The Form

To begin, there is a window that appears in the center of the screen labeled **Form1**. This is the window that we're designing. Visual Basic refers to windows that you customize as *forms*. As you can see, the form we begin with has the appearance of a normal window. In fact, this is the way our window will look when the application we're writing starts. Notice that Form1 already has a system menu box and a title bar, both minimize and maximize boxes, a border, and a client area.

As you can see, the client area is filled with dots at regular intervals. These dots form a grid that will help us to align buttons and boxes when we're designing

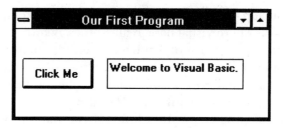

Figure 1-4. Our First Program

our window (and they'll disappear at run-time). In fact, our window is already viable as it stands. As a program, it will work, but it won't do much. If we tell Visual Basic to run this program, this window, labeled **Form1**, will appear on the screen. The parts of the window that you already see — including the system menu, maximize, and minimize boxes — will all be active. This is part of what Visual Basic provides for us. Let's give this a shot. Move up now to the menu bar in the Visual Basic display (we'll cover the different menus in this menu bar soon), and select the Run menu. This menu appears in Figure 1-6.

Choose the Start option in this menu. When you do, the screen changes, and **Form1** appears just like a normal window, as in Figure 1-7.

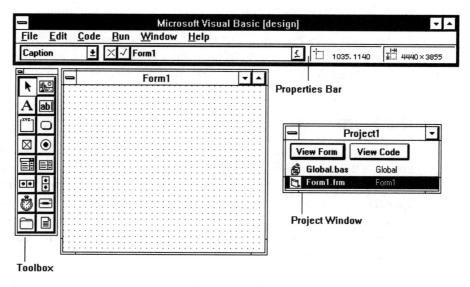

Figure 1-5. The Visual Basic Display

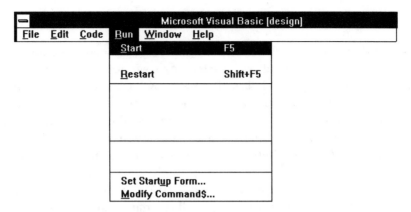

Figure 1-6. Visual Basic's Run Menu

Already, our program is running although it's not very spectacular. You can move the window **Form1** around the screen, and resize it just like a normal window. The minimize and maximize buttons work as you would expect, minimizing **Form1** down to an icon or expanding it so that it takes up the whole page. In addition, note that the grid of dots in the window that was present when we started Visual Basic is now gone. These dots are present only at design-time, to help us align objects on the window (in fact, we can remove the grid altogether with the Grid Settings... menu item in the Edit menu). End the program now by opening the system box in the window we've designed and selecting the Close option, or by selecting the End option in Visual Basic's Run menu.

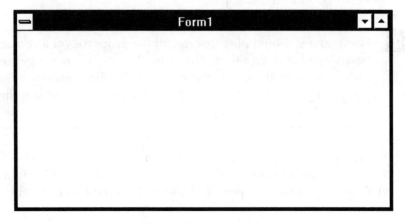

Figure 1-7. Form1 Running

Properties

The window — that is, the form — that we've been designing so far has been pretty plain. So far, all we have is a single window named **Form1**; now let's start customizing it. Visual Basic treats windows under design — forms — as well as boxes and buttons as *objects*, and each different type of object can have certain *properties*. For example, our object named **Form1** has properties associated with it that are normal for a window, such as the title or caption, color, visibility (that is, whether or not it is visible on the screen), a certain screen position, and so on. A text box might have a different set of properties, including, for example, what text is currently displayed in it. In other words, an object's properties represent all the data that is normally associated with that object.

Let's change the caption property of **Form1** so that the caption reads "Our First Program" instead of **Form1**. To do that, we have to use the *property bar* on the screen, which is the bar under Visual Basic's menu bar (see Figure 1-5; note that the property bar is separate from the menu bar — for example, the property bar is only present when we're designing our programs, not when we're running them).

As we work through the design process, we'll introduce more and more objects on the screen, objects such as buttons, list boxes, radio buttons, and labels. Each of these objects has a specific set of properties; that is, data that can be associated with them. As we work on the different objects, the property bar will let us change the properties of the object we're working on. For example, we're working on **Form1** now, so the property bar holds the properties connected with this object.

NOTE   However, we should note that not all the properties of a certain object may be available at design-time. For example, one of the properties associated with a filename list box is the name of the file currently selected, but, at design-time, no file is selected, so that property will not appear in the property bar for us to work on.

Currently, the property bar reads **Caption** and **Form1**. This is the first property associated with this window; that is, the caption of this window is **Form1**. If we move up to the property bar now and open the left-hand list box in it (by

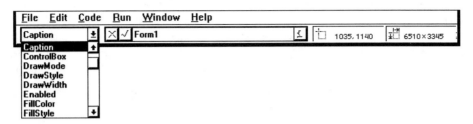

Figure 1-8. The Property Bar

clicking on the down arrow to the right of the caption), we see an entire list of properties connected with this window, as in Figure 1-8.

We'll explore these options more thoroughly later. Just make sure **Caption** is selected for now and appears in the property bar. The second box in the property bar gives the current value of the selected property, which is **Form1**. We can change that now simply by selecting or clicking on that text box and overwriting the text there to read "Our First Program." As you do, note that the caption of the window itself changes to read the same thing. At this point, we've renamed our window as Our First Program, which means that running it will produce that caption in the caption bar. That's fine as far as it goes, and we'll see that you can also change a window's color, but let's press on to more interesting topics now as we add a text box to our window.

Controls

So far, we've seen how to work on the elementary properties of a form. There are two types of objects in Visual Basic, however, both forms and *controls*. Controls refer to all the graphical objects that we can design and place on a form, such as list boxes, buttons, labels, and even timers (timers tell you how much time has elapsed, and they're represented graphically at design-time in Visual Basic). In other words, a control is any object that the user can manipulate that is not itself a window. These terms are important. A form is the window we're designing and creating, a control is used for I/O with the user, like boxes and buttons. Forms and controls together are called objects in Visual Basic because they are both treated like graphical objects. And objects have properties associated with them, which is the same as saying that an object has data associated with it.

NOTE If you're familiar with object-oriented programming, then you'll already know that objects such as these not only have data associated with them, but built-in procedures too, which can be used to, say, move a button around the window. In C++, these object-connected procedures are called member functions; in Pascal and Visual Basic they're called methods, and we'll meet them soon.

Let's see an example of a control. For example, we can add a text box to our first window. To do that, we can use the Visual Basic toolbox.

The Toolbox

Since this is Visual Basic, we're going to draw the controls we want right on the form we're designing. This process works much like it does under a paint program, where you select a drawing tool and then draw with it. Here, we select a control tool, and then paint controls with it. We do that by selecting a tool from the Visual Basic toolbox, which is shown in Figure 1-9.

The toolbox will play a big part in this book, because it allows us to draw all the controls we'll need. We want to draw a text box at this point, so select the text box tool — the second tool down on the right in Figure 1-9. There are two ways to draw controls in Visual Basic. The first way is to select a tool from the tool box (click on it once). When you do, the Visual Basic pointer changes

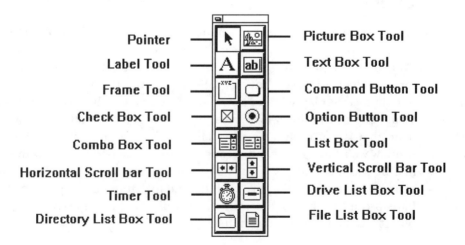

Figure 1-9. The Visual Basic Toolbox

from an arrow to a cross when you move over to a form under design. You can position the cross anywhere on the form, click once to anchor that end of the control (the top-left end), then move the pointer to the other end of the control (the bottom-left end), and click again. The control appears. The second method, which we'll use more often, is simply to double-click on the tool in the toolbox. When you do, the control you want appears in the center of the form, ready to be moved and shaped.

Our goal now is to create a text box: Double-click on the text box tool and a default-sized text box appears in the middle of the form, as shown in Figure 1-10.

Note that the property bar now displays "**CtlName**" and "**Text1**." The **CtlName** is the name of a control (**CtlName** is a contraction of Control Name), and it's the way we'll refer to it in our program. That is, the **CtlName** is the name of our control as far as Visual Basic is concerned. In this case, the default name for our text box is **Text1**. As you can also see, there are eight small black squares on the periphery of our new text box. These squares, called *sizing handles*, allow you to manipulate the size of the controls that you're designing. Using them, you can stretch a control in any of the eight directions. Also, you can move the control itself simply by clicking on it and dragging it.

Move the text box and resize the window until it corresponds roughly to Figure 1-11. Since the text box is selected, the property bar is ready to display

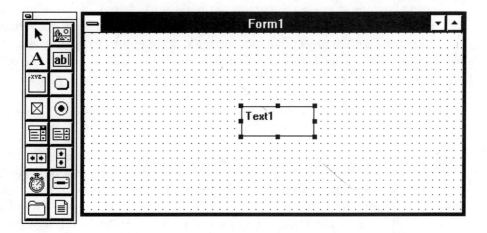

Figure 1-10. Default Text Box

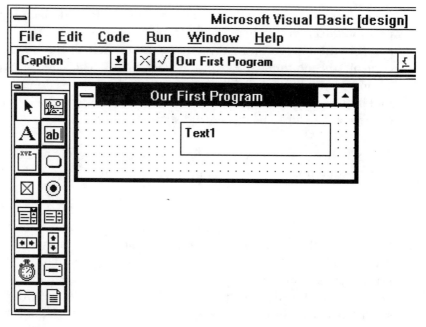

Figure 1-11. Text Box Moved

the properties of the text box that we can set. As mentioned above, not all properties associated with an object are available at design-time, but we'll find that many useful ones are.

Let's take a look at the properties (i.e., the data items) that we can set for our text box now. Click on the arrow to the right of the box in the properties bar marked **CtlName**, and a list appears, as in Figure 1-12. This list presents all the properties of an object that you can set at design-time. You can scroll through to see what's available. Some of these features are **BackColor** (the background color behind the text); **FontName**; **Left** and **Top** (the position of the top-left corner of the text box); and **Width** and **Height**. If you select a property such as **Width**, the current width of the text box appears in the middle box in the properties bar.

That's how it works. You select a property of the object you're dealing with first, and the current setting of the property appears in the middle box. The downward pointing arrow in the middle box opens up to display a list of all the possible options that you can set the current property to. In this way, you don't have to remember long lists of numbers or codes — just select an object, select

Place First Class
Postage Here
Post Office
Will Not Deliver
Without Postage

College Marketing Group
50 Cross Street
Winchester, MA 01890

ATT: **Cheryl Read**

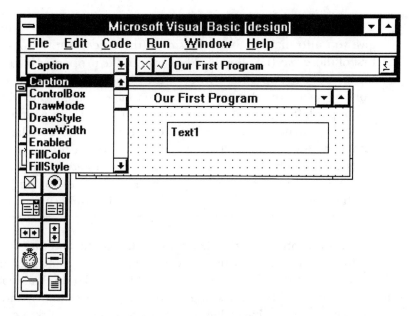

Figure 1-12. Properties List

a property in the leftmost box (from the list provided if you forget what properties are available), and then set the property as you want it to be when your program starts. In fact, if you do check the **Width** property, you may be surprised to find that your text box has a width of something like 2,295.

The obvious next question is 2,295 what? That is, what is the unit of measurement here? You might first assume that measurements on the screen would be in terms of pixels, the individual dots on the screen. Although they can be in pixels if you like (we'll get to this topic later), the default measuring system for a Windows application should apply to all possible display devices, not only to the screen. For example, a laser printer typically prints 300 dots to the inch, so we'd need some unit of measurement that's finer than that. Visual Basic uses *twips*, and there are 1,440 of them to the inch for the display on the corresponding device. We'll see more about such measurements later. In the meantime, we'll simply design our interface using the toolbox tools rather than concern ourselves with the actual location of controls on our forms. However, we might notice that we can change the **Width** property, like all the properties available at design-time, simply by editing the text in the middle box of the properties bar. For example, if you changed it to 1,440, you'd see your text box grow or shrink to 1,440 twips, or one inch wide.

TIP   The other two boxes in the properties bar (see Figure 1-5) automatically give you information about the size of the object you're working on. The first of these two (i.e., the third box over in the properties bar) indicate the location of the upper-left corner of the object you're working on. If you're working on a form, the upper-left corner measurements are with respect to the upper-left corner of the screen. If you're working with a control, the upper-left corner measurements are with respect to the client area (i.e., under the menu bar, excluding the scroll bars) of the present form. The units are the default units (in this case, twips). In addition, the second box (i.e., the rightmost box in the properties bar) gives you with height and width of the current object, also in the default numbering system, twips.

We can take advantage of this flexibility to change the text that appears in our text window. Right now, it simply reads Text1, which is not very interesting. Let's change it to read "Welcome to Visual Basic." To do that, make sure the text box is selected (i.e., the sizing handles appear around it), and then move up to the properties bar. Click the down arrow in the first box, called the *properties list.* The property we want to change is called **Text**. Find and select it.

When you do, the properties list box displays the word **Text**, and the box next to it, which is called the *settings box,* displays the current setting of that property, which is **Text1**, as in Figure 1-13.

TIP   Sometimes, the list of properties is a long one. To locate the correct property can take a good deal of scrolling. One good shortcut here is that you can type the first letter of the property you're looking for when the property list is displayed, and Visual Basic will move you down to the first property that begins with that letter automatically.

Now just edit the text in the Settings box (i.e., "Text1"), changing it to "Welcome to Visual Basic." As you type, the text in the text box automatically changes, following each keystroke. Now we've changed a property of the text box; that is, we've changed the text in it from "Text1" to "Welcome to Visual Basic." This new data becomes part of the object, and, when we make this into a program, this new text will appear in the text box. As we'll see in a few pages, we can also reach the properties of controls like this text box from our programs. In the meantime, select the Start option in the Run menu. At run-time, the window we've been creating now looks like the one in Figure 1-14.

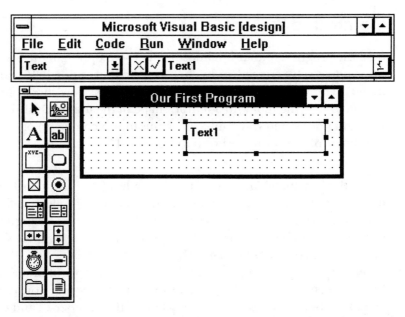

Figure 1-13. Setting Text in a Text Box

Note that when you run our program, the caption bar of Visual Basic itself, which has been displaying "Microsoft Visual Basic [design]," becomes "Microsoft Visual Basic [run]," indicating that the program is now running. (In addition, you might notice two other windows that appear on the screen, one labeled PROJECT1, and the other labeled Immediate Window, and we'll get to those later.) As you can see, the new text appears in the text box: "Welcome to Visual Basic."

So far, then, our program is a success — we've displayed our own message — but it's still not very interesting. Let's add a command button now that we can click to display the text in the text box, instead of having the text present immediately when we run the program.

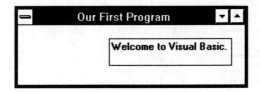

Figure 1-14. Initialized Text Box

Command Buttons

Stop the program (either by choosing the Close option in the System menu of the window we've created, or by choosing the End option in Visual Basic's Run menu). The Visual Basic design screen reappears. Now choose the command button tool — the tool with a button shape in the toolbox, third tool down on the right side. When you double-click this tool, a command button appears in the center of our form, as shown in Figure 1-15.

Move the command button to the left side of the form so that it doesn't obscure the text box. Because the command button is selected, the properties bar contains all of its properties that we can work with at design-time. As you can see by looking through the properties list, this includes **CtlName**, the name of this control, **Left**, **Top**, **Height**, and **Width** as before, **FontName** and other properties having to do with fonts, and a number of other properties we haven't seen before, such as **TabStop** (whether or not you can reach this command button by using the <Tab> key on the keyboard), and **Index** (which will let us coordinate the actions of several buttons).

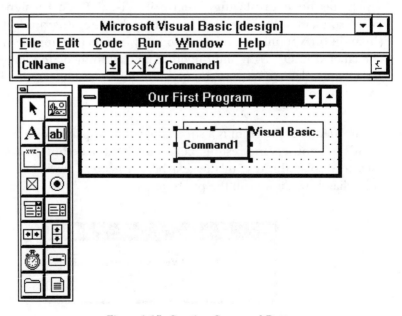

Figure 1-15. Creating Command Buttons

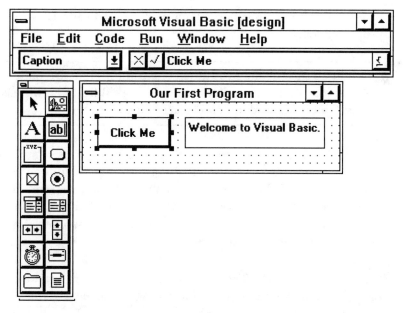

Figure 1-16. Click Me Graphic

In this case, let's change the caption of this button so that it says "Click Me." Just select the **Caption** property for this command button in the properties bar, and edit the text in the Settings box to "Click Me," as shown in Figure 1-16. As you do, "Click Me" appears on our new command button. Next, erase the text in the text box by selecting it, choosing the **Text** property in the Properties List Box, and deleting all the characters there so that the text box is blank.

Now we've got to connect the command button to the text box somehow so that when we click the button, the text "Welcome to Visual Basic" appears in the text box, and this is where we'll start writing our first lines of actual Basic code. Our goal is to reach the text property of the text box from inside our program. To do that, we have to know how Visual Basic refers to the properties of the various controls we have in our program.

It turns out that if we have a text box whose name (that is, whose **CtlName**) is **Text1**, then we can simply refer to the text in it (its **Text** property) as **Text1.Text**. In other words, the usual way to refer to a property in a Visual Basic program is **Object.Property**, where **Object** is the name of the object —

form or control — that has this property, and **Property** is the name of the property itself.

NOTE   When we start dealing with the code routines that are built-in for many of our screen objects — called methods — we'll find that we access them like this: **Object.Method**, much like accessing a property.

We should note that it's important not to get a control's caption or some other text confused with its actual control name. The control name is the internal name of that control for a Visual Basic program, and the default control name for our text box is **Text1** (a second text box would automatically be named **Text2** and so on). You can see this by checking the **CtlName** property of the text box, as in Figure 1-17.

We want to set **Text1**'s **Text** property in our program, and we can do that in a Basic statement when the Click Me button is pushed like this:

```
Text1.Text = "Welcome to Visual Basic."
```

If we delete the text in the text box at design-time, then, when the program starts, the text box will be empty. When we execute the above statement; however, the text "Welcome to Visual Basic." will appear in it.

As you know, our programs are going to be event driven; that is, broken up into sections specifically written to handle certain events, such as button pushes. This means that we have to connect our single line of code to the correct event. In this case, when the user clicks our command button. To find the events associated with any object, just double-click that object while designing your program. A new window opens up, called the *code window*, as shown in Figure 1-18.

Using the Code Window

The code window has a template for every event procedure (i.e., connected with a specific object) that we can write. This is exceptionally handy for two reasons; one is that it will save us some time setting up the outlines of the procedures we want to write, and the other is that the code window indicates

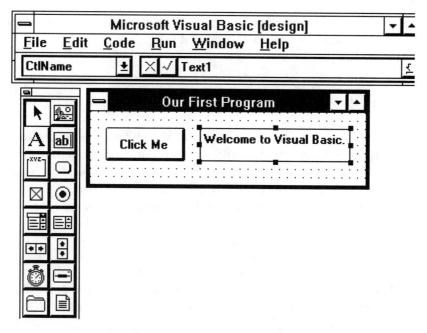

Figure 1-17. Text Box Control Name

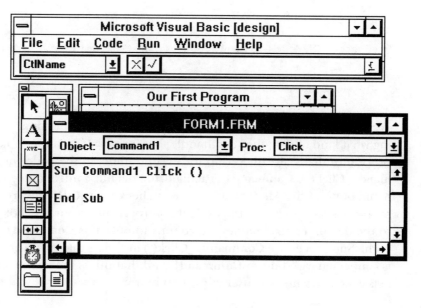

Figure 1-18. The Code Window

what kind of events there are that we can respond to. As you can see in Figure 1-18, this outline is already prepared for us:

```
Sub Command1_Click ()

End Sub
```

There are two types of procedures in Visual Basic: Sub procedures and Function procedures. The two differ in that Function procedures can return values, and Sub procedures cannot, just as in normal Basic. For example, INKEY$ is a popular Basic function (which, incidentally, is not supported in Visual Basic) that we have already seen. It returns a value that we can check like this:

```
WHILE INKEY$ = "": WEND
PRINT "Hello from Basic."
```

Just as in standard Basic, Sub procedures and Function procedures take arguments passed to them in Visual Basic:

```
Sub MySub (A As Integer, B As Integer)
    :
    :
End Sub

Function MyFunc (C As Integer, D As Integer)
    :
    :
End Function
```

We'll see how to set up our own Sub procedures and Functions later, including what kind of data they can handle, but for now let's take a look at the Sub procedure that's already set up for us, in outline, in the code window: **Command1_Click( )**. **Command1** is actually the default control name of our command button Click Me (as you can see by checking its **CtlName** property in the properties bar) — just as the default control name of our text box was **Text1**, so the default control name of a command button is **Command1**. The name of the Sub procedure **Command1_Click( )** indicates that this event procedure is connected with button **Command1**, and that this is the Sub procedure that gets executed when the user clicks that button.

There are other events associated with command buttons as well. Take another look at the code window in Figure 1-18. The box on the right, below the caption bar, is called the *procedure box*, and it indicates what procedures are available for a particular object. If you click on the down arrow next to the procedure box, you'll see a useful list of the available procedures, as in Figure 1-19.

The code window also lists all the objects that we've created so far in the leftmost box just under the caption bar, the *object box*. Clicking on it reveals the names of the objects that we can attach event procedures to, as in Figure 1-20.

You can see that **Text1** is there, as is **Command1**, our text box and command button. In addition, the form itself is listed, because there are several events that can take place with forms. For example, when a form is first used by a program, it's considered an event (**Form_Load( )**), as it is when the user clicks on the form during run-time (**Form_Click( )**). In addition, there is another entry in the object list called **general**. This is where our internal procedures will go when we write them; that is, the Sub and Function procedures we might write to do the real work of a program, where the rest is largely connected to I/O.

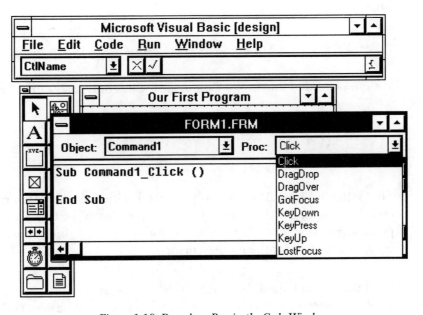

Figure 1-19. Procedure Box in the Code Window

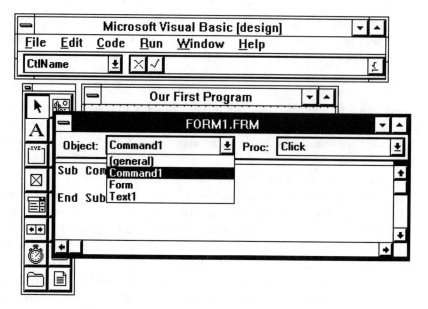

Figure 1-20. Object Box in the Code Window

In our case, however, our code is entirely I/O related and consists of this single line:

```
Text1.Text = "Welcome to Visual Basic."
```

We can place that line in the **Command1_Click** Sub procedure like this:

```
Sub Command1_Click ()
    Text1.Text = "Welcome to Visual Basic."
End Sub
```

To do that in Visual Basic, we only have to position the insertion point in the code window and enter the text as shown in Figure 1-21. (In Windows, the place where new text will go is called the insertion point or caret; the term cursor is reserved for the mouse cursor.)

Note that we indented the single code line by pressing the <Tab> key first. While not necessary, it's good programming practice to indent code lines like this, and, when our code gets more complex and includes multiple levels of

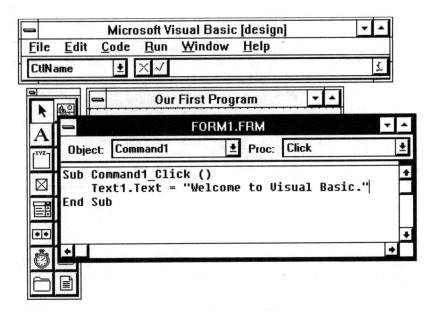

Figure 1-21. Entering Basic Code

control, we'll see that indenting helps make the code much easier to understand.

That's it as far as the code necessary for **Command1_Click( )** is concerned. Close the code window by choosing the Close option in the system menu. Make sure the text was cleared from the text box by selecting the text box and editing its text property (i.e., deleting the text there now).

There's an easy way to keep track of which events have code associated with them: If you look at the procedure list in the code window (i.e., the drop down list connected to the procedure box), you'll see that Visual Basic prints the names of all events that you've added code to in boldface, making them easy to pick out.

Now we're ready to run. To do so, simply choose the Start option in Visual Basic's Run menu. The window we've been creating appears on the screen along with the command button (labeled Click Me) and the text box (now empty). Just click the button, and the text "Welcome to Visual Basic." will

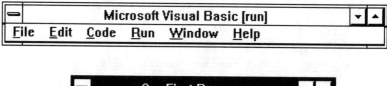

Figure 1-22. Running Our First Program

appear in the text box, as shown in Figure 1-22. End the program before continuing by clicking End in the Visual Basic Run menu.

In fact, we don't need to run our program under Visual Basic. We can make it into a standalone Windows application. All we need to do is to choose the Make Exe File... option in Visual Basic's File menu, as shown in Figure 1-23.

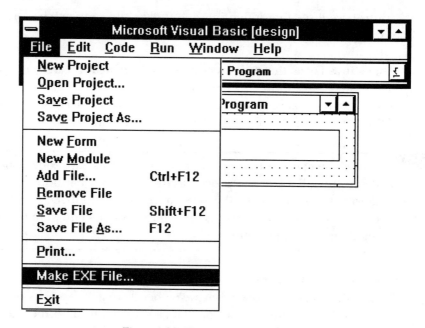

Figure 1-23. Visual Basic's File Menu

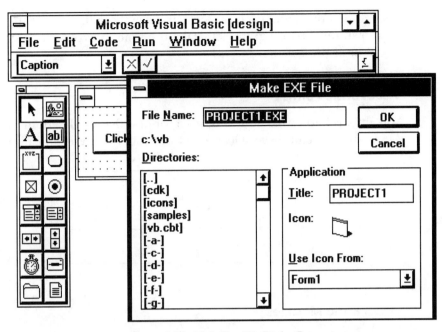

Figure 1-24. Make Exe File Dialog Box

When you choose this option, a dialog box opens, as shown in Figure 1-24. Click the OK button, and Visual Basic creates a file called Project1.Exe, which you can run under Windows directly, and which will produce our fully functioning window. Congratulations! You've created your first complete Windows application.

NOTE   Project1.Exe is not completely standalone; Visual Basic .Exe files require the file Vbrunxxx.Dll to run, where xxx corresponds to the version number (e.g., Vbrun100.Dll).

Visual Basic Projects

You may wonder why Visual Basic gave the name Project1.Exe to our application. The reason is that Visual Basic organizes tasks by *projects*, not by forms. An application can have a number of forms associated with it — i.e., multiple windows — and collecting everything together into a single project wraps it up into one easily managed package. Visual Basic only allows one project to be open at one time, and each project can have three different parts. Now that we've run our first program, let's take the time to explore what makes up a Visual Basic project.

Visual Basic Forms

You already know what a form is; it's a window that we design in Visual Basic. Applications usually have at least one form (but it's not technically necessary):

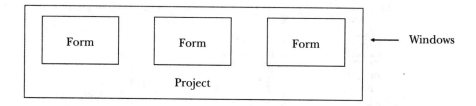

Visual Basic Modules

A Visual Basic *module* is made up of Basic code — but it's code that's not directly associated with a particular form. The procedures in a module can be reached from anywhere in the application. For example, you might want to define a Sub procedure that sorts data. This procedure is not directly concerned with input or output, but it can be vital to some applications. To avoid the necessity of having all code tied to some form, Visual Basic introduced the idea of a module, which was designed only to hold code. To create a module, as we'll do later, use the New Module... item in Visual Basic's File menu. Usually, larger applications use modules to store procedures that are used throughout the application:

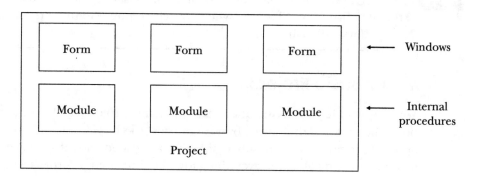

Visual Basic Global Modules

A global module is also shared by the entire application, but it holds declarations, not code. That is, you can declare variables in Basic, as well as constants, and you can also define types. Putting these declarations into the global module (there is only one global module) makes them accessible to the rest of the application:

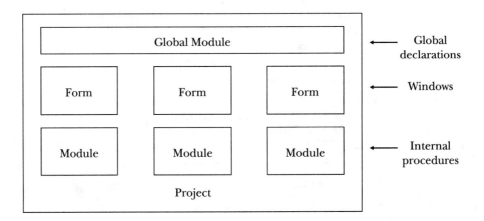

This has a great deal to do with the scope of constants and variables, and we'll put off that discussion until the next chapter, when we discuss what variable types are available.

Using Visual Basic Projects

When you start Visual Basic, then, it starts or creates Project1 automatically. To rename the project, select the Save Project As... item in the File menu. To work on some project that already exists, you can use the Open Project... item in the File menu, as shown in Figure 1-25. To keep track of the current project, Visual Basic maintains the *project window*. The contents of the project window for our application are shown in Figure 1-26.

The project window is useful when you have multiple forms or code modules. Here, we only have a single form, so we haven't made much use of it. As you can see in Figure 1-26, the project window also allows you to switch to the

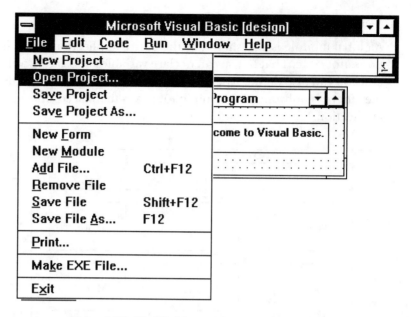

Figure 1-25. The File Menu with the Open Project Item

global module so that you can add global (that is, application wide, as we'll see in Chapter 2) declarations of constants, variables, or types.

You might also notice in the project window that the default name of our form is Form1.Frm. The .Frm extension is normal for forms, just as the .Bas extension is normal for Basic files. When Form1.Frm is selected in the project window, you can jump back and forth between looking at the form itself and looking at the code window (which holds all the code associated with the objects in this project) by choosing the buttons in the project window: View Form or View Code. (However, it's just as easy to double-click on an object to open up the code window.)

Figure 1-26. The Project Window

Finally, projects themselves are saved as .Mak files (although the associated .Frm and .Bas files are stored separately). Initially, when you create a new project, including new forms and even modules, Visual Basic doesn't automatically create the corresponding files on disk. Instead, it's up to you to save the files you want (although Visual Basic will prompt you to save files when you leave, if you haven't already done so). Now that we've created our own project, let's make sure that we can save it to disk so that nothing is lost.

Saving Your Work on Disk

There are five different Save items in the Visual Basic menu system: Save Project, Save Project As..., Save File, Save File As..., and Save Text.... The Save Project item saves all the files associated with the current project in Visual Basic's binary format on disk. To save a project, however, you should first give it a name (unless you don't mind using the default name, Project1 — but be careful that it's not overwritten by a later project this way), and you can do that with the Save Project As... item, which opens a dialog box. With this option, you can choose a name for the current project, and save all the associated files on disk. Once the project is named, the Save Project item will save your work under that name as well.

In addition, you can use the Save File item to save the currently selected form or module (as opposed to the current project), but, once again, you should give it a name before doing so, which you can do with the Save File As... item. This menu item opens a dialog box, and you must specify the name of the file you want to save. Storing files this way makes them inaccessible to you outside Visual Basic because Visual Basic stores them in its own binary format.

However, you might want to edit the code files yourself outside Visual Basic. This is a common thing to do, especially when the code you're writing is long and not directly I/O connected. To do that, use the Save Text... option, which is in the Code menu, not in the File menu. In this case, all the code connected with the object-oriented events you've written, as well as modules (application-wide procedures) and the global module (declarations) can be stored as normal text, which is easy to work with and edit.

TIP If you have Basic code you're moving over from QuickBASIC or the Microsoft Basic Professional Development System, the best two options for importing and checking it are the Load Text... and Save Text... pair in Visual Basic's Code menu.

Saving Our Project

To save our current project, then, give names to and save both files in the project window, which are currently named Global.Bas (the global module) and Form1.Frm (the single form in our application). It's best to use new names for these files because these are the Visual Basic defaults, and they might easily be overwritten by later projects. Next, use the Save Project As... item in the File menu to save the whole project, again selecting some name other than the default Project1.Mak, such as MyProg.Mak. That's it. The next time you start Visual Basic, you can reload this project by using the Open Project... item in the File menu and opening MyProg.Mak.

Adding More Power to Our Text Box

Before we finish with our first application, you might notice that, since the text ("Welcome to Visual Basic.") appears in a text box, the user is free to edit it, even after we've displayed our message (i.e., just like a normal Windows text box). However, we can modify our program so that we're appraised if any change is made to the text. It turns out that changing the text in a text box is one of the events we can write code for.

TIP   If you don't want the user to change the text that you display on a form, use a label instead. As we'll see, you can write to a label at run-time, but the user can't change the displayed text, which means labels can act as read-only text boxes.

When the text in a text box is edited, a *text box change* event occurs. Because our text box is named **Text1**, this event will be called **Text1_Change( )**. We can intercept that change by going back to the Visual Basic design screen and double-clicking on the text box. The code window for the text box opens up, as shown in Figure 1-27. The text change event is already selected, so we're ready to write code:

```
Sub Text1_Change()

End Sub
```

For example, if the text is edited, a text box change event is generated, and we might want to allow the user the option of restoring it to the original welcome

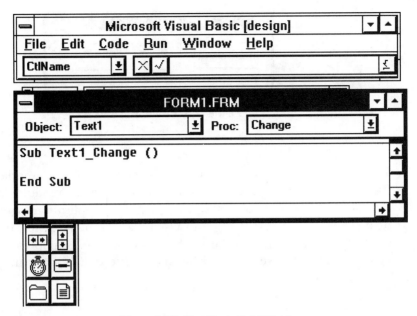

Figure 1-27. Text Box's Code Window

message. We can do that by changing the caption of the command button from "Click Me" to, say, "Restore Msg." This is easy because the caption of the command button is simply a property of the command button, which we can reach from our program. In particular, since the button's control name is **Command1**, we can simply make this Basic assignment: **Command1.Caption** = "Restore Msg", where we assign the string "Restore Msg" to the Caption property of the button. We do that by making this change to the Sub procedure **Text1_Change( )**:

```
Sub Text1_Change()
    Command1.Caption = "Restore Msg"
End Sub
```

Now, when we run the program, the usual window appears, along with the Click Me button and the empty text window. However, as soon as the user changes the text in the text box, the caption of the button changes to "Restore Msg," as shown in Figure 1-28, indicating that the original message can be restored by pressing this button.

Figure 1-28. Restore Msg Button

That's it for this chapter. In it, we've gotten many of the essentials of Visual Basic down, including the terms form, control, object, module, project, and others. And we've put our first working Windows application together. In the next chapter, we'll start to dig into Visual Basic in more depth. In particular, we'll explore all there is to know about two of its most popular objects, two objects, in fact, that we've already been introduced to: buttons and text boxes.

Using Buttons and Textboxes

Two of the most common Windows controls are certainly text boxes and buttons. In fact, we've already used both of these controls in the first chapter. Text boxes are the important text I/O controls in Visual Basic, and buttons are one of the chief command I/O controls (the other being, of course, menus, which we'll see in Chapter 3). For those reasons, we'll see how to use both text and buttons in this chapter in some depth.

It's important to realize that text boxes are the primary means of character string input in Visual Basic, and that means that they take the place of the standard Basic instructions INKEY$, LINE INPUT, INPUT$, and INPUT, which can be used to read from the keyboard in other Basics. Here, we have to use the Windows method of reading text, which is with text boxes. In addition, they are a primary means of character string output as well, which means they can take the place of other Basic instructions such as PRINT or PRINT USING. Given this importance to both user character input and output, they make up one of the first topics we should cover in this book.

The whole idea of text I/O — that is, character string input and output — brings us closer to the heart of programming in Visual Basic. That is, to understand handling text, and how to display data from our programs, we'll have to examine how to store it in the first place, and that will bring us to the topic of variables. In fact, our first application in this chapter will be a simple calculator that operates in its own window so that we can learn how to accept and display numeric values in text boxes.

In addition, we'll learn about the difficulties of displaying graphic text characters in Windows (e.g., the width of each character can be different, so it's hard to know exactly how far you've printed on the screen, and other concerns). It turns out that text boxes also have some pretty advanced capabilities that we should look into as well: For example, we can set up text boxes with more than one line — what Visual Basic calls multiline text boxes — that include word wrap and scroll bars, and we can also retrieve specific text that the user has marked. Later on, in our file handling chapter, we'll put together a small file editing program, and we can get that started here by writing a notepad application that takes keystrokes and lets you store text. That's the plan for this chapter: handling all kinds of character string input and output with text boxes and getting commands from the user with command buttons. Let's begin the chapter now with our calculator example.

A Calculator Example

Our calculator is going to be remarkably simple since we're focusing on text boxes and not on how to write larger applications. We'll just have two text boxes, one for the first operand and one for the second, a button marked with an equals sign, and a text box to hold the result of adding the two operands together. When the user clicks the equals button, the result of the addition will appear in the result text box.

To begin, start Visual Basic and change the caption property of the default window (which now reads **Form1**) to **Calculator** by editing its **Caption** property in the properties bar (i.e., the property that is displayed there when Visual Basic starts). Next, save this form as, say, Calc.Frm by choosing the Save File As... item in the File menu. Now save the whole project as Calc.Mak using the Save Project As... item, also in the File menu. These are the typical beginning steps of writing a new application because the only way to name files in Visual Basic is with the Save options (Visual Basic does not even create files for the form and project until you save them). It's also a good idea to save your work periodically, which you can do now with the Save Project item alone.

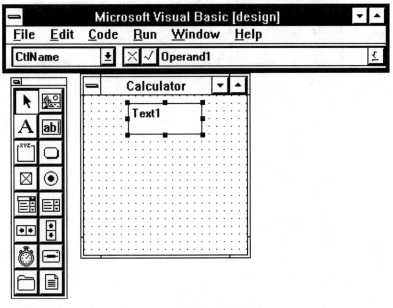

Figure 2-1. Calculator Form

Next, choose (that is, double-click) the text box tool. A text box appears in the center of the form. Move it up to the top of the form and change its control name (**CtlName** in the properties bar) to **Operand1**, as shown in Figure 2-1.

This text box, **Operand1**, is going to receive the first operand. The next text box will receive the second, and then there will be a button marked with an equals sign and a result text box. For simplicity's sake, this calculator will only perform addition, adding **Operand1** to **Operand2** to get a result, but it's a simple matter to add buttons for subtraction, multiplication, and division if you want to.

Next, double-click on the text box tool again, and place the second text box under the first one, changing its **CtlName** to **Operand2**, as shown in Figure 2-2 (note that Visual Basic gives it the default **CtlName Text1** just like the first text box, since we've renamed the first box **Operand1**). Now place a command button under the two boxes, and give it an equals sign for a caption. Finally, place one last text box under the command button, and give it a control name of **Result**, as shown in Figure 2-3.

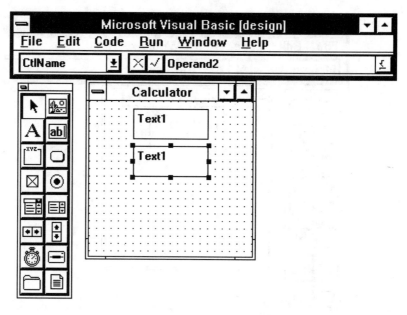

Figure 2-2. Calculator with Second Text Box

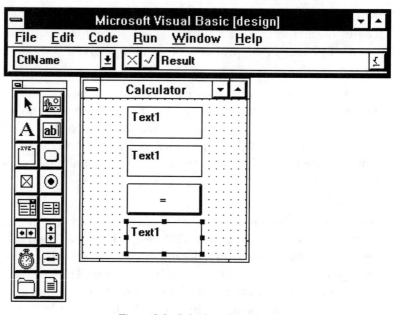

Figure 2-3. Calculator Template

There are two more things to do, and we will have designed the calculator's appearance completely. First, remove the text from each text box (i.e., "Text1") by selecting their **Text** properties and deleting what's there. We should also add a plus sign, +, in front of the second text box (**Operand2**) to indicate what operation we're performing, like this:

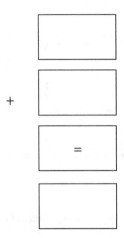

To do that, we can place a *label* on the form.

Labels

Labels are usually used, as their name implies, to label other controls on a form. Although your program can change the text in a label by referring to its caption property, the user cannot.

TIP   While labels often appear only as text, you can also put a box around them, making them look just like a text box. You do that by setting the **BorderStyle** option to 1 (recall that all possible settings for a property are displayed in the settings box in the properties bar). However, you should note that it's only possible to set the value of this property at design-time; that is, a program cannot add or remove a label's border at run-time.

The label we want to add to our calculator is very simple. It's only a plus sign. We can do that by choosing the label tool, which is the second tool down on the left-hand side of the toolbox and is marked with a large uppercase "A." A label appears in the middle of the form; change its **Caption** property from

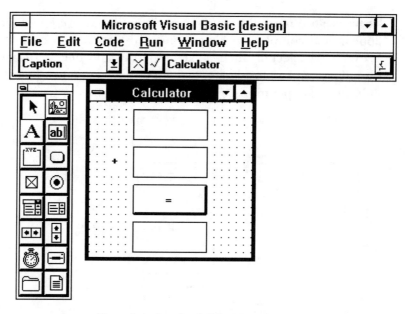

Figure 2-4. Completed Calculator Template

"Label1" to "+" in the properties bar, and move it next to the **Operand2** text box, as shown in Figure 2-4.

TIP   Another way of placing text directly on a form is printing directly to that form (as opposed to printing to a label), as we'll see when we cover graphics later.

Now the calculator template is complete. All that remains is to write the code. The action here is simple: When the user clicks the command button marked =, we want to take **Operand1**, add it to **Operand2**, and place the result in **Result** (the bottom text box). However, to do this poses a problem: So far, we've only dealt with text in text boxes. How do we interpret the text there as a number? For that matter, how do we display numbers? And how do we store them in our program?

This is going to be very important for us. How can we manipulate the input we receive from the user in our text boxes, especially if that input is supposed to represent numbers and not just text? In other words, our job now is to translate the text in the text boxes **Operand1** and **Operand2** into numbers, add them in our program, and then display the result. And all this internal handling of data brings up our next topic, variables, which we'll need to explore before proceeding.

Variables in Visual Basic

The types of variables Visual Basic uses are much like the variables in QuickBASIC or in the Basic Professional Development System. Like those compilers, variable names can be up to 40 characters long (including letters, numbers, and underscores), and they have only two naming rules: The first character must be a letter (so Visual Basic doesn't assume this is a numeric value), and we cannot use Visual Basic reserved words (such as Sub or Function) as variable names. The data types that are built into Visual Basic are shown in Table 2-1, along with their ranges of allowed values.

TIP   Besides the built-in data types, you can also define your own aggregate data types with Type, which defines data structures, as we'll see when we work with files.

Type Conventions for Variables

If you're a QuickBASIC user, you might not have seen the currency type before. Although originally designed to hold currency values, the currency type is attractive for other reasons as well — it stores numbers with 15-place accuracy to the left of the decimal place, and four places to the right. These numbers are fixed point numbers; that is, they always have four places to the left of the decimal point.

Type	*Number of bytes*	*Character*	*Range*
Integer	2	%	-32,768 to 32,767
Long	4	&	-2,147,483 to 2,147,483,647
Single	4	!	-3.37E+38 to 3.37E+38
Double	8	#	-1.67D+308 to 1.67D+308
Currency	8	@	-9.22E+14 to 9.22E+14
String	varies	$	Not applicable

Table 2-1. Visual Basic Data Types

Like other Basic compilers, there are certain characters (e.g., ! or %, as indicated in Table 2-1) that you can use to indicate what type of variable you intend when you first use it. For example, if you want to use an integer value named **my_int**, you can indicate to Visual Basic that **my_int** is an integer by adding a % character to the end of it like this: **my_int%**. Similarly, if you want to use a single-precision floating-point number called my_float, you can call it **my_float!**. In fact, you can even leave it as **my_float** since the default type for variables is single in Visual Basic (as it is in QuickBASIC and the Basic Professional Development System).

TIP   You can change the default data type with a Deftype statement: DefInt A–Z indicates that you want all variables beginning with letters A to Z to be integers. Other options include DefLng, DefSng, DefDbl, DefCur, and DefStr.

In fact, there are two ways of indicating to Visual Basic that you want to use a certain name as a variable name. The first is simply to use the name where you want it, like this:

```
my_int% = 5
```

If Visual Basic hasn't seen **my_int%** before, this becomes an *implicit declaration*. As we've seen, the last character of the variable can determine the variable's type. If the last character is not a special type-declaration character (i.e., %, &, !, #, @, or $), then the default type is single.

The other way (and more proper from a programming point of view) is to use the Dim statement to declare a variable specifically at the beginning of a procedure (we'll see how to declare variables in the global module later). Here are some examples:

```
Dim my_int As Integer
Dim my_double As Double
Dim my_variable_string As String
Dim my_fixed_string As String * 20
```

Note in particular the last two variables, **my_variable_string** and **my_fixed_string**. The first one, **my_variable_string**, is a string with variable length (up to 65,535 characters in Visual Basic), and the second one is explicitly declared as fixed length by adding "* 20" to the end of the declaration, which makes it a string of exactly 20 characters, just as in other Basic compilers. (We'll take a closer look at strings later in this chapter, when we deal with the built-in string statements and functions in Visual Basic.)

There are several places to put such declarations, and the placement of a variable's declaration affects the variable's *scope*, a reference to the portion of the program to which the variable is visible. Let's look into that next, and then we'll be ready to complete our calculator example.

Scope of Variables in Visual Basic

As mentioned, a variable's scope refers to the regions in the application that can access it. It turns out that there are four different levels of variable scope because there are four different places to declare variables.

The first place to declare variables, either with the Dim statement or implicitly (i.e., just by using it), is at the procedure level. There are two kinds of procedures in Visual Basic, Sub procedures and Function procedures, and each can have variable declarations in them. When you declare a variable in a procedure, however, that variable is *local* to that procedure. In other words, its scope is restricted to the procedure in which it's declared. Such variables are called *local variables* in Visual Basic:

```
┌─────────────────┐      ┌─────────────────┐
│    Procedure    │      │    Procedure    │
│                 │      │                 │
│      Local      │      │      Local      │
│    Variables    │      │    Variables    │
└─────────────────┘      └─────────────────┘
```

One important note is that local variables don't outlast the procedure they're defined in; that is, every time you enter the procedure, the local variables are reinitialized. In other words, don't count on retaining the value in a local variable between procedure calls.

TIP   You can, however, make local variables permanent by declaring them *static*. Visual Basic will not reinitialize a static variable at any time. To make a variable static, declare it with the keyword Static instead of Dim (e.g., Static **my_int** As Integer).

The next two places where you declare variables are at the form and module levels (recall that a module can hold the general, non-I/O code associated with an application). If you declare a form-level variable, that variable is accessible to all procedures in that form. The same goes for code modules: If you declare a module-level variable, that variable is accessible to all procedures in that module:

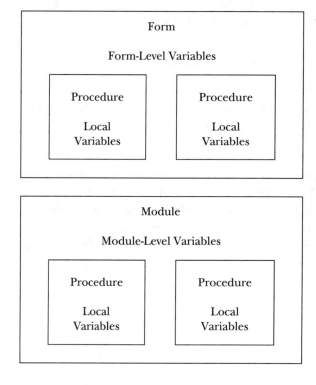

In particular, you might notice that this lets you share information between procedures. The way to declare a variable at the form or module level is to place it into the declarations part of the general object that we saw before, in the code window (we'll see this later). And, the way you create new modules is simply by selecting the New Module... item in Visual Basic's File menu (as we'll also see later). These new variables are static variables by default; that is, although procedure level variables are reinitialized each time the procedure is entered, variables at the form and module (and global variables as well) are static.

The final level, of course, is the global level. Every procedure or line of code in an application has access to these variables (i.e., these variables are application wide). To declare a variable global, place it in the global module (which only takes global declarations, not code) by switching to it in the project window (the default name for the global module is Global.Bas), clicking on the View Code button of the project window, and then declaring your variables. An important note is that you declare them with the keyword Global, not Dim, like this:

```
Global my_int As Integer
Global my_double As Double
Global my_variable_string As String
Global my_fixed_string As String * 20
```

Those are then the four places to declare variables: the procedure, form, module, or global levels:

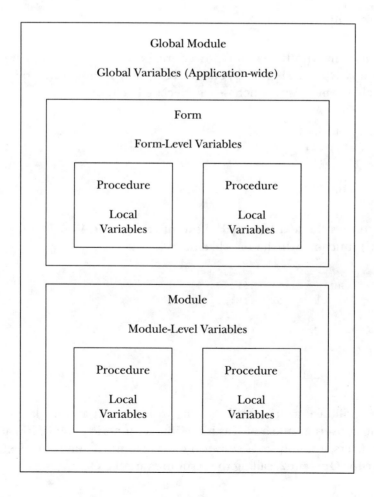

In our case, that is, in our calculator example, we'll be able to use procedure level (i.e., local) variables. Let's get back to that application now.

Storing the Calculator's Data

If we wish, we can store the calculator's data — the numbers typed by the user and the result — as single-precision numbers. The way we've designed things, all action takes place when the user clicks the = button, so let's take a look at that procedure. Double-click the command button we've labeled =, bringing up the code window and displaying the Sub procedure for a click event associated with it (note that Visual Basic's default name for it is **Command1**):

```
Sub Command1_Click()

End Sub
```

So far, there's nothing in this procedure. Let's begin by reading the text in the text box **Operand1** (i.e., **Operand1.Text**) and storing it in a single-precision variable named Op1 which we can declare like this:

```
Sub Command1_Click()
    Dim Op1 As Single
        :

End Sub
```

To convert the text **Operand1.Text** into a number, Visual Basic provides the Val( ) function, which works like this:

```
        Sub Command1_Click()
            Dim Op1 As Single

→           Op1 = Val(Operand1.Text)
                :

        End Sub
```

Val( ) will take a string and, starting from the left and working towards the right, convert as much of it as it can into a numeric value (if it reaches illegal characters, it simply stops converting the text into a number). Next, we do the same for **Operand2**, calling the resulting variable **Op2**:

```
      Sub Command1_Click()
          Dim Op1 As Single
  →       Dim Op2 As Single

          Op1 = Val(Operand1.Text)
  →       Op2 = Val(Operand2.Text)

          :

      End Sub
```

Besides the Val( ) function, Visual Basic also has the Str$( ) function, which goes the other way, converting a number into a text string. In other words, we can add the two numbers and display the results in **Result.Text** like this:

```
      Sub Command1_Click()
          Dim Op1 As Single
          Dim Op2 As Single

          Op1 = Val(Operand1.Text)
          Op2 = Val(Operand2.Text)

  →       Result.Text = Str$(Op1 + Op2)
      End Sub
```

And that's all the code we'll need; our calculator is ready (if not powerful). Just select the Start item in the Run menu, and the calculator will function, as in Figure 2-5. You can type in floating-point numbers for the first two operands, and, when you click the = button, the two will be added (it might even be a good idea to make the **Result** text window into a label so the user can't modify it). In fact, the user can even modify the two operands after typing them (i.e., to correct mistakes), since we're using text boxes.

As is usual in Windows, the user can switch from text box to text box by pressing <Tab> (not <Enter>) in addition to using the mouse. However this includes the **Result** box; that is, the user can tab to the **Result** box. Since that's not convenient for data entry, one change we might make to the program is to make sure that the <Tab> key will not move the *focus* to the **Result** box. When a control has the insertion point in Windows, it's called "having the focus." The way to make sure that the **Result** box no longer gets the focus by tabbing around the text boxes is to set its **TabStop** property to False (the default for text boxes and command buttons is True).

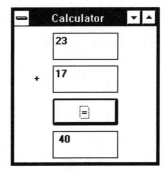

Figure 2-5. Calculator Running

We can do that by selecting the **TabStop** property for the **Result** text box in the properties bar and by setting it to False, as in Figure 2-6 (note that the two options offered by the settings list are True or False, so the choice is easy).

There's one more change that we might make here, which will also indicate another capability of command buttons. Since the user won't use the <Enter> key for anything else here, we can make the equals button the *default button.* In other words, when the user presses <Enter>, it will be the same as clicking the

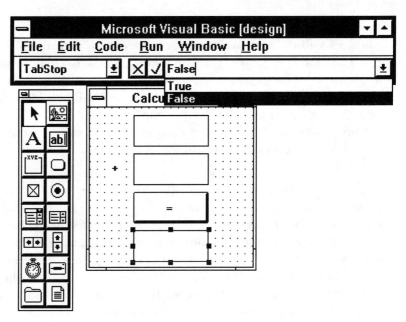

Figure 2-6. The TabStop Property

equals button. As is standard in Windows, the default button is surrounded by a thick black border so that the user knows exactly which button is the default.

We can make the equals button into the default button simply by setting its **Default** value to True at design-time, as in Figure 2-7. Now when the user runs the program, the equals button may be selected simply by pressing <Enter>.

TIP The constants True and False, by the way, are predefined in Visual Basic, along with a number of other constants, and they appear in the file CON-STANT.TXT. To use this file, as we'll see later, you must load it into the global module. If you don't want to load this file, you can use the actual values that Visual Basic uses for True (-1) and False (0). You may not have expected True to have a value of -1. It does because, in a computer, -1 as an integer is represented as 1111111111111111 in binary; that is, as &HFFFF, and all bits are set, the exact opposite of 0 (False).

The full version of the calculator, then — complete with default equals button (note the thick black border) — appears in Figure 2-8. We've made a good deal of progress as far as numeric I/O is concerned, but there's more that follows. In particular, since text boxes are so important for displaying data (in

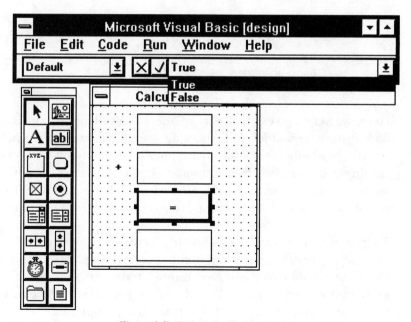

Figure 2-7. Calculator Button Design

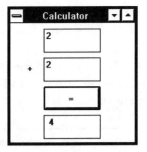

Figure 2-8. Calculator Application

addition to reading it), and this is our text box chapter, we should explore some of that added capability next.

Formatting Text

As we've seen, one way to display numbers as text in a text box is to use the Str$( ) function:

```
Sub Command1_Click()
      Dim Op1 As Single
      Dim Op2 As Single

      Op1 = Val(Operand1.Text)
      Op2 = Val(Operand2.Text)

→     Result.Text = Str$(Op1 + Op2)
  End Sub
```

Here, we set the **Text** property of the **Result** object to Str$(**Op1** + **Op2**). Str$( ) does a good job of formatting numeric data in most cases; that is, it adds a space before and after the number it is to print out, and it even handles floating-point numbers (i.e., if numbers get too big, it will print them out with an exponent, such as: 1.2E+07). However, this is essentially unformatted output. We have no real control over the format of the text in our **Result** text box.

To give us more control, Visual Basic includes the Format$( ) function. With Format$( ), we can indicate the number of decimal places that a number must have, the number of leading or trailing zeroes, as well as the capability of formatting currency values. The way to use Format$( ) is like this (where the square brackets indicate that the format string is optional):

```
text$ = Format$(number [, format_string$])
```

Character	Means
0	Digit placeholder; print a digit or a 0 at this place
#	Digit placeholder; do not print leading or trailing zeroes
.	Decimal placeholder; indicates position of the decimal point
,	Thousands separator
- +$( )Space	A literal character — displayed literally

Table 2-2. Format String Characters

The format string here can be made up of any of the characters in Table 2-2. Let's take a look at some examples like this to get an idea of how Format$( ) works:

```
Format$(1234.56, "######.#")     =    1234.5
Format$(1234.56, "00000.000")    =    01234.560
Format$(1234.56, "###,###.0")    =    1,234.56
Format$(1234.56, "$#,000.00")    =    $1,234.56
```

As you can see, the # symbol is a placeholder, telling Format$( ) how many places you want to retain to around the decimal point. The 0 symbol acts the same way, except that if there is no actual digit to be displayed at the corresponding location, a 0 is printed. In addition, you can specify other characters, such as $ or commas to separate thousands.

Let's add thousands separators to our calculator. We can do that simply by changing the Str$( ) statement to a Format$( ) statement like this:

```
Sub Command1_Click()
    Dim Op1 As Single
    Dim Op2 As Single

    Op1 = Val(Operand1.Text)
    Op2 = Val(Operand2.Text)

→   Result.Text = Format$(Op1 + Op2, "###,###,###.#####")
End Sub
```

The resulting change to the calculator is shown in Figure 2-9.

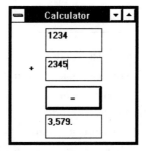

Figure 2-9. Calculator with Thousands Separator

Displaying Date and Time

Visual Basic also makes it easy to display the time and date with the Format$( ) function. In fact, we can use the built-in Visual Basic function named Now to return the current time and date in numeric form, and we can use Format$( ) to display that date and time. In this case, we can use special formatting characters: h, m, s and m, d, and y. Format$( ) is capable of producing text strings from Now in many different ways, depending on how you use these characters, and how many you use. Here are some examples:

```
Format$(Now, "m-d-yy")                 =   "4-5-92"
Format$(Now, "m/d/y")                  =   "4/5/92"
Format$(Now, "mm/dd/yy")               =   "04/05/92"
Format$(Now, "ddd, mmmm d, yyyy")      =   "Thu, April 5, 1992"
Format$(Now, "dddd, mmmm d, yyyy")     =   "Thursday, April 5
Format$(Now, "d mmm, yyyy")            =   "5 Apr, 1992"
Format$(Now, "hh:mm:ss mm/dd/yy")      =   "16:00:00 04/05/92"
Format$(Now, "hh:mm:ss AM/PM mm-dd-yy") =  "4:00:00 PM 04-05-92"
```

As you can see, there is a variety of formats available. In fact, if you use "ddddd" for the day and "ttttt" for the time, you will get the day and time in an appropriate format for the country that the computer is in (as set in the Windows control panel). For example, Format$(Now, "ttttt ddddd") might be "4:00:00 PM 04-05-92" in the United States, but in some European countries, it would be "92-04-05 16.00.00."

At this point, we've had a good introduction to the use of text boxes and control buttons with our calculator, but we can move on to even more powerful applications. For example, our next project is to build a windowed notepad, complete with text boxes that include scroll bars.

A Notepad Example — Complete with Cut and Paste

Putting together a functioning notepad application might be easier than you think in Visual Basic. In fact, a notepad is really just a multiline text box, and Visual Basic supports multiline text boxes automatically. To see how this works, start a Visual Basic project and give the form that appears the caption **Pad** from the properties bar. Next, save both the form itself as Pad.Frm (using Save File As...) and the project as Pad.Mak (using Save Project As...).

To produce our multiline text box, simply double-click the text box tool and stretch the resulting text box until it takes up most of the form (leaving room for a row of buttons at the bottom), as shown in Figure 2-10. Now find the **Multiline** property in the properties bar; there are two settings allowed for this property, as indicated by the settings list (which drops down from the arrow next to the settings box): True and False. The default is False, which means that textboxes can only handle a single line of text by default. Set this property to True, which gives our pad multiline capability.

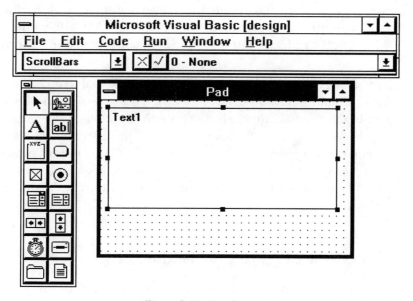

Figure 2-10. Pad Prototype

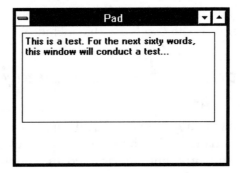

Figure 2-11. Pad at Run-Time

At this point, our pad is already functional; just delete the text in the text box (i.e., "Text1") using the properties bar, and run the program. The pad appears, as in Figure 2-11, and you can write in it. In fact, it comes complete with word wrap — when you get to the end of a line, the current word gets "wrapped" whole to the next line instead of being broken in the middle.

However, there's a great deal more that we can do here; for example, we can add a vertical scroll bar to the text box just by changing its **Scrollbars** property. In fact, we can add horizontal scroll bars as well, but if you add horizontal scroll bars to a multiline text box, word wrap is automatically turned off, so we won't. Unlike the scroll bars that we'll see later in this book, multiline text box scroll bars are managed entirely by Visual Basic. And adding them is easy: To add vertical scroll bars, just find the **Scrollbars** property in the properties bar.

The settings list indicates what's available: horizontal scroll bars, vertical scroll bars, or both, as indicated in Figure 2-12. To add vertical scroll bars to the text box in our notepad, just select the **Vertical** option, and a vertical scroll bar appears as in Figure 2-13. Now we can scroll through a much larger document in our new notepad — up to 64K in fact, which is the maximum length of strings in Visual Basic. So far, all we've done has been quite easy, so let's press on and add more capabilities to the pad; specifically, let's add cut and paste, where the user can select text, cut it, and paste it back in somewhere else.

Using Selected Text in Text Boxes

As is usual for a text box, the user can mark, or select text in Visual Basic text boxes. For example, they can simply place the (mouse) cursor at some loca-

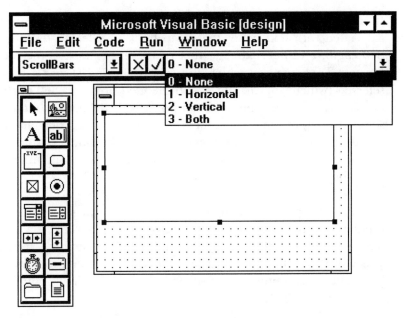

Figure 2-12. Scroll Bar Options

tion, hold down the left button, move the cursor to another location, and release it. In that case, the text between the two points is automatically highlighted; i.e., Visual Basic has already given this capability to our text boxes. We already know that we can refer to the text in a text box as, say **My_text.Text** (i.e., **My_text** is the name we gave to the text box control), but how can we refer to selected text?

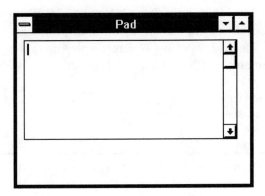

Figure 2-13. Pad with Vertical Scroll Bar

It turns out that this is also easy under Visual Basic. There are three properties associated with text boxes that keep track of selected text for us: **SelStart**, **SelLength**, and **SelText**. The first of these, **SelStart**, is the location in the **My_text.Text** string at which the selected string starts. If there is no text selected (which you can check with the next property, **SelLength**), this property indicates where the insertion point is. If **SelStart** is 0, the selected text starts just before the first character in the text box. If **SelStart** is equal to the length of the text in the text box then it's indicating a position just after the last character in the text box. Note that **SelStart** is a long integer (because it has to be able to handle numbers up to 64K).

The next property, **SelLength**, is also a long integer, and it indicates the number of characters that are selected. Finally, **SelText** is a string that contains the selected characters from the text box (if there are no characters selected, this is the empty string, " "). In fact, your program can set these properties at run-time (e.g., **SelStart** = 0 : **SelLength** = 5 would highlight the first five characters).

We'll use these properties to add cutting and pasting to our notepad by adding some command buttons. In particular, we can add three specific functions: Clear All, which deletes everything in the notepad's text box; Cut, which cuts the selected text; and Paste, which pastes the selected text at the insertion point.

The first button, Clear All is easy. All we have to do is to set the **Text** property of the text box to the empty string, " ". To start, let's change the name of the pad's text box to **PadText** in the properties bar. (We'll find as programs get longer and longer that it's advisable to end an object's name with an indication of what type of object it is.) Now add a command button with the caption "Clear All" and the name (i.e., **CtlName**) **ClearButton**. Position the button in the lower-right corner of the form and double-click on it to open the code window. The code window opens, displaying a template for the click event (i.e., **ClearButton_Click( )**), which is exactly what we want, so add this line:

```
        Sub ClearButton_Click()
 →          PadText.Text = ""
        End Sub
```

| TIP | If you change the name of a control part way through the design process, you should know that Visual Basic does *not* go through your code and change the names of the procedures you've already written to match — you're responsible for doing that. |

Now you can run the program. When you do, the button becomes active, and clicking it deletes the text in the text box. However, once you've selected an object in Windows — by clicking it, for example — the focus (i.e., the active control, and the location of the insertion point) is transferred to that object. This is always the default action in Windows — if you click on an object, that object gets the focus. In our case, that means that the Clear All button retains the focus even after clearing the pad (and it is surrounded by a thick black border to indicate that it still has the focus). To get back to the pad, the user has to press a <Tab> key or click on the text window, which seems less than professional.

We can fix that problem, however, with the **SetFocus** method. Programmers familiar with object-oriented languages know that there are two types of programming constructions that you can associate with an object: data and procedures. In Visual Basic, an object's data items are referred to as properties, and the procedures connected with it are called methods. We'll see more about methods throughout this book. In the meantime, what concerns us here is the **SetFocus** method that is built into most controls. With it, we can give the focus back to the text box simply with the statement **PadText.SetFocus**.

That is, you refer to methods the same way you refer to properties: with the dot (.) operator. (Later on, we'll see that some methods take arguments.) When we transfer the focus back to the text box, the insertion point appears there again and starts blinking. Here's how **ClearButton_Click( )** should look:

```
      Sub ClearButton_Click()
          PadText.Text = ""
  →       PadText.SetFocus
      End Sub
```

That's all there is to it. Your pad should now look like the one in Figure 2-14. Now, let's move on to cutting selected text in a text box.

How to Cut Selected Text

To start the process of cutting text, add another command button in the lower-left corner of the form, which we can name **CutButton**, and give it the caption "Cut." When the user presses this button, they want the text that is selected in the text box to be cut. Actually, we'll place it into a temporary buffer so that we can paste it later if required. Let's begin by creating this temporary buffer, which should itself be a String type, and which we can call **CutText**. Since we want both the Cut and Paste procedures to have access to

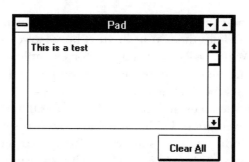

Figure 2-14. Pad with Clear All Button

this buffer, let's make **CutText** a global variable, making it accessible from all parts of our notepad application.

To make a global declaration, we have to open the global module, and you can do that simply by clicking on Global.Bas in the project window. When you do, the global module window opens, as shown in Figure 2-15. Declare **CutText** as shown:

```
Global CutText As String
```

(Recall that you use the Global keyword in the global module, not Dim.)

Now that our buffer, **CutText**, is ready, we are prepared to cut the string itself in the pad's text box. Before we do, however, we should save the selected text to the **CutText** string. To do that, click the Cut button to open the Sub procedure template in the code window:

```
Sub CutButton_Click()

End Sub
```

Then save the cut text like this:

```
Sub CutButton_Click()
    CutText = PadText.SelText

        :

End Sub
```

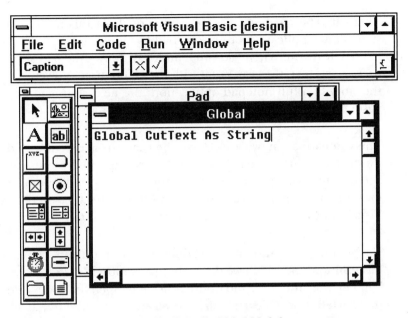

Figure 2-15. Pad's Global Module

The next step is to cut the selected string itself. That turns out to be surprisingly easy. All we have to do is to replace **PadText.SetText**, the selected text, with an empty string, " " (if no text was selected, no text is cut) like this:

```
      Sub CutButton_Click()
          CutText = PadText.SelText
  →       PadText.SelText = ""

              :

      End Sub
```

Finally, we give the focus back to the text window using the **SetFocus** method:

```
      Sub CutButton_Click()
          CutText = PadText.SelText
          PadText.SelText = ""
  →       PadText.SetFocus
      End Sub
```

NOTE   There are events connected with getting and losing the focus as well: **GotFocus** and **LostFocus**. These can be useful to check if the user has tabbed away from a text box or pushed the <Enter> key.

That's it. The cut button is now functional. At this point, you can make a standalone application out of our pad by choosing the Make Exe File... item in the File menu. When you run it under Windows, the pad appears. When the user selects text, they can cut it with the Cut button. However, that's only half the story of a full notepad application; the next step is to allow the user to paste the text back in.

This can happen in two ways. First, the user can select some additional text in the text box, and when they paste, we're supposed to paste over that text. Second, the user might simply position the insertion point at a particular location, and then we're supposed to insert the text there. As it happens, Visual Basic takes care of these two cases almost automatically.

To begin, we'll have to introduce another button, which we can call **PasteButton**, and which we might give the caption "Paste." Place this button in between the other two, and double-click it to open the code window. You'll see that **PasteButton_Click( )** is already selected. It turns out that all we have to do here is to replace the selected text in the text window, **PadText.SelText**, with **CutText** (the global string that holds the cut text). Visual Basic handles the details: If there is some text selected, it is replaced with **CutText**; if no text was selected, then **CutText** is inserted at the insertion point, exactly as it should be. Here's the code for **PasteButton_Click( )** (note that we return the focus to the text box here too):

```
Sub PasteButton_Click()
    PadText.SelText = CutText
    PadText.SetFocus
End Sub
```

We're almost done with the Paste button; the working pad application so far appears in Figure 2-16. However, there are still a few problems. One is that when the application is first started, there's nothing to paste yet, but the Paste button can still be pushed. Even though it does nothing, it would be better still if we could grey the button caption out; that is, disable the Paste button in the standard Windows fashion before there is something to paste.

In fact, we can do this too. One of the properties associated with a command button is the **Enabled** property. When set to True, the button is enabled and can be clicked; when set to False, the button does not respond to the user, and its caption is greyed. We can take advantage of this immediately. First, set the **Enabled** property of the Paste button to False in the properties bar. We want

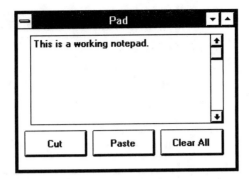

Figure 2-16. Pad Application with Paste Button

to enable this button only when text has been placed in the **CutText** buffer. Since that's only done when the Cut button has been clicked, we can simply add a line to **CutButton_Click( )** like this:

```
     Sub CutButton_Click()
         CutText = PadText.SelText
         PadText.SelText = ""
→        PasteButton.Enabled = -1 'Set to True
         PadText.SetFocus
     End Sub
```

Now, when you start the application, the pad appears as in Figure 2-17, with the Paste button greyed and disabled. However, as soon as you cut some text with the Cut button, the Paste button becomes active once again.

Loading CONSTANT.TXT

Notice that we set **PasteButton.Enabled** to -1, which is the value Visual Basic uses for True. On the other hand, the constant True is defined in the file CONSTANT.TXT already, and we can simply load that file into our global module (as we'll do frequently throughout the book). To do that, open the global module by double-clicking Global.Bas in the project window (note that our declaration of **CutText** is already in Global.Bas). Next, select the Load Text... item in the Code menu. A number of .TXT files will be displayed in the file box there. Select CONSTANT.TXT and select the Merge option. When you do, CONSTANT.TXT is loaded into the global module of our application. Now we're free to use the constant True instead of -1, like this:

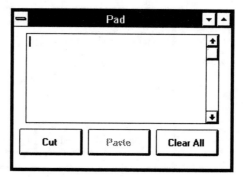

Figure 2-17. Pad with Paste Button Greyed

```
Sub CutButton_Click()
      CutText = PadText.SelText
      PadText.SelText = ""
→     PasteButton.Enabled = True
      PadText.SetFocus
End Sub
```

NOTE Now that we've placed text in Global.Bas, we should also save it under another name, such as Pad.Bas, to avoid overwriting it later with another project.

In fact, since we've gone this far, we might as well enable the Cut and Clear All buttons only when it makes sense. In particular, we can enable these buttons after the user has started typing something into the pad (i.e., at which time there is text available to cut or clear). In this case, we can work with the text box's **Change** event, which is one of the primary programming events of a text box, as we saw in the last chapter. Whenever the contents of a text box change (e.g., when characters are typed in it, or if your program affects the text box's **Text** property), a corresponding **Change** event is generated. We can take advantage of that here to enable the Cut and Clear All buttons in our pad after text has been typed for the first time.

To begin, set the **Enabled** property for both **CutButton** and **ClearButton** to False at design-time. Now, when the notepad appears for the first time, all three buttons, Cut, Paste, and Clear All will be greyed. Next, double-click the text box to open the code window; this sub procedure appears:

```
Sub PadText_Change()

End Sub
```

Now just put this code in:

```
Sub PadText_Change()
    CutButton.Enabled = True
    ClearButton.Enabled = True
End Sub
```

That's it. The first-time the user types, and the two buttons will be enabled. Our notepad is getting to be quite a polished application. While we're on the topic of command buttons, however, we should note that we can supply our buttons with *access* keys.

Using Access Keys

An access key is used in a menu or command button as a shortcut key that you can press along with the <Alt> key. For example, if we made C the access key for our Cut button, the user could press <Alt-C> to click the button.

Adding access keys is very easy: All we have to do is to specify which letter we want to have stand for the access key by placing an ampersand (&) in front of it in the control's caption. For example, to make <C> the access key for the Cut button, change the button's caption to "&Cut." To make <P> the access key for the Paste button, change the Paste button's caption to "&Paste." Finally, to change the Clear All button's access key to <A> (since we've already used <C> with the Cut button — each access key should be unique among the currently available buttons or menu items), change its caption to "Clear &All." When you do, Visual Basic changes the caption of each button, underlining the access key, as shown in Figure 2-18. It's that easy to set access keys in Visual Basic.

That's it for our pad for now (we'll come back to it later); the code, event by event, appears in Listing 2-1. Next, we can turn to another application: a windowed alarm clock.

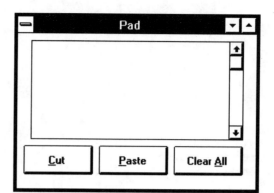

Figure 2-18. Pad with Access Keys

Listing 2-1. Pad Application

```
Pad.Bas (Global Module) -----------------------------

    Global CutText As String

Pad.Frm ---------------------------------------------

Sub ClearButton_Click ()
    PadText.Text = ""
    PadText.SetFocus
End Sub

Sub CutButton_Click ()
    CutText = PadText.SelText
    PadText.SelText = ""
    PasteButton.Enabled = True
    PadText.SetFocus
End Sub

Sub Pastebutton_Click ()
    PadText.SelText = CutText
    PadText.SetFocus
End Sub

Sub PadText_Change ()
    CutButton.Enabled = True
    ClearButton.Enabled = True
End Sub
```

An Alarm Clock Example

There is still a good deal to learn about text boxes and buttons. For example, we can actually read keystrokes as they're typed in a text box, or even change display fonts. For that matter, we can use an entirely different kind of button: option buttons (the small round buttons that are also called radio buttons). Let's take advantage of some of those capabilities with a new application: a digital alarm clock that lets you display the time and will notify you when a certain amount of time is up. The application we're aiming for appears in Figure 2-19.

Start a new Visual Basic project and give the caption "Alarm" to the default form; save the form, global module (i.e., Global.Bas in the project window); and project as Alarm.Frm, Alarm.Bas, and Alarm.Mak. Now we're ready to start. The first thing we can do is to set up the text box that will accept the alarm setting (e.g., the alarm setting in Figure 2-19 is 09:30:00). That's easy enough; just double-click the text box tool in Visual Basic's toolbox and place the text box in a position roughly corresponding to that in Figure 2-19 (i.e., the lower-left corner of the form).

We can call this text box, say, AlarmSetting. In addition, you should clear the default text in the text box ("Text1") so that the text box is clear when the user starts the application. To keep this example relatively simple, we're only going to accept the time in this box in a restricted format, like this: "hh:mm:ss," the same way that the Time$ function of Basic will return it. (In a professional application, of course, we'd have to be more forgiving.) We haven't restricted user input before, but Visual Basic allows us to do so by reading each keystroke as it's typed.

Figure 2-19. Alarm Clock Application

Interpreting Individual Keystrokes

There are three events that occur each time the user types a key in a control or form that has the focus: **KeyDown**, **KeyUp**, and **KeyPress**. The **KeyPress** event is the one we'll be using here because it returns the standard type of character values that we're used to dealing with in Basic. The **KeyDown** and **KeyUp** events are generated when the user presses and releases the key, and each event procedure receives two arguments: *KeyCode* and *Shift*. KeyCode here is the *ANSI* code (not ASCII) for the key that was pressed or released, and Shift holds the state of the <Shift>, <Alt>, and <Ctrl> keys. It turns out that ANSI, not ASCII, is the standard Windows character set, and, while the two character sets have considerable overlap, they are not the same; however, they're the same for letters (like "a") and numbers (like "5").

In addition, **KeyDown** and **KeyUp** do not differentiate between lowercase ("z") and uppercase ("Z") except in the Shift argument; that is, the only way to tell if a character is lower- or uppercase is to look at Shift. This argument has a value of 1 if the <Shift> key is down, 2 if the <Ctrl> key is down, 4 if the <Alt> key is down, or a sum of those values if more than one of those keys are down (e.g., <Shift+Alt> would give a value in the Shift argument of 5).

The reason that **KeyDown** and **KeyUp** are useful is that they can read keys that have no standard ASCII value, such as the arrow keys or the function keys. For example, if the user pressed the <F1> key, **KeyCode** will be equal to Key_F1 as defined in CONSTANT.TXT; if the user pressed <F2>, **KeyCode** will equal Key_F2 and so forth. However, both **KeyDown** and **KeyUp** are advanced events, so we'll stick with **KeyPress** here.

Our intention is to restrict the user's keystrokes to those allowed in the AlarmSetting text box. Those characters are "0–9" and ":". We'll check to make sure that the typed key is in that range. To set up our procedure, double-click the text box to open the code window, then select the **KeyPress** event from the procedures box. The following procedure template appears:

```
Sub AlarmSetting_KeyPress (KeyAscii As Integer)

End Sub
```

As you can see, Visual Basic passes one argument to a **KeyPress** event — *KeyAscii*, the typed key's ASCII value. While **KeyDown** and **KeyUp** use ANSI key codes, **KeyPress** uses the ASCII set that most programmers are used to. In other words, this is just like a normal Sub procedure with one argument passed to us, KeyAscii. That means we can make use of it immediately, checking the value of the just-typed key like this:

```
Sub AlarmSetting_KeyPress (KeyAscii As Integer)
    Key$ = Chr$(KeyAscii)
    If((Key$ < "0" OR Key$ > "9") AND Key$ <> ":") Then
        :

End Sub
```

First, we convert the ASCII code in KeyAscii to a character (i.e., a string of length one) using the Basic Chr$( ) function like this: Key$ = Chr$(KeyAscii). Then we check the value of that character against the allowed range. Recall that < and > work for string comparisons as well as numeric comparisons in Basic; that is, they compare strings in alphabetic order, so "0" is less than "1" and "c" is greater than "b."

TIP   Although we're restricting the user to the characters "0–9" and ":", it's a good idea in practice to allow text-editing characters as well, such as the <Backspace> and <Del> keys (just get their ASCII codes from the Visual Basic documentation). Also, it's worth pointing out that the opposite of Chr$( ) is Asc( ); that is, Asc( ) returns the ASCII value of the first character of its argument string, and it's also useful when checking to see if characters are in a certain range.

If the key that was typed is not in the allowed range, we should do two things: delete it and beep to indicate an error. We can beep with the Basic Beep statement, and it turns out that deleting the key is easy. We just have to set KeyAscii to 0:

```
      Sub AlarmSetting_KeyPress (KeyAscii As Integer)
          Key$ = Chr$(KeyAscii)
          If((Key$ < "0" OR Key$ > "9") AND Key$ <> ":") Then
→             Beep
→             KeyAscii = 0
          End If
      End Sub
```

That's it for checking the typed keys, so that's it for **AlarmSetting_KeyPress( )**. In addition, we should place the label "Alarm Setting:" above the text box to indicate what it's for. To do that, just click on the label tool (the capital A) in

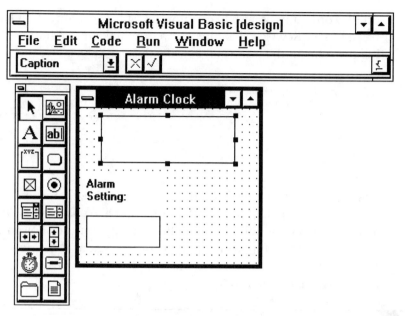

Figure 2-20. Clock Template

Visual Basic's tool box, and place the label above the text box, setting its caption to "Alarm Setting:" (see Figure 2-19). Now we're set as far as recording and storing the alarm setting goes; our program will be able to read the alarm setting directly from the text box's **Text** property.

Displaying the Time

The next step in assembling our alarm clock is to set up the clock's display itself. Since we don't want the clock display to be edited from the keyboard (that is, it will use system time), we can use a label, not a text box here. Click on the label tool once again, and enlarge the label until it is roughly the size of the one in Figure 2-20. Delete the characters in the **Caption** property, and then take a look at the **BorderStyle** property in the properties bar.

Normally, labels do not have a border, but they can have the same type of border that text boxes have. If you open the settings list next to the settings box, you'll see that the two options for **BorderStyle** are None and Fixed Single. Select Fixed Single to give the clock's display a border. In addition, we can give this label a name. Let's call it **Display**. To display the time, then, we can just use the Basic function Time$ like this:

```
Display.Caption = Time$.
```

The question, however, is how to keep the time updated. In other words, what kind of event occurs often enough, and regularly enough, to make sure that the time in **Display.Caption** is current? Visual Basic has another type of control for exactly this kind of use: timers.

Visual Basic Timers

A timer is just that: It can produce a specific event, called a Timer event, at a predetermined interval. Its control symbol is a small clock, both on the form (although it is not visible at run-time) and in the toolbox. Double-click the timer tool now and position the timer roughly in the same position as in Figure 2-21. Visual Basic gives the timer a default name of **Timer1**.

The next step is to set the timer's **Interval** property; that is, how often the Timer event occurs. Make sure the timer is selected and open the properties list in the properties bar. Highlight the **Interval** property and move over to the settings box. The **Interval** property is measured in milliseconds; that is, in thousandths of a second. Since we don't want to put a significant burden on

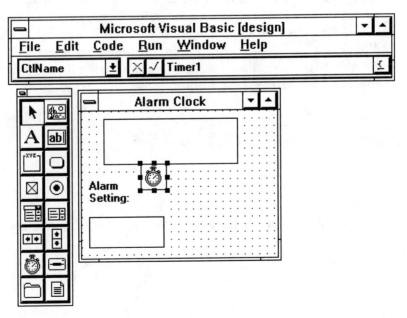

Figure 2-21. Clock Template with Timer

the rest of the system, we'll update the clock only once a second, so choose 1,000 for the **Interval** property of the timer.

NOTE Although there is a temptation to use timers to make sure your code gets control as often as possible, you should avoid using them unless necessary (as with, for example, a clock) because overuse goes against the spirit of event-oriented processing. That is, continual use of a timer can come very close to sequential (non-Windows) processing, where one application uses all the available computing time.

Now we're ready to write the actual procedure that will be run every time the timer ticks (i.e., once a second). Double-click the timer to open the code window. The procedure that's already displayed in outline — **Timer1_Timer( )** is the one we want:

```
Sub Timer1_Timer()

End Sub
```

We can start by checking if the time is up; that is, if the string returned by the Basic function Time$ is the same as the time which the alarm is set for (in other words, if Time$ equals **AlarmSetting.Text**), we should sound an alarm. In fact, this is not a safe thing to do. If Windows is performing some action, or if our clock's window is being moved, the timer may not be called for a while. For that reason, we should actually check whether Time$ is greater than or equal to **AlarmSetting.Text**, like this:

```
Sub Timer1_Timer()
    If (Time$ >= AlarmSetting.Text) Then

        :
End Sub
```

If the condition is True, then we can just use the Beep statement this way:

```
      Sub Timer1_Timer()
          If (Time$ >= AlarmSetting.Text) Then
→             Beep
          End If
      End Sub
```

That's it. When the time has elapsed, this procedure will make the clock beep, and, since it's called once a second, the clock will keep beeping, once a second. However, this is incomplete as it stands. Alarm clocks usually have two settings: alarm on and alarm off (now that the alarm is on, we've got to shut it off).

For that reason, we can add two option buttons labeled Alarm On and Alarm Off (see Figure 2-19). The procedure connected with those buttons can communicate with the current procedure, **Timer1_Timer( )**, through a global variable, which we might call **AlarmOn**. In other words, if **AlarmOn** is True *and* Time$ >= **AlarmSetting.Text**, then we should beep, which we can do like this:

```
      Sub Timer1_Timer()
→         If (Time$ >= AlarmSetting.Text AND AlarmOn) Then
              Beep
          End If
      End Sub
```

The last thing to do here is to update the display (i.e., because this procedure is called when the time changes), and we can do that like this:

```
      Sub Timer1_Timer()
          If (Time$ >= AlarmSetting.Text AND AlarmOn) Then
              Beep
          End If
→         Display.Caption = Time$
      End Sub
```

As mentioned, since this procedure is called once a second, the beeping will continue until the Alarm Off button is clicked (which will make **AlarmOn** False). Now let's set up **AlarmOn** itself. We can put it into the global module (making it shared by the whole application — recall that only declarations, no code, can go in the global module) by clicking Alarm.Bas in the project window.

The global module window opens, and since we're going to define **AlarmOn** as True or False, it's a good idea to include CONSTANT.TXT in this module first because that's where the values of True and False are stored. As before, you do that by using the Load Text... item in the Code menu of Visual Basic, selecting CONSTANT.TXT, and then choosing the Merge option. In addition to the contents of CONSTANT.TXT, declare **AlarmOn** in the global module like this:

```
Global AlarmOn As Integer
```

We declare it global because declarations in the global module must use the Global keyword instead of Dim; we declare it an integer because both True and False are integers in Visual Basic.

NOTE   If you're familiar with the *Boolean* type in other languages, then you should know that the boolean type becomes the integer type in Visual Basic.

At this point, our timer is ready, and our clock is ready to function (that is, a clock display will appear on the screen, although in a smaller font than in Figure 2-19). We compare the alarm setting to the current time, and we update the display on the screen: Everything is ready, except for the **AlarmOn** variable. The last step is designing the two option buttons that make **AlarmOn** active because, without it, the alarm part of the clock cannot work.

Using Option (Radio) Buttons

Option buttons — often called radio buttons — work in a group; that is, only one of the option buttons that appear on a form can be selected at once. You use option buttons to select one option from among several mutually exclusive choices (i.e., choices where it's either one or the other, such as Transparent and Opaque).

TIP   Another way of making option buttons work as a group is to enclose them in a *frame*, by using the frame tool in the Visual Basic toolbox (the frame tool has a frame drawn on it with xyz in the upper-left corner). The option buttons in such a frame are separate from the rest of the option buttons on the form.

Visual Basic takes care of the details of turning option buttons on and off for us. If one of a group of option buttons is clicked, the other one that was on (i.e., with a black dot in the center) will automatically be turned off. We can add two option buttons to our alarm clock easily. Just double-click the option button tool (fourth down on the right in the toolbox), and position the two

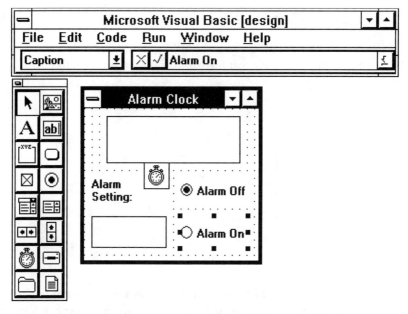

Figure 2-22. Alarm Clock Template with Option Buttons

option buttons under the Display label, giving them the captions "Alarm Off" and "Alarm On" as in Figure 2-22.

Together, these two make up an option button group. Because they are part of the same form (and not enclosed in separate frames), Visual Basic will turn them on and off so that only one is selected at a time. Note that we should have the Alarm Off option selected when the user starts the clock. Each option button has a **Value** property associated with it, indicating whether or not the button is selected — True if selected (i.e., with a black dot in the center); False if not. We can set the **Value** property at both design-time and at run-time, so set the Alarm Off button's **Value** to True in the properties bar now.

In addition, we need names for these new buttons. We can give them their own names, such as **AlarmOnButton** and **AlarmOffButton**, and then write the corresponding procedures when one of them is clicked; that is, we can set the variable **AlarmOn** to True or False by checking the values of **AlarmOnButton.Value** and **AlarmOffButton.Value**. However, groups of buttons (in fact, groups of controls) like this are usually handled in a different way in Visual Basic, and that is by making the group of buttons into a *control array*.

Arrays of Controls

Control arrays are the way to handle groups of controls in Visual Basic. For example, imagine that you have a number of buttons like this:

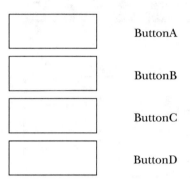

In this case, you would have to write a separate event handler for each button. For example, if you were interested in the Click event, you'd have **ButtonA_Click( )**, **ButtonB_Click( )**, **ButtonC_Click( )**, and **ButtonD_Click( )**. This can be awkward if the buttons perform essentially the same action with a few variations (as groups of controls usually do). The easier way to handle such groups of buttons like this is to give them all the same name. If you do, Visual Basic automatically gives them separate **Index** numbers (you might have noticed the **Index** property associated with most controls in the properties bar). For example, if you called each button **MyButton**, Visual Basic gives the first one an index of zero, the next an index of one, and so on:

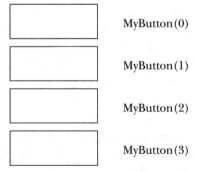

Now, instead of four separate event procedures (like **ButtonA_Click( )** to **ButtonD_Click( )**), there is only one procedure for each event, and Visual

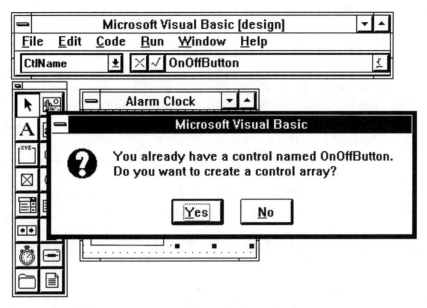

Figure 2-23. Control Array Box

Basic automatically passes the index corresponding to the button that was clicked: **MyButton_Click(Index As Integer)**.

Let's see this in action. Name the top option button (Alarm Off) as, say, **OnOffButton**; that is, make its **CtlName OnOffButton**. Next, do the same for the other option button (Alarm On). When you do, Visual Basic pops up a box saying: "You already have a control named **OnOffButton**. Do you want to create a control array?" as in Figure 2-23. Answer yes and then double-click on either option button to open the code window.

This is the procedure template that appears in the code window:

```
OnOffButton_Click(Index As Integer)

End Sub
```

Notice the first line: Because we've set up **OnOffButton** as a control array, Visual Basic passes the **Index** of the button pushed. That is, since we named the Alarm Off button as **OnOffButton** first, it will have **Index** 0. The Alarm On button will have **Index** 1 (if you wonder what a control's **Index** value is, just check it in the properties bar).

This means that if we check the value of **Index**, we'll be able to determine which button was pushed, letting us write one procedure for both buttons, which is precisely the idea behind creating groups of controls. When a set of controls handle similar functions, you should try to make them into a group and create a control array (since Visual Basic handles all the details, it's easy). All the current procedure has to do is determine which button was clicked by checking **Index** (0→Alarm Off; 1→Alarm On) and then set the global variable **AlarmOn** correctly (i.e., that's the job of these option buttons — to set the global variable **AlarmOn**). We can do that like this:

```
OnOffButton_Click(Index As Integer)
    If (Index = 1) Then
        AlarmOn = True
    Else
        AlarmOn = False
    End If
End Sub
```

And that's all there is to it. Our alarm clock is almost done. The last change we'll make will be to the clock display itself. As it stands, the time is displayed in standard system font characters, but we can improve that significantly.

TIP   One more point is worth mentioning here. If you had designed the clock in a slightly different order than we have here, and put the alarm setting text box on the form after the option buttons, then there would be a small problem. When the application started, the option button that was placed on the form first would have the focus, not the alarm settings box. To give the alarm settings box the default focus, set it first in the *tab order*. That is, one of the properties of controls that can get the focus is called **TabIndex**. The control with a **TabIndex** of 0 gets the default focus, and you can tab around the form to the other controls at will (the other controls have tab indices of 1, 2, 3, and so on). In fact, using the **TabIndex**, you can rearrange the way the user tabs from control to control on your form.

Selecting Fonts

Some of the properties associated with labels and text boxes have to do with fonts; here they are:

FontName	Name of font to use for text (such as Courier)
FontSize	Font size in points (1/72 of an inch)
FontBold	Make text bold
FontItalic	Make text italic
FontStrikeThrough	Overstrike text with dashes
FontUnderline	Underline the text

By selecting these properties at design-time, we can set the type of font in the clock's display. In our case, we'll just use the standard font (although there are eight fonts available, including Helvetica, Modern, Roman, and System), except that we'll expand the font size from 8.25 to 24 points (a point is 1/72 of an inch). To do that, select the Display label and then open the settings list for the **FontSize** property, as in Figure 2-24.

Finally, change the value of the **FontSize** setting to 24 points from 8.25. That will make the display size to 24 points, filling the **Display** label with the clock display. And that's it for the alarm clock. The working application appears in Figure 2-19, and the code, event by event, appears in Listing 2-2.

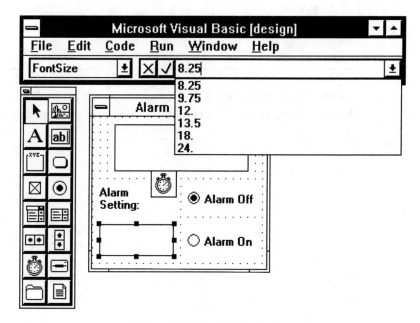

Figure 2-24. FontSize Settings

Listing 2-2. Alarm Application Code

```
Alarm.Bas (Global Module) -------------------------

    Global AlarmOn As Integer

Alarm.Frm -----------------------------------------

Sub Timer1_Timer ()
    If (Time$ > AlarmSetting.Text And AlarmOn) Then
        Beep
    End If
    Display.Caption = Time$
End Sub

Sub OnOffButton_Click (Index As Integer)
    If (Index = 1) Then
        AlarmOn = True
    Else
        AlarmOn = False
    End If
End Sub

Sub AlarmSetting_KeyPress (KeyAscii As Integer)
    Key$ = Chr$(KeyAscii)
    If ((Key$ < "0" Or Key$ > "9") And Key$ <> ":") Then
        Beep
        KeyAscii = 0
    End If
End Sub
```

We'll continue our exploration of I/O with the user under Visual Basic in the next chapter, when we start really digging in, by using menus in our programs.

Menus

——

The next step in creating useful applications is to add menus. If you're a Windows user, you're certainly familiar with menus. In fact, we've already used many menus in Visual Basic. For example, Visual Basic's File menu appears in Figure 3-1, with the various parts labeled.

There are a number of elements in a menu that we should be familiar with before starting our own discussion of how to build them. The first, of course, is the *menu bar*, which indicates all the currently available menus in an application. Selecting a name in the menu bar pops down (or up if you're at the bottom of the screen) the associated menu. Each line in a menu lists a unique *menu item*. If that item is highlighted, it is selected.

Releasing the mouse button while an item is selected chooses that item; if the item has an *ellipsis* (...) after it, it opens a dialog box that can read more information from the user. In addition, items can be *greyed* (disabled) or *checked* (a check mark next to them) indicating that a certain option has been turned on (for example, making text bold in a word processor). Finally, menu items can be grouped together with a *separator bar*, as shown in Figure 3-1. In other words, all the menu items having to do with, say, text color can fit into one group, and all the items having to do with font size can appear in another. We'll see all these parts — menu bars, menu items, disabled items, checked

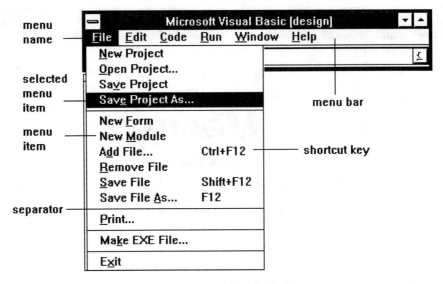

Figure 3-1. Visual Basic's File Menu

items, separator bars, and more in this chapter — however, we'll save the ellipsis items, which usually open a dialog box, for Chapter 4.

Designing and implementing menus in Visual Basic is not difficult. In this chapter, we'll see a number of examples. In particular, we'll start a small file editing program that we'll be able to finish later on (after we've covered the mechanics of loading and saving files), as well as updating our alarm clock into a menu-driven program. However, our first example will be a game, a tic-tac-toe game. We don't have the space here to develop the code necessary to let the computer play — games can be long programs to write — so this will be a game for two (human) players.

A Menu-driven Tic-Tac-Toe Game

We can begin the tic-tac-toe game by beginning a new project (i.e., start Visual Basic or choose the New Project item in Visual Basic's File menu). Change the form's caption to "Tic-Tac-Toe," and place nine command buttons on it as shown in Figure 3-2 (we'll use command buttons rather than text boxes because there is no Click event for text boxes, which means the user would have to type "x" or "o").

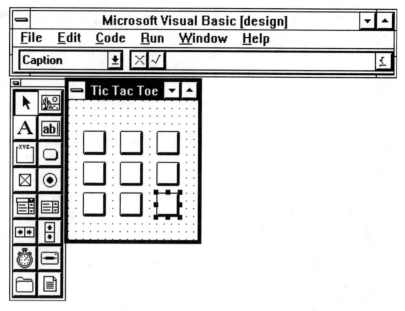

Figure 3-2. Tic-Tac-Toe Template

Clear the **Caption** property of each command button, and name them all, say, "TTT" for "Tic-Tac-Toe." When Visual Basic asks you whether you want to set up a control array, answer yes; writing one click procedure is going to be easier than writing nine. In fact, we can write that procedure immediately. Just double-click on a command button, and the code window opens, displaying this Sub procedure template:

```
Sub TTT_Click(Index As Integer)

End Sub
```

Because we've put the **TTT** buttons together into an array, Visual Basic passes an Index argument as well. If you've arranged the buttons in random order on the form, don't worry. It doesn't matter which index belongs to which button because we can set the caption of a button like this: **TTT(Index).Caption** = "x". This is the way you can change the text or caption of a control when you're working with a control array — simply refer to the name of the array and add the index in parentheses afterwards. In our case, that means that we'll be able to refer to the caption of each button as **TTT(Index).Caption**.

However, we have to know whether we should put an "x" at the current place, or an "o." Let's declare a global variable named **XTurn**; when it's True, it's x's turn; when it's False, it's o's turn. We can declare that variable by opening the global module — Global.Bas — and making this declaration:

```
Global XTurn As Integer
```

In addition, merge the file CONSTANT.TXT with the global module by using the Load Text... item in the code menu, and the Merge option after that so that we can use the constants True and False. You should also save this file with a unique name, such as TicTac.Bas, as well as saving the form as TicTac.Frm, and the project itself as TicTac.Mak. At this point, setting the button's caption to x or o is easy; we can just do it like this:

```
Sub TTT_Click(Index As Integer)
    If (Xturn) Then
        TTT(Index).Caption = "x"
        XTurn = False
    Else
        TTT(Index).Caption = "o"
        XTurn = True
    End If
End Sub
```

This will keep the characters that appear alternating when the user clicks the various command buttons (notice that in this simple program we did not check whether the button already had been clicked or whether someone has won the game — two things you should do if you intend to develop this into a tournament-level Tic-Tac-Toe game).

Now we have to provide the user with some way of starting over by adding a New Game option, which involves initializing the **XTurn** variable and clearing all the command buttons that make up the places on the Tic-Tac-Toe board. This is where we'll start working with menus because New Game is exactly the kind of item that you might find in a menu. In addition, we'll add an Exit item to our menu since all applications that have menus should have an Exit item.

Adding a Menu to the Tic-Tac-Toe Game

Designing menus in Visual Basic is not as hard as you might expect. In fact, each menu item is a control itself, and the primary event associated with it is

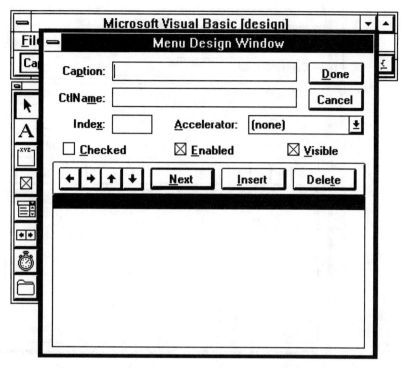

Figure 3-3. The Visual Basic Menu Design Window

the Click event. However, to get this new type of control onto our form, we have to design them first using the Menu Design Window (i.e., we can't just paint them with toolbox tools).

To pop that window onto the screen, open the Visual Basic Window menu and select the Menu Design Window item. That window appears, as shown in Figure 3-3.

We can start by specifying the caption of our menu. In particular, we can call it File because applications often have a file menu and because that's where the user expects to find the Exit item (and, if you wish, you can modify the Tic-Tac-Toe game to save the current game to a file after we learn about file handling). To create a File menu (i.e., "File" will appear in the menu bar), type File in the **Caption** text box at the top of the Menu Design Window, as shown in Figure 3-4. In addition, each menu has to be given a control name (**CtlName**) so that the program can refer to it (which will allow us to switch menus around in the menu bar, or change them altogether, as we'll see later).

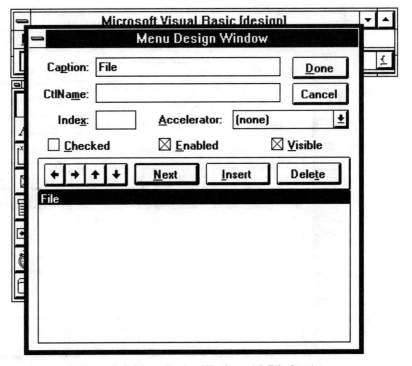

Figure 3-4. Menu Design Window with File Caption

In our case, we can give the File menu the **CtlName FileMenu**, which we should type in the **CtlName** text box.

You might note that as we typed File in the **Caption** box, the same word appeared in the main list box below it (i.e., File is shown highlighted in the main list box at the bottom of figure 3-4). This is where the menu(s) that we are designing will appear. So far, we only have the caption of one menu: File. The next step is to add the New Game and Exit items.

The insertion point should be right after the last name you typed — **FileMenu** in the **CtlName** text box. Press <Enter> to end this item and to move the highlight bar in the list box down one line; the **Caption** text box and the **CtlName** text boxes are cleared in preparation to receive the new menu item. Type New Game in the **Caption** text box, and, say, **NewItem** (meaning the New Game item in this menu) in the **CtlName** text box. Again, the text — New Game — appears in the list box at the bottom of the window. If we left it this way, however, New Game would be a menu name just like File, and would

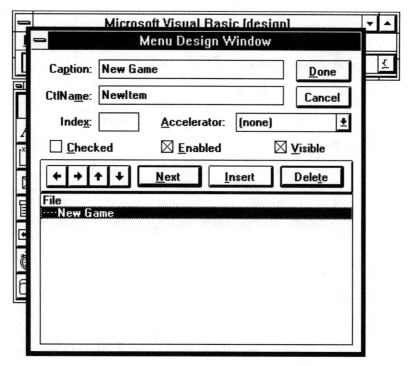

Figure 3-5. Menu Design Window, New Game Indented

appear in the menu bar. Instead, we want this to be the first menu item in the File menu, so click the right arrow in the bar above the list box (i.e., the second arrow from the left in the group of four). When you do, the New Game entry is indented four spaces in the list box, as shown in Figure 3-5.

This means that New Game is an *item* in the File menu, not a menu itself. In fact, New Game is the first item. Next, press <Enter> again so that the high-light bar in the list box moves down one more line. Again, the **Caption** and **CtlName** text boxes are cleared.

TIP   Visual Basic allows you to even have menus within menus, where selecting a menu item will pop open a new menu. You do this by successive levels of indentation, and you can have five such levels.

The next item in the File menu is Exit, so type **Exit** as the **Caption** and, say, **ExitItem** as the **CtlName**. Notice that you did not have to click the right arrow

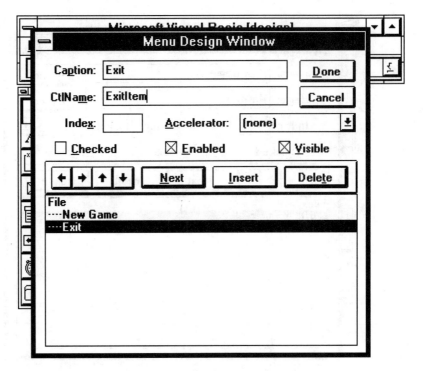

Figure 3-6. The Completed Menu Design Window

again to indent Exit in the list box. It was automatically indented now that we're adding names to the File menu (to remove the automatic indentation, click the left arrow above the list box). The menu design is now complete, as shown in Figure 3-6.

Close the Menu Design Window by clicking on the Done button. When you do, you'll see that a File menu has been added to our Tic-Tac-Toe game template, as in Figure 3-7.

As mentioned, the design process is primarily to add controls to our template. Now that we've added the controls, we can treat them like any others; that is, we can attach code to them as easily. Let's see how this works. For example, click on the File menu in the Tic-Tac-Toe menu bar, and the menu opens, showing the two items we've put in it, New Game and Exit, as shown in Figure 3-8.

These two items are now simply controls, like buttons or text boxes. To open the code window, for example, just double-click the New Game item. The

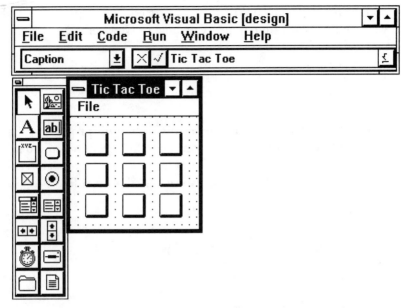

Figure 3-7. Tic-Tac-Toe Template with File Menu

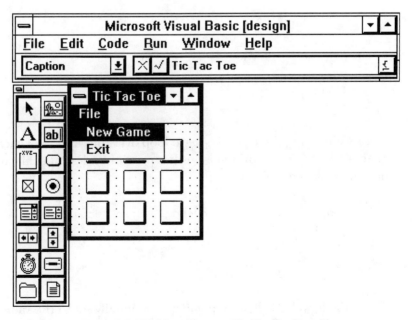

Figure 3-8. File Menu Open on Tic-Tac-Toe Template

code window opens, holding a Sub procedure template like this (recall that we gave the New Game item a **CtlName** of **NewItem**):

```
Sub NewItem_Click()

End Sub
```

When the user chooses this item, this is the Sub procedure that will be executed. In other words, we'll be using the Click event for menu items, just as we did for buttons. In our case, the user wants to start a new Tic-Tac-Toe game, so we'll have to reset the variable we've called **XTurn** like this (i.e., "o" will go first):

```
Sub NewItem_Click()
    XTurn = 0                 'Set XTurn False
        :
End Sub
```

In addition, we need to set the caption property of all the command buttons to " ". As an added touch, we can set the focus (that is, the thick black outline that appears around a command button) to the top-left button, although this is not necessary:

```
Sub NewItem_Click()
    XTurn = 0
    For loop_index = 0 To 8
        TTT(loop_index).Caption = ""
    Next loop_index
    TTT(0).SetFocus
End Sub
```

Here, we're using the Basic *for loop* to loop over the caption of each button. In general, the for loop works like this (we present Basic syntax like this throughout the book as a review only):

```
for loop_index = begin To end [, Step stepsize]
    :
    [body of for loop]
    :
Next loop_index
```

The variable we've called **loop_index** is originally set to the value **begin**, and tested against the value **end**. If it's less than **end**, the body of the loop is executed, and **loop_index** is incremented by 1 — unless you include the Step keyword and a **stepsize** (which can be negative). In that case, **stepsize** is added to **loop_index** instead (if **stepsize** is negative, the loop ends when the value in **loop_index** is less than **begin**). In our case, we're simply setting the caption of buttons **TTT(0)** to **TTT(8)** to the empty string, " ", in the body of the loop:

```
       Sub NewItem_Click()
           XTurn = 0
→          For loop_index = 0 To 8
→              TTT(loop_index).Caption = ""
→          Next loop_index
           TTT(0).SetFocus
       End Sub
```

Now the New Game option in the File menu is active. That's all there is to it. Making the Exit option active is even easier. Open the File menu on the Tic-Tac-Toe form once again and double-click on the Exit item; a new Sub procedure template appears:

```
  Sub ExitItem_Click()

  End Sub
```

All we want to do here is to end the application if the user selects this item, and we can do that with the Basic End statement like this:

```
       Sub ExitItem_Click()
→          End
       End Sub
```

When Visual Basic executes the End statement, it ends the program and removes the window from the screen, just like selecting Close in the system menu. And that's it for our Tic-Tac-Toe game; everything is ready to go. It was that quick. The full, operating version appears in Figure 3-9, and the code appears in Listing 3-1. Every time the user clicks a command button, an x or an o (in alternating sequence) appears. To start over, you can select the New Game item in the File menu. To stop completely, you can select Exit. Note that this is only a demonstration program, of course. As mentioned, the program allows you to click a command button that's already been clicked, and doesn't stop even when someone wins. The idea here is to demonstrate menus, and we've already put them to work for us.

Figure 3-9. Tic-Tac-Toe Application

Listing 3-1. Tic-Tac-Toe Game

```
TicTac.Bas ----------------------------------------

Global XTurn As Integer

TicTac.Frm ----------------------------------------

Sub TTT_Click(Index As Integer)
    If (Xturn) Then
        TTT(Index).Caption = "x"
        XTurn = False
    Else
        TTT(Index).Caption = "o"
        XTurn = True
    End If
End Sub

Sub NewItem_Click()
    XTurn = 0
    For loop_index = 0 To 8
        TTT(loop_index).Caption = ""
    Next loop_index
    TTT(0).SetFocus
End Sub

Sub ExitItem_Click()
    End
End Sub
```

There are times when you should use command buttons for options, and there are times when you should use menus instead. Generally, you use command buttons when the options they represent are so frequently used that it's acceptable to have them continually presented to the user. On the other hand, commands such as the ones we've used in our notepad last chapter — i.e., Cut, Paste, and Clear All are usually part of a menu, and are not displayed as command buttons. In fact, let's modify our notepad so that it uses menus instead of command buttons. It will point out how close command buttons and menus are from a Visual Basic programming point of view, and it will get us started on an application that we will complete when we discuss files, a file editor.

Beginning Our Editor Example

The notepad we've developed is fine as far as it goes, but it is of very limited utility. In particular, the contents of the notepad disappear when you close the application. Instead, it would be much better if we could save our work on disk, and even read in preexisting files to modify them.

Toward that end, let's modify our Pad project to start working with menu selections. Later, we'll be able to add the actual mechanics of Visual Basic's file handling. To begin, then, read in the Pad project and save it as, say, Editor.Mak. Change the caption of the form from Pad to Editor, and save the other files as Editor.Bas and Editor.Frm, respectively. Now let's design our Editor's menu system.

Again, just select the Menu Design Window from the Window menu in Visual Basic; the Menu Design Window opens. The leftmost menu is usually the File menu in Windows applications, so type File first, as the Caption of that menu. Give this menu a **CtlName** of, say, **FileMenu**. After you've entered these two names, press <Enter> to move down to the first of the entries that will go in this menu. The first item might be, say, Load File..., so type that as the caption, then indent it by clicking on the right arrow in the group of four arrows above the main list box. In addition, give this Menu item the **CtlName LoadItem**. We can also make a provision to save files with a Save File... item, so add that next, giving it a **CtlName** of **SaveItem**. After that, we'll need a final menu item of Exit, which is expected in the File menu.

However, since Exit doesn't fit in with Load File... and Save File..., we can set it off as its own group by placing a menu separator in our menu. A separator is one of the horizontal lines that runs across a menu (as shown in Figure 3-1; note that Exit is set off from the rest of the menu items with a separator in Visual Basic's File menu as well) and divides menu items into groups. You

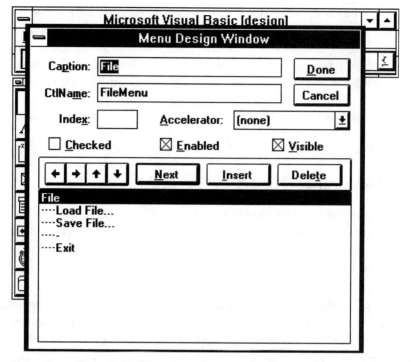

Figure 3-10. Menu Design Window for Editor, Stage 1

specify that you want a menu separator simply by typing a hyphen (-). Type a hyphen as the caption now and anything as the **CtlName**, such as **Separator**. Finally, enter Exit as the last item in the File menu. At this point, the Menu Design Window should look like Figure 3-10. Close the Menu Design Window by clicking Done; the Editor should now look like Figure 3-11.

As you can see, the separator was inserted, setting the Exit option off from the others. It is often a good idea to group menu items this way, since it makes it simpler for the user to find commands that are connected with each other.

Unfortunately, the only File menu item that we can make active at this time is the Exit item, since we'll have to wait until we have expertise with files before handling Load File... and Save File.... Double-click the Exit item and this template appears:

```
Sub ExitItem_Click()

End Sub
```

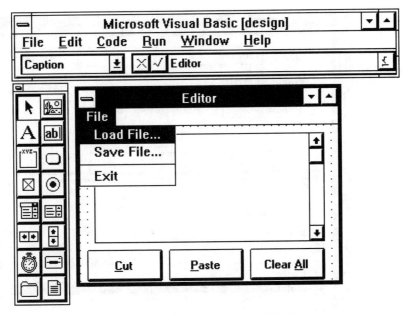

Figure 3-11. Editor Template with File Menu

Just add the End statement here, so that we can quit the application if the user chooses to:

```
Sub ExitItem_Click()
→     End
End Sub
```

The menu following the File menu is usually the Edit menu in word processors and editors, so let's add that now. Open the Menu Design Window again, and click on the blank line in the main list box below the last entry (i.e., Exit) so that it's highlighted. Now move up to the caption box and type Edit; give this menu a **CtlName** of **EditMenu**. Note that since we left the Menu Design Window and came back, the automatic indentation was turned off (i.e., Edit is made a menu bar item).

Since we'll be supplanting the notepad's command buttons with menu items here, the three items in the Edit menu should be Cut, Paste, and Clear All. Enter them one at a time, making sure they're indented and giving them the **CtlNames CutItem**, **PasteItem**, and **ClearItem**, respectively. At this point, the

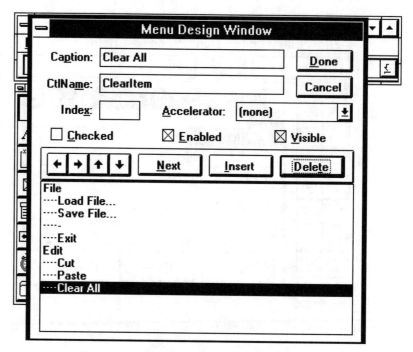

Figure 3-12. Menu Design Window with Edit Menu

Menu Design Window should look like Figure 3-12. Close the window. Now the Editor template should look like Figure 3-13.

Now the only work remaining is to transfer the procedures from the command buttons Cut, Paste, and Clear All to the menu items. Each of them are Click events, so they can be transferred whole. This is also easy to do in Visual Basic; just double-click the first button, Cut, to open the code window, as in Figure 3-14.

We've called this control **CutButton**, so the Sub procedure that appears looks like this:

```
Sub CutButton_Click()
    CutText = PadText.SelText
    PadText.SelText = " "
    PasteButton.Enabled = True
    PadText.SetFocus
End Sub
```

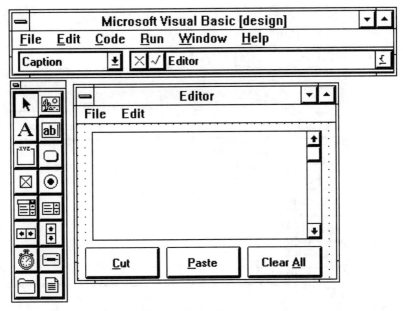

Figure 3-13. Editor Template with Edit Menu

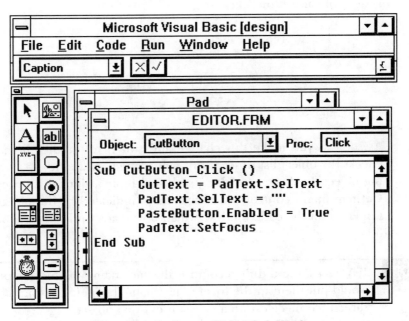

Figure 3-14. CutButton_Click( ) Code Window

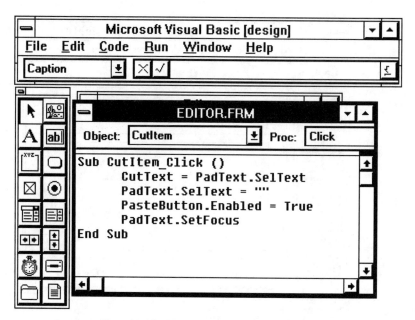

Figure 3-15. CutItem_Click( ) Code Window

Much of this will be the same under the menu system, so we can just change the name to **CutItem_Click( )** (the name of the cut item in the Edit menu) instead of **CutButton_Click( )**:

```
→    Sub CutItem_Click()
         CutText = PadText.SelText
         PadText.SelText = ""
         PasteButton.Enabled = True
         PadText.SetFocus
     End Sub
```

As soon as you make this change and switch to another line, Visual Basic checks the object list to see if this new name corresponds to an already existing object. In this case it does, so Visual Basic assigns this procedure to the **CutItem** menu control. Note that this is indicated by the object box in the upper-left of the code window, which now reads **CutItem**, as shown in Figure 3-15.

NOTE   If Visual Basic didn't recognize the new name of the our procedures, it would put them in the form object named general, assuming that it's not directly connected with an already existing object.

Next, we can do the same thing for the other buttons. The Paste button procedure, **PasteButton_Click( )**, looks like this now:

```
Sub PasteButton_Click()
    PadText.SelText = CutText
End Sub
```

(You might recall that we save the cut text in a global string named **CutText**, and that here we're just pasting it back in.) We can change this to **PasteItem_Click( )** easily enough; just edit the name of the Sub procedure until you have this:

```
→    Sub PasteItem_Click()
         PadText.SelText = CutText
     End Sub
```

That's it. We can handle the Clear All button the same way. Click on it (you don't have to close the code window first; the code in it will simply change to display **ClearButton_Click( )**) to pop up this procedure in the code window:

```
Sub ClearButton_Click()
    PadText.Text = ""
    PadText.SetFocus
End Sub
```

Change this to Sub **ClearItem_Click( )** instead:

```
Sub ClearItem_Click()
    PadText.Text = ""
    PadText.SetFocus
End Sub
```

Now we've made our menu items active and we can start making the changes to the code itself. First, we'll no longer need to set the focus to other objects because, in the absence of buttons, the text box will always have it. For that reason, remove the **PadText.SetFocus** line in all the procedures, until they look like this:

```
Sub CutItem_Click()
    CutText = PadText.SelText
    PadText.SelText = ""
    PasteButton.Enabled = True
End Sub
```

```
Sub PasteItem_Click()
    PadText.SelText = CutText
End Sub

Sub ClearItem_Click()
    PadText.Text = ""
End Sub
```

Next, you may recall that we started our pad with all three buttons greyed, and that we enabled the Cut and Clear All buttons only after the user typed something; that is, after there was a change in **PadText**, we executed these lines:

```
Sub PadText.Change()
    CutButton.Enabled = True
    ClearButton.Enabled = True
End Sub
```

It turns out that menu items have an enabled property just as buttons do. In fact, you're probably more used to seeing menu items greyed out than button captions. All we have to do is to change our references to button **Enabled** properties into menu item Enabled properties. In other words, what was **CutButton.Enabled** will become **CutItem.Enabled**, and what was **ClearButton.Enabled** becomes **ClearItem.Enabled**:

```
        Sub PadText.Change()
→           CutItem.Enabled = True
→           ClearItem.Enabled = True
        End Sub
```

In addition, you might recall that we enabled the Paste button only after some text had been cut (i.e., in the procedure **CutButton_Click( )**). We can change that reference also from **PasteButton.Enabled** to **PasteItem.Enabled** like this:

```
        Sub CutItem_Click()
            CutText = PadText.SelText
            PadText.SelText = ""
→           PasteItem.Enabled = True
        End Sub

        Sub PasteItem_Click()
            PadText.SelText = CutText
        End Sub

        Sub ClearItem_Click()
            PadText.Text = ""
        End Sub
```

Now all the references to buttons in the code have been replaced by references to menu items, so you can cut the buttons, removing them from the form. To do that, click on them and then select the Cut item in the Edit menu, readjusting the size of the form to absorb the space left by their absence.

At this point, we're almost done. The final step is to make sure that all the menu items in the Edit menu (Cut, Paste, Clear All) are greyed out when the application starts (i.e., before the user has started typing). As you might expect, we can do that at design-time in the Menu Design Window. Open that window by selecting it in the Window menu, and move the highlight bar in the main list box until the Cut item is highlighted. Then click on the **Enabled** check box — the middle check box in the row of three — to turn it off (the x in the box disappears), as shown in Figure 3-16.

Next, do the same for the other two menu items in the Edit menu, Paste, and Clear All, and click on the Done button. Now, when you run the Pad application, the Edit menu items originally appear greyed out, as in Figure 3-17.

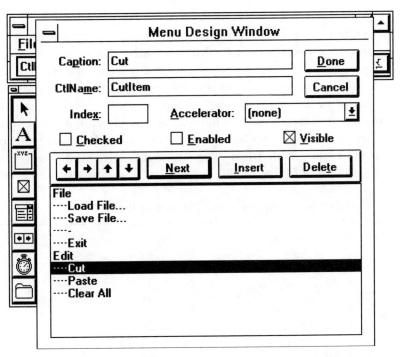

Figure 3-16. Menu Design Box with Enabled Option Off

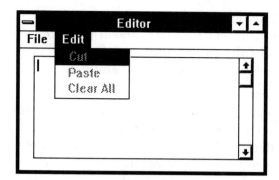

Figure 3-17. Pad with Edit Menu Greyed Out

When you start typing, however, the Cut and Clear All items are made active; when you actually do cut something, the Paste item is enabled as well.

That, then, is the way to enable or disable menu items — with the **Enabled** property. Setting it to True enables the menu item, and setting it False disables it. This capability is often extremely valuable to make sure that the user doesn't choose an impossible option, for example, attempting to save a file before there is any text in the text window.

However, you must keep track of the items you've disabled, and you should also realize that it's unattractive and frustrating to the user to present large menus where almost all items are greyed out (this has the flavor of operating in modes again — that is, drastically restricting the user's options — and Windows is all about presenting all the possible options so that the user has maximum freedom). If you have many greyed items, a better option might be to remove those items from your menus altogether, and replace them when they become enabled again (we'll see how to do this in Visual Basic later). All the code in our Editor so far appears in Listing 3-2, event by event.

Listing 3-2. Editor Application Code Version 1

```
Editor.Bas ---------------------------------------------

CutText As String

Editor.Frm ---------------------------------------------

Sub ExitItem_Click()
     End
End Sub
```

Listing 3-2. (continued)

```
Sub CutItem_Click()
    CutText = PadText.SelText
    PadText.SelText = ""
    PasteItem.Enabled = True
End Sub

Sub PasteItem_Click()
    PadText.SelText = CutText
End Sub

Sub ClearItem_Click()
    PadText.Text = ""
End Sub

Sub PadText.Change()
    CutItem.Enabled = True
    ClearItem.Enabled = True
End Sub
```

However, there are still some ways to improve our editor. One is to add another menu to it so that the user can select the actual font used in the text. This operation will expose us to more of what menus are all about from a programmer's point of view, so let's look into that next.

Selecting Fonts from Menus

You may have worked with word processors before that allowed you to switch fonts, in which case you know that they are exactly the kind of option that you should put into a menu, not into a set of command buttons (because users usually do not change fonts often enough to make it worthwhile having all the font options in front of them at all times). There are eight standard fonts available in Visual Basic: Courier, Helvetica, Roman, Modern, Script, Symbol, System, and Terminal, as shown in Figure 3-18. We can change the text in the editor text box to any one of these fonts simply by changing the **FontName** property of the text box. However, there is a drawback: When you change the font in a text box, all the text is automatically changed to that font. In other words, you can only use one font in a text box. With that restriction, however, let's add a font menu to our editor.

Courier	abcdefg
Helv	abcdefg
Modern	abcdefg
Roman	abcdefg
Script	abcdefg
Symbol	abcdefg
System	αβχδεφγ
Terminal	abcdefg

Figure 3-18. Visual Basic Standard Fonts

TIP   If you want to use different fonts in the same document, use the **Print** method, which applies to forms and picture boxes. In fact, **Print** is the general purpose way of displaying text in Visual Basic, and you can use it, for example, if you want to write an editor that can handle more than 64K of text (which is the limit for text boxes). In that case, however, you're responsible for such operations as scrolling and selecting text yourself. We'll see how to use **Print** later in this book, when we cover graphics.

To add a Font menu, open the Menu Design Window and add a new menu, Font (with the **CtlName FontMenu**), and give it eight items: Courier, Helvetica (Helv), Roman, Modern, Script, Symbol, System, and Terminal, as shown in Figure 3-19. We could write a separate Click event procedure for each menu item, but now that we have eight of them, it would be easier to set up a control array — meaning that we want Visual Basic to pass an **Index** to the event procedure — as we've done for buttons earlier.

In fact, it's as easy to have Visual Basic pass an index to a menu event procedure as it was to pass an index to a button event procedure. To do this, give each menu item (i.e., Courier, Helv, Roman, Modern, Script, Symbol, System, and Terminal) the same control name of, say, **FFF** in the **CtlName** text box (under the **Caption** text box). Now, as far as Visual Basic is concerned, each menu item has the same name. To distinguish between them, it will need an **Index**; however, Visual Basic does not automatically assign indices to menu items as it did to our buttons earlier. Instead, we can use the **Index** text box (see Figure 3-19) to set an Index for each menu item. In this case, we can simply assign the **Index** 0–7 to distinguish each of the eight fonts, as shown in

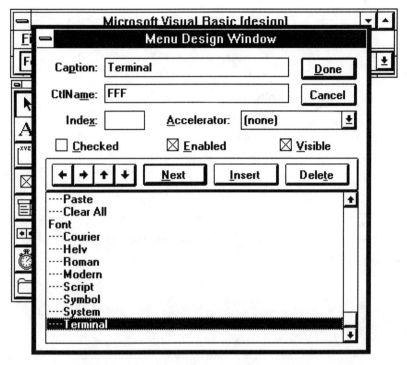

Figure 3-19. Menu Design Window with Font Menu

Table 3-1. To do that, just select each menu item in turn and fill in the **Index** text box.

Close the Menu Design Window; now we're ready to write some code. As you see, a new menu, Font, has been added to the Editor form, as shown in Figure 3-20. Click on any of the menu items in this menu and the code window opens with a template for **FFF_Click( )** like this:

```
Sub FFF_Click (Index As Integer)

End Sub
```

Our goal here is to select the appropriate font, depending on which selection was made. Since the menu item's index was passed to us, we can use it to set the font. The name of the text window in the Editor is **PadText**, so the

Menu Item	CtlName	Index
Courier	FFF	0
Helv	FFF	1
Roman	FFF	2
Modern	FFF	3
Script	FFF	4
Symbol	FFF	5
System	FFF	6
Terminal	FFF	7

Table 3-1. Font Menu Items

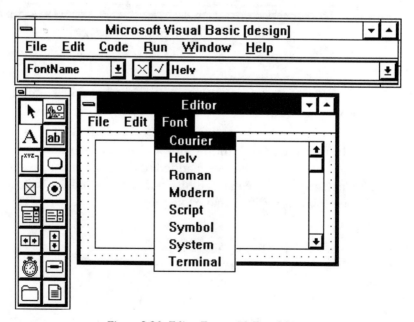

Figure 3-20. Editor Form with Font Menu

property we want to set is **PadText.FontName**. We can do that with a Select Case statement; in general, that statement works like this:

```
Select Case test_variable
    Case constant1
        [Statements...]
    [Case constant2]
        [Statements...]
        :
    [Case Else]
        [Statements...]
End Select
```

Here, what action is taken is determined by the value in **test_variable**. If that value matches one of the constants in a Case statement, the statements corresponding to that case are executed. If no case matches, the statements in the Else case are executed (if there is an Else case, which is optional). In **FFF_Click( )**, that will look like this:

```
Sub FFF_Click (Index As Integer)
    Select Case Index
        Case 0
            PadText.FontName = "Courier"
        Case 1
            PadText.FontName = "Helv"
        Case 2
            PadText.FontName = "Roman"
        Case 3
            PadText.FontName = "Modern"
        Case 4
            PadText.FontName = "Script"
        Case 5
            PadText.FontName = "Symbol"
        Case 6
            PadText.FontName = "System"
        Case 7
            PadText.FontName = "Terminal"
        End Select
    End Sub
```

That's all there is to selecting a font, and this makes the Font menu active. When you run the Editor, you'll find that you can select the font from this menu (and that all the text changes at once). However, there's no easy way to tell from the font menu which font is the current font (the default in Visual Basic is Helv). This is usually indicated in Windows applications with a check mark (applications often put a check mark next to the menu item in the menu to indicate which option is currently active). As you might expect, we can do this too, so let's add this capability to our Editor.

Marking Menu Items with Check Marks

Open the Menu Design Window again. Since the Helv option is the default font for text boxes in Visual Basic, that item should appear checked when the Editor first starts. To make sure it does, click the Check box for the Helv font as shown in Figure 3-21. This is the property we'll use to add check marks to menu items: the **Checked** property. When True, the item appears checked; when False, it appears without a check mark.

When the user selects a new font, we should first remove the check mark in the Font menu, which we can do by looping over each menu item and setting the **Checked** property (**FFF(0-7).Checked**) to False like this:

```
Sub FFF_Click (Index As Integer)
    Select Case Index
        Case 0
            PadText.FontName = "Courier"
        Case 1
            PadText.FontName = "Helv"
        Case 2
            PadText.FontName = "Roman"
        Case 3
            PadText.FontName = "Modern"
        Case 4
            PadText.FontName = "Script"
        Case 5
            PadText.FontName = "Symbol"
        Case 6
            PadText.FontName = "System"
        Case 7
            PadText.FontName = "Terminal"
    End Select

→       For loop_index = 0 To 7
→           FFF(loop_index) = False
→       Next loop_index
        :
    End Sub
```

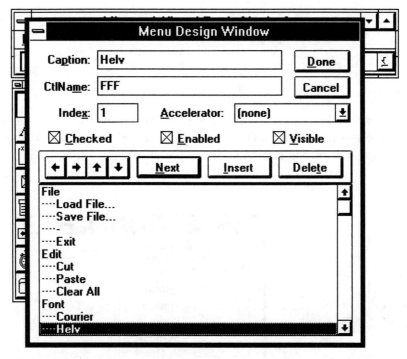

Figure 3-21. Menu Design Window with Helv Checked

Finally, we should check the new font, which is simply menu item **FFF(Index)**, like this:

```
Sub FFF_Click (Index As Integer)
    Select Case Index
        Case 0
            PadText.FontName = "Courier"
        Case 1
            PadText.FontName = "Helv"
        Case 2
            PadText.FontName = "Roman"
        Case 3
            PadText.FontName = "Modern"
        Case 4
            PadText.FontName = "Script"
        Case 5
            PadText.FontName = "Symbol"
        Case 6
            PadText.FontName = "System"
        Case 7
            PadText.FontName = "Terminal"
    End Select
```

```
        For loop_index = 0 To 7
            FFF(loop_index).Checked = False
        Next loop_index

→       FFF(Index).Checked = True
    End Sub
```

Now the Font menu is fully functional. When the user clicks a new font — not Helv — the check mark is removed from Helv and placed in front of the new font, as shown in Figure 3-22. In this way, the user can keep track of which font is currently selected. The code for our Editor so far appears in Listing 3-3.

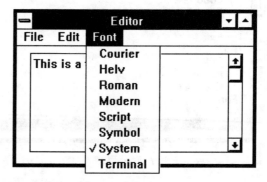

Figure 3-22. Check Marks in Editor's Font Menu

Listing 3-3. Editor Application Code Version 2

```
Editor.Bas ------------------------------------------

CutText As String

Editor.Frm ------------------------------------------

Sub ExitItem_Click()
    End
End Sub

Sub CutItem_Click()
    CutText = PadText.SelText
    PadText.SelText = ""
    PasteItem.Enabled = True
End Sub
```

Listing 3-3. (continued)

```
Sub PasteItem_Click()
    PadText.SelText = CutText
End Sub

Sub ClearItem_Click()
    PadText.Text = ""
End Sub

Sub PadText.Change()
    CutItem.Enabled = True
    ClearItem.Enabled = True
End Sub

Sub FFF_Click (Index As Integer)
    Select Case Index
        Case 0
            PadText.FontName = "Courier"
        Case 1
            PadText.FontName = "Helv"
        Case 2
            PadText.FontName = "Roman"
        Case 3
            PadText.FontName = "Modern"
        Case 4
            PadText.FontName = "Script"
        Case 5
            PadText.FontName = "Symbol"
        Case 6
            PadText.FontName = "System"
        Case 7
            PadText.FontName = "Terminal"
    End Select
    For loop_index = 0 To 7
        FFF(loop_index).Checked = False
    Next loop_index

    FFF(Index).Checked = True
End Sub
```

The Editor application is looking better, but a number of features are still missing from it (besides its obvious inability to work with files yet). In most complete Windows applications which use menus, you can also use access keys (i.e., one letter of a menu name or item is underlined, indicating that typing that letter will select the corresponding option) and shortcut keys (e.g., like <Ctrl+A>). Naturally, we can add those options to our Visual Basic programs also.

Adding Access Keys to Menus

Adding access keys — the underlined letter in a name or caption — to menus is as easy as it was with buttons; we just place an ampersand (&) in front of the letter that we want to use. For example, we can change Cut to &Cut to make C the access key for the Cut item in the Edit menu. Note again that the access keys should be unique on their level; that is, no two menu names in the menu bar should have the same access key, and no two menu items in the same menu should have the same access key either.

In fact, we'll use the first name of each item or menu name as its access key, with a few exceptions: Since there are two menu names that begin with F — File and Font — we can use F for the File menu access key, and, say, o for the Font menu. In addition, both Cut and Clear All appear in the Edit menu, so we can use C for the Cut item's access key and A (as before when we were designing our notepad) for Clear All. Also, we won't give access keys to the fonts because we don't expect the user to switch fonts often enough to need them. Finally, we give the access key x to the Exit option, even though it begins with E, which is unique in the File menu; the Windows convention is that Exit be given x as an access key, and many users have become accustomed to using it that way (and few menu items are likely to begin with x). All the access keys we'll use for Editor are marked with an ampersand, and they appear in Figure 3-23.

Now when you run the Editor, you'll see the access keys underlined, as in Figure 3-24. Now our editor is looking more professional, but there is one last change still to be made: adding shortcut keys.

Adding Shortcut Keys to Menus

You've probably seen shortcut keys in menus already. For example, Visual Basic's File menu in Figure 3-1 has three shortcut keys for handling file operations. <Ctrl+F12> is a shortcut for adding a file; <Shift+F12> is a shortcut for saving a file; and <F12> is a shortcut for the Save File As... menu item. We can add shortcuts like this to our Editor as well.

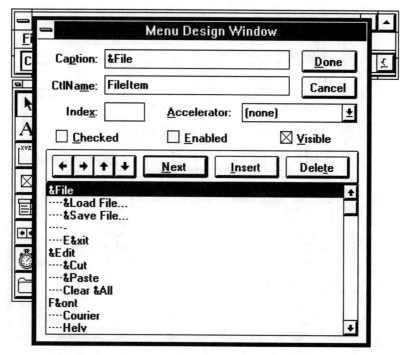

Figure 3-23. Editor Menu Design Window with Access Keys

To do that, open the Menu Design Window again. You select shortcut keys with the Accelerator box that appears on the right-hand side. As in most cases, Visual Basic is capable of presenting you with all the options available here (that is, instead of having to look it up, the options are displayed on the screen

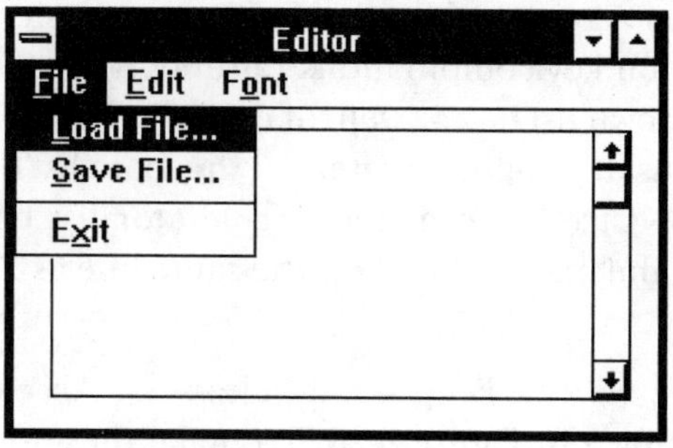

Figure 3-24. Editor Template Access Keys

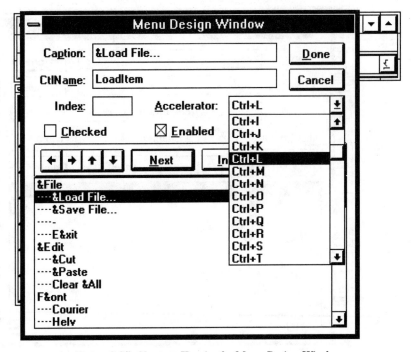

Figure 3-25. Shortcut Keys in the Menu Design Window

for your immediate use); just click on the arrow next to the Accelerator box. When you do, a list of the possible shortcut keys appears, as shown in Figure 3-25.

The first menu item we might give a shortcut key to is the Load File item in our File menu. Since we'll have no use for the <Ctrl> key combinations (like <Ctrl+A> or <Ctrl+B>) in our application, we can use them as shortcut keys. <Ctrl+Letter> key combinations are often easier for the user to remember than function key combinations (although those are available in the Accelerator drop-down list box as well, of course). To connect <Ctrl+L> with the Load File item, just highlight that item in the main list box (as shown in Figure 3-25) and select <Ctrl+L> from the Accelerator list box. When you do, <Ctrl+L> appears in the main list box on the same line as Load File....

In this way, we can keep going, choosing Accelerator keys for most of the items, as shown in Figure 3-26. To make these shortcut keys active, just click

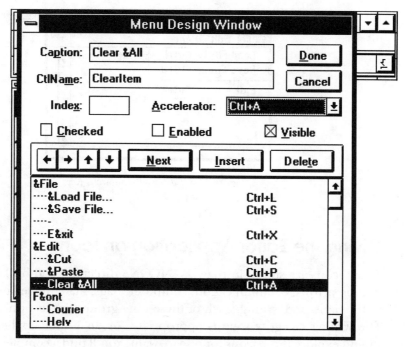

Figure 3-26. Accelerator Keys for the Editor Application

the Done box in the Menu Design Window and run the Editor application. As you can see in Figure 3-27, our shortcut keys are now displayed in the menus themselves, next to the items they represent.

> **NOTE** Keep in mind that, while you have to have a menu open to use the access keys in that menu, shortcut keys like <Ctrl+X> or <Shift-F3> are valid even when the menu is closed, so they should be unique over all menus, not just the one they're defined in.

That's it for developing the Editor for now. It's shown us a great deal about menu design, including how to grey items in a menu to show they're inactive; how to mark menu items with a check mark; how to use access keys and separator bars; and now how to use shortcut keys. In fact, the Editor application has come the closest we've gotten so far to producing a polished application, so, for that reason, let's give it its own icon. It turns out that this is easy enough to do. Visual Basic has a library of some 400 icons, ready for us to use.

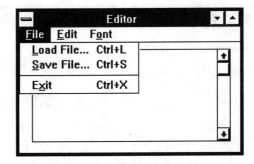

Figure 3-27. Editor with Shortcut Keys

Giving the Editor Application an Icon

These icons are stored in the C:\VB\ICONS directory, and broken into nine groups: arrows, communication, computer, flags, mail, miscellaneous, office, traffic signs, and writing; each of these nine groups has its own subdirectory. The writing category sounds appropriate for an Editor application, so we should explore those icons for one we want. You'll find a complete copy of the icon library in the Visual Basic documentation. Some of the icons from the writing library appear in Figure 3-28. Note that the icon labeled Default is Visual Basic's default icon for applications; that is, the icon each of our .Exe files has had until now, and it's not actually part of the Visual Basic icon library.

The Pencil01 icon looks good for our purposes: It's just a simple pencil icon. To use that icon, we must associate it with the Editor application's form. Click on the form itself and look at the **Icon** property in the properties bar. An

Figure 3-28. Some Visual Basic Writing Icons

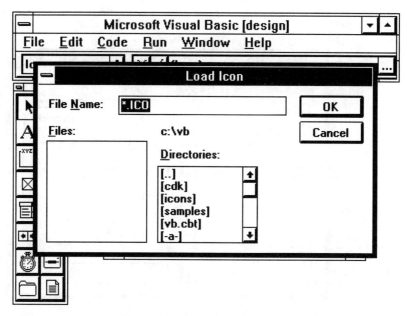

Figure 3-29. Load Icon Dialog Box

ellipsis (three dots) appears in the button next to the settings window; click on it and a Load Icon dialog box opens as in Figure 3-29.

Use the Directories box in this dialog box to switch to the C:\VB\ICONS\WRITING directory, and load the Pencil01 icon by highlighting Pencil01 and clicking the OK button. At this point, the Pencil01 icon is associated with the Editor application's form, which still has the default name of **Form1**. This is where Visual Basic takes the icon that it will associate with the .EXE file (again, by default). Select the Make EXE File... item in Visual Basic's File menu, and the Make EXE File dialog box opens, as shown in Figure 3-30.

As you can see, Pencil01 has become the icon for our Editor application. After you create Editor.Exe, you can add it to the applications displayed in Windows' Program Manager window by selecting the New... item in the File menu of the Program Manager. When you do, a dialog box labeled New Program Object opens; click the Program Item option button, followed by the OK button. The Program Manager then asks for the program item properties in a new dialog box. In the Description dialog box, type Editor; in the Command Line dialog box, type the location and name of the Editor application's .Exe file (if you're using the default Visual Basic settings, that will be

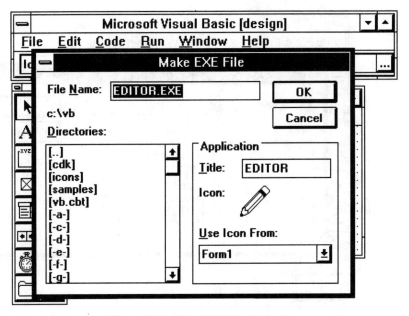

Figure 3-30. Make EXE File Dialog Box

C:\VB\EDITOR.EXE) and click the OK button. The Editor's icon will appear in the Program Manager window, along with the other icons already there. And, when you click it, the Editor will start.

That's it for the Editor for now; we'll return to it later when we're able to add file support. In the mean time, there is more to learn about menus. For example, we can change menu items at run-time. Let's take a look at this by adapting one of our old programs, the alarm clock.

Changing Menu Items at Run-Time

As you may recall, the alarm clock program had two option buttons, Alarm Off and Alarm On. We can convert this application to use a menu, just as we did

Figure 3-31. Editor Icon with Others

for the editor. In particular, our goal here will be to have one menu — Alarm — with one item in it. At first, that item will be Alarm Off, but when you select it at run-time, it will change to Alarm On, and so on, toggling back and forth as required.

To do that, we can open the Alarm project and the Menu Design Window in that project. All we'll need here is a single menu named Alarm, with a **CtlName** of, say, **AlarmMenu**, and with one item in it: Alarm Off, which we can give the **CtlName** of **OnOffItem** to (i.e., the option buttons were named **OnOffButton**). Now we can double-click one of the option buttons to open the code window and display this code:

```
Sub OnOffButton_Click (Index As Integer)
    If (Index = 1) Then
        AlarmOn = True
    Else
        AlarmOn = False
    End If
End Sub
```

As you may recall, the variable **AlarmOn** was a global variable that determined whether or not the program would beep when the allotted time elapsed. We can change this Sub procedure code, rewriting it like this:

```
Sub OnOffItem_Click()
    If (AlarmOn) Then
        AlarmOn = False         'Toggle alarm
        OnOffItem.Caption = "Alarm Off"
    Else
        AlarmOn = True          'Toggle alarm
        OnOffItem.Caption = "Alarm On"
    End If
End Sub
```

That's it. We can delete the option buttons now (using the Visual Basic Edit menu), since all reference to them in the code has been removed. By changing the **Caption** property of the single menu item, we're able to change that menu item at run-time. When you run the clock now, you'll see the menu name Alarm in the menu bar. Opening it will reveal the Alarm Off item. Clicking that item both closes the menu and changes it to Alarm On, as shown in Figure 3-32. In this way, we're able to toggle the caption of the Alarm On/Off item to match the alarm setting.

Figure 3-32. Alarm Clock with Menu

There is another way to do this as well. We could have used the **Visible** property of menu items instead. For example, if we had two menu items, **AlarmOnItem** (Alarm On) and **AlarmOffItem** (Alarm Off), setting the **AlarmOnItem.Visible** property to True would display the Alarm On menu item, and setting the **AlarmOffItem.Visible** property to False would hide it:

```
      Sub OnOffItem_Click()
          If (AlarmOn) Then
              AlarmOn = False            'Toggle alarm
  →           AlarmOnItem.Visible = False
  →           AlarmOffItem.Visible = True
          Else
              AlarmOn = True             'Toggle alarm
  →           AlarmOnItem.Visible = True
  →           AlarmOffItem.Visible = False
          End If
      End Sub
```

This is the way you can hide options in your menus when necessary (for example, to avoid presenting too many greyed out options). That is, setting the **Visible** property this way can be an important part of menu design.

Or, if we prefer, we can make our alarm clock function with check marks (i.e., check marks are designed for cases where you toggle options on and off). To put a menu with check marks into the alarm clock, we can open the Menu Design Window and again set up a menu with the **Caption Alarm** and **CtlName AlarmMenu**. Then we put one item into this menu: **OnItem**, with the caption "Alarm On" (i.e., when this item is checked, the alarm will be on).

Figure 3-33. Alarm Clock Application with Check Marks

Close the Menu Design Window and click on the Alarm On menu item to open the code window with this Sub procedure template:

```
Sub OnItem_Click()

End Sub
```

We can check the Alarm On item and set **AlarmOn** appropriately like this:

```
Sub OnItem_Click()
    If (AlarmOn) Then
        AlarmOn = False
        OnItem.Checked = False
    Else
        AlarmOn = True
        OnItem.Checked = True
    End If
End Sub
```

This way, the Alarm On item toggles between being checked and unchecked, corresponding to the state of the alarm, as in Figure 3-33 (alternatively, you can have two items: Alarm On and Alarm Off, placing a check mark in front of the appropriate one).

As we've seen, then, it's possible to change a menu item's caption at run-time, as well as make it visible or invisible. However, this doesn't take care of all possibilities. What if you wanted to add or delete entirely new menu items at run-time? We'll look into this possibility next.

Adding and Deleting Menu Items

Let's say that you wanted to write a menu-driven phone book application; that is, you wanted a program which you could use to keep track of your friends' phone numbers. Such an application might have two text boxes in it: one holding a name, and the other one holding the matching phone number. If all the stored names appeared in a menu, it would be easy to select among them: When you chose a name, it would appear in the name text box, and the corresponding phone number would appear in the phone number text box. However, we'll have to take into account that such a list of names (as displayed in our menu) can grow or shrink.

In Visual Basic, you can add menu items with the *Load* statement, and you can remove them with the *Unload* statement (as we'll see, Load and Unload can be used for many Visual Basic controls). However, to do this, the menu items must be part of a control array (i.e., they must use the same click procedure, although their indices will be different). The reason for this is that you cannot add entirely new code for a new click procedure at run-time (i.e., when you want to add a new item to a menu). Instead, Visual Basic must already have the code necessary to handle the new menu item.

Using Load and Unload is not difficult. For example, if we had a menu item named, say, **my_item**, whose index was 0, we could add another item named **my_item(1)** like this:

```
Load my_item(1)
```

This adds another item right below the last item. To add a new item to the menu itself, we can load a string into **my_item(1)**'s **Caption** property like this:

```
      Load my_item(1)
→     my_item(1).Caption = "Asparagus"
```

Similarly, we can unload items using Unload. Let's say that we had added these vegetables to a menu like this:

```
Load my_item(1)
my_item(1).Caption = "Asparagus"
Load my_item(2)
my_item(2).Caption = "Potato"
Load my_item(3)
my_item(3).Caption = "Spinach"
```

```
Load my_item(4)
my_item(4).Caption = "Corn"
```

Now let's say that we wanted to remove the Asparagus item. Visual Basic only allows you to remove the last item in a control array with Unload, so we'd have to do that by moving all the other items up and then deleting the last item like this:

```
Load my_item(1)
my_item(1).Caption = "Asparagus"
Load my_item(2)
my_item(2).Caption = "Potato"
Load my_item(3)
my_item(3).Caption = "Spinach"
Load my_item(4)
my_item(4).Caption = "Corn"
```

```
→   For loop_index = 1 To 3
→       my_item(loop_index).Caption = my_item(loop_index + 1).Caption
→   Next loop_index

→   Unload my_item(4)
```

Note also that in this case, the indices of each surviving item is decremented by one, so you would have to account for that in code. In addition, note that we did nothing with the first item in the array, **my_item(0)**. This is the conventional defect of using Load and Unload for menu items: You can't unload items created at design-time, nor can you set up a control array unless you have at least one element in place at design-time. In other words, no matter what we do, we'll always have to have one element of the control array in the menu. But, since we don't know what items we want to place in our menu before run-time (i.e., the names of our friends), what caption should we give it at design-time?

The usual solution to this, when designing a menu, is to give the 0th item — the one that starts the control array — an invisible menu item as a caption. That way, all subsequent menu items that you add will come after this invisible 0th item. Let's see how this works in practice.

We can start a new project named, say, Phone.Mak (with Phone.Bas and Phone.Frm in it). Add two text boxes and labels (Name: and Number:), as shown in Figure 3-34, and then open the Menu Design Window. We can call

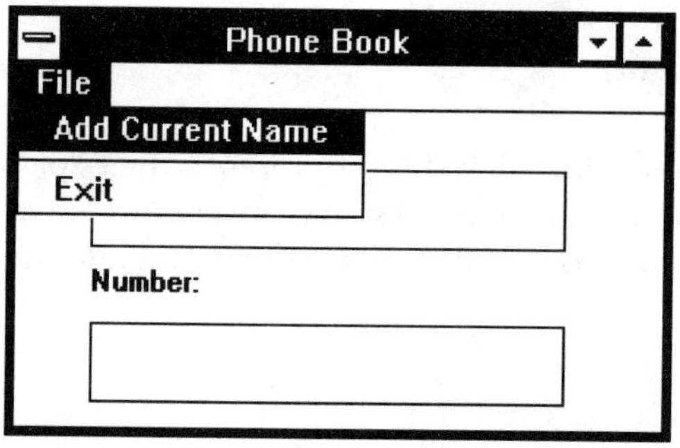

Figure 3-34. Phone Project Template

the menu in our phone book application File, because it can conceivably be expanded to save phone directories on disk. Give the first item in that menu the caption Add Current Name, and a **CtlName** of **AddNameItem**. Next, put in a separator bar by typing a hyphen (-), give it the **CtlName** of, say, **separator**. After that, add another item with any caption (except a null string, " "), even a space. Give this dummy item — the first item in our control array — a **CtlName** of, say, **NNN**. In addition, give it an **Index** of 0 (by putting 0 in the box marked Index), and make it invisible (by clicking the Visible box so the X disappears). In other words, our control array will be named **NNN( )**, and we can refer to specific items in it as **NNN(1)**, **NNN(2)**, and so on (note that **NNN(0)** will always remain invisible, so you can give it any name you like). Finally, add the last item of any File menu, Exit, with a **CtlName** of **ExitItem**.

If you run the program, you'll see a menu, as in Figure 3-34. This is how we want the program to work: The user should be free to type a name in the name text box, and a phone number in the number text box. Then they can select the Add Current Name menu item, and the program should add that name to the menu; i.e., it should appear right below the separator bar. After the user is finished entering names this way, they can select a name from the menu, and that name, along with the corresponding phone number, should appear in the text boxes.

We can start with the Add Current Name item in the menu. Double-click that item to open the code window, which displays this Sub procedure template:

```
Sub AddNameItem_Click()

End Sub
```

The first thing we'll want to keep track of is the number of menu items we have, so we can declare a variable named **NumberNames** as Static (i.e., its value won't change between successive calls):

```
      Sub AddNameItem_Click()
→         Static NumberNames
                :
      End Sub
```

Since we're adding a name in this procedure, our first action might be to simply increment **NumberNames** by one (static variables are initialized to 0) and load a new menu item like this:

```
      Sub AddNameItem_Click()
          Static NumberNames
→         NumberNames = NumberNames + 1
→         Load NNN(NumberNames)
                :
      End Sub
```

Next, we can load the name which is now in the name text box into the new menu item's **Caption** property this way (assuming we left the name text box's **CtlName** as **Text1**). We can also set that item's **Visible** property to True (-1):

```
      Sub AddNameItem_Click()
          Static NumberNames
          NumberNames = NumberNames + 1
          Load NNN(NumberNames)
→         NNN(NumberNames).Caption = Text1.Text
→         NNN(NumberNames).Visible = -1
                  :
      End Sub
```

Now we have to store the names and numbers themselves. To do that, we can set up two string arrays, named, say, **Names( )** and **Numbers( )**. These arrays will have to have broader scope than just our current procedure because, when the user clicks a name in the menu to retrieve data, we'll have to read from these arrays in the corresponding Click procedure to fill the name and number text boxes. For that reason, we can declare **Names( )** and **Numbers( )** as form-level arrays (or we could place them in the global module). To do that, click on the general item in the object box of the code window, and make

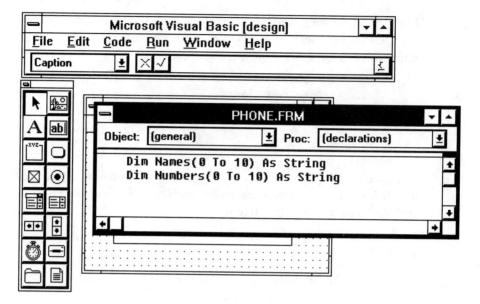

Figure 3-35. The General Object

sure that the declarations item is showing in the procedure box (the box on the right). Then add the following declarations, as shown in Figure 3-35:

```
Dim Names(1 To 10) As String
Dim Numbers(1 To 10) As String
```

Placing these arrays in the general object makes them form-level arrays, accessible to all procedures in the form. Now we can go back to **Add-NameItem_Click( )** and complete it like this to store the current name and number:

```
Sub AddNameItem_Click()
    Static NumberNames
    NumberNames = NumberNames + 1
    Load NNN(NumberNames)
    NNN(NumberNames).Caption = Text1.Text
    NNN(NumberNames).Visible = -1
→   Names(NumberNames) = Text1.Text      'Data from name text box
→   Numbers(NumberNames) = Text2.Text    'Data from number text box
End Sub
```

Now **AddNameItem_Click( )** is complete, so we're able to add our friends' names to the File menu at run-time. The next step after adding names is retrieving them on demand, and we do that when the user clicks a name in the menu. When that happens, an **NNN_Click( )** event occurs (i.e., **NNN( )** is the name we've given to our menu item array). Note that the first item, **NNN(0)**, is simply the place-holding dummy item, but the next item, **NNN(1)**, corresponds to the first name in the menu under that bar; **NNN(2)** corresponds to the next name, and so on. To write the **NNN_Click( )** Sub procedure, then, find and click **NNN** in the object box of the code window. This Sub procedure appears:

```
Sub NNN_Click(Index As Integer)

End Sub
```

When the user clicks a name in the menu, this procedure is called with an index number that corresponds to the item chosen. Since we've stored the names and numbers with the same index as the menu items themselves, we can display the requested name and number on the screen like this:

```
Sub NNN_Click(Index As Integer)
    Text1.Text = Names(Index)
    Text2.Text = Numbers(Index)
End Sub
```

That's all there is to it. If we add an End statement to make the Exit item active, we're done. The complete code appears in Listing 3-4.

Listing 3-4. Phone Book Application

```
Phone.Frm ---------------------------------------------

    Dim Names(1 To 10) As String     'Form-level array--general object
    Dim Numbers(1 To 10) As String   'Form-level array--general object

Sub AddNameItem_Click ()
    Static NumberNames
    NumberNames = NumberNames + 1
    Load NNN(NumberNames)
    NNN(NumberNames).Caption = Text1.Text
    NNN(NumberNames).Visible = -1
    Names(NumberNames) = Text1.Text
```

(continued)

Listing 3-4. (continued)

```
    Numbers(NumberNames) = Text2.Text
End Sub

Sub ExitItem_Click ()
    End
End Sub

Sub NNN_Click (Index As Integer)
    Text1.Text = Names(Index)
    Text2.Text = Numbers(Index)
End Sub
```

Run the phone application. You can store names and numbers by typing them in the text boxes and selecting the Add Current Name item. Each time you do, another name is added to the menu, as shown in Figure 3-36. To retrieve the number for any name, just select that menu item.

We've come far in our work with menus in this chapter. However, there is one significant thing that we didn't do: We didn't make items like Load File... and Save File... active. Usually, a menu item with an ellipsis like this pops open a dialog box when selected, and, for that reason, we'll cover dialog boxes next.

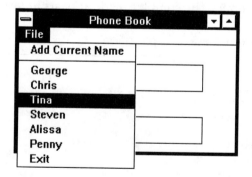

Figure 3-36. Functioning Phone Book Application

Using Dialog Boxes

So far, all our programs have involved a single window; that is, a single form. However, it's common for applications to use many windows — dialog boxes, message boxes, warning boxes, help windows, and all sorts of other windows. Probably the most common types of such windows are dialog boxes. And, we'll learn a lot about other types of multiple-form applications in this chapter.

In fact, Visual Basic provides some built-in windows that we can use for just this purpose: **MsgBox( )** and **InputBox$( )**. These two Visual Basic statements display a message and get string input from the user, respectively. Using them is easy, so we'll start with them first. Next, we'll see how to work with multiple forms in general: how to create a second form when designing our application; how to display it; how to address the properties of other forms; and how to hide them again.

After that, we'll see how to create and use dialog boxes in general. If you've used Windows, you know that dialog boxes play an integral part in getting information from the user. So far, we've handled tasks like numeric input, string input, and option selection by using buttons and menus. But, in real applications, these same tasks are often handled with dialog boxes. We'll also spend a good deal of time in this chapter with some of the controls that are often associated with dialog boxes: combo boxes and list boxes. With all that in mind, then, let's start with **MsgBox( )** and **InputBox$( )**, the two simplest types of dialog boxes available.

Displaying a Message Box with MsgBox( )

The first function we'll cover, **MsgBox( )**, really only allows a restricted dialog; you place a message on the screen in a window, and the user is restricted to communicating back through buttons. The way you use **MsgBox( )** is like this:

```
RetVal% = MsgBox (message$ [,type [,title$]])
```

where message$ is the message you want to display (e.g., "Error Number 5" or "That button is already selected."); type indicates what buttons and/or icons you want in the message box; and title$ is the string you want placed in the message box window's caption (this string is truncated after the 255th character).

The type argument lets you select from a number of options, such as displaying OK buttons; Abort, Retry or Ignore buttons; Cancel buttons; or even icons, such as a Stop sign, an information symbol (a lowercase "i" in a circle), or others as indicated in Table 4-1. The values in that table can be added together. For example, to display Yes, No, and OK buttons along with a Stop sign, you'd use a type value of 4 + 16 = 20. Note that even if you don't specify a value for type, Visual Basic still places an OK button in the message box so that the user can close it. The return values for this function (allowing you to determine what button the user pushed) appear in Table 4-2.

Let's put all this to use. Some common uses for message boxes are: help messages, about boxes (describing the application and the application's authors), and error messages. Let's begin with a help message. Start up Visual Basic and put a command button into the middle of the default form (**Form1**) with the caption Help, and double-click on it. The following Sub procedure template appears:

```
Sub Command1_Click ()

End Sub
```

Value	Means
0	OK button only
1	OK button and Cancel button
2	Abort, Retry, Ignore buttons
3	Yes, No, Cancel buttons
4	Yes, No buttons
5	Retry, Cancel buttons
16	Stop sign
32	Query sign (question mark in a circle)
48	Warning sign (exclamation point in a circle)
64	Information icon ("i" in a circle)
0	First button has default focus
256	Second button has default focus
512	Third button has default focus

Table 4-1. Type Argument for MsgBox( ) Function

Value	Means
1	OK button was pressed
2	Cancel button was pressed
3	Abort button was pressed
4	Retry button was pressed
5	Ignore button was pressed
6	Yes button was pressed
7	No button was pressed

Table 4-2. MsgBox( ) Return Values

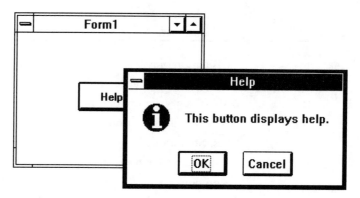

Figure 4-1. A Trial Help Message Box

We can use MsgBox to display a simple help message: "This button displays Help." along with an information symbol — an "i" inside a circle (type = 64) — as well as an OK button and a Cancel button (type = 1) like this:

```
Sub Command1_Click ()
    MsgBox "This button displays Help.", 65, "Help"
End Sub
```

(Notice that we can also use **MsgBox( )** as a statement, not a function, which we do here since we're not interested in its return value.) When clicked, the Help button puts our message box on the screen, as shown in Figure 4-1. That's it; we're using elementary dialog boxes already.

We can see an example of an error message box if we modify our Tic-Tac-Toe game. You may recall that the user could click on any button, changing it to an x or an o whether or not something was already there. We can fix that by checking the clicked button's caption and displaying an error message if the button had already been clicked. We called the control array that handles the button clicks **TTT**, and this was the corresponding event procedure:

```
Sub TTT_Click (Index As Integer)

    If (Xturn) Then
        TTT(Index).Caption = "x"
        Xturn = False
    Else
```

```
            TTT(Index).Caption = "o"
            Xturn = True
        End If

    End Sub
```

We can add an error message with a warning symbol (an exclamation point inside a circle, type = 48), and leave the Sub procedure if the button was already clicked like this:

```
        Sub TTT_Click (Index As Integer)

→           If(TTT(Index).Caption <> "") Then
→               MsgBox "That button was already clicked.", 48, "Error"
→               Exit Sub
→           End If

            If (Xturn) Then
                TTT(Index).Caption = "x"
                Xturn = False
            Else
                TTT(Index).Caption = "o"
                Xturn = True
            End If

        End Sub
```

This way, if the user clicks a button that already had an x or an o displayed, an error box is displayed as in Figure 4-2, and the button is not changed. Now the user can simply click the OK button and click another button in the game instead.

Because the icons and general appearance of message boxes like these look like standard message boxes in normal Windows applications, using **MsgBox( )** in your programs can make them seem more professional. And, as indicated, you can receive a limited amount of information back from **MsgBox** telling you which button a user clicked. However, that limits the user's input options to: Yes, No, Cancel, Abort, Retry, Ignore, and OK. On the other hand, the next function that we'll explore, **InputBox$( )**, has no such restriction.

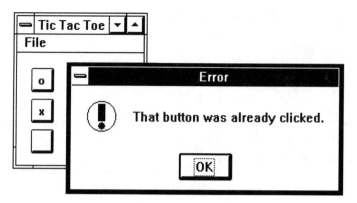

Figure 4-2. An Error Message Box

An InputBox$( ) Application — A Windows Shell

We can see how **InputBox$( )** functions by creating an application that uses it; in this case, we'll use Visual Basic's Shell( ) function, with which you can start Windows applications. The way you use Shell( ) is like this:

```
RetVal = Shell (command$ [, windowtype$])
```

Here, **command$** is the command string, just as you might type after the command Win when you start Windows (e.g., Win Vb.Exe starts Visual Basic). In particular, command$ must be the name of a file that ends in .EXE, .BAT, .COM, or .PIF. The windowtype$ argument indicates the startup options you want for the application's window (e.g., minimized or maximized), as indicated in Table 4-3. If the shell function was able to execute the program, it returns the task ID of the program (a unique number that identifies the program, which we won't make use of here).

We can create our own application called, say, Windows Shell, which will start applications on request. To get the name and path of the application to start, we can use the InputBox$( ) function. That function looks like this in general:

```
RetString$ = InputBox$(prompt$ [,title$ [,default$ [,x% [,y%]]]])
```

Here, **RetString$** is the string that the user typed (i.e., the input from the input box); **prompt$** is the prompt we display to indicate what type of input is desired; **title$** is the caption we want to give the input box, **default$** is the

Value	*Means*
1	Normal window, with focus
2	Minimized, with focus
3	Maximized, with focus
4	Normal window, without focus
7	Minimized, without focus

Table 4-3. Shell Function's Window Types

default string that first appears in the input box's text box (i.e., if the user types no other response, **default$** is returned); and the optional **x%** and **y%** arguments indicate the position of the input box as measured from the upper-left corner of the screen (in twips, 1/1440 of an inch).

Let's see all this in action. Start a new Visual Basic project called Windows Shell and open the Menu Design window. We can create one menu named File, with two items in it: Run... and Exit, giving them the **CtlNames RunItem** and **ExitItem** as shown in Figure 4-3.

Now click on our Run... menu item, opening the code window, which displays the template for **RunItem_Click( )** like this:

```
Sub RunItem_Click()

End Sub
```

We want to get a string for input here, so we can use **InputBox$( )**. In fact, because the menu item here has an ellipsis (Run...), the user is expecting a dialog box to appear. When we get a string back from **InputBox$( )**, we can just pass it on to Shell( ) like this:

```
Sub RunItem_Click()
    RetVal = Shell(InputBox$("Application to run:", "Run..."), 1)
End Sub
```

In this case, we're asking for an input box that has the prompt "Application to run:" and the caption "Run..." in the title bar. We can then pass the string that was typed back to the Shell( ) function, along with a **windowtype%** argument

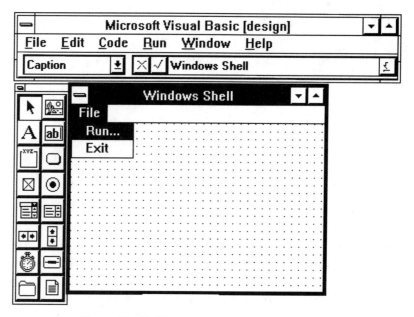

Figure 4-3. File Menu for Windows Shell Application

of 1, requesting a normal window. In addition, we should make the Exit item in our File menu active as well by placing the End statement in the **ExitItem_Click( )** Sub procedure like this:

```
Sub ExitItem_Click()
    End
End Sub
```

At this point, we're set. When you run the Windows Shell application, you'll see a simple window on the screen with a File menu. When you open that menu, there are two items available: Run... and Exit. When you click on Run..., a dialog box opens up — as it should — as shown in Figure 4-4. We can then type the name of a Windows application to run, say, Sol.Exe to start the solitaire game that comes with Windows. The application is started, and functions normally.

However, the appearance of our dialog box is less than optimal, which can always be a problem unless we can design our windows explicitly ourselves. As you can see, the prompt appears in the top of the dialog box, and the text box itself some distance away, at the bottom. In other words, although InputBox

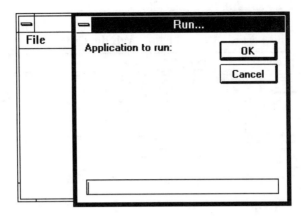

Figure 4-4. Windows Shell Application

works, you may be surprised at the results. A better option is designing the
dialog box you want to use yourself, so let's look into that next.

Creating Applications with Multiple Windows

As you might expect, it's not difficult to create multiple-form programs under
Visual Basic. Let's revise the Windows Shell program to use a dialog box of our
own creation. To do that, we'll need a new form, which is easily created — just
select the New Form item in the File menu, and a new form, called **Form2**,
appears on the screen, as shown in Figure 4-5.

The name of a form, like **Form1** or **Form2**, is not a **CtlName** property (because a form is not a control). Instead, it is a form name, held in the
FormName property. Until now, we haven't paid much attention to
FormNames, but now that we're using multiple forms, they will become important. For example, now you'll be able to switch between forms using the
project window: Just click on the name of the form you want to work on.

NOTE   Even if we had changed the **FormName** and **Caption** of **Form1**, the second
form would still have been named **Form2**.

The First Form

When there are multiple forms involved, a natural question is, "which one
does Visual Basic start first when the application starts?" It would be awkward

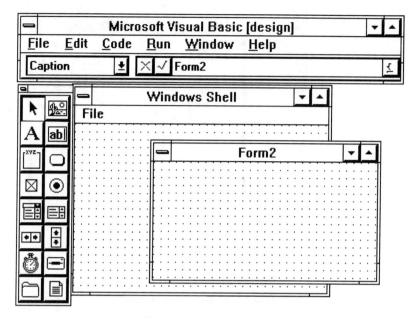

Figure 4-5. Visual Basic with a Second Form

if it decided to place our dialog box on the screen by itself. It turns out that, as you might expect, the default here is that the first form created when you're creating an application is the first form that is started when the application runs.

> **TIP**   If you want to indicate specifically which of a number of windows to place on the screen first, you can use the Set Startup Form... item in Visual Basic's Run menu.

Note that when the first form is started, a Form_Load event is generated for that form. This is a special event that occurs when a form is about to appear, so you can often do initialization of your entire application here. In particular, if your application depends on a number of windows being on the screen at the same time, you can use the Form_Load event of the first window (i.e., the one Visual Basic displays first) to display the others. (We'll see a great deal about the Form_Load event later.)

The question now is, "how do we display other windows?" After we've designed our dialog box, how will we be able to place it on the screen when we want it?

Visual Basic has several ways of handling this task. For example, two statements, Load and Unload, load and unload forms into and out of memory. In this way, Load and Unload work much the same way as they did with menu items in the last chapter. Here, however, we can load and unload forms by using their **FormName** properties like this:

```
Load Form2
UnLoad Form2
```

However, we should note that simply loading a form does not display it. Displaying is handled by the **Show** method. As we've seen before (with the **SetFocus** method), a method is like a procedure, except that it's tied to an object (a control or form), just like a property. In other words, a property is made up of data attached to the object, and a method is a procedure attached to the object.

To show a form named **Form2**, then, we'd just have to execute this statement: **Form2.Show** [**modal%**], where the optional argument **modal%** can take on two values (0 or 1). If it's 0, the user is free to use other forms even when this form (**Form2** here) is on the screen. If it's 1, all other forms in our application become inactive, and the user cannot switch to them. In the latter case, the form is said to be modal (i.e., the user's course of action is restricted), and dialog boxes are mostly modal — for example, **InputBox$( )** places a modal dialog box on the screen. Note that if you omit the form name, the reference is assumed to be to the current form.

One more point is important to mention about Show: You must have loaded a form before you can display it but, if a form is not loaded, **Show** loads it before displaying it. (For that reason, we'll be able to use the **Show** method alone to display forms, not Load followed by Show.)

TIP In fact, if you simply execute any code that uses a property or method of a form which is not loaded into memory, Visual Basic automatically loads it in before executing that statement.

Besides the Show method, there is the **Hide** method, which, predictably, hides the form from the screen once again. Together, Show and Hide are the two methods that handle dialog box appearances and disappearances. For example, we can change the name of our dialog box's form from **Form2** to, say, **RunDialog**. To load and display this form, we'll only have to execute the

RunDialog.Show 1 statement (where we're making this dialog box modal by passing an argument of 1 to the **Show** method).

When there are a number of forms on the screen, you may wonder how to refer to the controls and properties of a specific one. The solution to that is simply to use the form as part of that control or property's name, like this: **Form1.ExitItem** or **Form2.Text2**. Until now, when we've been dealing with only one form, we didn't need to specify the form name when referring to a control. Visual Basic simply assumed that the current form was the one we wanted. However, with multiple forms, all we'll need to do is to specify the form name along with the property or method we want to access.

In other words, we used to refer to a control's set of properties like this: **control.property**. Now, however, we might have a number of forms to choose among, so we can specify the same thing like this: **form.control.property**. In addition, now that we know a little about methods, we can refer to them by form as well, like this: **form.method**. Let's see some of this in action.

Creating Custom Dialog Boxes

The first step is to design our dialog box the way we want it. That is, we can start working on the second form, **RunDialog**, in the Visual Basic environment. To begin, change its form name property from **Form2** to **RunDialog** using the **FormName** property in the properties bar (click on the second form first if you have to). Also, give it the caption Run..., just as we labeled the **InputBox$( )** dialog box before.

The job of this dialog box is to accept a string (i.e., the name of a Windows application to run), so we'll need a text box in it. For that reason, place a text box in the upper half of the form, as shown in Figure 4-6, and remove the default text in it so that it appears blank. Also, we won't need minimizing or maximizing buttons here, since this is a modal dialog box (i.e., the user can't do anything else in our application until they deal with this box), so find the **MinButton** and **MaxButton** properties of the Run... dialog box and set them to False. When you do, the buttons will disappear from the form at run-time.

In addition, just like most dialog boxes, this dialog box need not be resized, so change its BorderStyle property to Fixed Single; that is, a fixed size, single width border (when you select a fixed border type, Visual Basic also removes the Size option in that form's system menu). We'll also want two buttons here:

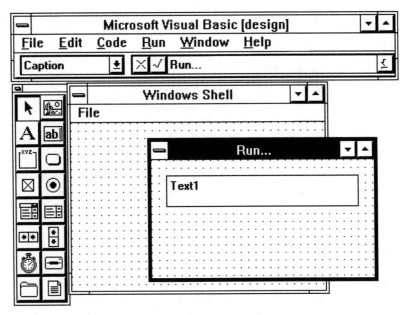

Figure 4-6. Text Box Position in Run... Dialog Box

OK and Cancel. In particular, you should note that most dialog boxes should have Cancel options in them (especially if the dialog box is modal). This gives the user a way out if the choices they've made until now have been in error or were unintentional. For that reason, double-click on the command button tool twice, once for each new button and position them below the text box, labeling one OK and the other Cancel. We can give **CtlNames** to these buttons of, say, **OKButton** and **CancelButton**.

Now that we've designed the dialog box's appearance, let's go back and start working on the code that will make this box active. In particular, the event that should make the dialog box appear is the **RunItem_Click( )** event (where **RunItem** is the **CtlName** of the Run... item in the application's File menu). Double-click on that option in the File menu and open up that procedure:

```
Sub RunItem_Click()
    RetVal = Shell(InputBox$("Application to run:", "Run...") ,1)
End Sub
```

This is the actual Shell statement that we put in earlier, but which is now going to be used only if the user presses the OK button in our dialog box. In other words, this procedure should be changed to simply display the dialog box, like this:

```
Sub RunItem_Click()
    RunDialog.Show 1
End Sub
```

Recall that even if the **RunDialog** form is not in memory when the **Show** method is executed, Visual basic will automatically load it. In fact, you can run the program right now. When you click on the Run... item in the File menu, our Run... dialog box will appear. On the other hand, there's no way to get rid of it now, since it is modal (which means that, if you try to switch to other windows in the same application, you'll get a beep — although you can switch to other Windows applications).

End the program (using the Visual Basic End item in the Run menu, not the menus in the Windows Shell form) and bring up the second form so we can work on it (i.e., click on Form2.Frm in the project window), as shown in Figure 4-7. The real action here takes place in the click procedures associated with the buttons. When the user clicks the OK button, the program is sup-

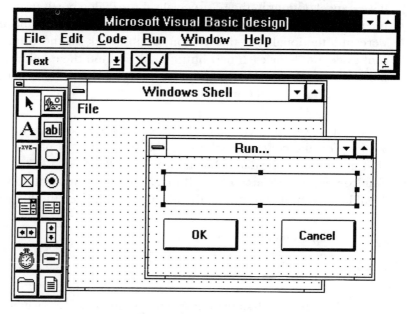

Figure 4-7. Run Dialog Box

posed to execute the Windows application whose path and name were typed in the text box.

Click on the OK button to bring up the code window; the following Sub procedure template appears:

```
Sub OKButton_Click()

End Sub
```

Since this is the procedure connected with the OK button, we are supposed to run the application here. The path and name of that application are presumably in the dialog box's text box, which is still named **Text1**. For that reason, we can simply put this line in the procedure:

```
Sub OKButton_Click()
    RetVal = Shell(Text1.Text, 1)
End Sub
```

However, before doing so, we should hide the dialog box. That way, when the Windows application finishes, we'll return to the original Windows Shell application, not to the dialog box:

```
      Sub OKButton_Click()
→         RunDialog.Hide
          RetVal = Shell(Text1.Text, 1)
      End Sub
```

Now, immediately after the user clicks the OK button, the dialog box disappears, and the application they wanted to start begins. In addition, while we're here, we should make the OK button the default (i.e., display it with a thick black border), so that the user only has to type the name of the application they want to start and press <Enter>, since pressing <Enter> clicks the default button. To do that, set the button's **Default** property to True in the properties bar.

TIP You can check to see if a form is hidden or not with the Visible property: If **Form.Visible** is True, the form is visible; if False, invisible.

The other button in our dialog box is the Cancel button; if it's clicked, we should just hide the dialog box and return to the original form, the Windows Shell application. That procedure can look like this:

```
Sub CancelButton_Click()
    RunDialog.Hide
End Sub
```

This returns us to the original form and restores the focus to it — nothing else is required. That's all there is to it; the complete code for the whole program appears in Listing 4-1.

Listing 4-1. Windows Shell Application

```
Shell.Frm  -------------------------------

Sub RunItem_Click ()
    RunDialog.Show 1
End Sub

Sub ExitItem_Click ()
    End
End Sub


Form2.Frm  ------------------------------

Sub OKButton_Click ()
    RunDialog.Hide
    RetVal = Shell(Text1.Text, 1)
End Sub

Sub CancelButton_Click ()
    RunDialog.Hide
End Sub
```

As you can see, it's quite short, only five lines of actual code, each line tied to its own event. In this way, event-driven programming can save us a good deal of work when it comes to I/O handling. (So far, we've been dealing mostly with I/O, but in the next chapter, when we start working with files, we'll start adding more code to our programs for internal processing of data behind the scenes.) Earlier in this chapter, we saw how to use InputBox$( ) as a dialog box of sorts, but now we've seen that it's almost as easy to create our own dialog boxes, and the result is usually worth the trouble in Visual Basic (compare Figure 4-7 to Figure 4-4).

In fact, there are many types of controls that you can find in dialog boxes, and buttons and text boxes are only two of them. For example, our next application will include a control panel, that will let us set various aspects of the main window with various controls including scroll bars (control panels are very popular in large scale Windows applications). Let's look into that next.

Adding a Control Panel to Our Applications

We can start a new application to demonstrate how control panels work in Windows applications. As you probably know, a control panel is used to customize certain aspects of an application. In our case, we'll use it to set some properties of the main window: the background color, the height and width of the window, and the main window's caption. Let's call this application Panel.Mak. This program will give us experience with changing the properties of another window besides the current one, as well as a new type of control: scroll bars.

We can leave the form name of the main window as Form1 so that the control panel we develop is quite generic. Start this project and create a new form (i.e., select the New Form item in the File menu) and give it the name (i.e., **FormName**) **ControlPanel** with a **Caption** of **Control Panel**. We should also save all files at this point as Panel.* so that our project doesn't inadvertently write over earlier files. Let's put a text box, which we might name **NewCaption** into the control panel, with the label "Application Caption:", as shown in Figure 4-8.

TIP   If the text you want to put into a label is too long for the label's width, don't worry: Like multiline text boxes, labels have automatic word wrap.

Delete the text now in the text box (i.e., "Text1"). This will be where the user can change the name of the main window if they want to. These kinds of changes will go into effect when the user clicks the OK button, which we can give the **CtlName OKButton** to. Let's add that at the bottom of the control panel, along with a Cancel button, which we can call **CancelButton**. As an added touch, we can give the OK button the focus (which is usually the case in control panels) by setting its Default property to True in the properties bar.

As you might expect, the code for **CancelButton** does nothing more than hide the control panel like this:

```
Sub CancelButton ()
    ControlPanel.Hide
End Sub
```

On the other hand, we'll do more work in the **OKButton** procedure because of the way our control panel will work: Rather than keep track of the changes made by the user, we'll just set the relevant properties of the main window, Form1, after they press the OK button. For example, here's how to set the main window's new caption in **OKButton_Click( )**:

```
      Sub OKButton_Click ()
→         Form1.Caption = NewCaption.Text
          ControlPanel.Hide
      End Sub
```

Notice the first line here: **Form1.Caption** = **NewCaption.Text**. In general, that's the way we refer to the properties of another form: by using the form name first. If we had wanted to change the properties of one of **Form1**'s controls, we could have referred to it as **Form1.Control.Property**.

Note that we should also load the current settings of the main window's properties into the control panel's controls when the user opens it (e.g., when

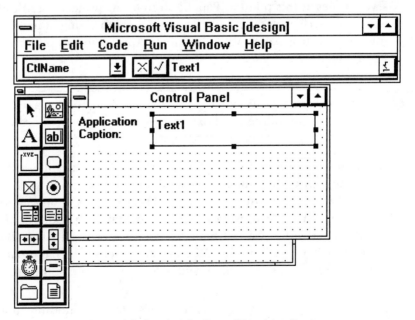

Figure 4-8. Starting the Control Panel Application

the user starts the control panel the first time, the text box should say: "Form1," which is the current caption of the main window) because that's the way a control panel usually works. Let's manipulate the size of the main window next.

Using Scroll Bars

The default measuring system in Visual Basic is twips, or 1/1,440 of an inch, which means that the two properties we are interested in changing — the main window's height and width — are measured in twips. We could, of course, just use a text window in the control panel and have the user set new sizes in terms of twips, which means that we could read in the values using Val( ) and set the two appropriate **Form1** properties, **Form1.Height** and **Form1.Width**, directly. However, it's not so easy to get a feel for 1/1,440 of an inch. Instead, we can use a popular Windows control for converting a numerical value into a smooth range that's easily manipulated graphically, scroll bars.

You've seen scroll bars many times in Windows applications. In fact, we've used them ourselves already, when we developed our multiline text box for the Editor application. However, Visual Basic took care of all the details there. Now it's up to us. There are five primary properties of scroll bars that we'll be interested in here: **Min**, **Max**, **Value**, **LargeChange**, and **SmallChange**.

Min is the numerical value that you assign to the top or left of a scroll bar (all of these properties can go from 0 to 32,767); **Max** is the value you assign to the right or bottom; and **Value** is the current value corresponding to the position of the thumb, the box that moves inside the scroll bar, also called the scroll box. You set **Min** and **Max** yourself. The scroll bar then indicates the position of the thumb by placing a value in its **Value** property, which we can read directly (**Min** <= **Value** <= **Max**). For example, if the thumb was all the way to the left in a horizontal scroll bar, the scroll bar's **Value** property would be equal to the value you put in the **Min** property.

The **LargeChange** property indicates the amount that **Value** should change each time the user clicks the bar above or below the thumb in the scroll bar; i.e., how far the thumb moves. **SmallChange** is the amount that **Value** should change when the user clicks one of the arrows at the top and bottom of the scroll bar. With the exception of **Value**, we can set all these properties at design-time.

The main event with scroll bars is the Change event, which occurs every time the thumb is moved. However, we don't want our changes to take effect unless the user clicks the OK button, so we won't read the value of our scroll bars until then. Let's see how this works in practice. Click on the vertical scroll bar tool in the Visual Basic toolbox (i.e., the sixth tool down on the right side), and a scroll bar appears in our control panel. We'll be using a total of five scroll bars in the control panel (corresponding to the height and width of the main window, and the three colors — red, green, and blue — to use for its background color), so place this first scroll bar over to the left in the control panel.

Next, we have to decide the **Min** and **Max** values for this scroll bar. Since there are 1,440 twips to an inch, we can actually design our window size in inches. For this example, let's have a minimum window size of 1" × 2" (height × width) and a maximum of 5" × 7", which translates into a twip range of 1,440 × 2,880 to 7,200 × 10,080. This first scroll bar can set the main window's height, and we might call it **NewHeight**, which means that the properties we should set at design-time are: **NewHeight.Min** = 1440 and **NewHeight.Max** = 7200 (similarly, when we design a scroll bar to change the main window's width, we can call it **NewWidth**; **NewWidth.Min** will be 2880, and **NewWidth.Max** will be 10080).

To set those properties, click on the **Min** property in the property bar: The default value is 0; set it to 1440. Next, click on the **Max** property: It's default value is 32767; set it to 7200. In addition, we'll have to specify values for **LargeChange** (when the user clicks the scroll bar above or below the thumb) and **SmallChange** (when the user clicks the arrows at the end of the scroll bar). For the purposes of this demonstration, we can use **Newheight.LargeChange** = 1000, and **NewHeight.SmallChange** = 500. Now the scroll bar will be active when we run the program (that is, we'll be able to read its setting simply by reading **NewHeight.Value**), so we should label the scroll bar. Put a label above it that says "New Height," as in Figure 4-9.

Next, create a new vertical scroll bar, giving it the CtlName NewWidth and a label above it that says "New Width." Place it next to the first scroll bar, and give it the **Min** and **Max** properties of 2880 and 10080, respectively. For the **LargeChange** and **SmallChange** values, we can use 1000 and 500 again. Now let's add the necessary code to the OK button. When the user clicks the OK button, they want the main window properties **Height** and **Width** set to **NewHeight.Value** and **NewWidth.Value**, respectively, so we can just add these lines to **OKButton_Click( )**:

```
    Sub OKButton_Click ()
        Form1.Caption = NewCaption.Text
→       Form1.Height = NewHeight.Value
→       Form1.Width = NewWidth.Value
        ControlPanel.Hide
    End Sub
```

Let's see this code in action. To do that, we'll have to add code to the main window to pop up the control panel in the first place. Go back to the main window, **Form1**, and open the Menu Design window. In this case, we can create a single menu, named File (menu name: **FileMenu**), which has two items in it: Control Panel... (**CtlName: ControlPanelItem**) and Exit (**CtlName: ExitItem**).

In fact, while we're here, we can add access keys and shortcut keys to our menu (say <Ctrl+C> for the control panel and <Ctrl+X> to exit). After creating the menu, close the Menu Design window and open the **Control-PanelItem_Click( )** in the code window, like this:

```
Sub ControlPanelItem_Click()

End Sub
```

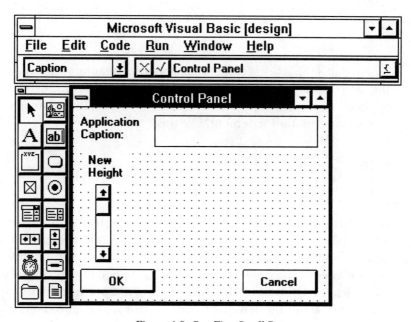

Figure 4-9. Our First Scroll Bar

When the user selects this item, we should load the control panel's controls with the current settings of the main window and then display the control panel on the screen. In other words, we want to load **ControlPanel.New-Caption.Text** (recall that we gave the control panel the form name of **ControlPanel**) with **Form1.Caption**, **ControlPanel.NewHeight.Value** with **Form1.Height**, and **ControlPanel.NewWidth.Value** with **Form1.Width**, like this (the thumb in the scroll bars will move, matching the number we place in their **Value** property):

```
Sub ControlPanelItem_Click()
    ControlPanel.NewCaption.Text = Form1.Caption
    ControlPanel.NewHeight.Value = Form1.Height
    ControlPanel.NewWidth.Value = Form1.Width
        :
End Sub
```

Then, after loading the defaults, we want to show the control panel, which we can do like this (note that the control panel does not have to be on the screen for us to change its properties):

```
      Sub ControlPanelItem_Click()
          ControlPanel.NewCaption.Text = Form1.Caption
          ControlPanel.NewHeight.Value = Form1.Height
          ControlPanel.NewWidth.Value = Form1.Width
  →       ControlPanel.Show
      End Sub
```

Again, that's the way to refer to the properties of another form, by referring to the properties' full name, including form. In addition, before starting the application, we should make the Exit item in the File menu active, which we can do with the End statement, like this:

```
Sub ExitItem_Click()
    End
End Sub
```

Now start the application and click on the Control Panel... item in the File menu. When you do, the control panel opens and displays the current defaults for both the main window's caption and size. You might try changing the size to see if the program works. If you change the text in the text box and then click the OK button, the control panel disappears and the caption in the main window will be changed to match your new caption. Or, if you use the scroll bars, you can reset the size of the window (which is really no great savings because the main window can be resized as easily by dragging its edges, but as an example it's still impressive to see).

In fact, we should really give some indication of the new size of the main window as the user manipulates the scroll bars. It's always best to give as much visual feedback in a Windows application as possible. Since we don't want to actually change the size of the main window while the user is using the scroll bars (they might still click the Cancel button), a good idea here might be to draw a rectangle in the control panel representing the screen, and another one representing the main window to show their relative sizes (and we'll learn how to draw rectangles in Chapter 6).

Now let's work on changing the color of the main window. The background color — that is, the color behind the text — is kept in the **BackColor** property, and that's the one we want to manipulate (the foreground color — the color of the text itself — is kept in the **ForeColor** property).

We should notice, however, that colors in Windows are determined by three independent settings: a red setting, a green setting, and a blue setting. To take care of all three, we'll need three vertical scroll bars, so create them now by clicking on the vertical scroll bar tool and position them next to the two we already have. Label the first one Red (placing the label above it, as with New Height and New Width), the second on Green, and the third one Blue. For control names, we can call them **NewRed**, **NewGreen**, and **NewBlue**.

In addition, we can actually provide the user with some direct visual feedback, indicating the color they're selecting, and doing so will introduce us to the scroll bar change event at the same time. Create a label named, say, **New-Color**, and place it in the space between the OK and Cancel buttons at the bottom of the control panel, giving it a fixed single border by changing its **BorderStyle** property (by default, labels don't have a border), as shown in Figure 4-10. This is where we'll display the color as selected with the scroll bars. Now let's explore how to actually deal with colors in Visual Basic.

Setting Colors in Visual Basic

As mentioned, there are three color settings in a color value under Visual Basic. Each one can range from 0 to 255, and they are put together to form a long integer, which is what we can place in properties like **Form1.BackColor** (or **NewColor.BackColor**, where **NewColor** is the **CtlName** of the label we've

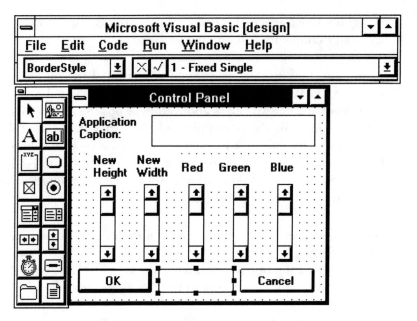

Figure 4-10. Complete Control Panel Template

added to show the color combination represented by the scroll bar values). In fact, there is an easy way to combine these values; Visual Basic provides a special function, the RGB function, to do exactly that. For example, we could set the background color of the **NewColor** label like this, where **New-Red.Value**, etc., are the names of the **Value** properties of the scroll bars:

```
NewColor.BackColor = RGB(NewRed.Value, NewGreen.Value,
NewBlue.Value)
```

In other words, we just need to pass the three color values red, green, and blue, in order, to RGB( ), and RGB( ) will return a setting that we can use in the **BackColor** (and **ForeColor**) properties. For that reason, we should give each of the color value scroll bars a **Min** property of 0 and a **Max** property of 255. We can also use **SmallChange** and **LargeChange** values of, say, 10 and 20. After setting these values in the scroll bars themselves, click on the first scroll bar (which sets the amount of red in the color we're designing) to open this Sub procedure template:

```
Sub NewRed_Change()

End Sub
```

This is the event procedure that is called whenever **NewRed.Value** is changed. Although we could simply read this value when the OK button is clicked and change **Form1.BackColor** accordingly, we can use this event to keep track of the currently selected color and display it in the **NewColor** label, which we do simply like this:

```
Sub NewRed_Change()
    NewColor.BackColor = RGB(NewRed.Value, NewGreen.Value, NewBlue.Value)
End Sub
```

Now, whenever the user changes the setting of the Red scroll bar, the color in the **NewColor** label changes to match. In fact, we can do the same thing in all three color scroll bar's change event procedures:

```
Sub NewRed_Change()
    NewColor.BackColor = RGB(NewRed.Value, NewGreen.Value, NewBlue.Value)
End Sub

Sub NewGreen_Change()
    NewColor.BackColor = RGB(NewRed.Value, NewGreen.Value, NewBlue.Value)
End Sub

Sub NewBlue_Change()
    NewColor.BackColor = RGB(NewRed.Value, NewGreen.Value, NewBlue.Value)
End Sub
```

Make these changes and run the program. When you do, you'll find that you can manipulate the color in the **NewColor** label simply by moving the scroll bars around, adjusting the color components in it. In addition, we'll need to make the color we've designed this way into the background color of the main window when the user clicks the OK button. We can do that by adding this line to the OK_Button_Click event:

```
      Sub OKButton_Click ()
          Form1.Caption = NewCaption.Text
          Form1.Height = NewHeight.Value
          Form1.Width = NewWidth.Value
→         Form1.BackColor = RGB(NewRed.Value, NewGreen.Value, NewBlue.Value)
          ControlPanel.Hide
      End Sub
```

Now the user is able to select the color of the main window and see what color they're selecting at the same time. When they press they OK button, the change is made instantly to the main window's **BackColor** property, turning it whatever color they choose. That's almost it for our control panel application. At this point, most of it is functional. The last step is to load the original background color from the main window into the control panel when it first starts; that is, to load the default color into the control panel. To do that, we can take the original color, **Form1.BackColor**, and load it into **Control-Panel.NewColor.BackColor** (since this is only a demonstration program, we're not going to dissect this color into separate settings for each of the color scroll bars). Because the control panel pops up when the Control Panel... item is selected in the File menu, we can do that like this:

```
        Sub ControlPanelItem_Click()
            ControlPanel.NewCaption.Text = Form1.Caption
            ControlPanel.NewHeight.Value = Form1.Height
            ControlPanel.NewWidth.Value = Form1.Width
  →         ControlPanel.NewColor.BackColor = Form1.BackColor
            ControlPanel.Show
        End Sub
```

And that's it. We've completed the control panel application, which let us customize our main window through the use of scroll bars. Its code appears in Listing 4-2.

Listing 4-2. The Control Panel Application

```
Form1 ----------------------------------------------

Sub ControlPanelItem_Click()
    ControlPanel.NewCaption.Text = Form1.Caption
    ControlPanel.NewHeight.Value = Form1.Height
    ControlPanel.NewWidth.Value = Form1.Width
    ControlPanel.NewColor.BackColor = Form1.BackColor
    ControlPanel.Show
End Sub

Sub ExitItem_Click()
    End
End Sub

ControlPanel --------------------------------------

Sub NewRed_Change()
    NewColor.BackColor = RGB(NewRed.Value, NewGreen.Value,
        NewBlue.Value)
End Sub
```

Listing 4-2. (continued)

```
Sub NewGreen_Change()
    NewColor.BackColor = RGB(NewRed.Value, NewGreen.Value,
        NewBlue.Value)
End Sub

Sub NewBlue_Change()
    NewColor.BackColor = RGB(NewRed.Value, NewGreen.Value,
        NewBlue.Value)
End Sub

Sub OKButton_Click ()
    Form1.Caption = NewCaption.Text
    Form1.Height = NewHeight.Value
    Form1.Width = NewWidth.Value
    Form1.BackColor = RGB(NewRed.Value, NewGreen.Value,
        NewBlue.Value)
    ControlPanel.Hide
End Sub

Sub CancelButton ()
    ControlPanel.Hide
End Sub
```

Scroll bars are not the only controls you find in dialog boxes, of course; other common controls include list boxes and combo boxes, and we'll take a look at them next, starting with list boxes.

Creating List Boxes

You use list boxes when you have a number of choices to present to the user, and you want to limit the choices to what you present (by contrast, a combo box is used more for suggested choices; that is, users can enter their own choice in the combo box's text box if they want to). For example, you might have a list of customized Windows applications that your program is capable of starting, so you can present the choices in a list box. Or you might want to present the various file attribute options (plain file, read-only, hidden, and so on) when writing to a file. In general, list boxes can be useful anywhere there are a number of choices to choose from. And, because list boxes can have scroll bars, the number of such choices can be significantly greater than you can present in a menu (which makes them popular in dialog boxes).

As an example, let's put together a mini-database program. Databases usually sort their data records according to some key, and we'll find we can do that here with a list box. Let's say that this database program is meant to keep track of stock inventory; for that reason, we might want to keep track of these things:

Name of the product
Number of the product
Additional space for comments

For example, if we had seven apples that had to be sold before they spoil next Thursday, our data might look like this:

Name of the product: "Apples"
Number of the product: "7"
Additional space for comments: "Sell by Thursday."

Each of these data items: "Apples," "7," and "Sell by Thursday." is called a *field* in a database. Together, they make up a *record*. To set up our application, we can add a menu to our main window with an item named Find Record...; when selected, a dialog box will open with a list box that lists the names associated with each record — e.g., Apples, Bananas, Cantaloupe, and so on:

By double-clicking on one of these names, the user can bring up the corresponding record (i.e., the dialog box will disappear and the record's data will be placed into text boxes in the main window). One of the properties of list boxes that will help us here is the **Sorted** property; if True, Visual Basic keeps all the items in the list box sorted alphabetically. In other words, Visual Basic will handle the sorting of our products automatically.

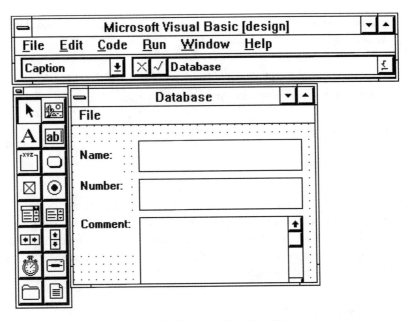

Figure 4-11. Database Template Window

To design this application, start Visual Basic, call this project Database.Mak and give the form the caption "Database." We'll need three text boxes on this main form, which we can label Name:, Number:, and Comment:, and which we can give the **CtlNames NameField**, **NumberField**, and **CommentField**. In fact, we can make the comment box a multiline text box so that a considerable amount of text can be stored there. Next, we can add a menu named File with several items in it: Add Item, Find Item..., Save File..., Load File..., and Exit. At this point, the main window should look like the one in Figure 4-11.

For the first menu choice, Add Item, let's use the **CtlName AddAnItem** (Add Item is a reserved word, as we're about to see). This item is available so the user can fill the database with data. After editing the three text boxes, the user can select Add Item to add this data to a new record in our database. We can use the **CtlName FindItem** for the next menu choice, Find Item.... This item is the one that will open the dialog box (the dialog box will contain the list box which holds the product names of each record, sorted alphabetically). When the user double-clicks on an item in the list, the dialog box will disappear and the correct record will appear in the main window. We'll be able to add the code for the next two menu items, Save File... and Load File..., in our chapter about files. In the meantime, give them the **CtlNames SaveItem** and **LoadItem**.

Let's write the **AddAnItem_Click( )** procedure first. Click on the Add Item menu choice, opening this Sub procedure template:

```
Sub AddAnItem_Click()

End Sub
```

When the user clicks on Add Item, they want the current contents of the text boxes to be stored in the database. We can do that by setting up some global variables (note that they should be global, not form-level, variables, since our dialog box — an entirely separate form — will have to reach them as well) like this in the global module:

```
Global Names(100) As String
Global Numbers(100) As String
Global Comments(100) As String
Global TotalRecords As Integer
```

In this way, we're setting aside enough space to hold records for 100 products. Also note that we're keeping track of the total number of records in a global integer named **TotalRecords**. Simply click on the global module in the project window, put the above declarations into it, and save that module as, say, Database.Bas. Now we're free to fill those arrays with data (because the user has placed the data we'll need in the main window's text boxes before clicking Add Item). That is, we can store data in our database arrays this way in **AddAnItem_Click( )** (note we increment **TotalRecords** first because we're adding a new record):

```
Sub AddAnItem_Click()
    TotalRecords = TotalRecords + 1
    Names(TotalRecords) = NameField.Text
    Numbers(TotalRecords) = NumberField.Text
    Comments(TotalRecords) = CommentField.Text
        :
End Sub
```

For example, if we were about to create the first record, and this was the data in the main window's text boxes:

Name of the product: "Apples"
Number of the product: "7"
Additional space for comments: "Sell by Thursday."

Then **Names(1)** would be set to "Apples," **Numbers(1)** to "7," and **Comments(1)** to "Sell by Thursday." Now that we've stored the data, we have to add the name of this product — Apples — to our (automatically alphabetized) list box so that the user can select records easily. We do that with the *AddItem* method. Note that this is a method, which means that we have to attach it to the name of the list box we want to change. For example, we can call the list box that holds all the product's names **NameList**, which means that we'd include this line in **AddAnItem_Click( )**:

```
Sub AddAnItem_Click()
    TotalRecords = TotalRecords + 1
    Names(TotalRecords) = NameField.Text
    Numbers(TotalRecords) = NumberField.Text
    Comments(TotalRecords) = CommentField.Text
→   Form2.NameList.AddItem NameField.Text
End Sub
```

Where **Form2** is the name of the second form, which will appear when the user wants to select a record. In general, this is the way you use **AddItem** in Visual Basic:

```
form.listbox.AddItem string$ [, index]
```

The optional argument named index specifies the new entry's position in the list box, 0 (at the top of the list box) is the first position, the next down is 1, and so on. Since our list box will be automatically sorted, we won't specify an index for our entries. Correspondingly, to remove an item, you can use the **RemoveItem** method:

```
form.listbox.RemoveItem index
```

Here, an index is not optional: You must use it to specify which item in the list you want to remove. That's it for adding an item. The next step is to find items on demand. Click on the Find Item... menu choice to bring up this template:

```
Sub FindItem_Click()

End Sub
```

The actual work of finding a record will be done by the second form, **Form2**, so we can pop that up on the screen now:

```
Sub FindItem_Click()
    Form2.Show
End Sub
```

And that's it for **FindItem_Click( )**. Let's design the dialog box named **Form2** now. Create **Form2** by clicking on the New Form item in Visual Basic's File menu, and give it a caption of Find Item.... Also, we should remove the **Min** and **Max** buttons, and give it a fixed border by selecting the **BorderStyle** property. Next, create a list box by clicking the list box tool in the toolbox (fifth tool down on the right). Give this list box the **CtlName** that we've already used, **NameList**, and set the **Sorted** property to True so that the entries in it will appear in alphabetical order. (Note that the **CtlName**, **NameList**, appears in the list box. It will be gone at run-time.) There are no scroll bars on this list, but they will appear automatically if the list is too long for the list box.

Now add the two normal control buttons for a dialog box, OK and Cancel, as shown in Figure 4-12, with the **CtlNames OKButton** and **CancelButton**. It's a good idea to make the OK button the default (i.e., set its default property to True) as well. As before, it's easy to write the Cancel Button procedure. All we have to do is to hide Form2 like this:

```
     Sub CancelButton_Click()
→        Form2.Hide
     End Sub
```

Now let's work on the dialog box's **OKButton_Click( )** procedure:

```
OKButton_Click()

End Sub
```

When the user clicks the OK button — or double-clicks an item in the list box — they've selected an item in the list box, and we should display the corresponding record. For example, if this was our dialog box:

Then clicking Apples should fill the text boxes in the main window with the data we've already stored by using Add Item:

Name of the product: "Apples"
Number of the product: "7"
Additional space for comments: "Sell by Thursday."

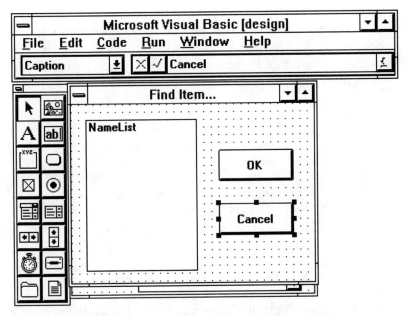

Figure 4-12. Find Item... Dialog Box Template

In general, we can determine what item is selected in a list box (one item is always selected in list boxes) by using these list box properties:

Text	The currently selected item
List	Array of String containing all the items
ListIndex	The index of the selected item (0-based)
ListCount	Total number of items in the list

The most commonly used property is **Text**, a string that holds the currently selected item. However, the others are very useful too (and we might notice that **Text** = **List(ListIndex)**). In our case, we'll have to find the record corresponding to the selection and display it. We can find the correct record with a loop like this in **OKButton_Click( )**:

```
Sub OKButton_Click()
    For Loop_Index = 1 To 100
        If (Names(loop_index) = NameList.Text) Then Exit For
    Next loop_index
        :
```

Here, we're just comparing the selected product name with the product names of each record. When we find the one we want (it must be in the list because the list box simply displays these names), we leave the for loop with the Visual Basic Exit For statement. At this point, we can fill the fields on the main form correctly and hide **Form2**, like this:

```
        Sub OKButton_Click()
            For loop_Index = 1 To 100
                If (Names(loop_index) = NameList.Text) Then Exit For
            Next loop_index

→           Form1.NameField.Text = Names(loop_index)
→           Form1.NumberField.Text = Numbers(loop_index)
→           Form1.CommentField.Text = Comments(loop_index)

→           Form2.Hide
        End Sub
```

We should note that the important events for list boxes are Click, when the user makes a selection, and DblClick, when the user makes a choice. That means that double-clicking an item is the same as clicking the OK button, so we can add the same procedure there:

```
Sub NameList_DblClick()
    For loop_Index = 1 To 100
        If (Names(loop_index) = NameList.Text) Then Exit For
    Next loop_index

    Form1.NameField.Text = Names(loop_index)
    Form1.NumberField.Text = Numbers(loop_index)
    Form1.CommentField.Text = Comments(loop_index)

    Form2.Hide
End Sub
```

The only remaining thing to do is to make the Exit item active in the main window's menu, which we do in the usual way, with the Visual Basic End statement:

```
Sub ExitItem ()
    End
End Sub
```

The completed program appears in Figure 4-13, ready to run. You use it by typing data into the text boxes in the main window. When you want to read a record back, you can select Find Item... in the File menu to pop our dialog box on the screen. Select the item in the list box there and click the OK button, or double-click the item in the list box, and that item's records appear in the main window. The database is a success.

However, we might note here that we had to duplicate the same code in both **NameList.DblClick( )** and **OKButton_Click( )** (i.e., both display the selected product's records). One way of avoiding this is to place this code into a *module*, and call it from these two procedures. For example, if we created a Sub procedure that contained all this code called **GetItem( )**, we could change both **NameList.DblClick( )** and **OKButton_Click( )** to this:

```
Sub NameList.DblClick()
    Call GetItem
End Sub

Sub OKButton_Click()
    Call GetItem
End Sub
```

That is, you use a *Call* statement to reference **GetItem( )**. Let's see how to add such modules before moving on to combo boxes.

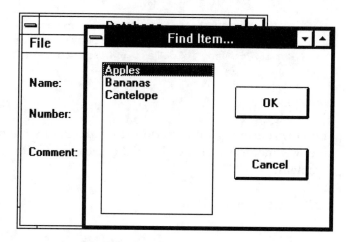

Figure 4-13. Database Application

Creating a Module in Visual Basic

To create a module, select the New Module item in Visual Basic's File menu. A code window opens up. The code we put here can be reached from anywhere in our entire application. We can place GetItem( ) in this module very simply: Just type the following code into the code window (Visual Basic takes the name of this new procedure, **GetItem**, from the declaration in the first line: Sub GetItem( )). However, we should note that each time we refer to a control on some form, we have to include the form's name (since this code is not attached to any form), such as this reference to **NameList**, which becomes **Form2.NameList**:

```
Sub GetItem()
    For loop_Index = 1 To 100
→       If (Names(loop_index) = Form2.NameList.Text) Then Exit For
    Next loop_index

    Form1.NameField.Text = Names(loop_index)
    Form1.NumberField.Text = Numbers(loop_index)
    Form1.CommentField.Text = Comments(loop_index)

    Form2.Hide
End Sub
```

(The global arrays **Names( )**, **Numbers( )**, and **Comments( )** aren't attached to any form, of course.) This module is just like any other file associated with the current project; that is, it is saved and loaded along with the others. That's it. The code for the entire database program, form by form (recall that we have not added any code for the Save File... or Load File... items yet), appears in Listing 4-3.

Listing 4-3. The Database Program

```
Global Names(100) As String
Global Numbers(100) As String
Global Comments(100) As String
Global TotalRecords As Integer

    Form1 ----------------------------------------

Sub AddAnItem_Click ()
    TotalRecords = TotalRecords + 1
    Names(TotalRecords) = NameField.Text
    Numbers(TotalRecords) = NumberField.Text
    Comments(TotalRecords) = CommentField.Text
    Form2.NameList.AddItem NameField.Text
End Sub

Sub FindItem_Click ()
    Form2.Show
End Sub

Sub ExitItem_Click ()
    End
End Sub

    Form2 ---------------------------------

Sub OKButton_Click ()
    Call GetItem
End Sub

Sub NameList_DblClick ()
    Call GetItem
End Sub

Sub CancelButton_Click ()
    Form2.Hide
End Sub
```

(continued)

Listing 4-3. (continued)

```
      Module1 ---------------------------------------

  Sub GetItem ()
      For loop_index = 1 To 100
          If (Names(loop_index) = Form2.NameList.Text) Then Exit For
      Next loop_index

      Form1.NameField.Text = Names(loop_index)
      Form1.NumberField.Text = Numbers(loop_index)
      Form1.CommentField.Text = Comments(loop_index)

      Form2.Hide
  End Sub
```

However, there's one more important point here, and it has to do with data organization.

Creating Our Own Data Types

The way the data base program stands, we're maintaining three arrays of data:

```
Global Names(100) As String
Global Numbers(100) As String
Global Comments(100) As String
```

In fact, such fields like this are usually gathered together into their own *type*, and that introduces us to a powerful Visual Basic concept. In general, such a type declaration (which is always declared in the global module) looks like this:

```
Type typename
    elementname As variabletype
    [elementname As variabletype]
    [elementname As variabletype]
        :
End Type
```

For example, we can make a Record type for our database like this:

```
Type Record
    Name As String * 50
    Number As String * 20
    Comment As String * 200
End Type
```

This defines a new data type, **Record**, which contains the individual fields as shown above. Note that we are giving each string a definite size here — that's what the * 50 or * 200 characters mean. **Name** As String * 50 means that the string called **Name** will be exactly 50 characters long. We can declare an array of this type called, say, **Database( )**, like this (in the database's global module):

```
Type Record
    Name As String * 50
    Number As String * 20
    Comment As String * 200
End Type

Global Database(100) As Record
```

NOTE Strings do not need to have a fixed length in a type declaration like this, except when they're used to set up records for random-access files, as we'll do in the next chapter.

Now we have an array, **Database( )**, of 100 such records:

```
┌─────────────────────────────────┐
│ Name As String * 50             │
│ Number As String * 20           │   Database(1)
│ Comment As String * 200         │
├─────────────────────────────────┤
│ Name As String * 50             │
│ Number As String * 20           │   Database(2)
│ Comment As String * 200         │
├─────────────────────────────────┤
│ Name As String * 50             │
│ Number As String * 20           │   Database(3)
│ Comment As String * 200         │
└─────────────────────────────────┘
                 ⋮
                 ⋮
```

And we can reach any one of them using the dot (.) operator (just as we do to reach a Visual Basic property):

```
Database(3).Name = "Carrots"
Database(3).Number = "287"
Database(3).Comment = "Price too high?"
```

Let's use this new array in our database application to combine all three separate arrays (**Names( )**, **Numbers( )**, and **Comments( )**) together into one array (**Database( )**). After setting up the new record type, Record, and the array of that type, Database( ), we've got to change the matching references in our program. For example, **Names(TotalRecords)** becomes **Database(Total-Records).Name**. There are only two Sub procedures to change, as it turns out, the procedure in which we store the data, and the procedure in which we retrieve it. In **Form1**, the procedure for adding an item should be changed from this:

```
Sub AddAnItem_Click ()
    TotalRecords = TotalRecords + 1
    Names(TotalRecords) = NameField.Text
    Numbers(TotalRecords) = NumberField.Text
    Comments(TotalRecords) = CommentField.Text
    Form2.NameList.AddItem NameField.Text
End Sub
```

To this:

```
        Sub AddAnItem_Click ()
            TotalRecords = TotalRecords + 1
→           Database(TotalRecords).Name = NameField.Text
→           Database(TotalRecords).Number = NumberField.Text
→           Database(TotalRecords).Comment = CommentField.Text
            Form2.NameList.AddItem NameField.Text
        End Sub
```

Here, we just change **Names(TotalRecords)** to **Database(TotalRecords).Name** and so on. Also, in our module, we should change the procedure for looking up an item, **GetItem( )**, from this:

```
Sub GetItem ()
    For loop_index = 1 To 100
        If (Names(loop_index)=Form2.NameList.Text) Then Exit For
    Next loop_index
```

```
        Form1.NameField.Text = Names(loop_index)
        Form1.NumberField.Text = Numbers(loop_index)
        Form1.CommentField.Text = Comments(loop_index)

        Form2.Hide
    End Sub
```

To this:

```
      Sub GetItem ()
          For loop_index = 1 To 100
→             If (Rtrim$(Database(loop_index).Name) =
                  Rtrim$(Form2.NameList.Text)) Then Exit For
          Next loop_index

→         Form1.NameField.Text = Database(loop_index).Name
→         Form1.NumberField.Text = Database(loop_index).Number
→         Form1.CommentField.Text = Database(loop_index).Comment

          Form2.Hide
      End Sub
```

Note that we're using a fixed length string for all fields, and, since Visual Basic pads such strings with spaces to the right, we had to remove those spaces with the Basic function Rtrim$( ) (which simply trims any spaces off the right side of strings — its counterpart for trimming spaces off the left is Ltrim$( )) before comparing to the item in the list box:

```
      For loop_index = 1 To 100
→         If (Rtrim$(Database(loop_index).Name) =
              Rtrim$(Form2.NameList.Text)) Then Exit For
      Next loop_index
```

That's it. The revised data base program, complete with its own data type (i.e., Record) appears in Listing 4-4.

Listing 4-4. Revised Database Program

```
      Type Record
          Name As String * 50
          Number As String * 20
          Comment As String * 200
      End Type

      Global Database(100) As Record
      Global TotalRecords As Integer
```

(continued)

Listing 4-4. (continued)

```
      Form1 -----------------------------------------

Sub AddAnItem_Click ()
    TotalRecords = TotalRecords + 1
    Database(TotalRecords).Name = NameField.Text
    Database(TotalRecords).Number = NumberField.Text
    Database(TotalRecords).Comment = CommentField.Text
    Form2.NameList.AddItem NameField.Text
End Sub

Sub FindItem_Click ()
    Form2.Show
End Sub

Sub ExitItem_Click ()
    End
End Sub

      Form2 ------------------------------

Sub OKButton_Click ()
    Call GetItem
End Sub

Sub NameList_DblClick ()
    Call GetItem
End Sub

Sub CancelButton_Click ()
    Form2.Hide
End Sub

      Module1 ---------------------------------------

Sub GetItem ()
    For loop_index = 1 To 100
        If (Rtrim$(Database(loop_index).Name) =
            Rtrim$(Form2.NameList.Text)) Then Exit For
    Next loop_index

    Form1.NameField.Text = Database(loop_index).Name
    Form1.NumberField.Text = Database(loop_index).Number
    Form1.CommentField.Text = Database(loop_index).Comment

    Form2.Hide
End Sub
```

That's it for our database program and list boxes. Let's move on to combo boxes next.

Creating Combo Boxes

The difference between combo boxes and list boxes is that combo boxes combine a list box with a text box (which is why they're called combo boxes), so that users can type their own text if they don't want to select one of the choices offered. There are three different styles of combo boxes, and they appear in Figure 4-14. The first style — style 0 — is a standard combo box, where the arrow is detached from the text box. When the user clicks the arrow, the list of items to choose from drops down. The second style — style 1 — is the same, except that the list box is always displayed. The third style — style 2 — with the arrow attached is actually not a combo box at all: It's a list box. It is called a drop-down list box, and it's the same as a normal list box (that is, the user cannot edit the selections as they can in a combo box), except that the list is hidden until the user clicks the arrow.

Because style 2 combo boxes are really list boxes, let's cover them first before working with straight combo boxes. It's easy to adapt our database application to use drop-down list boxes instead of normal list boxes. All we have to do is to delete the list box named **NameList** on **Form2** and replace it with a combo box, style 2, named **NameList**. To do that, click on the original list box, and select Cut in the Edit menu. Next, click on the combo box tool in the toolbox (next to the list box tool), select style 2, and position it correctly. The result appears in Figure 4-15. As you can see, it allows the Find Item... dialog box to be considerably more compact. Using a drop-down list box is that easy.

Now let's get into combo boxes themselves. Since the user can change or edit the item in the text box that forms part of the combo box, the two important events connected with combo boxes are Click and Change (the Change event occurs when the text in the text box is changed). In addition, a simple combo box — style 1, no drop down box — recognizes the DblClick event, but the other combo box — style 0 — does not. Here are the properties associated with combo boxes:

Text	The currently selected item
List	Array of String containing all the items
ListIndex	The index of the selected item (0 based; -1 if the user entered text rather than selected this item)
ListCount	Total number of items in the list

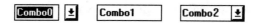

Figure 4-14. Combo Box Styles

In fact, the properties of a combo box are much like the properties of a list box, with one difference: If the user typed in the current selection instead of selecting it from the available list (an option that does not exist with list boxes), then the ListIndex property is set to -1. As for the rest of the details of combo boxes — maintaining the selected text, marking text, and so on — Visual Basic performs them for you.

To see how this works, let's alter our database program to display its product names in a combo box instead of a list box. This has the advantage that the user can then simply type the name of the product they're looking for instead of searching through what might be a long list, but it has the disadvantage that it introduces the possibility that the selected entry doesn't correspond to a record at all (i.e., in case the user mistyped the product name).

That's something we'll have to check for when the user clicks the OK button. In the meantime, open the database application in Visual Basic again and select the drop-down list box we just put in. Since Visual Basic treats it as a combo box of style 2, we can change it to another type of combo box without replacing it. Let's use combo box style 1, which is the same as style 0, except

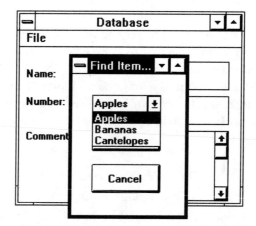

Figure 4-15. Database with a Drop-down List Box

that the list of selected choices is always visible (i.e., this is the style in the middle of Figure 4-14). Although we should rename it from **NameList** to **NameCombo**, it's more convenient to leave the name as **NameList**, since the code already refers to it that way. In fact, since this is the style that recognizes double-click events (combo box style 0 does not), we can leave the code in **NewList_DblClick( )** (as well as **OKButton_Click( )**) alone.

Now we've got to make sure that the selection actually corresponds to one of the records. To do that, we can add this code in our Sub procedure **GetItem( )**:

```
       Sub GetItem ()

→          Matched = False
           For loop_index = 1 To 100
               If (Rtrim$(Database(loop_index).Name) =
                   Rtrim$(Form2.NameList.Text)) Then
→                  Matched = True
                   Exit For
               End If
           Next loop_index

→          If (Matched) Then
               Form1.NameField.Text = Database(loop_index).Name
               Form1.NumberField.Text = Database(loop_index).Number
               Form1.CommentField.Text = Database(loop_index).Comment
               Form2.Hide
→          Else
→              MsgBox "Sorry, I cannot find that record.", 48, "Database"
→          End If

       End Sub
```

Here, if we can't find the record that was typed, we pop up an error message box and let the user start over. Note that we should also merge CON-STANT.TXT into the global module (use the Load Text... item in Visual Basic's Code menu, followed by the Merge button) so that True and False (used by **Matched**) are defined. After these changes, the program functions as before, except now the user can type in the name of the record they're looking for as a shortcut, as in Figure 4-16. However, if the user enters the name of a record that doesn't match one of the existing records, an error box appears, as shown in Figure 4-17.

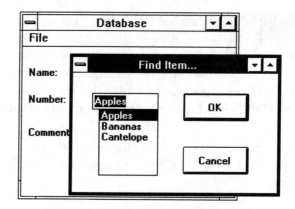

Figure 4-16. Database Application

That's it for our database application, and with it, we finish this chapter on dialog boxes. We've come far. We've seen message boxes, then input boxes, and then we've moved on to multiple forms in order to design our own dialog boxes. We also covered the typical kind of controls you find in dialog boxes: scroll bars, list boxes, and combo boxes. There are, however, some other types of controls that you often find in dialog boxes, directory boxes and file list boxes, and we'll see how they work in the next chapter, when we start working with files.

Figure 4-17. Database Application with Error Box

CHAPTER 5

What about Files?

You may recall that our Editor program had two menu choices that we never supported: Load File... and Save File.... Now, however, we'll be able to change that because this is our chapter on file handling. Until now, all the data that our programs have handled has been very temporary. When the application ended, it was gone. Files, of course are the most common way to store data in the PC, so they are vitally important to most computer applications.

The file system in Visual Basic is very similar to the one in QuickBASIC as far as the actual file manipulation statements go, so if you're familiar with Open, Close, Input$, and Seek, you already have a considerable head start. As you might expect, however, things are very different when it comes to interacting with the user. For example, the user usually picks file names to load data from or save to from dialog boxes in Windows applications (which, incidentally, is why we covered dialog boxes before covering files), and we'll see how to do that in this chapter as we set up our own file dialog boxes.

Two of these dialog boxes will be for the Save File... and Load File... items from our Editor application, and we'll see how to make these items work in this chapter. In addition, we'll see how to work with structured files in this chapter, where the data is broken up into specific records, as it was in our database application in the last chapter. In fact, we'll be able to modify that application in this chapter so that it can save its data to disk. With this and other topics coming up, let's get started immediately.

Saving Data in a File

If we wanted to add file support to our editor application, we might start with the Save File... item (after all, the user has to create files before reading them back in). When the user selects the Save File... item, we could pop a dialog box onto the screen with a list box and two buttons: OK and Cancel. The user could then type the name of the file he wanted to save his document to, and our program would then take that name, create the file (if necessary), and then store the document there. Let's put this into practice.

Start Visual Basic and open the Editor project. If you take a look at the File menu, you'll see that the Save File... menu item already exists, so click on it to bring up the following template:

```
Sub SaveItem_Click ()

End Sub
```

When the user clicks this menu item, she wants to save the current document, which means that our goal here is to place the Save File... dialog box on the screen. Let's name that dialog box (i.e., give it a **FormName** of) **SaveForm**. To display it, all we need to do is this:

```
Sub SaveItem_Click ()
    SaveForm.Show
End Sub
```

Next, we should put together that dialog box (i.e., still in the Editor project), giving it a **FormName** of **SaveForm**, a caption that reads Save File..., and saving our work as, say, SaveForm.Frm. In addition, we should add a text box (which we can call **FilenameBox**) to this new form; a label above the text box with the caption Save File As... (so the user knows that a file name is expected); an OK button with the **CtlName OKButton** (and we should set its default property to True so that it has a thick black border when the dialog box first appears); and a Cancel button (**CtlName: CancelButton**), as shown in Figure 5-1. Finally, because this is a dialog box, we can remove the **Min** and **Max** buttons, as well as making the **BorderStyle** fixed double.

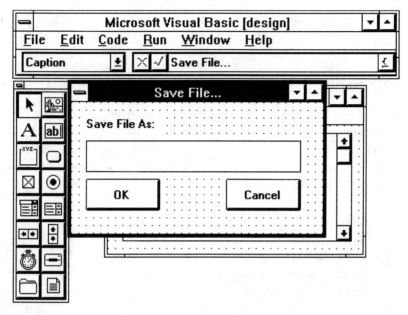

Figure 5-1. Save File... Dialog Box

The Cancel button procedure is easy, so we can do that first. All we want to do if the user decides to cancel is to conceal the form again, so put this in **CancelButton_Click( )**:

```
Sub CancelButton_Click ()
    SaveForm.Hide
End Sub
```

The real work is done when the user clicks the OK button. Click on that button now to open the OK button's click procedure:

```
Sub OKButton_Click ()

End Sub
```

When we reach this point in the program, we can suppose that the text in **FilenameBox** holds a file name and that we're supposed to save the current document — that is, the string named **Form1.PadText.Text**, where **PadText** is the name of the main multiline text box that the document is stored in — to this file. There are three steps in this process: opening the file (or creating it if it does not exist); writing the data to the file; and closing it. We can take a look at each of these three steps in order as we build **OKButton_Click( )** because each step tells us something about the Visual Basic file system.

Opening Files in Visual Basic

The way to open or create a file in Visual Basic is simply to use the Open statement; however, we have to give some consideration to the *way* we open or create that file. In particular, there are five ways of opening files in Visual Basic, corresponding to the five different ways we can use them. Here's a list of the available *file modes*:

Sequential Input
Sequential Output
Sequential Append
Random Input/Output
Binary Input/Output

Types of Visual Basic Files

The first three file modes all have to do with one type of file: sequential files. Sequential files are usually used for text files, where you write the file from beginning to end and read it the same way; that is, you don't jump around inside the file. Working with sequential files is like using cassette tapes. If you want to hear something at the end of the tape, you have to pass by everything in front of it first. In the same way, if you want some of the text at the end of a file opened for *sequential access*, you have to read all the text that comes before it first.

If sequential-access files are like cassette tapes, then random-access files — the next type — are like compact discs. Although you have to fast forward to the parts you want in a cassette tape, you can simply move around at will on a CD, without going through all the intervening tracks. In the same way, you can move around in a *random-access* file at will, taking data from whatever location you want. The price you pay is that the data in a random-access file has to be carefully sectioned into *records*, so that you know exactly where the data is that you want. For example, if the records we developed for our database application were all the same size, they would work perfectly in a random-access file. When we wanted the 20th record, we could simply skip over the first 19 and then start reading. However, text — such as the text we're storing in the

Access	Common Visual Basic Statements
Sequential	Open, Line Input #, Print #, Write #, Input$, Close
Random	Type...End Type, Open, Put #, Len, Close, Get #
Binary	Open, Get #, Put #, Close, Seek, Input$

Table 5-1. Visual Basic File Statements

Editor application — is not neatly sectioned into records of the same size. For that reason, we will place the text that we're about to save in a sequential file.

The third type of files are binary files, and here Visual Basic does not interpret the contents of the file at all. For example, executable (.Exe) files are binary files, and we treat them on a byte-by-byte basis in Visual Basic. To copy such a file over, we would read in every byte of the original file (the source file) and then send them to the new file (the destination or target file). While we can set the amount of data we want to read under sequential- or random-access files, binary files are always dealt with byte by byte.

Each of these three types of file access has its own set of Visual Basic statements, as we'll see in this chapter. Since that can get confusing, you'll find a collection of the most common Visual Basic file handling statements organized by file type in Table 5-1 for easy reference later.

Our job here is to save the Editor's current document, and we'll do that by opening a sequential file (although it could actually be treated as a binary file, it is easier to write and read strings from sequential files). There are three ways of opening sequential files: for Input, Output, and Append. We open a file for input if we want to read from it, for output if we want to write to it, and for append if we want to add to the end of it. These three modes are consistent with the idea of opening the file and then working with the data from beginning to end (i.e., sequentially). For example, if we opened a file for sequential output, wrote a string to it, and then followed it with a second string, the second string would go directly after the first, and so on for any subsequent strings, one after the other. If you wanted to read them in again, you'd have to close the file and open it for input, and then you could read the data back from beginning to end.

Random files, where you can move around in the file at will, don't have any such restrictions. When you open a file for random access, it's for both input and output (on the other hand, recall that you have to section the data up into records in random files). In this case, where we're writing our Editor document to disk, we'll open our file for sequential output. In general, Visual Basic's file Open statement looks like this:

```
Open fff$ [For mmm] [Access aaa] [lll] As [#] nnn% [Len = rrr%]
```

Where this is what the arguments mean:

fff$	The filename (including an optional path)
mmm	Mode: Can be Append, Binary, Input, Output, or Random
aaa	Access: Can be Read, Write, or Read-Write
lll	Lock: Restricts access of other applications to this file to: Shared, Lock Read, Lock Write, Lock Read-Write
nnn%	Filenumber (1–255): The number we'll use to refer to this file from now on
rrr%	Record length for random files, or size of the buffer you want Visual Basic to use for sequential files

In our case, the user wants to write to the filename now in FilenameBox.Text, so we can use this Open statement to open that file:

```
Open FilenameBox.Text For Output As # 1
```

In fact, this file might not even exist; the user might want us to create it. That is actually handled automatically by the Open statement: If the file does not exist and we're trying to open it for anything but Input, Visual Basic will create the file for us. On the other hand, note that when we open an already existing file for output and then write to it, the original contents of the file are destroyed (if you want to add to the end of a sequential file while retaining what was there before, open the file for Append). Now we can start the Editor's Save File... dialog box with this line in the OK button's click procedure:

```
Sub OKButton_Click ()
    Open FilenameBox.Text For Output As # 1      'Open file
        :
End Sub
```

From this point on, we'll be able to refer to this file as file # 1 when we want to write to it or close it, just as in standard Basic. However, we should note that there is the possibility of error(s) when opening a file this way: The user may have specified an invalid path, for example, or misspelled the file name. To handle such errors, we can include an *On Error GoTo* statement, like this:

```
        Sub OKButton_Click ()
→           On Error GoTo FileError
            Open FilenameBox.Text For Output As # 1      'Open file
              :
              :
```

The way this statement works is this: If an error occurs, we'll automatically jump to the label FileError, where we can place a message box on the screen, and then execute a Resume statement, which jumps back to the line that caused the error, allowing the user to try again:

```
        Sub OKButton_Click ()
            On Error GoTo FileError
            Open FilenameBox.Text For Output As # 1      'Open file
              :
              :
            Exit Sub

→       FileError:
→           MsgBox "File Error", 48, "Editor"    'MsgBox for file error.
→           Resume
            End Sub
```

NOTE If we hadn't placed this statement in our code, we wouldn't have caught these errors — called *trappable* errors — in which case Visual Basic often notifies the user of the error directly, with a message box (this is undesirable in most applications).

TIP We'll go into more depth about the specific kinds of errors that can occur in this and other situations in our chapter on error handling and debugging. In that chapter, we'll see a great deal more about the On Error GoTo and Resume statements.

In other words, if the file name was legal, and the corresponding file can be opened or created, we do so. If there was a problem, we indicate that fact and let the user change the file specification for another attempt. At this point, then, the file is open. The next step is to write our document to it.

Writing to Files in Visual Basic

The usual way of writing to a sequential file is by using either the Print # or Write # statements. Here's the way to use them:

```
Print # nnn%, expressionlist
Write # nnn%, expressionlist
```

Here, nnn% is the file number (1 for us here), and expressionlist is a list of the variables (including strings) that you want to write to the file. The two statements, Print # and Write #, are different; Write # inserts commas between the separate items in the expressionlist as it writes them to the file, places quotation marks around strings, and inserts a new (blank) line at the end of the file. Since we don't want any of these added characters, we'll use Print # instead. In fact, we'll only want to send a single string to the file: **Form1.PadText.Text**, so our Print # statement should look like this:

```
Sub OKButton_Click ()
    On Error GoTo FileError
    Open FilenameBox.Text For Output As # 1      'Open file
→   Print # 1, Form1.PadText.Text                'Write document
       :
       :
    Exit Sub

FileError:
    MsgBox "File Error", 48, "Editor"    'MsgBox for file error.
    Resume
End Sub
```

That's all there is to writing the text into the file, now that it's been opened. In fact, closing the file isn't much harder. All we have to do is to use the Close statement, like this:

```
Sub OKButton_Click ()
    On Error GoTo FileError
    Open FilenameBox.Text For Output As # 1      'Open file
    Print # 1, Form1.PadText.Text                'Write document
```

```
→        Close # 1                                          'Close file
             :
         Exit Sub

    FileError:
         MsgBox "File Error", 48, "Editor"    'MsgBox for file error.
    End Sub
```

Here, Close # 1 closes file number 1, which is the file we're working on. After closing the file, we're done, so we exit the Sub procedure with an Exit Sub statement. At this point, the file has been successfully written to disk, or, if not, we've alerted the user to that fact; that is, if the Print # statement generated an error (e.g., the disk was full), we jump to the FileError label and pop our message box on the screen as before.

TIP If you use the Close statement without any file number — i.e., just Close — then Visual Basic closes all the files your application has open at once.

The final step, if the file handling has gone smoothly, is to hide the Save File... dialog box (i.e., **SaveForm**) like this:

```
    Sub OKButton_Click ()
        On Error GoTo FileError
        Open FilenameBox.Text For Output As # 1    'Open file
        Print # 1, Form1.PadText.Text              'Write document
        Close # 1                                  'Close file
→       SaveForm.Hide
        Exit Sub

    FileError:
        MsgBox "File Error", 48, "Editor"    'MsgBox for file error.
        Resume
    End Sub
```

Let's see this in action. After making the above changes, you might try typing some lines of text into the Editor and then saving them, as shown in Figure 5-2. When you do, you'll find that the text is indeed saved to disk in the file you choose.

You might also note one more thing here. The text in the file is simply stored as one long string without carriage returns — unless they were present in the

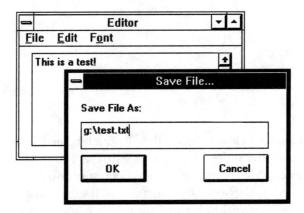

Figure 5-2. Saving a File with the Editor Application

original document — because the main text box itself stores it that way (and uses word wrap when it displays the text). That's it for our Save File... item; we've been able to write a sequential text file to disk, and our Editor application has become even more polished. However, the corresponding next step is to read files back in; that is, to make the Editor's Load File... item work also. Let's look into that process next.

Using the Visual Basic File Controls

The first step in reading the contents of a file is to get the name of that file. However, that's not just a simple matter of asking the user to type the name in a text box; we have to be able to search the disk (like other, similar Windows applications) and let the user select from what's already there. Visual Basic provides three special controls for doing exactly that, and they are *disk list boxes, directory list boxes,* and *file list boxes.*

The tools for creating these file controls appear at the bottom of the Visual Basic toolbox (along with the Timer tool). It turns out that these controls will do much of the work for us; that is, they'll search the drives and directories automatically, and we'll be able to work with various properties associated with them, instead of doing all the programming ourselves. Let's start this process by designing a dialog box for the Load File... option, which we can call Load-Form and save as, say, Loadform.Frm. First, let's connect it up to the Load File... menu item by clicking on that item in the Editor's File menu:

```
Sub LoadItem

End Sub
```

To display the Load File... dialog box (LoadForm), we can simply show it like this:

```
Sub LoadItem
    LoadForm.Show
End Sub
```

Now let's design **LoadForm**. Use the New Form item in Visual Basic's File menu to create the form; give it a **FormName** of **LoadForm**; give it a caption of Load File...; remove the **Min** and **Max** buttons; change the **BorderStyle** property to double fixed; and put two buttons on it, an OK button (OKButton), which should have its **Default** property set to True, and a Cancel Button.

Next, add a drive list box by double-clicking the drive list tool in the toolbox, which is next to the Timer tool. Notice that the drive list box is a drop-down list box, which will save us some space. We'll also need a directory list box and a file list box, so double-click on those tools too (the tools at the very bottom of the toolbox), and arrange them as you want them in the dialog box — something like Figure 5-3 (notice that all three list boxes are already active, showing the current drive, directory, and file list, respectively).

The user will be able to load any existing file this way, through the combination of the drive, directory, and file list boxes. They can use the drive list box to specify the drive, the directory list box to specify the directory in that drive, and the file list box to indicate the actual file they want to open. That file can be opened in two ways: by double-clicking on the filename in the file list box or by selecting (highlighting) it in the file list box and clicking the OK button.

And, as usual, making the Cancel button active is easy. We can just hide the dialog box when this button is clicked:

```
Sub CancelButton_Click()
    LoadForm.Hide
End Sub
```

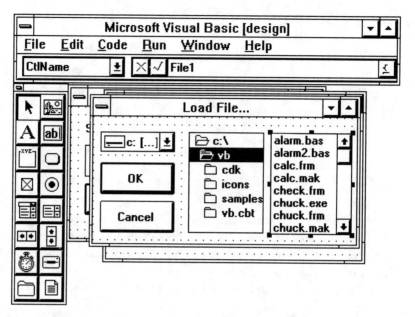

Figure 5-3. Load File... Dialog Box Template

Now let's turn to the file controls. At this point, the three list boxes (drive, directory, and file) are not communicating with each other; that is, they are just showing independent information for the current directory on disk. If we were to run this program and change the disk in the disk box list, the other two boxes wouldn't respond to the change. To get them to communicate, we have to know a little more about what the important events are for each of them, and we'll look into that next.

Drive List Boxes

The drive list box is a drop-down list box, as shown in Figure 5-3. The current drive is indicated in it. When the user clicks on the attached arrow, the list box drops down, showing what other drives are available to choose from. When the user picks one, a Change event occurs in the list box. Since we haven't set the name of our drive list box, it still has the default name of **Drive1** (the default for drive list boxes), so the event procedure is **Drive1_Change( )**. The property of our Drive1 box that holds the drive is simply **Drive1.Drive**, and our next task is to pass this new drive on to the directory list box, which still has its default name of **Dir1** (as is standard for directory list boxes). To do that, it turns out that we just need to pass the **Drive1.Drive** property on to the **Dir1.Path** property:

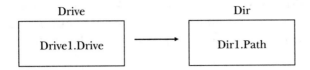

We can do that by clicking on the drive list box, which brings up the **Drive1_Change** procedure:

```
Sub Drive1_Change ()

End Sub
```

Just assign the **Drive** property of **Drive1** to the **Path** property of **Dir1** like this:

```
Sub Drive1_Change ()
    Dir1.Path = Drive1.Drive
End Sub
```

That's all it takes to connect the drive and directory boxes together. In fact, we can run the program at this point. When we do, we can click on the Load File... item of the Editor's File menu. The dialog box we've been designing, **LoadForm**, appears, displaying the current drive, directory, and files in that directory. If we click on the drive box, the drop-down list of all drives in the system appears. Clicking on one of those changes us to that drive, and the change ripples through to the directory list box, which also changes to list the directories on that new disk. The next step in our program now is to connect the directory list box with the file list box, so that when the directory is changed, the files displayed will be the files in that directory.

Directory List Boxes

The directory list box displays the directories available on a certain drive. It is a simple list box (that is, it is always displayed, not a drop-down list box like the drive list box); the working drive is displayed in the top line (e.g., c:\), and the directories of that drive appear underneath (e.g., vb). If there are more directories than we've allowed space for, a vertical scroll bar appears on the right of the box. The current directory appears as a shaded open folder, and its sub-directories appear as (nonshaded) closed folders just below it (e.g., icons), as you can see in Figure 5-3. When the user changes the directory by clicking on a new directory, a Dir1_Change event occurs, and the new path is placed in **Dir1.Path**. In addition, the way we've set things up, when the user changes drives, **Drive1.Drive** is loaded into **Dir1.Path**, which also generates a Dir1_Change event. In other words, the only event we need to be concerned about here is Dir1_Change, which now handles both drive and directory changes.

When such an event occurs, we need to communicate the news to the file list box, which we can do by passing on the **Dir1.Path** property to the **Path** property of the file list box, and since the file list box is still named **File1** (the default for file list boxes), we can do that like this:

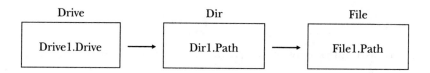

To do this in code, click on the directory list box to bring up this Sub procedure template in the code window:

```
Sub Dir1_Change ()

End Sub
```

Our goal here is to ripple any changes in the Dir1.Path property down to File1.Path, and we can do that simply like this:

```
Sub Dir1_Change ()
    File1.Path = Dir1.Path
End Sub
```

This way, every time there's a change in the working directory — or the working drive — the file list box will know about it. If we make this change and then start the program, we'll find that the list boxes are all connected together now. For example, we can click on the drive list box to change the drive, and the change will automatically be communicated to the directory list box, which changes to display the new set of directories. That change in turn is also communicated to the file list box, which then displays the files in the new working directory.

On the other hand, if we change the working directory in the directory list box, that change is also communicated to the file list box, which then displays the files in the new directory. In other words, the important events here were **Drive1_Change** and **Dir1_Change**, and the important properties that had to be transferred were **Drive1.Drive** → **Dir1.Path**, and **Dir1.Path** → **File1.Path**.

The way we actually read the filename that the user wants to load will be from the **FileName** property of **File1** — that is, **File1.FileName** — like this:

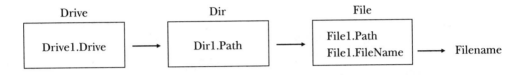

| NOTE | We might also note that, while you can select a new drive with a single click, it takes two clicks to select a new directory in the directory list box. This difference has to do with the difference between drop-down and straight list boxes. The reason you need two clicks in the directory list box is so that users can move up and down through the list using the arrow keys without changing the working directory to each highlighted entry along the way; that is, the change is postponed until they reach the directory they want. |

Our next task is to integrate the file list box into the program. When the user double-clicks on a file's name, we should open that file and load it into the Editor. Let's look at file list boxes next.

File List Boxes

The file list box shows the files in the current working directory. Like the directory list box, it is a simple list box, with its list always displayed. If the list is too long for the box, a vertical scroll bar appears. The files shown in the list box correspond to two properties: the **Path** and **Pattern** properties. The **Path** property holds the path name of the directory whose files you want to display, and the **Pattern** property holds the file specification — "*.EXE", for example (the default pattern is "*.*").

TIP   Although we're not going to do it in this demonstration program, you can include a text box to get a file specification from the user, transferring the appropriate text from the text box to the **Pattern** property of a file list box something like this: **File1.Pattern = Text1.Text** (note that you might have to separate the pattern string from a longer string if the user specifies both path and pattern in the same text box — e.g., "C:\MyData\Thesis.Phd"). A line of code like this can be put into the text box's Change event procedure.

File list boxes can respond to click or double-click events. In particular, it's normal to let the user select a file from a file list box and close the current dialog box by double-clicking a file's name, so we should add code to the **File1_DblClick( )** procedure. Note that this is the same as selecting a file and then clicking the OK button, so we should write one procedure that can be used by both events. We did that before by placing a procedure in a code module and then calling that general procedure from two event procedures, and we could do that again here. However, there's another way of doing the same thing, which we might demonstrate here. First, click on the file list box and select the **File1_DblClick( )** Sub procedure in the code window:

```
Sub File1_DblClick ()

End Sub
```

We want to make this the same as the **OKButton_Click( )** procedure, but since that's also a procedure, we can simply call it like this:

```
Sub File1_DblClick ()
    OKButton_Click
End Sub
```

(Note that if OKButton was part of a control array, we'd have to pass an index, like this: **OKButton(3)**.) That's all there is to it. Now let's write **OKButton_Click ( )**, where all the action is going to be. Click the **OKButton** to bring up this Sub procedure template in the code window:

```
Sub OKButton_Click ()

End Sub
```

At this point, the user is trying to open a file. The correct drive is in **Drive1.Drive**, and the correct path is **Dir1.Path**. Now we need the actual file name from the file list box. As mentioned above, the currently selected file name is kept in the file list box's **FileName** property, so now we have the file's complete specification. We're ready to open the file.

NOTE   Because the drive, directory, and file list boxes are still list boxes, you can also use their **List**, **ListCount**, and **ListIndex** properties as well.

TIP   Your program can change the **FileName** property of a file list box to set the drive, path, and pattern of the files displayed in the file list box all at once.

One way of opening the required file is to actually change to the new drive (**Drive1.Drive**) with the Basic ChDrive statement, change to the new path (**Dir1.Path**) with the Basic ChDir statement, and then open the file itself (**File1.FileName**). However, there is no need to change the default drive and directory at operating system level. Instead, we can assemble the complete file specification ourselves.

TIP   Changing the drive and directory like this is useful if you're about to run a program in that directory (with the Shell statement, for example), and the program itself will search for some supporting files (like .DLL or .DAT files) that it might need.

The Path property of the directory list box, **Dir1.Path**, usually represents a complete path, including the drive letter (e.g., "C:\vb\icons\arrows"), so we can add that to our file name, **File1.FileName**, if we add a backslash after the path like this (using Basic's standard method of joining strings together with a + sign):

```
Filename$ = Dir1.Path + "\" + File1.FileName
```

Here, **Filename$** is a local variable that we can use in our **OKButton_Click( )** procedure. However, this is not quite good enough. If we happen to be in the root directory of a drive, such as d:\, then **Dir1.Path** would be "d:\"; if the current file were Novel.Txt, then **Filename$** — equal to **Dir1.Path** + "\" + **File1.FileName** — would be "d:\\Novel.Txt". In other words, we would have one backslash too many. To avoid this, we should check the last character of **Dir1.Path**. If it's a backslash already, we won't have to add one ourselves:

```
If (Right$(Dir1.Path, 1) = "\") Then
    Filename$ = Dir1.Path + File1.FileName
Else
    Filename$ = Dir1.Path + "\" + File1.FileName
End If
```

Now **Filename$** holds the complete file specification of the file we're supposed to open, and we can open it with an Open statement. Since we're using sequential file access, and we want to read the file, we can open it for Input like this:

```
      If (Right$(Dir1.Path, 1) = "\") Then
          Filename$ = Dir1.Path + File1.FileName
      Else
          Filename$ = Dir1.Path + "\" + File1.FileName
      End If
→     Open Filename$ For Input As # 1
```

Once again, there is the possibility of errors here (for example, the diskette with the file might have been inadvertently removed), so we should put in some error handling code. That might look like this in the **OKButton_Click( )** Sub procedure:

```
      Sub OKButton_Click ()
→         On Error GoTo FileError
              :
          Exit Sub


→     FileError:
→         MsgBox "File Error", 48, "Editor"    'MsgBox for file error.
          Resume
      End Sub
```

Here, we simply display a message box if there was any kind of file error, allowing the user to try again after the problem has been fixed. Now we can add our file opening statements this way:

```
      Sub OKButton_Click ()
          On Error GoTo FileError
→         If (Right$(Dir1.Path, 1) = "\") Then
→             Filename$ = Dir1.Path + File1.FileName
→         Else
→             Filename$ = Dir1.Path + "\" + File1.FileName
→         End If
```

```
→        Open Filename$ For Input As # 1
              :
         Exit Sub

   FileError:
         MsgBox "File Error", 48, "Editor"    'MsgBox for file error.
         Resume
   End Sub
```

At this point, our use for the file controls is done. The file has been selected and opened. The next step is reading in the data, and we'll see how to do that next.

Reading from Files in Visual Basic

The standard ways of reading a sequential file in Visual Basic (see Table 5-1) are Input #, Line Input #, and Input$, and the way to use them is as follows:

```
Input # nnn%, expressionlist
Line Input # nnn%, stringvariable
Input$ (bbb%, [#] nnn%)
```

Here, **nnn%** is a file number (i.e., 1 for us), **bbb%** is the number of bytes to read, **stringvariable** is the name of a string variable to place data into, and **expressionlist** is a list of expressions that the data will be placed into.

For example, if we used Input # to fill **Form1.PadText.Text**, that might look like this: Input # 1 **Form1.PadText.Text**. However, the problem with Input # is that it expects the items in the file to be separated by commas, spaces, or the ends of lines (i.e., a carriage return). For numbers, this means that when Input # encounters the first comma, space, or end of line, it assumes that the current number is finished; for strings, Input # terminates the string when it reaches a comma or end of line. This is unacceptable to us, since the text of the document we're reading in may contain many commas. In fact, the user may have put in deliberate carriage returns into the document (although they are not required since the Editor's multiline text box has automatic word wrap), or they may be trying to read in another application's document that has carriage returns in it.

Similarly, the Line Input # function reads strings from files, until it encounters a carriage return, when it quits. That means that we'd have to read in each line

of the file (if it is divided into lines) separately. One way to do that would be
like this:

```
Do Until EOF(1)
    Line Input # 1, Dummy$
    Form1.PadText.Text = Form1.PadText.Text + Dummy$ + Chr$(13) + Chr$(10)
Loop
```

Here, we're using several capabilities of Visual Basic that we haven't used
before, including the Do Until loop, EOF( ), and Chr$( ). These all function
as in standard Basic; the Do Until loop has this general form:

```
Do Until condition
    [statements]
Loop
```

The statements in this loop, if there are any, are repeatedly executed until
condition becomes true, at which point execution stops (note that if the
condition is true at the beginning, the statements in the body of the loop are
not even executed once). In our case, we're using the EOF( ) function to
make up the condition for our loop. This function takes a file number as its
argument (for us, that would be EOF(1)), and returns a value of True when
we've reached the end of the file. In the above loop, then, we keep reading
lines from the file until we reach the end of that file. In addition, each time we
read a line, we add carriage return and line feed characters to the end of the
line, like this:

```
      Do Until EOF(1)
          Line Input # 1, Dummy$
→         Form1.PadText.Text=Form1.PadText.Text+Dummy$+Chr$(13)+Chr$(10)
      Loop
```

Here, we're using the Chr$( ) function, which returns the ANSI character
corresponding to the ANSI code passed to it. For example, Chr$(13) returns
a carriage return. The reason we have to add a carriage return line feed pair
at the end of each line is that Line Input # treats these two characters purely
as delimiters between strings, and deletes them. Since they are actually part of
the file, however, we can simply put them back.

A better option for us than either Input # or Line Input # is the Input$ function, which is specially made to read strings and which doesn't suppress carriage returns of line feeds. To use this function, however, we have to indicate the exact number of bytes we want to read. When we do, Input$ returns a string (which we can assign to **Form1.PadText.Text**). The number of bytes we want to read is simply the length of the file in bytes, and we can use another file function, LOF( ), to get that for us. Like EOF( ), LOF( ) takes a file number as an argument. LOF( ), however, returns the length of the indicated file in bytes (the file must be open for LOF( ) to work), so we can read in the whole thing like this, with the Input$( ) statement:

```
Form1.PadText.Text = Input$(LOF(1), # 1)
```

NOTE   The Input$( ) function is limited to reading files of 32,767 bytes if you open the file for sequential or binary access. However, if you want to use longer files, you can simply check the length of the file, LOF( ), and then read from the file several times in succession until you get all the data you need.

In fact, because you specify the number of bytes to read, you can also use this statement to read data from binary files. We can add our Input$ statement to **OKButton_Click( )** this way, where we place the string that's read in (i.e., the whole contents of the file) directly into the Editor's text box (**Form1.PadText.Text**):

```
Sub OKButton_Click ()
    On Error GoTo FileError
    If (Right$(Dir1.Path, 1) = "\") Then
        Filename$ = Dir1.Path + File1.FileName
    Else
        Filename$ = Dir1.Path + "\" + File1.FileName
    End If
    Open Filename$ For Input As # 1
→   Form1.PadText.Text = Input$(LOF(1), # 1)
        :
    Exit Sub

FileError:
    MsgBox "File Error", 48, "Editor"    'MsgBox for file error.
    Resume
End Sub
```

All that remains now is to close the file, and, of course, to hide the dialog box (**LoadForm**) at the same time. We can do that like this, ending **OKButton_Click( )**:

```
Sub OKButton_Click ()
    On Error GoTo FileError

    If (Right$(Dir1.Path, 1) = "\") Then          'Get file name
        Filename$ = Dir1.Path + File1.FileName
    Else
        Filename$ = Dir1.Path + "\" + File1.FileName
    End If

    Open Filename$ For Input As # 1               'Open file
    Form1.PadText.Text = Input$(LOF(1), # 1)      'Read file in

    Close # 1                      'Close file
    LoadForm.Hide                  'Hide dialog box

    Exit Sub

FileError:
    MsgBox "File Error", 48, "Editor"    'MsgBox for file error.
    Resume
End Sub
```

Now the Load File... dialog box is complete. To use it, simply start the program and select the Load File... item in the File menu. The Load File... dialog box opens, as shown in Figure 5-4. As you can see, the file list box presents the file names in alphabetical order. To open one of them, just double-click on it,

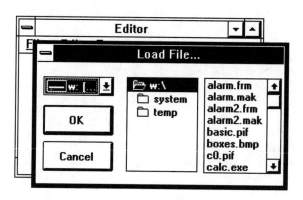

Figure 5-4. Editor with Load File... Dialog Box

or select it and click the OK button. When you do, the **OKButton_Click( )** procedure is executed, the file is opened, and read into the Editor. At that point, you can edit it and then save it to the disk again with the Save File... option.

That's the end of the entire Editor application. We've made all the parts operational. All the code, form by form, appears in Listing 5-1.

Listing 5-1. Editor Application's Code

```
Form1 -----------------------------------

Sub Command1_Click ()
    PadText.SelText = CutText
    PadText.SetFocus
End Sub

Sub PadText_Change ()
    CutItem.Enabled = True
    ClearItem.Enabled = True
End Sub

Sub CutItem_Click ()
    CutText = PadText.SelText
    PadText.SelText = ""
    PasteItem.Enabled = True
    PadText.SetFocus
End Sub

Sub ExitItem_Click ()
    End
End Sub

Sub ClearItem_Click ()
    PadText.Text = ""
    PadText.SetFocus
End Sub

Sub PasteItem_Click ()
    PadText.SelText = CutText
End Sub

Sub FFF_Click (Index As Integer)
    Select Case Index
        Case 0
            PadText.FontName = "Courier"
```

(continued)

Listing 5-1. (continued)

```
            Case 1
                PadText.FontName = "Helv"
            Case 2
                PadText.FontName = "Roman"
            Case 3
                PadText.FontName = "Modern"
            Case 4
                PadText.FontName = "Script"
            Case 5
                PadText.FontName = "Symbol"
            Case 6
                PadText.FontName = "System"
            Case 7
                PadText.FontName = "Terminal"
            End Select

            For loop_index = 0 To 7
                FFF(loop_index).Checked = False
            Next loop_index

            FFF(Index).Checked = True
    End Sub

    Sub SaveItem_Click ()
        SaveForm.Show
    End Sub

    Sub LoadItem_Click ()
        LoadForm.Show
    End Sub


            SaveForm ─────────────────────────────

    Sub CancelButton_Click ()
        SaveForm.Hide
    End Sub

    Sub OKButton_Click ()
        On Error GoTo FileError
        Open FileNameBox.Text For Output As #1
        Print #1, Form1.PadText.Text
        Close #1
        SaveForm.Hide
        Exit Sub

    FileError:
```

Listing 5-1. (continued)

```
      MsgBox "File Error", 48, "Editor"
      Resume
End Sub

        LoadForm ───────────────────────────

Sub CancelButton_Click ()
    LoadForm.Hide
End Sub

Sub Drive1_Change ()
    Dir1.Path = Drive1.Drive
End Sub

Sub Dir1_Change ()
    File1.Path = Dir1.Path
End Sub

Sub OKButton_Click ()
    On Error GoTo FileError
    If (Right$(Dir1.Path, 1) = "\") Then
        Filename$ = Dir1.Path + File1.Filename
    Else
        Filename$ = Dir1.Path + "\" + File1.Filename
    End If
    Open Filename$ For Input As #1
    Form1.PadText.Text = Input$(LOF(1), #1)
    Close #1
    LoadForm.Hide
    Exit Sub

FileError:
    MsgBox "File Error" + Str$(Err), 48, "Editor"
    Resume
End Sub

Sub File1_DblClick ()
    OKButton_Click
End Sub
```

At this point, we've covered opening sequential files both for Input and for Output. And, as mentioned earlier, if you want to add to the end of a sequential file, you can open it for Append — in that case, everything you write to the file goes at the end of the preexisting file contents.

That's it for our coverage for sequential files. Now let's move on to the next type: random files.

Using Random Files in Visual Basic

We're ready to move past sequential files to random-access files. These kinds of files usually break their data up into *records,* all of which have the same format, but (usually) different data. And, as you may remember, we set up the data in our database program in the last chapter into exactly those kinds of records, like this:

```
Type Record
    Name As String * 50
    Number As String * 20
    Comment As String * 200
End Type
```

Global Database(100) As Record

In other words, each record, **Database(n)**, looks like this:

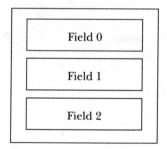

We can make well-organized files from such records, like this:

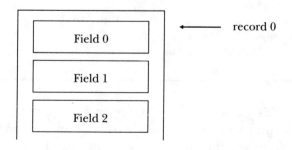

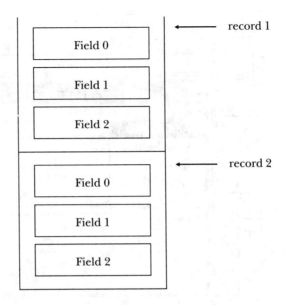

As you may recall, the database application had five items in its menu, as shown in Figure 5-5: Add Item (added the current item to the database); Find Item... (opened the Find Item... dialog box); Save File...; Load File...; and Exit. Everything works in this menu except the two file items, which we have left until now to complete, but now we can complete them as well because the database application is exactly where we should use random-access files.

Writing Random-Access Files

We can start by saving the file once the user selects the Save File... item in the File menu. That item's **CtlName** is **SaveItem**, and we can open **SaveItem_Click( )** by clicking on the item in the menu:

```
Sub SaveItem_Click ()

End Sub
```

When the user clicks this item, they want to save the database in a particular file, so we need to pop up a dialog box much like the one we designed earlier in this chapter for our Editor. In fact, we can use the *same* dialog box here. To load that form in, just open Visual Basic's File menu, select the Add File... item, and then give the name of the Save File... form (we used Saveform.Frm above). That file is loaded automatically. In this way, you can swap forms like

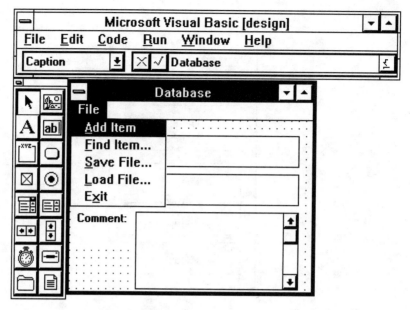

Figure 5-5. Database Application with Menu Open

dialog boxes between projects, saving you a great deal of design-time, and making your applications more uniform. Now we can pop that dialog box onto the screen this way in **SaveItem_Click( )**:

```
        Sub SaveItem_Click ()
→            SaveForm.Show
        End Sub
```

Next, we'll have to make some changes to SaveForm's code, since it is set up to store sequential files. Just switch to that form using the project window, and click on the main Sub procedure, **OKButton_Click ( )**, which currently looks like this:

```
Sub OKButton_Click ()
    On Error GoTo FileError
    Open FilenameBox.Text For Output As # 1        'Open file
    Print # 1, Form1.PadText.Text                  'Write document
    Close # 1                                      'Close file
    SaveForm.Hide
    Exit Sub
```

```
FileError:
    MsgBox "File Error", 48, "Editor"    'MsgBox for file error.
    Resume
End Sub
```

We're using a random file of records this time, not a sequential file of text, so we open the file as Random instead:

```
    Sub OKButton_Click ()
        On Error GoTo FileError
→       Open FilenameBox.Text For Random As # 1 Len = Len(Database(1))
        Print # 1, Form1.PadText.Text            'Write document
        Close # 1                                'Close file
        SaveForm.Hide
        Exit Sub

    FileError:
        MsgBox "File Error", 48, "Editor"    'MsgBox for file error.
        Resume
    End Sub
```

Here, we're indicating that the record length we'll be using is Len(**Database(1)**), which returns the length (in bytes) of our record size. Next, we want to write the entire array of records, **Database( )**, out to that file, so we should look into the options for writing random-access files.

The most common I/O statements for both binary and random-access files are Get # and Put #. These statements can get or put records from or to the file. In this case, we'll use Put #, whose syntax is like this:

```
Put [#] nnn% , [rrr%], vvv%
```

Here, **nnn%** is a file number, **rrr%** is the record number you want to put into the file, and **vvv%** is the variable we want to put there. If we do not specify a record number, Visual Basic simply places one record after the last into the file. The total number of records is stored in the global integer **TotalRecords**, so we can write that many records out like this (note that no records are written if **TotalRecords** is 0):

```
    Sub OKButton_Click ()
        On Error GoTo FileError
        Open FilenameBox.Text For Random As # 1 Len = Len(Database(1))
```

```
→          For loop_index = 1 To TotalRecords
→              Put # 1, , Database(loop_index)
→          Next loop_index
           Close # 1                                    'Close file
           SaveForm.Hide
           Exit Sub

    FileError:
        MsgBox "File Error", 48, "Database"    'MsgBox for file error.
        Resume
    End Sub
```

That's it. Now we can use the database's Save File... option as shown in Figure 5-6.

At this point, the file is written to disk (note that we also changed the error message box in the FileError section of the code, giving it the title "Database" instead of "Editor"). If we had wanted to, we could have written any given record instead of all of them by specifying a particular record number like this:

```
Put # 1, 5, Database(23)
```

This writes record 5 in the file, filling it with the record **Database(23)**. In this way, random access is truly random access because we have access to all records in the file. In other words, we can move around in the file at will, writing

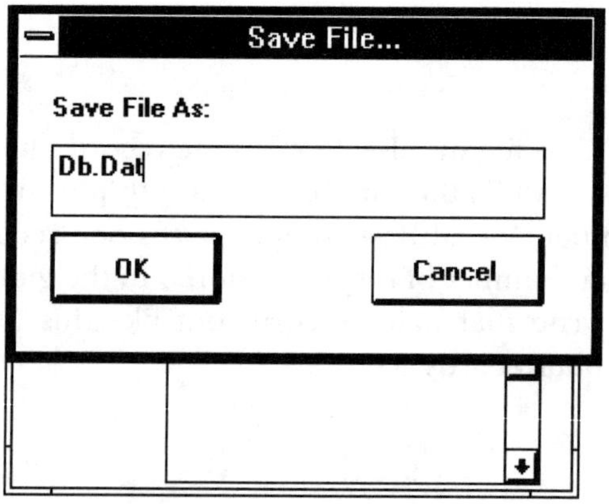

Figure 5-6. Database Application's Save File... Box

records in the order we want them. This works in a similar way with Get #, as we'll see next, when we read the file of records back in.

Reading Random-Access Files

We copied the Save File... dialog box from the Editor application to our database, and we can copy the Load File... dialog box as well (which is very useful since all the file controls on that dialog box are already connected together). Once again, select the Add File... item in Visual Basic's File menu, and then add the .Frm file containing the Load File... dialog box (we named it Loadform.Frm above). Next, make the Load File... item in the Database's File menu active like this:

```
     Sub LoadItem_Click()
→        LoadForm.Show
     End Sub
```

Now click on the OK button in that new form, LoadForm, to bring up the important procedure there — **OKButton_Click( )** — which currently looks like this:

```
Sub OKButton_Click ()
    On Error GoTo FileError

    If (Right$(Dir1.Path, 1) = "\") Then          'Get file name
        Filename$ = Dir1.Path + File1.FileName
    Else
        Filename$ = Dir1.Path + "\" + File1.FileName
    End If

    Open Filename$ For Input As # 1               'Open file
    Form1.PadText.Text = Input$(LOF(1), # 1)      'Read file in

    Close # 1                   'Close file
    LoadForm.Hide               'Hide dialog box

    Exit Sub

FileError:
    MsgBox "File Error", 48, "Editor"    'MsgBox for file error.
    Resume
End Sub
```

Once again, we open the file as before, for random access:

```
      Sub OKButton_Click ()
          On Error GoTo FileError

          If (Right$(Dir1.Path, 1) = "\") Then          'Get file name
              Filename$ = Dir1.Path + File1.FileName
          Else
              Filename$ = Dir1.Path + "\" + File1.FileName
          End If


→         Open Filename$ For Random As # 1 Len = Len(Database(1))
          Form1.PadText.Text = Input$(LOF(1), # 1)      'Read file in

          Close # 1                     'Close file
          LoadForm.Hide                 'Hide dialog box

          Exit Sub

      FileError:
          MsgBox "File Error", 48, "Editor"     'MsgBox for file error.
          Resume
      End Sub
```

Now we have to get records from the file using Get #, which you use to read from random and binary files, and whose syntax is like this:

```
Get [#] nnn% , [rrr%], vvv%
```

As with Put #, **nnn%** is a file number, **rrr%** is the record number you want to get from the file, and **vvv%** is the variable we want to place the data in. If we do not specify a record number, Visual Basic simply gets the next record from the current position in the file. Our first job here is to find out how many records there are in the file, and we can do that simply by dividing the length of the file by the size of each record. After we do, we can read the data in like this, record by record:

```
      Sub OKButton_Click ()
          On Error GoTo FileError

          If (Right$(Dir1.Path, 1) = "\") Then          'Get file name
              Filename$ = Dir1.Path + File1.FileName
          Else
              Filename$ = Dir1.Path + "\" + File1.FileName
          End If

          Open Filename$ For Random As # 1 Len = Len(Database(1))
```

```
  →        NumberFileRecords = LOF(1) / Len(Database(1))
  →        For loop_index = 1 To NumberFileRecords
  →            Get # 1, , Database(loop_index)
  →        Next loop_index

           Close # 1                      'Close file
           LoadForm.Hide                  'Hide dialog box

           Exit Sub

       FileError:
           MsgBox "File Error", 48, "Database"    'MsgBox for file error.
           Resume
       End Sub
```

(Note that, once again, we changed the name of the error box title in the FileError section of the code from "Editor" to "Database"). However, simply loading a file does not make the database active. In addition, we have to load the record names we've read into the database's sorted list box, where they can be selected by the user. That list box is maintained in the database's Find Item... dialog box; to load the record names into that list box, we must first erase all the current entries (using Visual Basic's **RemoveItem** method), and then we can reload them from **Database( )** (using the AddItem method):

```
       Sub OKButton_Click ()
           On Error GoTo FileError

           If (Right$(Dir1.Path, 1) = "\") Then        'Get file name
               Filename$ = Dir1.Path + File1.FileName
           Else
               Filename$ = Dir1.Path + "\" + File1.FileName
           End If

           Open Filename$ For Random As # 1 Len = Len(Database(1))
           NumberFileRecords = LOF(1) / Len(Database(1))
           For loop_index = 1 To NumberFileRecords
               Get # 1, , Database(loop_index)
           Next loop_index

           Close # 1                      'Close file

  →        For loop_index = 1 To TotalRecords
  →            Form2.NameList.RemoveItem 0
  →        Next loop_index
```

```
→          TotalRecords = NumberFileRecords    'After safely reading file

→          For loop_index = 1 To TotalRecords
→              Form2.NameList.AddItem Database(loop_index).Name
→          Next loop_index

→          Form1.NameField.Text = Database(1).Name
→          Form1.NumberField.Text = Database(1).Number
→          Form1.CommentField.Text = Database(1).Comment

           LoadForm.Hide                   'Hide dialog box

           Exit Sub

     FileError:
           MsgBox "File Error", 48, "Database"    'MsgBox for file error.
           Resume
     End Sub
```

That's it, then. We've read in the file and filled the program variables correctly. The database Load File... dialog box is now functional, as shown in Figure 5-7.

Note that we did not have to read in the whole array of records at once. In fact, we could have only read in one record at a time if we wanted to (saving a significant amount of memory). For example, if we always stored our data in a

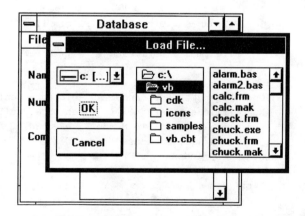

Figure 5-7. Database Load File Dialog Box

file named Db.Dat, we could change the Sub procedure that looks up records, **GetItem( )**, from this (which retrieves the data from the array **Database( )**):

```
Sub GetItem ()
    For loop_index = 1 To 100
        If (Rtrim$(Database(loop_index).Name) =
            Rtrim$(Form2.NameList.Text)) Then Exit For
    Next loop_index

    Form1.NameField.Text = Database(loop_index).Name
    Form1.NumberField.Text = Database(loop_index).Number
    Form1.CommentField.Text = Database(loop_index).Comment

    Form2.Hide
End Sub
```

to this (which retrieves the data from the Db.Dat file directly):

```
        Sub GetItem ()
            For loop_index = 1 To 100
                If (Rtrim$(Database(loop_index).Name) =
                    Rtrim$(Form2.NameList.Text)) Then Exit For
            Next loop_index

→           Open "Db.Dat" For Random As # 1 Len = Len(Database(1))
→           Get # 1, loop_index, Database(loop_index)
→           Close # 1

            Form1.NameField.Text = Database(loop_index).Name
            Form1.NumberField.Text = Database(loop_index).Number
            Form1.CommentField.Text = Database(loop_index).Comment

            Form2.Hide
        End Sub
```

In this way, we can move around in the file, retrieving the specific records we want. At this point, our file expertise is almost complete. However, we should note that we don't have to specify the record number in the Get # statement if we don't want to. We can use *Seek* instead. Let's look at Seek as our last file topic.

Using the Seek Statement

This statement can be extremely useful because it allows us to specify which record will be read from or written to next. Its syntax is like this:

```
Seek [#] nnn%, ppp&
```

Here, **nnn%** is the file number, and **ppp&** (a long integer) is the new position in the file. For sequential files, **ppp&** is measured in bytes; for random files, in record numbers. In other words, this line:

```
Get # 1, loop_index, Database(loop_index)
```

is the same as:

```
Seek # 1, loop_index
Get # 1, , Database(loop_index)
```

Using Get, Put, and Seek together, we have a great deal of control over our files. In particular, we can work byte by byte in binary files if we want to with these statements.

That completes our coverage of files, then. We've seen Visual Basic's file handling statements, we've seen how they work in practice, and now we've added file handling capabilities to two of our major applications. As you can see, working with files in Visual Basic is much like working with files in standard Basic, except that in Visual Basic we have the added advantage of three new types of file controls to make selecting files easier. This is very much the way Visual Basic is in general. It's just like standard Basic, except when it comes to communicating with the user. In fact, while we're on the subject of communicating with the user, let's turn to the next chapter, where we'll start working with one of Visual Basic's most exciting ways of doing just that: graphics.

Graphics

—

This is our chapter on graphics and graphical text output. You may not have been expecting to see text handling in a chapter on graphics, but, in an environment like Windows (that is, a Graphical User Interface, or GUI), everything is really graphics, including text. If you've read standard books on programming, you're probably used to seeing text treated differently than graphics, but here we'll see that Visual Basic treats it essentially the same way. If text is not in a specifically text-oriented control like a text box, label, or list box, text is treated simply as any other graphics would be.

Besides text, of course, we'll explore the rest of Visual Basic's graphics capabilities — and they're extensive. For example, we'll draw points, lines, rectangles, circles, ellipses, and other graphical objects in this chapter, showing how to change their color, width, and even the pattern they're filled with. We'll also see how we can protect drawings in case they're covered temporarily by other windows (a risk you don't have in standard Basic), and how to load pictures from files. In addition, we'll see how to send our graphics (including text) to the printer in this chapter, which is easier than you might imagine. With all this in store for us, then, let's jump in with both feet.

Drawing with Visual Basic

There are two types of objects that we can draw on in Visual Basic, forms and picture boxes. We're already familiar with forms (we can draw anywhere in the client area of a form); however, we haven't seen picture boxes yet. It turns out that picture boxes are simply boxes like any other (text boxes, for example), which we can place on forms, except they have one primary function that we haven't seen yet: to display graphics. Let's get started with a picture box and some elementary graphics that begin with drawing a single point.

Drawing Points

The Visual Basic graphics functions that actually draw on forms or in picture boxes are much like the matching QuickBASIC functions (i.e., if you're upgrading your code from QuickBASIC, you won't have much trouble with graphics). For example, the first graphics function we're going to look at is **PSet( )**, which sets a pixel on the screen.

To use **PSet( )**, start Visual Basic and name this project, say, Graphics.Mak, changing the caption of the default form, **Form1**, to Graphics. Next, find the **AutoRedraw** property in the properties bar, and set it to True. This property indicates that Visual Basic should redraw the graphics on the form if part or all of it is temporarily covered (and we'll see more about **AutoRedraw** later).

The coordinate system in Visual Basic uses twips (1/1,440 of an inch) by default. You may have wondered why twips are the default measurement instead of, say, screen pixels. The answer is that the Visual Basic environment is intended to operate in a manner that's as device independent as possible; that is, we'll be able to draw on the printer as easily as the screen. However, printers can have considerably higher resolution than screens (laser printers typically have at least 300 dots per inch resolution), so we need a measuring system that's even more precise than the best any of our devices can give us, which is why Visual Basic uses twips. Of course, as a programmer, you may be used to other units, such as pixels, centimeters, or even points (a point, often used in measuring the dimensions of a font, is 1/72 of an inch and a twip is 1/20 of a point), so it may take a little time to get used to twips. (We'll see later that we can switch the basic unit of measurement to pixels, centimeters, or other units if we need to.)

The coordinate system starts at (0, 0) in a form or picture box; x and y increase to the right and down, like this:

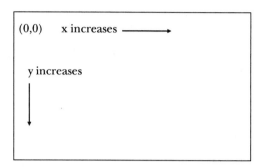

Let's make use of this fact in drawing our pixel, which we can place in the exact center of the form. To do that, we can get the size of the form from the properties bar if we wish (i.e., from the rightmost box in the properties bar); for example, we might have a form that's 4,320 twips high × 7,200 twips wide (i.e., 3 inches by 5 inches). In that case, our **PSet( )** statement might look like this:

```
Pset (4320 / 2, 7200 / 2)
```

This sets the pixel in the center of the form, the syntax of **PSet( )** is **PSet (x , y)**. However, there is another way that we might use to center the pixel without knowing the size of the form beforehand, and that's by using the **ScaleWidth** and **ScaleHeight** properties.

There are four built-in properties that can tell you the dimensions of a form or picture box: **Height, Width, ScaleHeight,** and **ScaleWidth**. It might seem that the natural properties to use to determine how to center a pixel are **Width** and **Height**, but these actually correspond to the outer width and height of the window (i.e., including title bar, menu bar, and so on). The actual dimensions of the client area — the area we have control of — is **ScaleWidth** wide and **ScaleHeight** tall (in twips), as shown in Figure 6-1. For that reason, our **PSet( )** statement might look like this:

```
PSet (ScaleWidth / 2, ScaleHeight / 2)
```

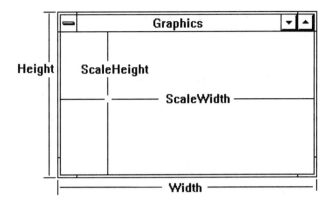

Figure 6-1. Height and Width Properties of Forms

We want to execute this line as soon as the form appears on the screen, so we'll put it into the **Form_Load( )** Sub procedure; this procedure is run when the form is first displayed. Click on the form itself, and find the **Form_Load( )** procedure in the code window:

```
Sub Form_Load()

End Sub
```

Next, place our **PSet( )** statement there:

```
Sub Form_Load()
    PSet (ScaleWidth / 2, ScaleHeight / 2)
End Sub
```

Now run the program. When you do, the pixel appears in the center of the form, as shown in Figure 6-2. (You can even resize this form, and the dot will stay in the center.) Note that there are other events that we could have used to display this pixel as well, such as the **Form_Click( )** event, which means that the dot would appear when you clicked any location on the form.

Let's do the same thing in a picture box next. Double-click the picture box tool (upper-right corner of Visual Basic's toolbox), size the picture box until it takes up most of the window, and set its **AutoRedraw** property to True. The default name for picture boxes is **Picture1**, so we can add this line to **Form_Load( )**:

```
Sub Form_Load()
    PSet (ScaleWidth / 2, ScaleHeight / 2)
→   Picture1.PSet (Picture.ScaleWidth / 2, Picture1.ScaleHeight / 2)
End Sub
```

In other words, **PSet( )** is actually a Visual Basic method; that is, it is connected to the object you want to draw on (this is also the case for the subsequent graphics routines in this chapter, such as the line-drawing routine Line). When you don't use it with an object name, the current form is assumed; if you do use an object's name, then that object is **PSet( )**'s target. Now run the program. When you do, you'll see the picture box with a dot in its center, as in Figure 6-3. Note that the picture box is obscuring the dot on the form. This is true in general: Any controls placed on a form will be placed on top of graphics already on the form, covering them up.

So far, nothing very exciting has happened: We've just drawn a single point in black. However, we can change the color of that point as well, and we'll see how to do that next.

Selecting Colors

There are several ways to set our own colors in Visual Basic. Probably the easiest is to use the predefined values in the file CONSTANT.TXT. Each color value in Visual Basic is a long integer, and many such values are ready for us to use, such as the constants named RED, BLUE, and so on, as shown in Table 6-1. In addition, we can find how the user has set the system colors (i.e., using the Windows control panel) and tailor our application to match by using the system color constants, as defined in Table 6-2. For example, you can set a

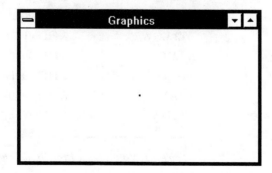

Figure 6-2. Graphics Application with Dot

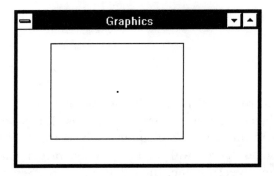

Figure 6-3. Picture Box with Dot

form's background color property (i.e., **BackColor**) to the current system-wide standard by setting it equal to WINDOW_BACKGROUND.

Let's have our program print out a red dot. The general syntax of **PSet( )** is:

```
[object.]Pset [Step] (x!, y!)[,color&]
```

Here, (**x!**, **y!**) represent the location of the pixel we want to work with. We should note that these variables are measured with respect to the object (form or picture box) we're drawing in. In other words, when we're setting pixels in a picture box, (**x! y!**) represents the location of the pixel with respect to the

BLACK	&H0&
RED	&HFF&
GREEN	&HFF00&
YELLOW	&HFFFF&
BLUE	&HFF0000
MAGENTA	&HFF00FF
CYAN	&HFFFF00
WHITE	&HFFFFFF

Table 6-1. Visual Basic Predefined Colors

SCROLL_BARS	&H80000000
DESKTOP	&H80000001
ACTIVE_TITLE_BAR	&H80000002
INACTIVE_TITLE_BAR	&H80000003
MENU_BAR	&H80000004
WINDOW_BACKGROUND	&H80000005
WINDOW_FRAME	&H80000006
MENU_TEXT	&H80000007
WINDOW_TEXT	&H80000008
TITLE_BAR_TEXT	&H80000009
ACTIVE_BORDER	&H8000000A
INACTIVE_BORDER	&H8000000B
APPLICATION_WORKSPACE	&H8000000C
HIGHLIGHT	&H8000000D
HIGHLIGHT_TEXT	&H8000000E
BUTTON_FACE	&H8000000F
BUTTON_SHADOW	&H80000010
GRAY_TEXT	&H80000011
BUTTON_TEXT	&H80000012

Table 6-2. Visual Basic System Colors

picture box's upper-left corner (which is (0, 0)). In addition, the color value, **color&**, is always a long integer.

The Step keyword is one we'll see in many of the drawing methods, and it indicates that the coordinates specified are with respect to the *current graphics position,* whose coordinates are stored in the **CurrentX** and **CurrentY** properties of forms and picture boxes. As we'll see, you can draw lines or other graphics figures using the current graphics position. To set that position, set the **CurrentX** and **CurrentY** properties. Also, using graphical methods like **PSet( )** can set the current graphics position. When you set a pixel with **PSet( )** in some object, the current graphics position is set to that pixel. We won't use Step here, however. To make our pixel red we can simply use the predefined constant RED, like this:

```
    Sub Form_Load()
       PSet (ScaleWidth / 2, ScaleHeight / 2)
→      Picture1.PSet (Picture.ScaleWidth/2, Picture1.ScaleHeight/2), RED
    End Sub
```

In addition, you must include CONSTANT.TXT in the global module (which you can do with the Load Text... option of the Code menu) because the constant RED is defined there. Running this program changes the pixel in the center of the picture box to red, so our program is a success. However, there are other ways to indicate what color we want in Visual Basic.

For example, we can specify the color using the RGB function, which we've already seen. This function takes three arguments, a red color value, a green color value, and a blue color value:

```
    RGB (RedVal%, GreenVal%, BlueVal%)
```

Each of these color values can go from a minimum of 0 (i.e., when the color is excluded entirely) to a maximum of 255 (when it's at its strongest). For a pure red dot, we can use **RedVal** = 255, **GreenVal** = 0, and **BlueVal** = 0, like this:

```
    Sub Form_Load()
       PSet (ScaleWidth / 2, ScaleHeight / 2)
       Picture1.PSet (Picture.ScaleWidth / 2,
→         Picture1.ScaleHeight / 2), RGB(255, 0, 0)
       End Sub
```

There are even more options for setting colors. For example, we could set the actual bytes in a long integer directly, and pass that as our color value. A long integer is made up of four bytes, and the three colors take the bottom three bytes. It's easiest to look at it in hexadecimal, where a color value is represented like this: &H00rrggbb&, where **rr** is the (hex) value of the red setting, **gg** is the green setting, and **bb** is the blue setting. (The reason that this is most convenient in hex is that, in hex, each byte takes up exactly two hex digits.) This means that to turn on red, we can give it the highest value a byte can have, &HFF (255):

```
    Sub Form_Load()
       PSet (ScaleWidth / 2, ScaleHeight / 2)
       Picture1.PSet (Picture.ScaleWidth / 2,
→         Picture1.ScaleHeight / 2), &H00FF0000&
    End Sub
```

Color Number	Color
0	Black
1	Blue
2	Green
3	Cyan
4	Red
5	Magenta
6	Yellow
7	White
8	Grey
9	Light Blue
10	Light Green
11	Light Cyan
12	Light Red
13	Light Magenta
14	Light Yellow
15	Bright White

Table 6-3. QuickBASIC Colors for the QBColor( ) Function

TIP If you want to specify one of the system default colors as in Table 6-2, such as the current background for windows, use &H80 for the top byte in the color value, not &H00.

This works as well, displaying a red dot in our picture box. The last way to specify colors in Visual Basic is with the QBColor( ) function. QuickBASIC has 16 predefined colors, and you can access them in Visual Basic as well (making it easier to move graphics code over to Visual Basic from QuickBASIC) by using the QBColor( ) function. This function returns a long integer corresponding to the correct Visual Basic RGB value. You use QBColor( ) like this: QBColor(**nnn%**), where **nnn%** is the QuickBASIC color number from 0 to 15 associated with the color you want, as shown in Table 6-3.

For example, we could turn our dot red this way:

```
Sub Form_Load()
    PSet (ScaleWidth / 2, ScaleHeight / 2)
```

```
           Picture1.PSet (Picture.ScaleWidth / 2,
    →          Picture1.ScaleHeight / 2), QBColor(4)
       End Sub
```

TIP   If you ever want to find out what color a particular position on the screen is, you can use the **Point** method — **[object].Point (x!, y!)**, which returns the corresponding long integer color value.

That's it for drawing points. Of course, that's just the beginning of Visual Basic's graphics capabilities. Let's move on now to drawing lines.

Drawing Lines

To draw lines, we can use the Line method, whose syntax is:

```
[object.]Line [[Step](x1!, y1!)]-[Step](x2!, y2!)[,[color&],B[F]]]
```

Again, notice that this is a method, which means that you can specify which object you want to draw lines on (as usual, if you don't specify an object, Visual Basic assumes you intend to use the current form). And, as before, we can use the Step keyword here if we want to. To draw a line, there are usually two points involved, the beginning and end of the line, (**x1!, y1!**) and (**x2!, y2!**), respectively. When you use Step in front of either of them, that indicates that point is to be taken with respect to the current graphics position, as specified by (**CurrentX, CurrentY**). In addition, we can specify the line's color with the color& argument. The last two arguments, **B** and **F**, are used to draw rectangles (boxes), and we'll look at them in the next section.

This means that if we wanted to draw a single line diagonally across a form, we could do so like this, using Line:

```
Line (0, 0) - (ScaleWidth, ScaleHeight)
```

That's all that's required, just the two end points of the line (Visual Basic draws the line so that the first endpoint, but not the second, is included). For example, let's remove the picture box from our Graphics application temporarily, and change the **Form_Load( )** Sub procedure to this:

```
Sub Form_Load()
    Line (0, 0) - (ScaleWidth, ScaleHeight)
End Sub
```

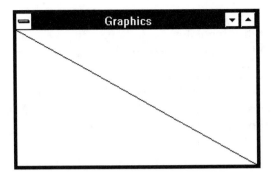

Figure 6-4. Graphics Window with a Diagonal Line

Now running the program results in a window as shown in Figure 6-4. In fact, we can make that a blue line by specifying a color like this (as long as CONSTANT.TXT has been loaded into the global module):

```
Sub Form_Load()
    Line (0, 0) - (ScaleWidth, ScaleHeight), BLUE
End Sub
```

There's another way of specifying that this line should be blue without passing a color value to the Line method, and that's by setting the object's **ForeColor** property first. All forms and picture boxes have this property, which you can think of as the drawing color. In fact, all controls that can display text also have this property, which determines the text's color (except for command buttons, which only have a **BackColor** property). When you draw text or other graphics figures without specifying a color, the foreground color is used as the default. We can specify that color for a particular object like this (recall that if we don't specify an object for some graphical method, the current form is used):

```
      Sub Form_Load()
→         ForeColor = BLUE
          Line (0, 0) - (ScaleWidth, ScaleHeight)
      End Sub
```

From now on, this object's drawing color will be blue, until changed again, that is. In other words, text and so on will be blue when you place it here; however, we should note that changing the foreground color does not change the color of text or other graphics already in graphical objects like forms or picture boxes. By specifying the **ForeColor** property, then, it's possible to have a number of different forms or picture boxes in your application, all with a different drawing color. In the same way, there are other drawing properties associated with such objects, and we'll explore some of them next.

TIP   A good way to get an idea of what properties are available for a specific object is to look at the list in the properties bar, but keep in mind that not all properties may be available at design-time, so that list may be incomplete. A better way is to search for that object type in Visual Basic's on-line help index; for each type of object, all of the properties are explicitly listed.

For example, a graphics *pen* is associated with each object that can display graphics, and this pen has a number of properties associated with it as well. One of them is the **DrawWidth** property, with which we can change the width of the line we draw (or the size of the dot that **PSet( )** draws). The default value for this graphics property is 1, which corresponds to the thinnest line, as in Figure 6-4. This line is actually 1 pixel wide on the screen; however, we can make this line thicker by specifying a higher value. **DrawWidth** = 2 results in a line 2 pixels wide and so on. To see some of these lines, we might set up a loop in the **Form_Load( )** Sub procedure like this:

```
Sub Form_Load()
    For i = 1 To 9
        DrawWidth = i
        Line (0, i * ScaleHeight / 10) - (ScaleWidth, i * ScaleHeight / 10)
    Next i
    DrawWidth = 1
End Sub
```

This gives us a window as shown in Figure 6-5, where the line across the form grows steadily thicker as we go down.

Besides affecting the width of the line, we can also affect the *style* of the line. In other words, we can specify whether the line is solid (the default) or is broken up into dots or dashes. There are seven different styles of lines, from solid to dotted to transparent, and they appear in Table 6-4.

The last line style, an *inside line* (DrawStyle 6) deserves some special mention. When you draw a box with a thick line, the line is normally centered on the edge of the box; that is, the box ends up slightly larger than intended because

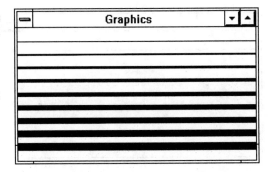

Figure 6-5. Graphics Window with Thickening Lines

the thick line is half in and half out of the box. On the other hand, an inside line is drawn so that it is entirely inside the box, even for thick lines (we'll see this in action shortly). Let's take a look at these line styles in our Graphics application, this time by modifying the **Form_Click( )** Sub procedure. Click on the form itself, and bring up the **Form_Click( )** Sub procedure:

```
Sub Form_Click ()

End Sub
```

By the time this Sub procedure is invoked; i.e., by clicking on the form, **Form_Load( )** has already put the thickening lines onto the form, as shown in

DrawStyle	Results In
0	Solid line (default DrawStyle value)
1	Dashed line
2	Dotted line
3	Dash-dot line
4	Dash-dot-dot line
5	Transparent line (does not appear)
6	Inside line

Table 6-4. Line Styles — DrawStyle Property

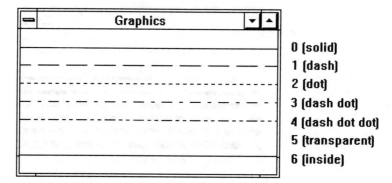

Figure 6-6. Graphics Window Showing Line Styles

Figure 6-5. We want to get rid of that pattern first, so we use the **Cls** (which originally stood for Clear Screen) method to start with:

```
Sub Form_Click ()
    Cls
      :
End Sub
```

This method works for both forms and picture boxes, clearing the object and blanking whatever graphics (including text) was already there. Next, we simply want to draw the seven line styles on the form, which we can do by looping:

```
Sub Form_Click()
    Cls
    For i = 1 To 7
        DrawStyle = i - 1
        Line (0, i * ScaleHeight / 8) - (ScaleWidth, i * ScaleHeight / 8)
    Next i
End Sub
```

The result of this program is that the window first appears as in Figure 6-5. Then, when you click it, it changes to that shown in Figure 6-6, showing all the different line styles.

NOTE   We should note here, however, that using a drawing width (**DrawWidth**) of greater than one makes line styles 1-4 produce solid lines, rather than series of dashes and/or dots.

DrawMode	*Name*	*Means*
4	Not Pen	Draws the inverse of the pen
6	Invert Pen	Inverts what's on the screen
7	Xor Pen	Xors pen and screen
11	No Pen	Draws nothing
13	Copy Pen	Draws pen directly (default)

Table 6-5. Visual Basic Pen Styles

So far, we've been able to change the thickness of lines, and their appearance (i.e., solid or not). In fact, we can go even farther and specify how what we draw affects what's already there. This is called the **DrawMode** property, and it affects what *type* of pen we use to draw.

As mentioned, you can think of each graphics object having a pen. This pen, in turn, can draw in different styles. For example, if you've set **DrawWidth** to 6, then the pen will draw six pixel wide lines or circles, or draw six pixel wide "dots" with **PSet( )** because the default for the pen is simply to draw in the foreground color (**ForeColor**), which corresponds to a **DrawMode** of 13. On the other hand, if we change **DrawMode** to 4, then the pen changes into a Not Pen, and it draws in the inverse of the foreground color. For example, if the foreground color is black, then a Not Pen draws in white. Altogether, **DrawMode** can take values from 1 to 16, and the most common settings are shown in Table 6-5.

Some of these pens deserve mention here. For example, the Invert Pen (**DrawMode** = 6), *color inverts* what's on the screen when it draws. That is, if we're drawing over a black area, white appears. If we're drawing over green, red appears (i.e., the color inverse of green). This can create some striking visual effects; let's make this change to **Form_Click( )** in our Graphics application, so that, when clicked, two broad diagonal bands appear on the form, inverting what's underneath them:

```
Sub Form_Click ()
    DrawMode = 6
    DrawWidth = 9
    Line (0, 0) - (ScaleWidth, ScaleHeight)
    Line (0, ScaleHeight) - (ScaleWidth, 0)
End Sub
```

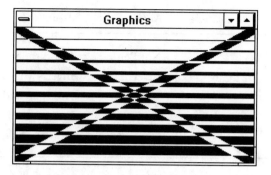

Figure 6-7. Invert Pen Example

When you run the application, the window appears at first as in Figure 6-5. However, when you click the window, the two diagonal bands appear, inverting whatever they draw over, as shown in Figure 6-7.

The Xor Pen also deserves mention since it's commonly used in animation. Xor — Exclusive Or — is a bitwise operator much like And and Or, which you're probably familiar with in Basic already. These operators compare the individual bits of two operands and produce a result based on a bit by bit comparison. For example, Oring two bits which are both 1, produce 1; Oring two bits, which are both 0, produce 0. The general action of these operators is shown in Table 6-6; for example, if we're working with two bytes, then the results, bit by bit, might look like this:

$$
\text{Or} \begin{array}{r} 01010101 \\ 10101010 \\ \hline 11111111 \end{array}
\qquad
\text{And} \begin{array}{r} 11111111 \\ 10101010 \\ \hline 10101010 \end{array}
\qquad
\text{Xor} \begin{array}{r} 11111111 \\ 10101010 \\ \hline 01010101 \end{array}
$$

Visual Basic's logical operators work like this:

And	0	1
0	0	0
1	0	1

Or	0	1
0	0	1
1	1	1

Xor	0	1
0	0	1
1	1	0

When you use the Xor Pen, the drawing color and the colors being overwritten on the screen are Xored together. If, for example, you're drawing on a white screen, then this ends up color inverting the drawing color (i.e., green becomes red and so on). That's because the color value of the drawing color is Xored with white, which has a color value of &HFFFFFF& — all 1s — and when you Xor anything with all 1s, you get its inverse (therefore inverting the color):

$$
\begin{array}{r}
11111111 \\
\text{Xor} \quad 10101010 \\
\hline
01010101
\end{array}
$$

On the other hand, if you Xor the result with the same pen again, you'll always get the original value back (white in this case):

$$
\begin{array}{r}
11111111 \\
\text{Xor} \quad 10101010 \\
\hline
01010101 \\
\text{Xor} \quad 10101010 \\
\hline
11111111
\end{array}
$$

This means that you can draw anything on the screen using the Xor Pen to make it appear, and, when you draw it a second time with the same pen, what you've drawn will disappear (i.e., the original display will be restored). This is often how animation works. On a white screen, for example, you can draw in white using the Xor Pen and the result will be black; drawing the same figure over again erases it, restoring the white screen (because any value Xored with another value twice is restored to its original value).

TIP Because Xoring a value twice restores the original value, the logical Xor operator can also be used to encrypt data. Just Xor the data, byte by byte, with some value or values (i.e., like the characters in a password) to encrypt it, and then Xor it again with the same value or values to reproduce the original exactly. This is called Xor encryption.

Let's move on now to a new capability of the **Line** method, drawing boxes.

Drawing Rectangles

It might seem odd that you only need to use the **Line** method once to draw a box, but that's exactly what the **B** option lets us do:

```
[object.]Line [[Step](x1!, y1!)]-[Step](x2!, y2!)[,[color&],B[F]]]
```

When you specify a line in Visual Basic, you specify the endpoints. Similarly, when you specify a rectangle, it makes sense that you only need to specify two points: the upper-left and lower-right corners:

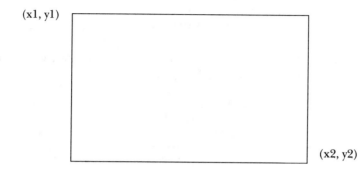

Since both patterns are uniquely specified by two points, Visual Basic (as well as many other types of Basic, including QuickBASIC) let you draw rectangles as well as lines with Line. Let's see how this works by modifying our Graphics application to draw a few rectangles, like this:

```
Sub Form_Load()
    DrawWidth = 8
    Line (0, 0) - (ScaleWidth / 2, ScaleHeight / 2), , B
    Line (ScaleWidth/4, ScaleHeight/4)-(3*ScaleWidth/4,
        3*ScaleHeight/4),,B
    Line (ScaleWidth / 2, ScaleHeight / 2) - (ScaleWidth,
ScaleHeight), , B
End Sub
```

This generates the window as shown in Figure 6-8. As you can see, the thick lines at the edges are half inside and half outside the client area. This can be fixed by using the Inside Line drawing style, like this:

```
      Sub Form_Load()
          DrawWidth = 8
→         DrawStyle = 6
          Line (0, 0) - (ScaleWidth / 2, ScaleHeight / 2), , B
          Line (ScaleWidth/4, ScaleHeight/4)-(3*ScaleWidth/4,
              3*ScaleHeight/4),,B
          Line (ScaleWidth / 2, ScaleHeight / 2) - (ScaleWidth,
              ScaleHeight), , B
      End Sub
```

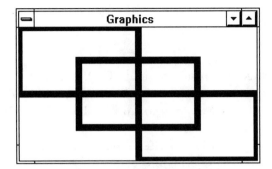

Figure 6-8. Graphics Rectangles

Now the rectangles are drawn so that the thick border is inside the boundaries, as shown in Figure 6-9. That's the way inside lines work. They don't overlap the figure's boundaries.

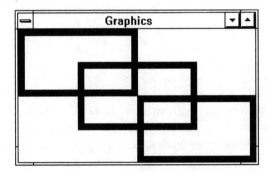

Figure 6-9. Graphics Rectangles with Inside Lines

We can also change the drawing mode (i.e., use a different pen setting) if we wish. For example, we can use an Invert Pen, which inverts what it draws over (**DrawMode** = 6):

```
Sub Form_Load()
    DrawWidth = 8
    DrawStyle = 6
→   DrawMode = 6
    Line (0, 0) - (ScaleWidth / 2, ScaleHeight / 2), , B
    Line (ScaleWidth/4, ScaleHeight/4)-(3*ScaleWidth/4,
        3*ScaleHeight/4),,B
```

```
            Line (ScaleWidth / 2, ScaleHeight / 2) - (ScaleWidth,
                ScaleHeight), , B
        End Sub
```

This produces the result in Figure 6-10. In general, we can produce all kinds of rectangles this way, as easily as we might draw lines. In fact, we can also fill the rectangles in if we want to, and we'll look into that next.

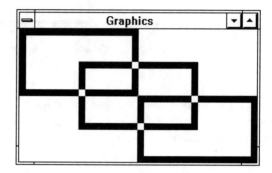

Figure 6-10. Rectangles

Filling Figures with Patterns

By drawing boxes, we've drawn enclosed graphics figures for the first time, but Visual Basic lets us go farther than that. We can specify a fill pattern so that our boxes are automatically filled in. In fact, our boxes have automatically been filled in already, but the default *fill pattern* is transparent. That's only one of the eight fill patterns available, however. The other ones include horizontal or vertical lines, diagonal lines, or, of course, filling our figures with solid color. These options appear in Table 6-6.

You select one of the fill patterns from Table 6-7 with the **FillStyle** property. Let's see this in action. We can draw eight rectangles on the main form of the Graphics application, and then fill them, one by one, with the different patterns corresponding to different **FillStyle** property settings. Again, let's use the **Form_Load( )** Sub procedure to see this working. We can change that procedure to draw two rows of four rectangles and fill each one with a different fill pattern:

```
Sub Form_Load()
        SX = ScaleWidth
        SY = ScaleHeight
```

```
        For i = 0 To 3
            FillStyle = i
            Line ((2*i+1) * SX/9, SY/5) - ((2*i+2) * SX/9, 2*SY/5), ,B
            FillStyle = i + 4
            Line ((2*i+1) * SX/9, 3*SY/5) - ((2*i+2) * SX/9, 4*SY/5), ,B
        Next i
    End Sub
```

As you can see, all the eight fill patterns appear, as shown in Figure 6-11. You can use these built-in patterns to create visual effects in your Visual Basic programs. Again, we're using the **B** option here to draw boxes. If you're familiar with QuickBASIC, you may have expected us to use the **F** option so that the rectangles were filled:

```
Line (0, 0) - (1000, 1000), , BF
```

In fact, the **F** option — for fillcolor — is only used to specify that the fill pattern be made the same color as the rectangle itself. If you don't specify **F** (and note that **F** can only be specified if you've already specified **B**), then the current **FillColor** is used. This color is just like the other colors that we've seen, **BackColor** and **ForeColor**, except that it's used exclusively as the color of the fill pattern. Like **ForeColor** and **BackColor**, it's a property of graphical objects like picture boxes and forms, and, like other properties, it remains set until you change it again. We'll see how to use the fill color soon, when we start drawing circles.

FillStyle Value	*Resulting Fill Pattern*
0	Solid
1	Transparent (the default)
2	Horizontal lines
3	Vertical lines
4	Upward diagonals
5	Downward diagonals
6	Crosshatch
7	Diagonal crosshatch

Table 6-6. Fill Options — FillStyle Property

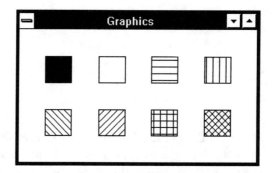

Figure 6-11. The Different FillStyle Options

Before leaving rectangles, however, it's worth noting something important: drawing solid white rectangles — with white borders — is a standard way of deleting text on forms and picture boxes. Because text is treated as graphics in both of these objects, you can't just erase it by selecting text and then deleting it (as you can in, say, text boxes). Instead, you have to remove it from the screen yourself, as you would with any graphics. We'll see more about text very soon. Before that, however, let's move on now to drawing circles.

Drawing Circles

As you might expect, you draw circles with the Circle method:

```
[object].Circle [Step] (x!, y!), radius! [,[color&][,[start!]
    [,[end!][, aspect!]]]]
```

Here, (**x!, y!**) represents the center of the circle, and radius! its radius (all in twips). In addition, you can draw arcs by specifying a start angle and end angle for drawing (in radians). Let's see this at work by drawing a few circles ourselves. We can start with a fill style of downward diagonals and a simple red circle like this:

```
Sub Form_Load()
    FillStyle = 5         'Downward diagonals
    ForeColor = RGB(255, 0, 0)   'Red
    Circle (ScaleWidth/4, ScaleHeight/4), ScaleHeight/5
End Sub
```

This produces a red circle filled with downward diagonals, but the fill pattern is black, not red. If we were drawing boxes, we could fix that with the **F** option, but there is no **F** option here. Instead, we can set the **FillColor** property to match the current **ForeColor** like this:

```
     Sub Form_Load()
         FillStyle = 5          'Downward diagonals
         ForeColor = RGB(255, 0, 0)    'Red
  →      FillColor = ForeColor
         Circle (ScaleWidth/4, ScaleHeight/4), ScaleHeight/5
     End Sub
```

Now both the circle and the fill pattern inside are red. However, the **Circle** method is more powerful still. We can draw ellipses and arcs with it as well. To draw ellipses, we use the *aspect* argument with Circle. The aspect ratio indicates the vertical to horizontal ratio for ellipses. When we're drawing a circle, this is set to its default value of 1; however, we can draw an ellipse as easily. For example, to draw a circle and then an ellipse that's twice as high as it is wide, we can use an aspect ratio of two:

```
     Sub Form_Load()
         Circle (ScaleWidth/4, ScaleHeight/4), ScaleHeight/5
         FillStyle = 2
  →      Circle (ScaleWidth/2, ScaleHeight/2), ScaleHeight/3,,,,2
     End Sub
```

The resulting graphics display appears in Figure 6-12. We can also draw arcs — that is, partial circles — by specifying start! and end! angles. These angles are measured in radians, which go from 0 to two pi. For example, let's add an arc that goes from 0 (i.e., the three o'clock position) to pi (i.e., going counterclockwise to the nine o'clock position) like this:

```
   Sub Form_Load()
       Circle (ScaleWidth/4, ScaleHeight/4), ScaleHeight/5
       FillStyle = 2
       Circle (ScaleWidth/2, ScaleHeight/2), ScaleHeight/3,,,,2   'Ellipse
       Circle (3*ScaleWidth/4, 3*ScaleHeight/4), ScaleHeight/5,,0,3.1415
   End Sub
```

The resulting figures appear in Figure 6-13 (note that even though we specified a fill pattern, the arc is not filled because it is not a closed figure).

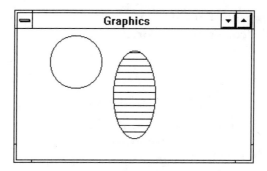

Figure 6-12. An Ellipse

That's it for the primary, built-in drawing methods, **PSet**, **Line**, and **Circle**. As we've seen, you can produce some interesting effects with them. However, Visual Basic also allows us to do many other things with graphics. For example, we can load predrawn pictures into either forms or picture boxes, and we'll explore this capability next.

Loading Pictures

You can load pictures into either picture boxes or forms using the LoadPicture( ) function and by assigning them to the object's **Picture** property. In particular, we can use LoadPicture( ) with three types of files, .ICO files (icons); .BMP files (bitmap files produced by such applications as Windows Paintbrush); and .WMF (Windows metafiles).

TIP   Just as you can load pictures with LoadPicture( ), so you can save them with SavePicture( ), as we'll see in the next chapter.

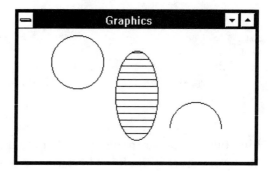

Figure 6-13. Circle, Ellipse, and Arc

Let's give this a try by loading an icon into a picture box. Visual Basic already has many icons set up for us to use. For example, the icon we want might be the stoplight icon which is stored in "C:\VB\ICONS\TRAF-FIC\TRFFC10A.ICO" (see the Visual Basic documentation for a complete listing of its icon library). To read that in, we could place a picture box on the Graphics application's form and then execute this line:

```
      Sub Form_Click()
→         Picture1.Picture = LoadPicture("C:\VB\ICONS\TRAFFIC\TRFFC10A.ICO")
      End Sub
```

In this way, we assign the icon to the picture property of Picture1. The result is in Figure 6-14. Note that the icon is placed in the upper left corner of the picture box. We can make the picture box grow or shrink to fit the image we've loaded into it by setting its **Autosize** property to True (its upper-left corner will not move). When we do, the picture box shrinks around the icon, as shown in Figure 6-15.

We can also load .BMP files as are produced by Windows Paintbrush this way (we won't examine .WMF — Windows metafiles — files here). This can be valuable if you want to customize the appearance of a window. First, you draw the figure you want in an application like Windows Paintbrush, and then save it in bitmap, .BMP, format. Next, you can read it in with a line like this:

```
      Sub Form_Click ()
→         Picture = LoadPicture("C:\WINDOWS\IMAGE.BMP")
      End Sub
```

For example, the window in Figure 6-16 was produced this way, by loading in a .BMP file directly with LoadPicture( ). At this point, we know how to use

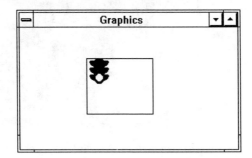

Figure 6-14. Loading a Stoplight Icon

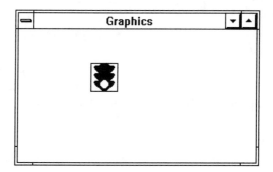

Figure 6-15. Same as 6-14, But with AutoSize Set True

graphics in Visual Basic pretty well, not to mention how to load graphics files (even those created by other applications) into our programs directly, so we're ready to start exploring how to deal with text, and that will be our next topic.

Before leaving nontext graphics, however, there is a point that deserves to be made here. In our Graphics application, we've been setting the Form's **AutoRedraw** property to true. This means that when the graphics in our application's form(s) or picture box(es) are temporarily obscured by other windows and then restored, Visual Basic takes charge of restoring the graphics itself. However, to do this, it needs to store the entire graphics image, which is very costly in terms of memory.

There's another way to do the same thing, but which involves restoring graphics images ourselves. To do that, you must redraw the image every time a form

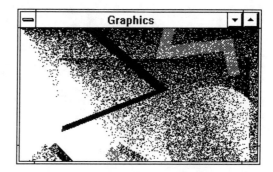

Figure 6-16. LoadPicture Example

Paint event occurs. This event is generated when an obscured part of our client area is uncovered, at which time we're supposed to "repaint" the image we want (the easiest way to do that is simply by redrawing everything in the client area). If you're going to use Paint events, however, you should know two more things: Paint events do not occur if **AutoRedraw** is True, and, if **AutoRedraw** is False, you cannot draw graphics in the **Form_Load( )** Sub procedure. That's it for nontext graphics. Let's turn to text as our next topic.

Displaying Text in Visual Basic

In Visual Basic, graphical text (i.e., text that does not appear in text-oriented controls) can be printed three places: on forms, in picture boxes, and on the printer. We'll take a look at all three in this chapter.

Before we start, however, it's important to understand that here, text is indeed treated as graphics. What that means is that the ANSI code of each character is not stored. When we print a character on a form, a picture of that character appears, and that's all. The text itself is not somewhere in memory as with a text or list box. If we want to write our own editor which doesn't use a text box as a base (and can therefore go beyond the 64K limit), we'd have to handle all the screen details ourselves.

We've already seen the Visual Basic fonts available when we designed our notepad application. Now it's important to concentrate on *how* to print when it comes to graphical text, rather than the specific fonts involved. Printing text can be more involved than you might think because most fonts in Windows don't have characters of the same width. Fonts in which all characters have the same width — called monospace fonts — do exist in Windows, but fonts with different character widths — called variable width fonts — are much more common. Since Windows normally uses the latter, we'll have to be careful about printing. If we want to add more text to the end of a printed string, for example, we'll have to figure out just where that string ends.

To print graphical text, then, we simply use the **Print** method (which is defined only for the types of objects we can print directly to: forms, picture boxes, and the printer). Since it's a method, you use it together with the name of an object (or, if you omit the object name, Visual Basic assumes you're referring to the current form). For example, we could print a string of text like this:

```
Form1.Print "No worries."
```

To see the result of this line, we can put it in the **Form_Load( )** Sub procedure of our Graphics application, and then run that application:

```
Sub Form_Load()
    Form1.Print "No worries."
End Sub
```

The result appears in Figure 6-17. As you can see, the text appears in the upper-left corner of the form. That is, the upper-left corner of the text appears at (0, 0). The reason for this is that text is printed at the current graphics output position, as set by the properties (**CurrentX**, **CurrentY**), where both quantities are measured in twips. If we wanted to start the text in the exact middle of the form, we could do this instead:

```
Sub Form_Load()
    CurrentX = ScaleWidth / 2
    CurrentY = ScaleHeight / 2
    Form1.Print "No worries."
End Sub
```

And the result appears in Figure 6-18. In general, this is the way we can use the Print method:

```
[object.]Print [expressionlist][{;¦,}]
```

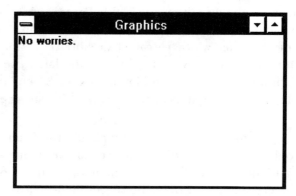

Figure 6-17. Graphics Application with First Text String

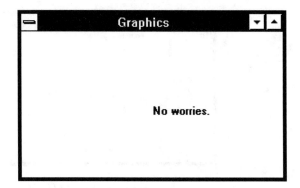

Figure 6-18. Text String Origin at Form Center

Here, **expressionlist** is a list of the strings we want to print. Notice that we can use either a comma or semicolon, if we want to, at the end of the expression list. Which one we use, if either, determines where we leave the text cursor when we're done printing. If we use a semicolon, the text cursor will be placed right after the text we print (so future text will immediately follow it); that is, this program will produce the same result as the one we just ran:

```
     Sub Form_Load()
         CurrentX = ScaleWidth / 2
         CurrentY = ScaleHeight / 2
  →      Form1.Print "No ";
  →      Form1.Print "worries."
     End Sub
```

On the other hand, if we use a comma, then a tab is inserted, which means that the text cursor is placed into the next *print zone*. The default length for a tab is the width of 14 average characters of the current font. For example, this program:

```
   Sub Form_Load()
       Form1.Print "No ", "worries."
   End Sub
```

produces the output that you see in Figure 6-19. In this way, you can print out tables of data in neat columns. In fact, we can set up our own tab widths with the Tab( ) function. For example, Tab(20) tabs over to a print zone that starts 20 average character widths instead of 14.

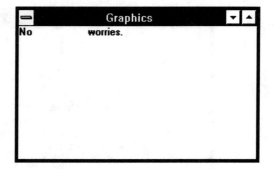

Figure 6-19. Tabbed Text Output

Let's see how this works. For example, we might want to print out this table:

```
Region              Product
----------------------
East                Apples
West                Tomatoes
North               Wheat
South               Oranges
```

We could do that with the **Print** method. To start, let's move down a few lines. Every time we use **Print** without an argument, we move to the next line, so we could skip three lines like this:

```
Sub Form_Load()
    Print
    Print
    Print
        :
End Sub
```

Next, we can place customized tabs into our table like this:

```
Sub Form_Load()
    Print
    Print
    Print
    Print Tab(10); "Region"; Tab(30); "Product"
    Print
    Print Tab(10); "East"; Tab(30); "Apples"
    Print Tab(10); "West"; Tab(30); "Tomatoes"
```

```
        Print Tab(10); "North"; Tab(30); "Wheat"
        Print Tab(10); "South"; Tab(30); "Oranges"
           :
    End Sub
```

We can even draw a box around our table like this:

```
Sub Form_Load()
    Print
    Print
    Print
    Print Tab(10); "Region"; Tab(30); "Product"
    Print
    Print Tab(10); "East"; Tab(30); "Apples"
    Print Tab(10); "West"; Tab(30); "Tomatoes"
    Print Tab(10); "North"; Tab(30); "Wheat"
    Print Tab(10); "South"; Tab(30); "Oranges"
    DrawWidth = 2
    Line(650, 400)-(3600, 2000), , B
    Line (650, 930)-(3600, 930)
End Sub
```

The final table appears in Figure 6-20, printed (as with all text) in the object's **ForeColor**. Of course, we can also print to picture boxes; double-click on the picture box tool and change the code in **Form_Load( )** to this:

```
Sub Form_Load()
    Picture1.Print "This is a very long string for such a
small picture box."
End Sub
```

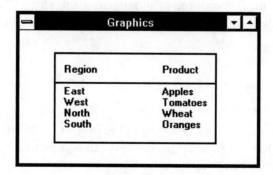

Figure 6-20. Tabbed Tabular Text Output

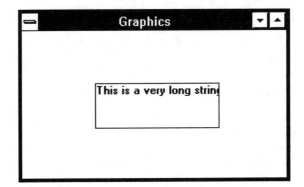

Figure 6-21. Truncated Text in a Picture Box

Now set the picture box's **AutoRedraw** property to true (if you do not, you will not be able to put graphics in it from the **Form_Load( )** Sub procedure). As you can see in Figure 6-21, the string is too long for the picture box to hold, so the text is cut off on the right (in fact, cut off in midcharacter). To fix this problem, we'd have to know when to skip to the next line — and to know that, we'd have to know the length of our text string as it's going to appear on the screen. We can find that out by using the **TextWidth** method.

How Long Is the String on the Screen?

There are two methods that we can use to determine the dimensions of a text string as it's going to appear (and in an environment that uses variable width fonts, these methods can be invaluable). They are called **TextHeight** and **TextWidth**. For example, the length of the string "Now is the time." in our picture box (using the current font and font size of the picture box) is equal to this:

```
StringLength% = Picture1.TextWidth("Now is the time.")
```

Let's say our picture box isn't big enough to print this string all on one line, and we have to break it up into two lines. To check where to break it up, we can use the **TextWidth** method.

> **TIP** Although **TextWidth** is the most commonly used of these two methods, you can use **TextHeight** to determine the height of a line of text by asking for the height of a string like: **Height% = TextHeight**("ABCDEFGHIJK"). Then, if you want to position yourself down five lines, you need only add 5 × **Height%** to **CurrentY**.

Let's start this example by setting up an array of type String:

```
Sub Form_Load
    Static My_Text(4) As String
       :

End Sub
```

Next, we load each word into the string array:

```
Sub Form_Load
    Static My_Text(4) As String

    My_Text(1) = "Now "
    My_Text(2) = "is "
    My_Text(3) = "the "
    My_Text(4) = "time."
         :
End Sub
```

Then we loop over each word, adding it to a string to print, and checking if it's too long:

```
Sub Form_Load
    Static My_Text(4) As String

    My_Text(1) = "Now "
    My_Text(2) = "is "
    My_Text(3) = "the "
    My_Text(4) = "time."

    Temp$ = ""
    First_Line$ = ""

    For Word% = 1 To 4
        Temp$ = Temp$ + My_Text(Word%)
```

```
            If Picture1.TextWidth(Temp$) > Picture1.ScaleWidth
                Then Exit For
            First_Line$ = Temp$
        Next Word%
            :
    End Sub
```

If the string was too long, then we have to create a second line like this:

```
    Sub Form_Load
        Static My_Text(4) As String

        My_Text(1) = "Now "
        My_Text(2) = "is "
        My_Text(3) = "the "
        My_Text(4) = "time."

        Temp$ = ""
        First_Line$ = ""
→       Second_Line$ = ""

        For Word% = 1 To 4
            Temp$ = Temp$ + My_Text(Word%)
            If Picture1.TextWidth(Temp$) > Picture1.ScaleWidth
                Then Exit For
            First_Line$ = Temp$
        Next Word%

        FirstWordSecondLine% = Word%

→       For Word% = FirstWordSecondLine% to 4
→           Second_Line$ = SecondLine$ + My_Text(Word%)
→       Next Word%
            :
    End Sub
```

Finally, we can print the text out:

```
    Sub Form_Load
        Static My_Text(4) As String

        My_Text(1) = "Now "
        My_Text(2) = "is "
        My_Text(3) = "the "
        My_Text(4) = "time."
```

```
Temp$ = ""
First_Line$ = ""
Second_Line$ = ""

For Word% = 1 To 4
    Temp$ = Temp$ + My_Text(Word%)
    If Picture1.TextWidth(Temp$) > Picture1.ScaleWidth
        Then Exit For
    First_Line$ = Temp$
Next Word%

FirstWordSecondLine% = Word%

For Word% = FirstWordSecondLine% to 4
    Second_Line$ = SecondLine$ + My_Text(Word%)
Next Word%
```

→   `Picture1.Print First_Line$`
→   `Picture1.Print Second_Line$`

```
End Sub
```

The result of all this work appears in Figure 6-22. Now we've done our own word wrap. This is a common problem in printing with variable width fonts. In fact, there are other font properties that you can vary when printing — including underlining text or making it bold or italic — that can make string widths even more unpredictable. These properties appear in Table 6-7.

Because formatting your text for output in a restricted picture box is such a common problem, let's develop a Sub procedure, PrintString( ), to do it for us (PrintString( ) will also introduce us to some new points in Visual Basic).

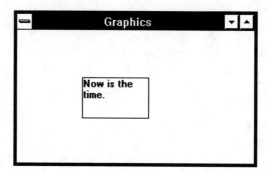

Figure 6-22. Word Wrap Example

Property	*Means*
FontName	Name of font, such as "Courier" or "Modern"
FontSize	Size of font in points (1/72 of an inch)
FontBold	Makes font bold if true
FontItalic	Makes font italic if true
FontStrikethru	Strikes through characters with a dash if true
FontUnderline	Characters are underlined if true

Table 6-7. Font Properties in Visual Basic

To begin, we'll want to pass two things to PrintString( ): the picture box we want it to print in, and the string of text to print. It turns out that we can actually pass a control, such as a picture box, by declaring it as type Control:

```
→   Sub PrintString(PBox As Control, PString As String)

    End Sub
```

Now we can refer to the picture box simply as **PBox**. In PrintString( ), we want to break the print string, **PString**, into lines that will fit in the picture box. To do that, we might set up a function named GetWord$( ) (which we'll write later), to return the next word in **PString** to us, and we can loop as long as it doesn't return " " (in which case we've exhausted the print string):

```
Sub PrintString(PBox As Control, PString As String)

    PrintLine$ = ""
    NextWord$ = GetWord$()

    Do While NextWord$ <> ""
         :

    Loop

End Sub
```

Here, we're using a Basic Do While loop. In it, we'll assemble the line to print **PrintLine$**, until it gets too long, at which point we'll print it and start over. We can check its length by creating a temporary string, which we might name

Temp$**; that is, **Temp$ will equal **PrintLine$** + **NextWord$**, and, if **Temp$** is too long for the picture box, it's time to print:

```
Sub PrintString(PBox As Control, PString As String)

    PrintLine$ = ""
    NextWord$ = GetWord$()

    Do While NextWord$ <> ""
→        Temp$ = PrintLine$ + NextWord$
→        If PBox.TextWidth(Temp$) > PBox.ScaleWidth Then
→            PBox.Print PrintLine$    'Print before it gets too long
        Else
            :

        End If
    Loop

End Sub
```

On the other hand, if the line wasn't too long, then we want to add the current word to **PrintLine$**, get the next word (if there is one) from **GetWord$( )**, and start over:

```
Sub PrintString(PBox As Control, PString As String)

    PrintLine$ = ""
    NextWord$ = GetWord$()

    Do While NextWord$ <> ""
        Temp$ = PrintLine$ + NextWord$
        If PBox.TextWidth(Temp$) > PBox.ScaleWidth Then
            PBox.Print PrintLine$    'Print before it gets too long
        Else
→            PrintLine$ = Temp$
        End If
→        NextWord$ = GetWord$()
    Loop

End Sub
```

That's it except for one last thing: We've been printing lines when they've gotten too long, but we have not yet printed the left over words that make up the last line (the last line is not long enough to run past the edge, so it hasn't been printed). We print out that remainder like this, and then we're done:

```
Sub PrintString(PBox As Control, PString As String)

    PrintLine$ = ""
    NextWord$ = GetWord$()

    Do While NextWord$ <> ""
        Temp$ = PrintLine$ + NextWord$
        If PBox.TextWidth(Temp$) > PBox.ScaleWidth Then
            PBox.Print PrintLine$    'Print before it gets too long
        Else
            PrintLine$ = Temp$
        End If
        NextWord$ = GetWord$()
    Loop

→   PBox.Print PrintLine$        'Print remainder
End Sub
```

The final step is to write the function GetWord$( ), the function that returns the next word in the string **PString** (the string that was passed for us to print). This function needs a copy of **PString** to get the successive words from, but we can't just pass it a copy of the string **PString** each time, since it would keep chopping off and returning the first word over and over. Instead, we can add a global string, **StringToPrint**, and let GetWord$( ) chop successive words off that. To do that, we declare **StringToPrint** global in the global module this way:

```
Global StringToPrint As String
```

Or, if we wished, we could make it a form-wide string by placing it in the declarations section of the **general** object like this:

```
Dim StringToPrint As String
```

We can fill **StringToPrint** immediately in PrintString( ) like this (giving GetWord$( ) access to it):

```
Sub PrintString (PBox As Control, PString As String)

→   StringToPrint = PString
    PrintLine$ = ""
    NextWord$ = GetWord$()

    Do While NextWord$ <> ""
        Temp$ = PrintLine$ + NextWord$
```

```
        If PBox.TextWidth(Temp$) > PBox.ScaleWidth Then
            PBox.Print PrintLine$    'Print before it gets too long
            PrintLine$ = NextWord$
        Else
            PrintLine$ = Temp$
        End If
        NextWord$ = GetWord$()
    Loop
    PBox.Print PrintLine$    'Print remainder.
End Sub
```

Now let's write GetWord$( ). Our task here is to chop off the first word of the string **StringToPrint**. In other words, to find the first space in that string and return everything up to and including it. If this was **StringToPrint**:

```
"Now is the time for all good men..."
```

then GetWord$( ) should return "Now ," leaving **StringToPrint** as "is the time for all good men...." Let's start with an easy case where **StringToPrint** has no spaces in it; that is, it is an empty string (just " ") or a single word. In that case, we can just return that single word or empty string. And, since we're chopping off words from **StringToPrint**, we make **StringToPrint** an empty string, indicating that there's nothing left:

```
Function GetWord$ ()
    If InStr(StringToPrint, " ") = 0 Then
        GetWord$ = StringToPrint
        StringToPrint = ""
            :
```

Here we're using the Basic InStr( ) function to determine whether or not there is a space in **StringToPrint**. As in other Basics, this function returns the place number of a substring in a string. In our case, that means that, if InStr(**StringToPrint**," ") equals 0, there is no space in **StringToPrint**. Notice also that we must return a value from the GetWord$ function. As is normal in Basic, we simply assign the value we want to return to the name of the function itself:

```
      Function GetWord$ ()                   'No words
          If InStr(StringToPrint, " ") = 0 Then
  →           GetWord$ = StringToPrint
              StringToPrint = ""
              :
```

On the other hand, if there is a space in **StringToPrint**, then that string has at least two words in it. We should return the first one and cut it off the string to prepare for the next time GetWord$ is called. We can do that like this, using the Left$(**String$**, **n**) and Right$(**String$**, **n**) Basic string functions, which return the leftmost or rightmost **n** characters of a string:

```
Function GetWord$ ()
    If InStr(StringToPrint, " ") = 0 Then        'No words
        GetWord$ = StringToPrint
        StringToPrint = ""
    Else
        GetWord$ = Left$(StringToPrint, InStr(StringToPrint, ""))
        StringToPrint = Right$(StringToPrint, Len(StringToPrint) -
            InStr(StringToPrint, " "))
    End If
End Function
```

That's it for GetWord$( ) and for PrintString( ) itself. Now we can use it to print to picture boxes, calling it from anywhere in the form, like this:

```
Sub Form_Load ()
    Call PrintString(Picture1, "Now is the time for all good men...")
End Sub
```

In this case, we're asking PrintString( ) to print "Now is the time for all good men..." in picture box **Picture1**, and the result appears in Figure 6-23. That's it for our Sub procedure PrintString( ). Its code appears in Listing 6-1.

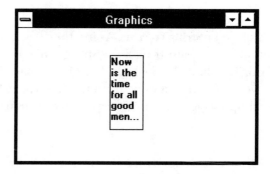

Figure 6-23. A Tight Text Squeeze

TIP As PrintString( ) stands, it is limited to printing in picture boxes; however, you can change it to work on forms if you pass a form and declare it As Form. In that case, you should put all the code into its own module.

Listing 6-1. The PrintString Sub Procedure

```
Form1 General Declarations --------------------------------

Dim StringToPrint As String          'Form-wide variable

Form1 -------------------------------

Sub Form_Load ()
    Call PrintString(Picture1, "Now is the time for all good men...")
End Sub

Form1 General -------------------------------

Sub PrintString (PBox As Control, PString As String)

    StringToPrint = PString
    PrintLine$ = ""
    NextWord$ = GetWord$()

    Do While NextWord$ <> ""
        Temp$ = PrintLine$ + NextWord$
        If PBox.TextWidth(Temp$) > PBox.ScaleWidth Then
            PBox.Print PrintLine$    'Print before it gets too long
            PrintLine$ = NextWord$
        Else
            PrintLine$ = Temp$
        End If
        NextWord$ = GetWord$()
    Loop

    PBox.Print PrintLine$    'Print remainder.
End Sub

Function GetWord$ ()
    If InStr(StringToPrint, " ") = 0 Then
        GetWord$ = StringToPrint
        StringToPrint = ""
```

(continued)

Listing 6-1. (continued)

```
        Else
            GetWord$ = Left$(StringToPrint, InStr(StringToPrint, " "))
            StringToPrint = Right$(StringToPrint, Len(StringToPrint) -
                InStr(StringToPrint, " "))
        End If
    End Function
```

That's it for our study of screen graphics for this chapter. Next, we're going to take a look at the printer.

TIP There are many other uses for **TextHeight** and **TextWidth**, of course. For example, you can center text on a form using them together with the **ScaleWidth** and **ScaleHeight** properties. Or, you can find the width of an average character by finding the width of a long string and dividing by the number of characters in it.

Using a Printer from Visual Basic

It turns out that you use the printer much as you might a picture box or form when it comes to graphics. In particular, you can simply use the **Print** method as before, but now we'll use it with the Printer object, which corresponds to the default printer that was loaded with the Windows control panel.

For example, if we wanted to print "Now is the time for all good men..." on the printer in underlined courier text, we could do that like this:

```
Sub Form_Load ()
    Printer.FontName = "Courier"
    Printer.FontUnderline = True
    Printer.Print "Now is the time for all good men..."
End Sub
```

Similarly, we can use **CurrentX** and **CurrentY** to position printer output on the page (as measured in twips):

```
    Sub Form_Load ()
→       Printer.CurrentX = 1440
→       Printer.CurrentY = 2880
```

```
        Printer.FontName = "Courier"
        Printer.FontUnderline = True
        Printer.Print "Now is the time for all good men..."
    End Sub
```

This doesn't move the printer head, but it does indicate where graphics should go on the next page. In fact, you can skip to the next page with the **NewPage** method like this:

```
    Sub Form_Load ()
        Printer.CurrentX = 1440
        Printer.CurrentY = 2880
        Printer.FontName = "Courier"
        Printer.FontUnderline = True
        Printer.Print "Now is the time for all good men..."
→       Printer.NewPage
    End Sub
```

In fact, because Visual Basic is designed to be device independent, there is little more to learn here. For example, the Printer object supports the other graphics methods we saw before: **PSet**, **Line**, and **Circle**, and it includes the normal graphical properties like **ScaleHeight** and **ScaleWidth**, so we can draw a circle like this:

```
    Sub Form_Load ()
        Printer.CurrentX = 1440
        Printer.CurrentY = 2880
        Printer.FontName = "Courier"
        Printer.FontUnderline = True
        Printer.Print "Now is the time for all good men..."
        Printer.NewPage
→       Printer.Circle (ScaleWidth/4, ScaleHeight/4), ScaleHeight/5
    End Sub
```

Because Visual Basic treats output in a relatively device-independent manner, that's almost all we have to know about the printer to use it fully. There is one method here, however, that we haven't seen before, and that is the **PrintForm** method, which lets you print a whole form, like this (if the form has graphics in it, set the AutoRedraw property True so that the graphics will print as well):

```
    Sub Form_Load ()
        Form1.PrintForm
    End Sub
```

Note, however, that this prints only with pixel resolution (i.e., as if it were a direct transcription from the screen). If you want higher resolution graphics, use the **Print** method.

That's it, then, for our coverage of graphics in this chapter. Let's move on now to incorporate the mouse together with our graphics capabilities when we write a mouse-driven Paint program in Chapter 7.

The Mouse and a
Mouse-driven Paint Program

In the last chapter, we explored the Visual Basic graphics system. In this chapter, we'll study the mouse, and we'll put them together by creating a mouse-driven paint program at the same time, which will let us draw figures on the screen and even print them out.

The mouse is one of the two most important user interface tools (the other is the keyboard) in Windows, and we've been using it throughout this book already by responding to the Click event for various controls. However, there's much more information here than we've been using so far. We can get the precise location of the mouse pointer (called the cursor or pointer in Windows) when the user clicks or releases a button. In fact, we can watch as they move the mouse around the screen. Let's start at once by investigating one of the basic mouse events, the MouseDown event.

MouseDown Events

When the user positions the mouse cursor somewhere on a form and presses a mouse button, a *MouseDown* event is generated. This event is not the same as a Click event. In a Click event, the user must press and release the mouse button. A MouseDown event occurs when the user simply presses a mouse button. These kinds of events are recognized by forms, picture boxes, labels, and any control that includes a list (list boxes, combo boxes, directory list boxes, and so on). Note that controls like buttons do not respond to MouseDown events, only to Click events.

In a MouseDown event, we get considerably more information than we did with the Click event. To see this, let's start putting together our Paint program right away. Start Visual Basic and create a new project, giving the default form (**Form1**) the **Caption** Paint, and setting its **AutoRedraw** property true. Now click on the form, bring up the code window, and find the **Form_MouseDown( )** event procedure in it. That procedure has this template already:

```
Sub Form_MouseDown (Button As Integer,Shift As Integer,X As
      Single,Y As Single)

End Sub
```

As you can see, there are a number of arguments passed to this procedure that we haven't seen before: **Button**, **Shift**, **X**, and **Y**. The **Button** and **Shift** arguments pass mouse button and keyboard shift state information to us, and the **X** and **Y** arguments report the position of the mouse cursor. We can make use of that information by, for example, reporting the cursor's position when you press a mouse button. To do that, create two new text boxes, **Text1** and **Text2**, and place them on the form. We can report the position, (**X, Y**), like this:

```
Sub Form_MouseDown (Button As Integer,Shift As Integer,X As
        Single,Y As Single)
    Text1.Text = Str$(X)
    Text2.Text = Str$(Y)
End Sub
```

Now run the program and press a mouse button (the MouseDown event occurs when any mouse button is pressed). When you do, the mouse cursor's position (in twips) is reported in the two text boxes. In this way, we're able to read direct information about the mouse cursor's position.

Now let's take a look at the two other arguments passed to us: **Button** and **Shift**, both integers. The **Button** argument describes which of the mouse buttons is pressed by encoding that information in its lowest three bits. That looks like this (recall that an integer is two bytes, 16 bits, long):

Button

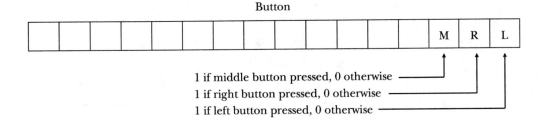

1 if middle button pressed, 0 otherwise ─────

1 if right button pressed, 0 otherwise ─────

1 if left button pressed, 0 otherwise ─────

Note that we can only test for one button being pushed, not two or three at a time. **Button** only reports which button was pushed first: right, left, or middle (although most mouse devices don't have middle buttons anymore). The event that we're going to examine next, the MouseMove event, does actually report when two or more buttons are pressed simultaneously. Here, however, the **Button** argument can only take one of three values, as shown in Table 7-1.

Note that **Button** cannot be 0 because at least one button must have been pushed to cause the MouseDown event. Let's make use of this information in our program. We can add another text box, **Text3**, to report which button caused the MouseDown event with a Select Case statement like this:

```
Sub Form_MouseDown (Button As Integer,Shift As Integer,X As
        Single,Y As Single)
    Text1.Text = Str$(X)
    Text2.Text = Str$(Y)
    Select Case Button
        Case 1
    Text3.Text = "Left Button"
        Case 2
    Text3.Text = "Right Button"
        Case 4
    Text3.Text = "Middle Button"
    End Select
End Sub
```

Now when you run the program, it reports not only the position of the mouse cursor when the MouseDown event occurred but also which button caused it. For example, if you use the left mouse button, you may see something like the window in Figure 7-1.

Besides **X, Y**, and **Button**, the **Shift** argument also returns some useful information. This integer indicates whether the <Ctrl> or <Shift> keys on the keyboard were pressed when the mouse button was clicked (some programs

Button Value	Binary	Means
1	0000000000000001	Left button was pushed
2	0000000000000010	Right button was pushed
4	0000000000000100	Middle button was pushed

Table 7-1. Values for the Button Argument (MouseDown, MouseUp)

distinguish between Click and <Shift>-Click, and there is no "ShiftClick" event in Visual Basic). This information is encoded in the last two bits of Shift like this:

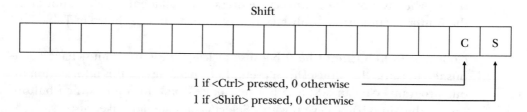

In other words, **Shift** can take on three values: 0 (meaning neither key was pressed), 1, or 2 as shown in Table 7-2.

So far, then, we've seen that the MouseDown event reports four things: the X position of the mouse cursor, the Y position of the mouse cursor, which one of the buttons were pushed, and which of the keyboard's shift or control keys

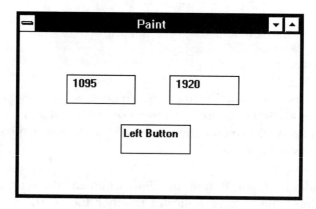

Figure 7-1. MouseInfo Window

Shift Value	Binary	Means
0	0000000000000000	Neither \<Shift\> nor \<Ctrl\> were down
1	0000000000000001	\<Shift\> key was down
2	0000000000000010	\<Ctrl\> key was down

Table 7-2. Values for the Shift Argument

(if either) were pushed. MouseDown also has an important use in paint programs. Usually MouseDown is used to start a drawing operation. For example, if we want to draw a line in a paint program, we might press the left mouse button once to indicate where we want the line to start, move to the other end of the line, and release the button. When we do, we expect the program to draw a line between the two locations.

In Visual Basic terms, we can translate that into saving the point where the MouseDown event occurred, which we can call the Anchor point, (**AnchorX**, **AnchorY**), setting the current graphics position to the same point, and then performing the drawing operation when the mouse button goes up. In other words, when the user presses a mouse button, we'll record that position. When they release it, we'll be able to draw a line or box, or whatever figure was required. That means that we should remove the three text boxes from the form and change **Form_MouseDown( )** to this:

```
Sub Form_MouseDown (Button As Integer,Shift As Integer,X As
        Single,Y As Single)
    If Button = 1 Then              'Left button
        AnchorX = X
        AnchorY = Y
        CurrentX = X
        CurrentY = Y
    End If
End Sub
```

We should also make **AnchorX** and **AnchorY** into global variables, so that any routine in the application can tell where the MouseDown event occurred. This will be useful if, for example, we're supposed to draw a line from the anchor point to the present location when the mouse button goes up. To make these variables global, place them into the global module:

```
Global AnchorX As Integer
Global AnchorY As Integer
```

Now we'll be able to tell where the anchor point is from anywhere in the application. In addition, we should add CONSTANT.TXT to the global module as well so that we can use the constants True and False. Let's put this to work and start drawing.

MouseMove Events

One capability of a paint program should be simply to draw continuously when the user moves the mouse cursor around. In other words, the user should be able to press the mouse button and move the mouse, creating a freehand drawing by leaving a trail of pixels. To do that, we'll need to know where the mouse cursor is at any given time. We can do that with the MouseMove event. Every time the mouse is moved across a form or selected controls (which are file list boxes, labels, list boxes, or picture boxes), a MouseMove event is generated. Actually, MouseMove events are not usually generated for each pixel over which the mouse cursor moves. Instead, Visual Basic only generates a certain number of such events per second. Still, that will be good enough for our application, as we'll see.

In addition, the **Button** argument in a MouseMove event reports the complete state of the mouse buttons; i.e., it can report if more than one button is being pressed (unlike MouseDown or the next event we'll examine, MouseUp). You'll find the values that it can report for **Button** in Table 7-3.

Let's make use of the MouseMove event to start drawing in our paint application. In particular, when the user presses the left mouse button, we set the anchor point — (**AnchorX**, **AnchorY**) — and set that location as the current graphics location. Next, when the user moves, still holding down the left mouse button, we want to draw on the screen, following the mouse cursor's movements. To do that, find the **Form_MouseMove( )** Sub procedure in the code window:

```
Sub Form_MouseMove (Button As Integer,Shift As Integer,X As
    Single,Y As Single)

End Sub
```

Button Value	Binary	Means
0	0000000000000000	No button is pushed
1	0000000000000001	Only left button is pushed
2	0000000000000010	Only right button is pushed
3	0000000000000011	Right and left buttons are pushed
4	0000000000000100	Only Middle button is pushed
5	0000000000000101	Middle and left buttons are pushed
6	0000000000000110	Middle and right buttons are pushed
7	0000000000000111	All three buttons are pushed

Table 7-3. Values for the Button Argument (MouseMove)

We want to make sure that we only draw when the left mouse button is down, so we can check the value of **Button** like this:

```
Sub Form_MouseMove (Button As Integer,Shift As Integer,X As
      Single,Y As Single)
    If Button = 1 Then          'Left button
        :

    End If
End Sub
```

Now we should draw on the form, following the mouse cursor. When we enter this procedure, the user has already moved from the original MouseDown location. However, since we set the graphics position to that position already, we only need to draw from the graphics position to the current position. We can do that with the **Line** method like this:

```
Sub Form_MouseMove (Button As Integer,Shift As Integer,X As
      Single,Y As Single)
    If Button = 1 Then          'Left button
        Line -(X, Y)
    End If
End Sub
```

That is, if you don't specify the first point with the **Line** method, it uses the current graphics position, which we were smart enough to set when the mouse

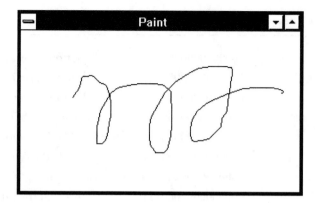

Figure 7-2. Freehand Drawing with the Paint Application

originally went down. Now we're free to draw on the form as much as we like, simply by holding the left mouse button down, as shown in Figure 7-2.

So far, then, we've only used two event procedures, MouseMove and MouseDown, but we've already been able to draw on the form:

```
Sub Form_MouseMove (Button As Integer,Shift As Integer,X As
      Single,Y As Single)
    If Button = 1 Then          'Left button
      Line -(X, Y)
    End If
End Sub

Sub Form_MouseDown (Button As Integer,Shift As Integer,X As
      Single,Y As Single)
    If Button = 1 Then          'Left button
      AnchorX = X
      AnchorY = Y
      CurrentX = X
      CurrentY = Y
    End If
End Sub
```

However, paint programs are supposed to draw all sorts of objects like lines and rectangles as well, and for those we'll need to determine the position where the mouse button went up.

MouseUp Events

To draw a line, the user moves the mouse cursor to the first endpoint (the anchor point) and presses the left mouse button, then moves to the other endpoint, and releases the button to complete the line. We already set the anchor point — (**AnchorX**, **AnchorY**) — when the user presses the left mouse button, so now we have to watch where it's released. We can do that with a MouseUp event, which looks like this:

```
Sub Form_MouseUp (Button As Integer,Shift As Integer,X As
    Single,Y As Single)

End Sub
```

Drawing Lines

In this procedure, we just check if the left mouse button was the button released, and, if so, we draw the line from (**AnchorX**, **AnchorY**) to the current position, (**X**, **Y**):

```
Sub Form_MouseUp (Button As Integer,Shift As Integer,X As
        Single,Y As Single)
    If Button = 1 Then
        Line (AnchorX, AnchorY) - (X, Y)
    End If
End Sub
```

However, this leaves us with a problem. Although the line is drawn, we're still drawing over all the intermediate positions with the MouseMove( ) Sub procedure:

```
Sub Form_MouseMove (Button As Integer,Shift As Integer,X As
        Single,Y As Single)
    If Button = 1 Then            'Left button
        Line -(X, Y)
    End If
End Sub
```

In other words, we're drawing freehand and lines at the same time. Usually, paint applications solve this problem by letting the user select only one drawing "tool" at a time. We can do the same thing by setting up a toolbox from

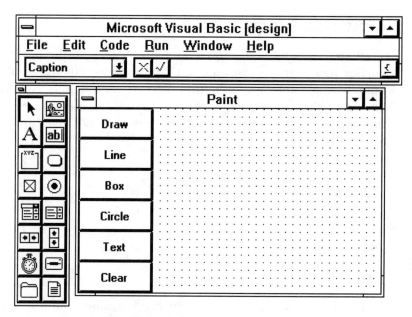

Figure 7-3. Paint Application Template with Buttons

which the user can select tools. To do that, we can create a toolbox of command buttons as shown in Figure 7-3, corresponding to the painting operations we'll support in this program: Draw, Line, Box, Circle, Text, and Clear (Clear is to clear the drawing area). Give each one a name to match its caption; that is, give the Draw button the **CtlName DrawButton**, the Line button **LineButton**, and so on.

TIP   If you prefer not to have a toolbox full of grey buttons (the default color) in your Paint application, you can change their color by changing their **BackColor** property.

In fact, we can do more here. Paint applications often have a different mouse cursor in the drawing area — a cross instead of an arrow — from the cursor with which you select tools from the toolbox. We can do that here too. Forms, and most controls, have a **MousePointer** property, which will allow us to specify the mouse cursor style as it passes over that form or control. We can change the cursor to any of these, using the property bar:

Default	Use form's default cursor
Arrow	Use arrow
Cross	Use a cross
I-Beam	Use an I-Beam (the insertion point cursor)
Icon	Use an icon
Size	Use a sizing arrow
Size NE SW	Use Northeast, Southwest arrow
Size N S	Use North-South arrow

Change the form's mouse cursor to, say, a Cross using the properties bar. However, this means that the buttons in the toolbox will use the same cursor since they use the default mouse cursor (i.e., the form's mouse cursor), unless we change that. However, we can switch them back to using an arrow cursor. To do that, find each button's **MousePointer** property in the property bar, display the list of available cursors, and choose the arrow cursor. Now we're set. The mouse cursor will switch to a cross in the drawing area, and an arrow in the toolbox.

We can make one of these buttons in the toolbox, the Clear button, active immediately. The Clear button simply clears the drawing area. That's done with the Cls statement in Visual Basic, so just add this line to **ClearButton_Click( )**:

```
     Sub ClearButton_Click()
→         Cls
     End Sub
```

In addition, we can have each button set a flag, indicating to the rest of the application which drawing tool is currently in use; that is, a MouseUp event means something different if we're drawing lines or rectangles. These flags should be global, so add them to the global module:

```
     Global AnchorX As Integer
     Global AnchorY As Integer
→    Global DrawFlag As Integer
→    Global LineFlag As Integer
→    Global BoxFlag As Integer
→    Global CircleFlag As Integer
→    Global TextFlag As Integer
```

In other words, we now have two kinds of data available to us anywhere in the program: the anchor point (**AnchorX**, **AnchorY**) and a set of flags that tell us which drawing tool is currently active. To set the flags, we can make each button in our toolbox set the corresponding flag while resetting the rest. This way, we will be able to tell from anywhere in the Paint program what drawing operation is currently being used. To do this, we need to put this code in the button's Sub procedures:

```
Sub DrawButton_Click()
    DrawFlag = True      'Turn drawing on
    LineFlag = False
    BoxFlag = False
    CircleFlag = False
    TextFlag = False
End Sub

Sub LineButton_Click()
    DrawFlag = False
    LineFlag = True      'Turn line drawing on
    BoxFlag = False
    CircleFlag = False
    TextFlag = False
End Sub

Sub BoxButton_Click()
    DrawFlag = False
    LineFlag = False
    BoxFlag = True       'Turn box drawing on
    CircleFlag = False
    TextFlag = False
End Sub

Sub CircleButton_Click()
    DrawFlag = False
    LineFlag = False
    BoxFlag = False
    CircleFlag = True    'Turn circle drawing on
    TextFlag = False
End Sub

Sub TextButton_Click()
    DrawFlag = False
    LineFlag = False
    BoxFlag = False
    CircleFlag = False
    TextFlag = True      'Turn text drawing on
End Sub
```

Now the buttons are done and our toolbox is finished. It only remains to use these flags with the mouse events. In other words, from now on, we can just check the global variables **DrawFlag**, **LineFlag**, **BoxFlag**, **CircleFlag**, and **TextFlag** to find out which drawing tool is active. For example, we can check whether the **DrawFlag** is true in the MouseMove event. If it is, we will draw:

```
        Sub Form_MouseMove (Button As Integer,Shift As Integer,X As
            Single,Y As Single)
          If Button = 1 Then         'Left button
→           If DrawFlag Then
→               Line -(X, Y)
→           End If
          End If
        End Sub
```

This solves the problem of drawing lines and drawing freehand at the same time. Now, if the user selects the Line tool, he can tack one end of the line down by pressing the mouse button, moving to the other end and releasing the button, which creates the line.

In fact, paint programs usually do more than this. They usually display the line after one end has been tacked down at the anchor point, giving the impression of stretching a line into a shape that becomes permanent when you release the mouse button. We can do that here, too, by checking if **LineFlag** is True in the MouseMove event Sub procedure:

```
        Sub Form_MouseMove (Button As Integer,Shift As Integer,X As
            Single,Y As Single)
          If Button = 1 Then         'Left button
            If DrawFlag Then
                Line -(X, Y)
            End If

→           If LineFlag Then
                    :

→           End If
          End If
        End Sub
```

The way to create the illusion of stretching (or dragging) a graphic object is with the Xor pen. To use that pen, we'll have to change the **ForeColor** and

DrawMode properties, so we can save them first. Then we set **ForeColor** to **BackColor** (we'll see why in a moment), and set **DrawMode** to 7, the Xor Pen:

```
Sub Form_MouseMove (Button As Integer,Shift As Integer,X As
        Single,Y As Single)
    If Button = 1 Then            'Left button
        If DrawFlag Then
            Line -(X, Y)
        End If

        If LineFlag Then
→           TempFore& = ForeColor
→           TempMode% = DrawMode
→           ForeColor = BackColor
→           DrawMode = 7                  'Xor mode
                :
        End If
    End If
End Sub
```

When we use the Xor Pen, the **ForeColor** is Xored with what is already on the screen. Because we want the line to show up as we stretch it, we'll want it to be a different color than the background. In fact, if we temporarily make the foreground color the same as the background color, Xoring the two will give black, so we'll end up with a black line on the standard white foreground. To erase that line and restore the background, we only need to draw it on the screen with the Xor pen again (and in the same place). In MouseMove, then, the plan is to erase the last line drawn from the anchor point to the mouse cursor, and draw a new line from the anchor point to the new mouse cursor's position. We can do that like this:

```
Sub Form_MouseMove (Button As Integer,Shift As Integer,X As
        Single,Y As Single)
    If Button = 1 Then            'Left button
        If DrawFlag Then
            Line -(X, Y)
        End If

        If LineFlag Then
            TempFore& = ForeColor
            TempMode% = DrawMode
            ForeColor = BackColor
            DrawMode = 7                  'Xor mode
→           Line (AnchorX, AnchorY)-(CurrentX, CurrentY)
```

```
→            Line (AnchorX, AnchorY)-(X, Y)
                   :
         End If
      End If
End Sub
```

Finally, we just replace the original values in the **ForeColor** and **DrawMode** properties, finishing the MouseMove event:

```
Sub Form_MouseMove (Button As Integer,Shift As Integer,X As
      Single,Y As Single)

   If Button = 1 Then           'Left button
      If DrawFlag Then
         Line -(X, Y)
      End If

      If LineFlag Then
         TempFore& = ForeColor
         TempMode% = DrawMode
         ForeColor = BackColor
         DrawMode = 7                 'Xor mode
         Line (AnchorX, AnchorY)-(CurrentX, CurrentY)
         Line (AnchorX, AnchorY)-(X, Y)
→         ForeColor = TempFore&
→         DrawMode = TempMode%
      End If
   End If
End Sub
```

That's it. Now the user can tack one end of a line down by pressing the left mouse button; moving around while stretching a line from that point; and then releasing the mouse button to make the line permanent.

Note that we also have to update our other event procedures to take the new flags into account. The MouseDown event procedure is not going to change because it only sets the anchor point and the current graphics location. However, we'll have to update the MouseUp event procedure so it only draws lines if **LineFlag** is true, and we can do that like this:

```
Sub Form_MouseUp (Button As Integer,Shift As Integer,X As
      Single,Y As Single)
   If Button = 1 Then

→         If LineFlag Then
```

```
                    Line (AnchorX, AnchorY) - (X, Y)
→               End If

        End
End Sub
```

That's it for lines and freehand drawing. All the code so far appears in Listing 7-1, and the application at run-time appears in Figure 7-4. We've made a good deal of progress. We've set up a Paint program that lets you draw freehand or create lines. However, as we know, it's as easy to draw rectangles or boxes as it is to draw lines, so let's do that next.

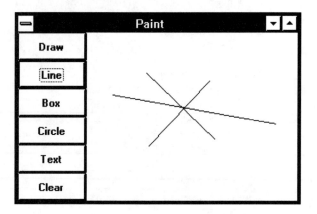

Figure 7-4. Line Drawing Paint Application

Listing 7-1. Paint Program with Drawing and Lines

```
Global Module-----------------------------------------------------

        Global AnchorX As Integer
        Global AnchorY As Integer
        Global DrawFlag As Integer
        Global LineFlag As Integer
        Global BoxFlag As Integer
        Global CircleFlag As Integer
        Global TextFlag As Integer


Form Form1--------------------------------------------------------


Sub Form_MouseDown (Button As Integer,Shift As Integer,X As
        Single,Y As Single)
```

Listing 7-1. (continued)

```
        If Button = 1 Then        'Left Button
            AnchorX = X
            AnchorY = Y
            CurrentX = X
            CurrentY = Y
        End If
    End Sub

    Sub Form_MouseMove (Button As Integer,Shift As Integer,X As
            Single,Y As Single)
        If (Button = 1) Then
            If DrawFlag Then
                Line -(X, Y)
            End If

            If LineFlag Then
                TempFore& = ForeColor
                TempMode% = DrawMode
                ForeColor = BackColor
                DrawMode = 7             'Xor mode
                Line (AnchorX, AnchorY)-(CurrentX, CurrentY)
                Line (AnchorX, AnchorY)-(X, Y)
                ForeColor = TempFore&
                DrawMode = TempMode%
            End If
        End If
    End Sub

    Sub Form_MouseUp (Button As Integer, Shift As Integer, X As
            Single, Y As Single)
        If Button = 1 Then

            If LineFlag Then
                Line (AnchorX, AnchorY)-(X, Y)
            End If

        End If
    End Sub

    Sub DrawButton_Click ()
        DrawFlag = True
        LineFlag = False
        BoxFlag = False
        CircleFlag = False
        TextFlag = False
    End Sub
```

(continued)

Listing 7-1. (continued)

```
Sub LineButton_Click ()
    DrawFlag = False
    LineFlag = True
    BoxFlag = False
    CircleFlag = False
    TextFlag = False
End Sub

Sub BoxButton_Click ()
    DrawFlag = False
    LineFlag = False
    BoxFlag = True
    CircleFlag = False
    TextFlag = False
End Sub

Sub CircleButton_Click ()
    DrawFlag = False
    LineFlag = False
    BoxFlag = False
    CircleFlag = True
    TextFlag = False
End Sub

Sub TextButton_Click ()
    DrawFlag = False
    LineFlag = False
    BoxFlag = False
    CircleFlag = False
    TextFlag = True
End Sub

Sub ClearButton_Click ()
    Cls
End Sub
```

Drawing Boxes

We can draw boxes by using the **Line** method as long as we specify the **B** parameter. In fact, it will be simple to add this capability to our code. Wherever we drew lines before, we can do the same thing for boxes (after testing **BoxFlag**, which is set by the Box drawing tool). The two places that we've used **Line** already are the MouseMove and MouseUp procedures:

```
Sub Form_MouseMove (Button As Integer,Shift As Integer,X As
        Single,Y As Single)
    If (Button = 1) Then
        If DrawFlag Then
            Line -(X, Y)
        End If


        If LineFlag Then
            TempFore& = ForeColor
            TempMode% = DrawMode
            ForeColor = BackColor
            DrawMode = 7              'Xor mode
            Line (AnchorX, AnchorY)-(CurrentX, CurrentY)
            Line (AnchorX, AnchorY)-(X, Y)
            ForeColor = TempFore&
            DrawMode = TempMode%
        End If
    End If
End Sub

Sub Form_MouseUp (Button As Integer, Shift As Integer, X As
        Single, Y As Single)
    If Button = 1 Then

        If LineFlag Then
            Line (AnchorX, AnchorY)-(X, Y)
        End If
    End If
```

All we need to do is to repeat the line code for boxes, using the **B** parameter and checking for **BoxFlag** like this:

```
Sub Form_MouseMove (Button As Integer,Shift As Integer,X As
        Single,Y As Single)
    If (Button = 1) Then
        If DrawFlag Then
            Line -(X, Y)
        End If

        If LineFlag Then
            TempFore& = ForeColor
            TempMode% = DrawMode
            ForeColor = BackColor
            DrawMode = 7              'Xor mode
            Line (AnchorX, AnchorY)-(CurrentX, CurrentY)
            Line (AnchorX, AnchorY)-(X, Y)
```

```
                              ForeColor = TempFore&
                              DrawMode = TempMode%
                          End If

→             If BoxFlag Then
                  TempFore& = ForeColor
                  TempMode% = DrawMode
                  ForeColor = BackColor
                  DrawMode = 7                'Xor mode
→             Line (AnchorX, AnchorY)-(CurrentX, CurrentY), , B
→             Line (AnchorX, AnchorY)-(X, Y), , B
                  ForeColor = TempFore&
                  DrawMode = TempMode%
              End If

          End If
      End Sub

      Sub Form_MouseUp (Button As Integer, Shift As Integer, X As
              Single, Y As Single)
          If Button = 1 Then

              If LineFlag Then
                  Line (AnchorX, AnchorY)-(X, Y)
              End If

→             If BoxFlag Then
→                 Line (AnchorX, AnchorY)-(X, Y), , B
              End If
```

That's it. That's the only change we have to make. Now our Paint application is able to draw freehand, as well as to draw lines and boxes. However, there are still other drawing routines in Visual Basic that we can make use of, for example, circles.

TIP   This is the code you can use to "stretch" rectangles on the screen if you want to. In fact, you can make the rectangle itself dotted as it's being stretched by setting its **DrawStyle** property to 1 and then resetting it back to its original value when you're done and the rectangle becomes permanent. You can even let users select portions of the drawing this way by letting them stretch a rectangle into place and reading all the enclosed pixels with the **Point( )** method. You can then transfer those pixels to other locations as desired by using **PSet( )**.

Drawing Circles

Drawing circles is not very difficult because we can use the **Circle** method. That is, we can use the anchor point as the center of the circle, and draw the circle out to the mouse pointer's location when the user releases the button. To start, we check if the **CircleFlag** (set by clicking the Circle tool) is set this way in the MouseUp event procedure, which is where we're supposed to draw the circle:

```
Sub Form_MouseUp (Button As Integer, Shift As Integer, X As
        Single, Y As Single)
    If Button = 1 Then

        If LineFlag Then
            Line (AnchorX, AnchorY)-(X, Y)
        End If

        If BoxFlag Then
            Line (AnchorX, AnchorY)-(X, Y), , B
        End If

→       If CircleFlag Then

→       End If
```

Next, we draw the circle, using (**AnchorX, AnchorY**) as the center point and the distance from (**AnchorX, AnchorY**) to the current location (**X, Y**) as the radius:

```
Sub Form_MouseUp (Button As Integer, Shift As Integer, X As
        Single, Y As Single)
    If Button = 1 Then

        If LineFlag Then
            Line (AnchorX, AnchorY)-(X, Y)
        End If

        If BoxFlag Then
            Line (AnchorX, AnchorY)-(X, Y), , B
        End If

        If CircleFlag Then
→           Radius! = Sqr((AnchorX - X)^2 + (AnchorY - Y)^2)
→           Circle (AnchorX, AnchorY), Radius!
        End If
```

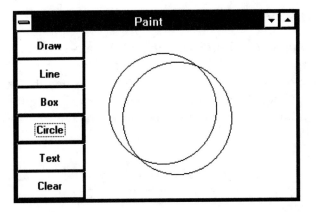

Figure 7-5. Drawing Circles with the Paint Application

Here we're using the standard Basic Sqr( ) function to find square roots, and the ^ operator to square quantities. The result is that we can now draw circles, as shown in Figure 7-5.

In fact, we can draw the intermediate circles as the user is moving the mouse cursor, as we did for lines and boxes. To do that, we have to modify the MouseMove event procedure. The code we add has to check whether or not the **CircleFlag** is set first:

```
If CircleFlag Then
     :

End If
```

Next, we save the foreground color and the current drawing mode, restoring them at the end:

```
If CircleFlag Then
    TempFore& = ForeColor
    TempMode% = DrawMode
    ForeColor = BackColor
    DrawMode = 7                     'Xor mode
        :

    ForeColor = TempFore&
    DrawMode = TempMode%
End If
```

As before, giving the appearance of stretching a graphics figure is really a matter of erasing the old figure and drawing the new one. To do that, we use the Xor Pen and draw the old circle. Assuming we stored the last mouse position in (**CurrentX**, **CurrentY**), that would look like this:

```
        If CircleFlag Then
             TempFore& = ForeColor
             TempMode% = DrawMode
             ForeColor = BackColor
             DrawMode = 7          'Xor mode
   →         Radius! = Sqr((AnchorX - CurrentX)^2 + (AnchorY - CurrentY)^2)
   →         Circle (AnchorX, AnchorY), Radius!
                  :

             ForeColor = TempFore&
             DrawMode = TempMode%
        End If
```

Next, we draw the new circle and store the mouse cursor's position in (**CurrentX**, **CurrentY** for next time):

```
        If CircleFlag Then
             TempFore& = ForeColor
             TempMode% = DrawMode
             ForeColor = BackColor
             DrawMode = 7          'Xor mode
             Radius! = Sqr((AnchorX - CurrentX)^2 + (AnchorY - CurrentY)^2)
             Circle (AnchorX, AnchorY), Radius!
   →         Radius! = Sqr(AnchorX - X)^2 + (AnchorY - Y)^2)
   →         Circle (AnchorX, AnchorY), Radius!
   →         CurrentX = X
   →         CurrentY = Y
             ForeColor = TempFore&
             DrawMode = TempMode%
        End If
```

And that's it. The whole MouseMove event procedure looks like this now where we have broken it up into specific drawing actions depending on which drawing tool is being used:

```
Sub Form_MouseMove (Button As Integer,Shift As Integer,X As
    Single,Y As Single)

If (Button = 1) Then
    If DrawFlag Then
        Line -(X, Y)
    End If

    If LineFlag Then
        TempFore& = ForeColor
        TempMode% = DrawMode
        ForeColor = BackColor
        DrawMode = 7              'Xor mode
        Line (AnchorX, AnchorY)-(CurrentX, CurrentY)
        Line (AnchorX, AnchorY)-(X, Y)
        ForeColor = TempFore&
        DrawMode = TempMode%
    End If

    If BoxFlag Then
        TempFore& = ForeColor
        TempMode% = DrawMode
        ForeColor = BackColor
        DrawMode = 7         'Xor mode
        Line (AnchorX, AnchorY)-(CurrentX, CurrentY), , B
        Line (AnchorX, AnchorY)-(X, Y), , B
        ForeColor = TempFore&
        DrawMode = TempMode%
    End If

    If CircleFlag Then
        TempFore& = ForeColor
        TempMode% = DrawMode
        ForeColor = BackColor
        DrawMode = 7            'Xor mode
        Radius! = Sqr((AnchorX - CurrentX)^2 + (AnchorY - CurrentY)^2)
        Circle (AnchorX, AnchorY), Radius!
        Radius! = Sqr(AnchorX - X)^2 + (AnchorY - Y)^2)
        Circle (AnchorX, AnchorY), Radius!
        CurrentX = X
        CurrentY = Y
        ForeColor = TempFore&
        DrawMode = TempMode%
    End If

End If
End Sub
```

The last of the tools is Text, which will let us draw text directly in the graphics area.

Drawing Text

We can draw text if we make use of the fact that, when the user clicks the Text button in our toolbox, that button gets the focus. From then on, we can read each key struck (until another tool is selected) by placing code in the **TextButton_KeyPress( )** Sub procedure:

```
Sub TextButton_KeyPress (KeyAscii As Integer)

End Sub
```

In fact, since text is printed at the current graphics position, and the user sets that position with a MouseDown event, all we need to do is to let the user select the Text tool/button, click somewhere in the graphics area, and then print whatever he types like this:

```
       Sub TextButton_KeyPress (KeyAscii As Integer)
→          Print Chr$(KeyAscii);
       End Sub
```

That's all there is to it. Everything the user types is sent to the current paint document as long as the Text toolbox button retains the focus, as it will until the user selects a new tool (which is exactly when we should stop printing characters). Now we can use text as well as figures, as shown in Figure 7-6. (If

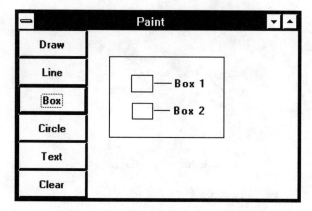

Figure 7-6. Paint Application with Text

you like, you can even add a text cursor — i.e., an insertion point — to this program with a little more work.) The whole program so far appears in Listing 7-2.

Listing 7-2. Paint Program: Drawing, Lines, Boxes, Circles, and Text

```
Global Module -------------------------------------

        Global AnchorX As Integer
        Global AnchorY As Integer
        Global DrawFlag As Integer
        Global LineFlag As Integer
        Global BoxFlag As Integer
        Global CircleFlag As Integer
        Global TextFlag As Integer


Form1 ----------------------------------------------

Sub Form_MouseDown (Button As Integer,Shift As Integer,X As
        Single,Y As Single)
    If Button = 1 Then        'Left Button
        AnchorX = X
        AnchorY = Y
        CurrentX = X
        CurrentY = Y
    End If
End Sub

Sub Form_MouseMove (Button As Integer,Shift As Integer,X As
        Single,Y As Single)
    If (Button = 1) Then
        If DrawFlag Then
            Line -(X, Y)
        End If

        If LineFlag Then
            TempFore& = ForeColor
            TempMode% = DrawMode
            ForeColor = BackColor
            DrawMode = 7                'Xor mode
            Line (AnchorX, AnchorY)-(CurrentX, CurrentY)
            Line (AnchorX, AnchorY)-(X, Y)
            ForeColor = TempFore&
            DrawMode = TempMode%
        End If
```

Listing 7-2. (continued)

```
        If BoxFlag Then
            TempFore& = ForeColor
            TempMode% = DrawMode
            ForeColor = BackColor
            DrawMode = 7                'Xor mode
            Line (AnchorX, AnchorY)-(CurrentX, CurrentY), , B
            Line (AnchorX, AnchorY)-(X, Y), , B
            ForeColor = TempFore&
            DrawMode = TempMode%
        End If

        If CircleFlag Then
            TempFore& = ForeColor
            TempMode% = DrawMode
            ForeColor = BackColor
            DrawMode = 7                'Xor mode
            radius! = Sqr((AnchorX - CurrentX) ^ 2 +
                (AnchorY - CurrentY) ^ 2)
            Circle (AnchorX, AnchorY), radius!
            radius! = Sqr((AnchorX - X) ^ 2 + (AnchorY - Y) ^ 2)
            Circle (AnchorX, AnchorY), radius!
            CurrentX = X
            CurrentY = Y
            ForeColor = TempFore&
            DrawMode = TempMode%
        End If

    End If
End Sub

Sub Form_MouseUp (Button As Integer, Shift As Integer, X As
        Single, Y As Single)
    If Button = 1 Then
        If LineFlag Then
            Line (AnchorX, AnchorY)-(X, Y)
        End If

        If BoxFlag Then
            Line (AnchorX, AnchorY)-(X, Y), , B
        End If

        If CircleFlag Then
            radius! = Sqr((AnchorX - X) ^ 2 + (AnchorY - Y) ^ 2)
            Circle (AnchorX, AnchorY), radius!
        End If
```

(continued)

Listing 7-2. (continued)

```
        End If
End Sub

Sub ClearButton_Click ()
        Cls
End Sub

Sub DrawButton_Click ()
        DrawFlag = True
        LineFlag = False
        BoxFlag = False
        CircleFlag = False
        TextFlag = False
End Sub

Sub LineButton_Click ()
        DrawFlag = False
        LineFlag = True
        BoxFlag = False
        CircleFlag = False
        TextFlag = False
End Sub

Sub BoxButton_Click ()
        DrawFlag = False
        LineFlag = False
        BoxFlag = True
        CircleFlag = False
        TextFlag = False
End Sub

Sub CircleButton_Click ()
        DrawFlag = False
        LineFlag = False
        BoxFlag = False
        CircleFlag = True
        TextFlag = False
End Sub

Sub TextButton_Click ()
        DrawFlag = False
        LineFlag = False
        BoxFlag = False
        CircleFlag = False
        TextFlag = True
End Sub
```

Listing 7-2. (continued)

```
Sub TextButton_KeyPress (KeyAscii As Integer)
    Print Chr$(KeyAscii);
End Sub
```

That's it for our toolbox. The next step is to add a File menu that will let us undertake such operations as saving our image on disk, reading it back in again, printing our image out, and selecting drawing colors. Let's start by saving the image on disk.

Saving Our Paint Image on Disk

We'll need a File menu in our Paint application, so bring up the Menu Design Window and create a menu with that caption (**CtlName: FileMenu**). Add three items to the menu: Save File... (**CtlName: SaveItem**), Load File... (**CtlName: LoadItem**), and Exit (**CtlName: ExitItem**). As before, the Exit item is easy to complete. We just need to use the End statement like this:

```
Sub ExitItem_Click ()
    End
End Sub
```

TIP   You can even add an Undo item to the Paint application's menu by adding another form which is never shown. For example, whenever the user chooses a drawing tool, copy the current Picture from Form1 to that form. When the user selects Undo, copy it back, restoring the image.

Now let's make the Save File... item active. Find the SaveItem_Click( ) Sub procedure in the code window, like this:

```
Sub SaveItem_Click ()

End Sub
```

When the user selects this item, we want to get a filename, and then we can save the image we've been working on there. In fact, we've already developed two forms that will deal with the problems of saving and loading files for us, LoadForm and SaveForm from our Editor application.

To save files, add the SaveForm.Frm file to the Paint application by using the Add File... item in the Visual Basic File menu. After loading the file, save it with a new name (e.g., Savpaint.Frm) so that you don't overwrite the Editor's dialog box. After the user types the name of the file in which she wants to save the image, we can save that image using the SavePicture statement when the OK button is clicked. Originally, OKButton_Click( ) looks like this in Save-Form:

```
Sub OKButton_Click ()
    On Error GoTo FileError
    Open FileNameBox.Text For Output As #1
    Print #1, Form1.PadText.Text
    Close #1
    SaveForm.Hide
    Exit Sub

FileError:
    MsgBox "File Error", 48, "Editor"
    Resume
End Sub
```

However, we want to use SavePicture instead, whose syntax is like this:

```
SavePicture [Object.]Image, FileName$
```

Here, **Image** is the name of a special property of the form, which stands for the picture itself. We can use SavePicture like this in our program:

```
      Sub OKButton_Click()
          On Error GoTo FileError
→         SavePicture Form1.Image, FileNameBox.Text
→         SaveForm.Hide
          Exit Sub

      FileError:
          MsgBox "File Error", 48, "Paint"
          Resume
      End Sub
```

(Note that we also changed the name in the error message from "Editor" to "Paint.") All that remains is to make the Save File... item active in the File menu. We can do that by clicking on it and adding this line to **SaveItem_Click( )**:

```
Sub SaveItem_Click()
    SaveForm.Show
End Sub
```

Now when the user decides to save her graphics work, she can click on the Save File... item (**CtlName: SaveItem**), which pops up **SaveForm**. The user then types a filename, which we read out of the text box and pass on the SavePicture. And that's it. Next, let's make sure that we've saved the file correctly by reading it back in.

Reading the Image Back from Disk

To read files from the disk, we can use the **LoadForm** dialog box from our Editor application. Add that file, LoadForm.Frm, to the Paint application, rename it, say, LodPaint, and bring up the **OKButton_Click ( )** Sub procedure in the code window. This button is clicked after the user has selected the file he wants to read in. We spend a little time in the procedure making sure that the pathname is correct, and then we read in files like this:

```
Sub OKButton_Click ()
    On Error GoTo FileError
    If (Right$(Dir1.Path, 1) = "\") Then
        Filename$ = Dir1.Path + File1.Filename
    Else
        Filename$ = Dir1.Path + "\" + File1.Filename
    End If
    Open Filename$ For Input As #1
→   Form1.PadText.Text = Input$(LOF(1), #1)
    Close #1
    LoadForm.Hide
    Exit Sub

FileError:
    MsgBox "File Error", 48, "Editor"
    Resume
End Sub
```

In the Paint application, of course, we'll change that to read in a picture instead of a text file. In particular, we'll use the LoadPicture function, which looks like this:

```
[Object.]Picture = LoadPicture(Filename$)
```

In other words, we have to assign the return value from LoadPicture( ) to the Picture property of an object (i.e., a Form or Picture Box). We can modify **OKButton_Click ( )** to that this way:

```
Sub OKButton_Click ()
    On Error GoTo FileError
    If (Right$(Dir1.Path, 1) = "\") Then
        Filename$ = Dir1.Path + File1.Filename
    Else
        Filename$ = Dir1.Path + "\" + File1.Filename
    End If
    Form1.Picture = LoadPicture(Filename$)
    LoadForm.Hide
    Exit Sub

FileError:
    MsgBox "File Error", 48, "Paint"
    Resume
End Sub
```

(Once again, we also changed the name in the error message from "Editor" to "Paint.") Finally, to make this form appear on the screen when the user clicks the Load File... item (**CtlName: LoadItem**) in our File menu, we can place a line like this in **LoadItem_Click ( )**:

```
Sub LoadItem_Click ()
    LoadForm.Show
End Sub
```

And that's it. Now we can save images to disk and retrieve them as well, as shown in Figure 7-7. However, there's more power that we can add to our application relatively easily. For example, we can change the drawing (i.e., foreground) color. Let's look into that next.

TIP   You can even exchange images with Microsoft Paintbrush for Windows this way. The disk format created by the SavePicture statement is a bitmap format, the same as is created by Paintbrush when it saves files in its .BMP format.

Changing the Drawing Color

Some pages ago, we designed a control panel application, complete with a control panel that lets you change a number of properties of the main win-

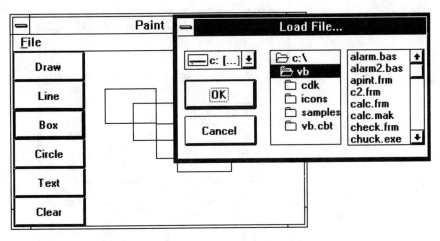

Figure 7-7. Paint Application with Load File... Box

dow, including its color. To do that, we had a number of scroll bars that the user could manipulate, while watching the result in a box in the control panel itself. It will be easy to modify that form for use here, allowing us to set the drawing color. (As you can see, once you've created some general purpose forms in Visual Basic, the usual thing to do is to use them over and over again.) Just load it into the Paint application with the Add File... item in Visual Basic's File menu (we called this file Panel.Frm a while ago). The panel appears, as in Figure 7-8.

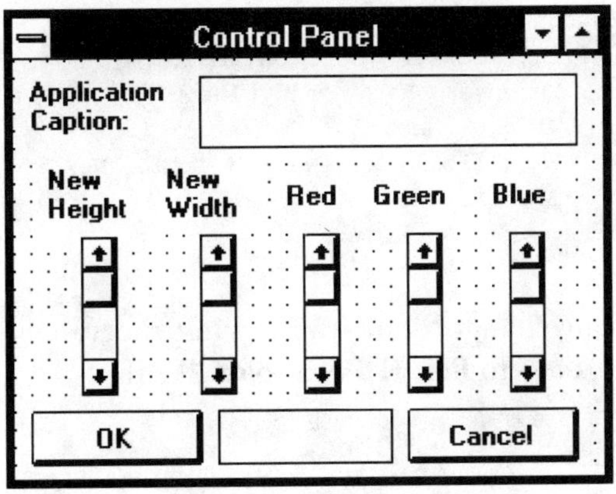

Figure 7-8. Customized Control Panel

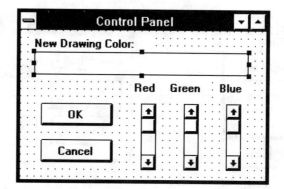

Figure 7-9. Paint Application Control Panel's Template

This control panel has a number of items that we won't need, which are the scroll bars for the main window's height and width and a text box for that window's new name. However, we can remove those controls and move around the color controls to fill up the box, as shown in Figure 7-9. In particular, notice that we enlarged the label that displays the new color (we called this label **NewColor**), and also labeled it "New Drawing Color:".

Now we've got scroll bars for color, and a box to indicate that color to the user. When they move the scroll bars (which we called **NewRed**, **NewGreen**, and **NewBlue**), the new drawing color is indicated in the box we've named **New-Color**. After the drawing color is set, the user will click the OK button to make it active. At that point, we want to set the new drawing color; that is, the **ForeColor** property of **Form1**. Originally, **OKButton_Click ( )** looks like this:

```
Sub OKButton_Click ()
    Form1.Caption = NewCaption.Text
    Form1.Height = NewHeight.Value
    Form1.Width = NewWidth.Value
    Form1.BackColor = RGB(NewRed.Value, NewGreen.Value, NewBlue.Value)
    ControlPanel.Hide
End Sub
```

Now we can change that, transferring the values of the scroll bars (**New-Red.Value**, etc.) to **Form1.ForeColor** like this:

```
Sub OKButton_Click ()
    Form1.ForeColor = RGB(NewRed.Value, NewGreen.Value, NewBlue.Value)
    ControlPanel.Hide
End Sub
```

The new control panel is set. All that remains is to make it active when the user selects an item in the File menu. Go back to the paint application's main window, and bring up the Menu Design Window. Move the highlight bar in the list box at the bottom to the last item — Exit — and click on the button labeled Insert. A new line will appear above Exit. Type New Drawing Color... as the name of the menu item that will bring up the new color control panel, and give this item the name of, say, **DrawingItem**. Then close the Menu Design Window by clicking Done, and click on the new menu item to bring up this Sub procedure template:

```
Sub DrawingItem_Click ()

End Sub
```

We want to do two things here: load the current drawing color into the color-displaying label in the control panel (**ControlPanel.NewColor**) and show the color control panel. We can do those things like this:

```
Sub DrawingItem_Click ()
    ControlPanel.NewColor.BackColor = ForeColor
    ControlPanel.Show
End Sub
```

And that's it. Now we can design the drawing color in our Paint application. Give it a try: When you select the Drawing Color... item in the File menu, the color control panel pops up. Manipulate the scroll bars until you have a new drawing color you like, then select the OK button. When you draw again, you'll find that the drawing color has been switched to the new color. The new program, including the code for changing colors, loading and saving files, and all the drawing tools, appears in Listing 7-3.

Listing 7-3. Paint Application with File Capability and Color Selection

```
         Global Module ------------------------------------

Global AnchorX As Integer
Global AnchorY As Integer
Global DrawFlag As Integer
Global LineFlag As Integer
Global BoxFlag As Integer
Global CircleFlag As Integer
Global TextFlag As Integer
```

(continued)

Listing 7-3. (continued)

```
          Form1 ----------------------------------------------

Sub Form_MouseDown (Button As Integer,Shift As Integer,X As
          Single,Y As Single)
     If Button = 1 Then        'Left Button
          AnchorX = X
          AnchorY = Y
          CurrentX = X
          CurrentY = Y
              End If
End Sub

Sub Form_MouseMove (Button As Integer,Shift As Integer,X As
          Single,Y As Single)
     If (Button = 1) Then
          If DrawFlag Then
               Line -(X, Y)
          End If

          If LineFlag Then
               TempFore& = ForeColor
               TempMode% = DrawMode
               ForeColor = BackColor
               DrawMode = 7                'Xor mode
               Line (AnchorX, AnchorY)-(CurrentX, CurrentY)
               Line (AnchorX, AnchorY)-(X, Y)
               ForeColor = TempFore&
               DrawMode = TempMode%
          End If

          If BoxFlag Then
               TempFore& = ForeColor
               TempMode% = DrawMode
               ForeColor = BackColor
               DrawMode = 7                'Xor mode
               Line (AnchorX, AnchorY)-(CurrentX, CurrentY), , B
               Line (AnchorX, AnchorY)-(X, Y), , B
               ForeColor = TempFore&
               DrawMode = TempMode%
          End If

          If CircleFlag Then
               TempFore& = ForeColor
               TempMode% = DrawMode
```

Listing 7-3. (continued)

```
            ForeColor = BackColor
            DrawMode = 7                'Xor mode
            radius! = Sqr((AnchorX - CurrentX) ^ 2 + (AnchorY -
                CurrentY)^ 2)
            Circle (AnchorX, AnchorY), radius!
            radius! = Sqr((AnchorX - X) ^ 2 + (AnchorY - Y) ^ 2)
            Circle (AnchorX, AnchorY), radius!
            CurrentX = X
            CurrentY = Y
            ForeColor = TempFore&
            DrawMode = TempMode%
        End If

    End If
End Sub

Sub Form_MouseUp (Button As Integer, Shift As Integer, X As
        Single, Y As Single)
    If Button = 1 Then
        If LineFlag Then
            Line (AnchorX, AnchorY)-(X, Y)
        End If

        If BoxFlag Then
            Line (AnchorX, AnchorY)-(X, Y), , B
        End If

        If CircleFlag Then
            radius! = Sqr((AnchorX - X) ^ 2 + (AnchorY - Y) ^ 2)
            Circle (AnchorX, AnchorY), radius!
        End If
    End If
End Sub

Sub ClearButton_Click ()
    Cls
End Sub

Sub DrawButton_Click ()
    DrawFlag = True
    LineFlag = False
    BoxFlag = False
```

(continued)

Listing 7-3. (continued)

```
        CircleFlag = False
        TextFlag = False
    End Sub

    Sub LineButton_Click ()
        DrawFlag = False
        LineFlag = True
        BoxFlag = False
        CircleFlag = False
        TextFlag = False
    End Sub

    Sub BoxButton_Click ()
        DrawFlag = False
        LineFlag = False
        BoxFlag = True
        CircleFlag = False
        TextFlag = False
    End Sub

    Sub CircleButton_Click ()
        DrawFlag = False
        LineFlag = False
        BoxFlag = False
        CircleFlag = True
        TextFlag = False
    End Sub

    Sub TextButton_Click ()
        DrawFlag = False
        LineFlag = False
        BoxFlag = False
        CircleFlag = False
        TextFlag = True
    End Sub

    Sub TextButton_KeyPress (KeyAscii As Integer)
        Print Chr$(KeyAscii);
    End Sub

    Sub ExitItem_Click ()
        End
    End Sub

    Sub SaveItem_Click ()
        SaveForm.Show
    End Sub
```

Listing 7-3. (continued)

```
Sub LoadItem_Click ()
    LoadForm.Show
End Sub

Sub DrawingItem_Click ()
    ControlPanel.NewColor.BackColor = ForeColor
    ControlPanel.Show
End Sub

        SaveForm --------------------------------------

Sub CancelButton_Click ()
    SaveForm.Hide
End Sub

Sub OKButton_Click ()
    'On Error GoTo FileError
    SavePicture Form1.Image, FileNameBox.Text
    SaveForm.Hide
    Exit Sub

FileError:
    MsgBox "File Error", 48, "Paint"
    Resume
End Sub

        LoadForm ---------------------------------

Sub CancelButton_Click ()
    LoadForm.Hide
End Sub

Sub Drive1_Change ()
    Dir1.Path = Drive1.Drive
End Sub

Sub Dir1_Change ()
    File1.Path = Dir1.Path
End Sub

Sub OKButton_Click ()
    On Error GoTo FileError
    If (Right$(Dir1.Path, 1) = "\") Then
        Filename$ = Dir1.Path + File1.Filename
    Else
```

(continued)

Listing 7-3. (continued)

```
        Filename$ = Dir1.Path + "\" + File1.Filename
    End If
    Form1.Picture = LoadPicture(Filename$)
    LoadForm.Hide
    Exit Sub

FileError:
    MsgBox "File Error", 48, "Editor"
    Resume
End Sub

Sub File1_DblClick ()
    OKButton_Click
End Sub

Sub CancelButton_Click ()
    ControlPanel.Hide
End Sub

        ControlPanel --------------------------------------

Sub OKButton_Click ()

    Form1.ForeColor = RGB(NewRed.Value, NewGreen.Value, NewBlue.Value)
    ControlPanel.Hide
End Sub

Sub NewRed_Change ()
    NewColor.BackColor = RGB(NewRed.Value, NewGreen.Value,
        NewBlue.Value)
End Sub

Sub NewGreen_Change ()
    NewColor.BackColor = RGB(NewRed.Value, NewGreen.Value,
        NewBlue.Value)
End Sub

Sub NewBlue_Change ()
    NewColor.BackColor = RGB(NewRed.Value, NewGreen.Value,
        NewBlue.Value)
End Sub
```

As polished as our Paint application is becoming, it's not very useful unless we can print the results out on the printer. However, it's not hard to do that, so let's examine how to do so next.

Printing the Paint Program's Graphics

We've already seen the Printer object in the last chapter. With it, we can use any of the graphics methods we've already seen: **Line**, **Circle**, **Print**, and so on. However, there is a very simple way that will let us print out all the predrawn graphics in our Paint document: the **PrintForm** method.

As we saw in the last chapter, this method prints all that is in the client area of a window (i.e., excluding menu bar, borders, and so on). However, this includes all the controls, such as buttons, that are on the form too. Since we don't want to print them out as well, we can make them temporarily disappear by setting their **Visible** property to False. Let's start by adding a Print item to our Paint program's File menu. Bring up the Menu Design Window and highlight the Exit item, clicking the Insert button as before. Add an item with the caption Print and the **CtlName PrintItem**, then close the Menu Design Window. Next, click on the new menu item, bringing up this Sub procedure template:

```
Sub PrintItem_Click ()

End Sub
```

First, we hide all the buttons in our toolbox:

```
Sub PrintItem_Click ()
    DrawButton.Visible = False
    LineButton.Visible = False
    BoxButton.Visible = False
    CircleButton.Visible = False
    TextButton.Visible = False
    ClearButton.Visible = False
        :
End Sub
```

Then we can print the form with **PrintForm** and show the buttons again:

```
     Sub PrintItem_Click ()
         DrawButton.Visible = False
         LineButton.Visible = False
         BoxButton.Visible = False
         CircleButton.Visible = False
         TextButton.Visible = False
         ClearButton.Visible = False
→        PrintForm
            :
```

```
        DrawButton.Visible = True
        LineButton.Visible = True
        BoxButton.Visible = True
        CircleButton.Visible = True
        TextButton.Visible = True
        ClearButton.Visible = True
    End Sub
```

When you print using **PrintForm**, Visual Basic even pops a small window on the screen, as shown in Figure 7-10, indicating that it is printing. This window even includes a button that lets the user cancel at any time. That's it for printing from the Paint application. The next, and last, capability we'll give to this program is to let it interact with the Window's clipboard.

Using the Windows Clipboard

The clipboard is a means of passing data back and forth between applications in Windows. For example, you can press the Print Screen (<PrtSc>) key in Windows to take a snapshot of the screen and paste it automatically into the clipboard. When you use Windows Paintbrush, you can then paste the snapshot of the screen into the current document. Let's add this kind of power to our Paint application.

Visual Basic supports a **Clipboard** object with the methods indicated in Table 7-4. There are two usual ways of using the **Clipboard** object: to pass text or to

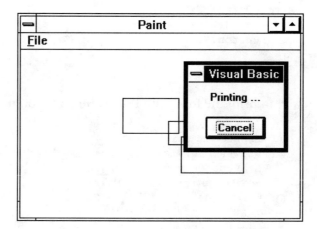

Figure 7-10. Visual Basic's Print Window

Method	Action
Clear	Clears the clipboard
GetText	Gets the text in the clipboard
GetData	Gets the graphics data in the clipboard
SetData	Pastes graphics data to the clipboard
GetFormat	Gets clipboard format (e.g., text or graphics)
SetText	Pastes text to the clipboard

Table 7-4. Clipboard Object Methods

pass graphics. Since we're designing a Paint application here, we'll be interested in graphics, and the two **Clipboard** methods we'll use are **GetData** and **SetData**.

To use the **Clipboard**, just add two items to the File menu: Paste from Clipboard and Paste to Clipboard by using the **CtlNames FromItem** and **ToItem**. We can make those items active by adding the appropriate lines to their procedures. To start, let's look at **GetData**, whose syntax is:

```
Clipboard.GetData ([format%])
```

Here, **format%** can take these values (defined with Const in CONSTANT.TXT):

```
CF_BITMAP      'Bitmap
CF_METFILE     'Metafile
CF_DIB         'Device Independent bitmap
```

If we omit **format%**, CF_BITMAP is assumed, which is the format we want here. This means that we can get the current picture from the Clipboard and paste it into our Paint application this way, in the Sub procedure FromItem_Click( ):

```
Sub FromItem_Click ()
    Picture = Clipboard.GetData()
End Sub
```

Now let's look at the process of pasting data into the Clipboard. To do that, we use the **Clipboard.SetData** method, whose syntax is:

```
Clipboard.SetData (data, [format%])
```

In our case, data refers to the Image property of our form, **Form1.Image**, and **format%** can be one of the following, as before:

```
CF_BITMAP          'Bitmap
CF_METFILE         'Metafile
CF_DIB             'Device Independent bitmap
```

That means that we can paste our form's picture to the Clipboard like this:

```
Sub ToItem_Click ()
    Clipboard.SetData Form1.Image
End Sub
```

Now we're able to paste to and from the clipboard, allowing us to communicate with other Windows applications. And that's it for the Paint application. The entire listing appears in Listing 7-4. We've come far with this program. We've seen how to use the mouse to draw freehand and draw lines, boxes, and circles, as well as how to position text with the mouse; how to save and retrieve graphics images to and from disk, print them, and use the clipboard.

TIP Of course, you can add further capabilities to the Paint application, even adding vertical and horizontal scroll bars if you like. The possibilities are endless.

Listing 7-4. Complete Paint Application

```
        Global Module -------------------------------------

Global AnchorX As Integer
Global AnchorY As Integer
Global DrawFlag As Integer
Global LineFlag As Integer
Global BoxFlag As Integer
Global CircleFlag As Integer
Global TextFlag As Integer
```

Listing 7-4. (continued)

```
        Form1 ---------------------------------------

Sub Form_MouseDown (Button As Integer,Shift As Integer,X As
        Single,Y As Single)
    If Button = 1 Then      'Left Button
        AnchorX = X
        AnchorY = Y
        CurrentX = X
        CurrentY = Y
    End If
End Sub

Sub Form_MouseMove (Button As Integer,Shift As Integer,X As
        Single,Y As Single)
    If (Button = 1) Then
        If DrawFlag Then
            Line -(X, Y)
        End If

        If LineFlag Then
            TempFore& = ForeColor
            TempMode% = DrawMode
            ForeColor = BackColor
            DrawMode = 7                'Xor mode
            Line (AnchorX, AnchorY)-(CurrentX, CurrentY)
            Line (AnchorX, AnchorY)-(X, Y)
            ForeColor = TempFore&
            DrawMode = TempMode%
        End If

        If BoxFlag Then
            TempFore& = ForeColor
            TempMode% = DrawMode
            ForeColor = BackColor
            DrawMode = 7                'Xor mode
            Line (AnchorX, AnchorY)-(CurrentX, CurrentY), , B
            Line (AnchorX, AnchorY)-(X, Y), , B
            ForeColor = TempFore&
            DrawMode = TempMode%
        End If

        If CircleFlag Then
            TempFore& = ForeColor
```

(continued)

Listing 7-4. (continued)

```
                TempMode% = DrawMode
                ForeColor = BackColor
                DrawMode = 7                'Xor mode
                radius! = Sqr((AnchorX - CurrentX) ^ 2 + (AnchorY -
                    CurrentY)^ 2)
                Circle (AnchorX, AnchorY), radius!
                radius! = Sqr((AnchorX - X) ^ 2 + (AnchorY - Y) ^ 2)
                Circle (AnchorX, AnchorY), radius!
                CurrentX = X
                CurrentY = Y
                ForeColor = TempFore&
                DrawMode = TempMode%
            End If

        End If
End Sub

Sub Form_MouseUp (Button As Integer, Shift As Integer, X As
        Single, Y As Single)
    If Button = 1 Then
        If LineFlag Then
            Line (AnchorX, AnchorY)-(X, Y)
        End If

        If BoxFlag Then
            Line (AnchorX, AnchorY)-(X, Y), , B
        End If

        If CircleFlag Then
            radius! = Sqr((AnchorX - X) ^ 2 + (AnchorY - Y) ^ 2)
            Circle (AnchorX, AnchorY), radius!
        End If
    End If
End Sub

Sub ClearButton_Click ()
    Cls
End Sub

Sub DrawButton_Click ()
    DrawFlag = True
    LineFlag = False
    BoxFlag = False
    CircleFlag = False
    TextFlag = False
End Sub
```

Listing 7-4. (continued)

```
Sub LineButton_Click ()
    DrawFlag = False
    LineFlag = True
    BoxFlag = False
    CircleFlag = False
    TextFlag = False
End Sub

Sub BoxButton_Click ()
    DrawFlag = False
    LineFlag = False
    BoxFlag = True
    CircleFlag = False
    TextFlag = False
End Sub

Sub CircleButton_Click ()
    DrawFlag = False
    LineFlag = False
    BoxFlag = False
    CircleFlag = True
    TextFlag = False
End Sub

Sub TextButton_Click ()
    DrawFlag = False
    LineFlag = False
    BoxFlag = False
    CircleFlag = False
    TextFlag = True
End Sub

Sub TextButton_KeyPress (KeyAscii As Integer)
    Print Chr$(KeyAscii);
End Sub

Sub ExitItem_Click ()
    End
End Sub

Sub SaveItem_Click ()
    SaveForm.Show
End Sub
```

(continued)

Listing 7-4. (continued)

```
Sub LoadItem_Click ()
    LoadForm.Show
End Sub

Sub DrawingItem_Click ()
    ControlPanel.NewColor.BackColor = ForeColor
    ControlPanel.Show
End Sub

Sub PrintItem_Click ()
        DrawButton.Visible = False
        LineButton.Visible = False
        BoxButton.Visible = False
        CircleButton.Visible = False
        TextButton.Visible = False
        ClearButton.Visible = False
        PrintForm
        DrawButton.Visible = True
        LineButton.Visible = True
        BoxButton.Visible = True
        CircleButton.Visible = True
        TextButton.Visible = True
        ClearButton.Visible = True
End Sub

Sub FromItem_Click ()
        Picture = Clipboard.GetData()
End Sub

Sub ToItem_Click ()
        Clipboard.SetData Form1.Image
End Sub

        SaveForm ----------------------------------------

Sub CancelButton_Click ()
    SaveForm.Hide
End Sub

Sub OKButton_Click ()
    'On Error GoTo FileError
    SavePicture Form1.Image, FileNameBox.Text
    SaveForm.Hide
    Exit Sub
```

Listing 7-4. (continued)

```
FileError:
    MsgBox "File Error", 48, "Paint"
    Resume
End Sub


        LoadForm ----------------------------------

Sub CancelButton_Click ()
    LoadForm.Hide
End Sub

Sub Drive1_Change ()
    Dir1.Path = Drive1.Drive
End Sub

Sub Dir1_Change ()
    File1.Path = Dir1.Path
End Sub

Sub OKButton_Click ()
    On Error GoTo FileError
    If (Right$(Dir1.Path, 1) = "\") Then
        Filename$ = Dir1.Path + File1.Filename
    Else
        Filename$ = Dir1.Path + "\" + File1.Filename
    End If
    Form1.Picture = LoadPicture(Filename$)
    LoadForm.Hide
    Exit Sub

FileError:
    MsgBox "File Error", 48, "Editor"
    Resume
End Sub

Sub File1_DblClick ()
    OKButton_Click
End Sub

Sub CancelButton_Click ()
    ControlPanel.Hide
End Sub
```

(continued)

Listing 7-4. (continued)

```
        ControlPanel ------------------------------------

Sub OKButton_Click ()

    Form1.ForeColor = RGB(NewRed.Value, NewGreen.Value, NewBlue.Value)
    ControlPanel.Hide
End Sub

Sub NewRed_Change ()
    NewColor.BackColor = RGB(NewRed.Value, NewGreen.Value,
        NewBlue.Value)
End Sub

Sub NewGreen_Change ()
    NewColor.BackColor = RGB(NewRed.Value, NewGreen.Value,
        NewBlue.Value)
End Sub

Sub NewBlue_Change ()
    NewColor.BackColor = RGB(NewRed.Value, NewGreen.Value,
        NewBlue.Value)

End Sub
```

Before leaving the subject of graphics, however, there is one more consideration that we should examine, and it involves the *scale* that we use.

Graphics Scaling

So far, we've used twips, the default unit of measurement in Visual Basic. However, we don't have to use twips forever. In fact, if you do a lot of graphics programming with Visual Basic, you'll find that there are times that you'll want to use other units. For example, if you want to draw a grid on the screen, you'll have to specify where your lines go. If you use twips, you'll find that your measurements are converted to pixels, and that can cause problems. If you specify a twip spacing between grid lines that turns out to be 36.7 pixels, those lines will not always be the same distance apart on the screen (and if the grid spacing is small, this effect will be very noticeable). Instead, the best thing here is to use a pixel scale, and work in pixels from then on. To do that, set the

ScaleMode	Means
0	User-defined; ScaleHeight, ScaleWidth already set
1	Twips (1,440 twips per inch)
2	Points (72 points per inch)
3	Pixels (dot on monitor screen)
4	Character (120 twips on x-axis; 240 twips on y-axis)
5	Inches
6	Millimeters
7	Centimeters

Table 7-5. ScaleMode Values

form's **ScaleMode** property as shown in Table 7-5 (the **ScaleMode** property is available for picture boxes, forms, and the **Printer** object).

| TIP | If you want to find the size of the current screen in pixels, use the **Screen** object, and check the **Screen.Width** and **Screen.Height** properties. |

Besides these predefined scales, you can even design your own scale. For example, this can make drawing graphs very easy if you set up a system of units so that both x and y directions are exactly 100 units. To plot a point at (56, 93) on your graph, you'd just have to use **PSet(56, 93)**. You can set such a scale simply by setting the **ScaleWidth** and **ScaleHeight** properties of the form or picture box yourself. For example, to make the form or picture box 100 × 100 units, set both **ScaleWidth** and **ScaleHeight** to 100.

This has another use too. If you've set up a custom scale and the user resizes the window, you don't have to make any changes in the way you send graphics to the screen. For instance, if you've made your window 100 × 100 units, and the user doubles the size of the window, it's still 100 × 100 units. If you want to know when the user has resized the window, you should watch for *Resize* events (which only occur if **AutoRedraw** is False). Every time the user resizes the window, one of these events occurs, allowing you to redraw what's on it if you like (for example, if you're using a custom scale of 100 × 100, you can simply redraw your whole graph as before, and Visual Basic will shape it to the new window's dimensions).

That's it for graphics, our Paint application, and the mouse. It's time to move on now for some behind-the-scenes work (non-I/O), and in the next chapter, we'll start looking at some advanced data handling.

Advanced Data Handling and Sorting in Visual Basic

In this chapter we'll work through just about all the ways there are of organizing data in Visual Basic (and then we'll add a few of our own). Organizing your data for easy access can be crucial in program development for speed in both program coding and execution. In fact, organizing your data at the beginning may win you more than half the battle of writing a program.

We'll work through the most helpful methods of arranging data, including arrays, data structures, linked lists, circular buffers, and binary trees. Programmers should be familiar with these common methods of organizing data and not continually have to reinvent the wheel. And, at the end of the chapter, we'll examine two fast sorting methods to get the most out of our data, as well as a fast searching algorithm to search through sorted arrays.

Variables

The most elementary method of organizing data is by storing it in simple variables. Table 8-1 shows the standard types used in Visual Basic.

Type	Symbol	Bytes	Range
Integer	%	2	-32,768 to 32,767
Long	&	4	-2,147,483,648 to 2,147,483,647
Single	!	4	-3.402823E38 to -1.40129E-45
Double	#	8	-1.79769313486232D308 to -2.2250738585072D-308
Currency	@	8	-\$922337203685477.5808 to \$922337203685477.5807
String	$	32K	Strings can range up to 32K characters (bytes)

Table 8-1. Standard Visual Basic Variable Types

We're familiar with all of these, except perhaps the Currency type. You use that type to store amounts of money. Here's an example (results are printed out to the nearest cent):

```
Sub Form_Load ()
    Savings@ = 6000.00
    Rent@ = 775.00
    Food@ = 124.50
    Bills@ = 513.72

    Savings@ = Savings@ - Rent@
    Savings@ = Savings@ - Food@
    Savings@ = Savings@ - Bills@

    Print "Money left: $"; Savings@
End Sub
```

This example prints out how much of your savings are left after paying rent and the bills. For most purposes, you can think of a Currency variable as a more accurate Long variable with four decimal places added on to it as well (although the last two decimal places are for internal accuracy only).

In many versions of Basic, the next step up in data handling is the Data statement, which you're probably familiar with, and which works like this, where we calculate the sum and product of the numbers 1-10, stored in a Data statement:

```
    Sum& = 0
    Product& = 1
```

```
      For i = 1 To 10
→            Read Number&
             Sum& = Sum& + Number&
      Next i

      Print "The sum of your data is:"; Sum&

→     Data 1, 2, 3, 4, 5, 6, 7, 8, 9, 10
```

However, there are a number of Basic statements that Visual Basic does not support, and Data (which is largely considered obsolete) is one of them. Instead, the next step up in data handling in Visual Basic is working with something we're already familiar with: arrays.

Arrays

We're all familiar with arrays, such as the one in this example (set the form's **AutoRedraw** property to True so we can draw text from the **Form_Load( )** procedure):

```
Sub Form_Load()
    Static Array(10, 2) As Currency   ←

    'Fill Array(n,1) with today's sales:

    Array(1, 1) = 10.00
    Array(2, 1) = 53.00
    Array(3, 1) = 7.17
    Array(4, 1) = 9.67
    Array(5, 1) = 87.99
    Array(6, 1) = 14.00
    Array(7, 1) = 91.19
    Array(8, 1) = 12.73
    Array(9, 1) = 1.03
    Array(10, 1) = 5.04

    'Fill Array(n,2) with yesterday's sales:

    Array(1, 2) = 9.67
    Array(2, 2) = 3.5
    Array(3, 2) = 8.97
    Array(4, 2) = 10.00
    Array(5, 2) = 78.33
    Array(6, 2) = 17.00
    Array(7, 2) = 91.36
```

```
        Array(8, 2) = 12.73
        Array(9, 2) = 16.12
        Array(10, 2) = 7.98

        Print "     SALES (in $)"
        Print "Yesterday" ; Tab(20) ; "Today"
        Print "---------" ; Tab(20) ; "-----"
        For loop_index = 1 To 10
                Print Array(loop_index, 1) ; Tab(20) ; Array(loop_index, 2)
        Next loop_index
        Print "---------" ; Tab(20) ; "-----"

        Sum1@ = 0
        Sum2@ = 0
        For loop_index = 1 To 10
            Sum1@ = Sum1@ + Array(loop_index, 1)
            Sum2@ = Sum2@ + Array(loop_index, 2)
        Next loop_index

        Print Sum1@ ; Tab(20) ; Sum2@ ; " = Total"

    End Sub
```

In this program, we're setting up an array of 10 rows and 2 columns to hold sales values for the last two days:

```
Static Array(10, 2) As Currency  ←

'Fill Array(n,1) with today's sales:

Array(1, 1) = 10.00
Array(2, 1) = 53.00
Array(3, 1) = 7.17
Array(4, 1) = 9.67
Array(5, 1) = 87.99
Array(6, 1) = 14.00
Array(7, 1) = 91.19
Array(8, 1) = 12.73
Array(9, 1) = 1.03
Array(10, 1) = 5.04

'Fill Array(n,2) with yesterday's sales:

Array(1, 2) = 9.67
Array(2, 2) = 3.5
```

```
Array(3, 2) = 8.97
Array(4, 2) = 10.00
Array(5, 2) = 78.33
Array(6, 2) = 17.00
Array(7, 2) = 91.36
Array(8, 2) = 12.73
Array(9, 2) = 16.12
Array(10, 2) = 7.98
  : :
```

And this is the array produced:

Col 1	Col 2
10.00	9.67
53.00	3.5
7.17	8.97
9.67	10.00
87.99	78.33
14.00	17.00
91.19	91.36
12.73	12.73
1.03	16.12
5.04	7.98

← Row 1 (10.00, 9.67)

← Row 2 (53.00, 3.5)

The reason we declare this array with Static instead of Dim is that in Visual Basic, you must use Static to declare a fixed size array in non-Static procedures (i.e., if you declare the whole procedure Static, you can use either Dim or Static). Declaring an array Static like this means that the values in this array won't change between calls to this procedure. Now we can reach each day's column of sales just by incrementing the column index. In this format, we can perform parallel operations on parallel sets of data, like adding the columns of sales to produce sums as in our example program:

```
Sub Form_Load()
    Static Array(10, 2) As Currency  ←

    'Fill Array(n,1) with today's sales:

    Array(1,  1) = 10.00
    Array(2,  1) = 53.00
    Array(3,  1) = 7.17
    Array(4,  1) = 9.67
    Array(5,  1) = 87.99
    Array(6,  1) = 14.00
    Array(7,  1) = 91.19
    Array(8,  1) = 12.73
    Array(9,  1) = 1.03
    Array(10, 1) = 5.04

    'Fill Array(n,2) with yesterday's sales:

    Array(1,  2) = 9.67
    Array(2,  2) = 3.5
    Array(3,  2) = 8.97
    Array(4,  2) = 10.00
    Array(5,  2) = 78.33
    Array(6,  2) = 17.00
    Array(7,  2) = 91.36
    Array(8,  2) = 12.73
    Array(9,  2) = 16.12
    Array(10, 2) = 7.98

    Print "     SALES (in $)"
    Print "Yesterday" ; Tab(20) ; "Today"
    Print "---------" ; Tab(20) ; "-----"
    For loop_index = 1 To 10
        Print Array(loop_index, 1) ; Tab(20) ; Array(loop_index, 2)
    Next loop_index
    Print "---------" ; Tab(20) ; "-----"

    Sum1@ = 0
    Sum2@ = 0
    For loop_index = 1 To 10
        Sum1@ = Sum1@ + Array(loop_index, 1)
        Sum2@ = Sum2@ + Array(loop_index, 2)
    Next loop_index

    Print Sum1@ ; Tab(20) ; Sum2@ ; " = Total"
End Sub
```

The results of this program appear in Figure 8-1.

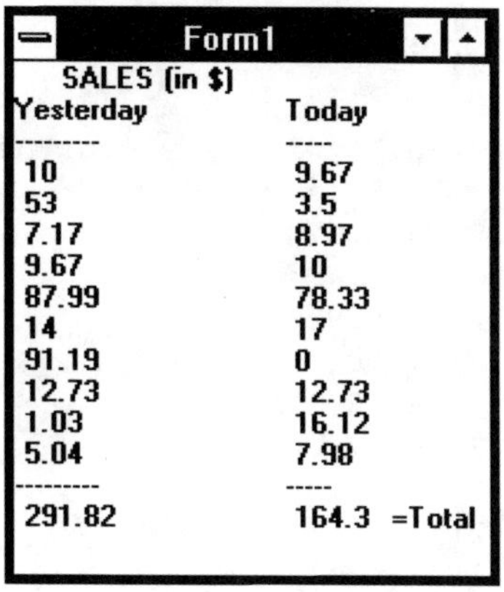

```
┌──────────────────────────────────┐
│ ═        Form1          ▼  ▲      │
│    SALES (in $)                   │
│ Yesterday          Today          │
│ ----------         -----          │
│ 10                 9.67           │
│ 53                 3.5            │
│ 7.17               8.97           │
│ 9.67               10             │
│ 87.99              78.33          │
│ 14                 17             │
│ 91.19              0              │
│ 12.73              12.73          │
│ 1.03               16.12          │
│ 5.04               7.98           │
│ ----------         -----          │
│ 291.82             164.3  =Total  │
│                                   │
└──────────────────────────────────┘
```

Figure 8-1. Array Example

In Visual Basic, you can also declare arrays as *dynamic,* which means that you can redimension them with the *ReDim* statement at run-time. To declare a dynamic array at the procedure level, just declare it using Dim and with no arguments in the parentheses:

```
Sub Form_Load()
    Dim Array() As Currency            ←
:
```

Now you can redimension it whenever you want to, and use it as we have before:

```
Sub Form_Load()
    Dim Array() As Currency

    ReDim Array(10, 2) As Currency     ←

    'Fill Array(n,1) with today's sales:

    Array(1, 1) = 10.00
    Array(2, 1) = 53.00
    Array(3, 1) = 7.17
    Array(4, 1) = 9.67
    Array(5, 1) = 87.99
    Array(6, 1) = 14.00
    Array(7, 1) = 91.19
    Array(8, 1) = 12.73
```

```
        Array(9, 1) = 1.03
        Array(10, 1) = 5.04

        'Fill Array(n,2) with yesterday's sales:

        Array(1, 2) = 9.67
        Array(2, 2) = 3.5
        Array(3, 2) = 8.97
        Array(4, 2) = 10.00
        Array(5, 2) = 78.33
        Array(6, 2) = 17.00
        Array(7, 2) = 91.36
        Array(8, 2) = 12.73
        Array(9, 2) = 16.12
        Array(10, 2) = 7.98
            :

    End Sub
```

The ReDim statement initializes all elements of the array to 0. In addition, you can't use ReDim to create arrays with more than eight dimensions, and there is a limit on the size of dynamic or static arrays in Visual Basic of 64K.

That's really it. Arrays don't get very complex in Visual Basic, unlike in C where array names are just pointers (and two-dimensional array names are just pointers to pointers). There you can really go wild, saving both time and memory by converting all array references to pointer references and making your code extremely hard to read at the same time.

As it is, we've gotten about as complex as arrays get in Visual Basic, so let's move on to the next most advanced way of organizing data after arrays: data structures.

Data Structures

As we've seen to some extent already, we can group the standard data types together and come up with a whole new type of our own. To define a Type named **Person**, we can do this:

```
Type Person
    FirstName As String * 20
    LastName As String * 20
End Type
    :
```

Note that we have to put this Type definition into the global module in Visual Basic since that's the only place Type is valid. In addition, we can actually use variables length strings in Type statements (except when we're using variables of this type as records in a random access file, as we saw before). The data structure we've created here just stores a person's first and last names. We can set up a variable of this type or, even more powerfully, an array of variables of this type (use Global in the global module, Static in non-static procedures):

```
Type Person
    FirstName As String * 20
    LastName As String * 20
End Type

→   Global People(10) As Person
    :
```

And then we reference them like this in our procedures:

```
People(1).FirstName = "Al"
People(1).LastName = "Einstein"

People(2).FirstName = "Frank"
People(2).LastName = "Roosevelt"

People(2).FirstName = "Charlie"
People(2).LastName = "DeGaulle"

Print People(1).FirstName
:
```

But that's not the end to working with data structures. If there is some connection between the elements of our array, we can connect them into a *linked list*.

Linked Lists

Linked lists are good for organizing data items into sequential chains, especially if you have a number of such chains to manage and want to use space efficiently.

They work this way: For each data item, there is also a *pointer* pointing to the next data item; that is, an index of some sort that references the next data item, as we'll see below. We find the next item in the list by referring to the pointer in the present item. At any time, you can add another data item to the list, as long as you update the current pointer to point to the new data item:

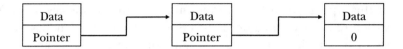

The last pointer in the chain is a null pointer with a value of 0 (so you know the list is done when you reach it). A prominent example of a linked list in your computer is the File Allocation Table (FAT) on disks. This is a list of the clusters allocated to files for storage. Files are stored cluster by cluster, and, for each cluster on the disk, there is one entry in the FAT.

NOTE   A cluster is the minimum size of disk storage allocation. On 360K diskettes, clusters are two sectors — 1,024 bytes — long. This means, incidentally, that the amount of free space on 360K diskettes is always reported in units of 1,024 bytes.

To see what clusters a file is stored in, you get its first cluster number from the internal data in its directory entry. Let's say that number is 2. That means that the first section of the file is stored in cluster 2 on the disk. This number is also the key to the FAT for us. We can find the *next* cluster occupied by the file by looking in cluster 2's entry in the FAT:

FAT Entry #	2	3	4	5	6	7	8	9	10	11	12	13
	3	4	6	32	7	End	29	10	End	0	0	0

That cluster's entry in the FAT holds 3, which is the number of the next cluster that the file occupies on the disk. To find the cluster after 3, check the entry in the File Allocation Table for that cluster:

FAT Entry #	2	3	4	5	6	7	8	9	10	11	12	13
	3	4	6	32	7	End	29	10	End	0	0	0

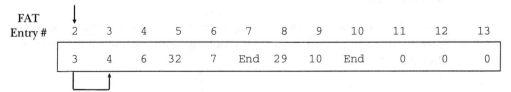

That holds 4, so the next section of the file is in cluster 4. To continue from there, check the number in the FAT entry for cluster 4:

FAT Entry #

2	3	4	5	6	7	8	9	10	11	12	13
3	4	6	32	7	End	29	10	End	0	0	0

That number is 6, and you continue on until you come to the end-of-file mark in the FAT:

FAT Entry #

2	3	4	5	6	7	8	9	10	11	12	13
3	4	6	32	7	End	29	10	End	0	0	0

In other words, this file is stored in clusters 2, 3, 4, 6, and 7. Notice that 5 was already taken by another file, which is also weaving its own thread of clusters through the FAT at the same time. Linked lists like this are used when you want to use memory or disk space efficiently and have to keep track of a number of sequential chains of data. For example, when this file is deleted, its entries in the FAT can be written over, and those clusters can be taken by another file.

Let's see an example of a linked list in Visual Basic. For example, we might have these two distinct career paths to keep track of:

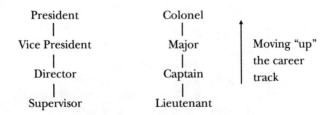

We can connect the various levels with a linked list. We start by setting up a variable of type **Person** in the global module as follows:

```
→   Type Person
→       Rank As String * 20
→       SuperiorPointer As Integer
→   End Type
```

Now we fill the Rank fields: We can fill them in any order; the **SuperiorPointers** will keep them straight:

```
Sub Form_Load ()

    'Linked List Example

    Static People(10) As Person

→   People(1).Rank = "Supervisor"
:   People(2).Rank = "Major"
:   People(3).Rank = "Director"
    People(4).Rank = "President"
    People(5).Rank = "Captain"
    People(6).Rank = "Vice President"
    People(7).Rank = "Colonel"
    People(8).Rank = "Lieutenant"
            :
```

For each entry in **People( )**, there's also a "superior" position. For example, the superior of the entry in **People(1)** — Supervisor — is in **People(3)** — Director. To link the entries in each of the two chains, we have to point to the superior rank by filling the pointers **Person().SuperiorPointer**:

```
Sub Form_Load ()

    'Linked List Example

    Static People(10) As Person

    People(1).Rank = "Supervisor"
    People(2).Rank = "Major"
    People(3).Rank = "Director"
    People(4).Rank = "President"
    People(5).Rank = "Captain"
    People(6).Rank = "Vice President"
    People(7).Rank = "Colonel"
    People(8).Rank = "Lieutenant"

→   People(1).SuperiorPointer = 3
:   People(2).SuperiorPointer = 7
:   People(3).SuperiorPointer = 6
    People(4).SuperiorPointer = 0
    People(5).SuperiorPointer = 2
    People(6).SuperiorPointer = 4
```

```
        People(7).SuperiorPointer = 0
        People(8).SuperiorPointer = 5
            :
```

Now that all the items in the two lists are linked, we can choose a number, 1 or 2, and work our way through the first or second linked list, printing out the various **Rank** names as we go. In this example, let's choose life track 1:

```
    Sub Form_Load ()

    'Linked List Example

        Static People(10) As Person

        People(1).Rank = "Supervisor"
        People(2).Rank = "Major"
        People(3).Rank = "Director"
        People(4).Rank = "President"
        People(5).Rank = "Captain"
        People(6).Rank = "Vice President"
        People(7).Rank = "Colonel"
        People(8).Rank = "Lieutenant"

        People(1).SuperiorPointer = 3
        People(2).SuperiorPointer = 7
        People(3).SuperiorPointer = 6
        People(4).SuperiorPointer = 0
        People(5).SuperiorPointer = 2
        People(6).SuperiorPointer = 4
        People(7).SuperiorPointer = 0
        People(8).SuperiorPointer = 5

→       Index = 1

→       Do
→           Print People(Index).Rank      'Print out results.
→           Index = People(Index).SuperiorPointer
→       Loop While Index <> 0

    End Sub
```

When this program runs, it prints out life track 1, and we see this list on the form:

Supervisor
Director
Vice President
President

Note that we must know in advance that chain 1 starts with entry 1 and chain 2 with entry 8. We always need the first entry to use as a key to the first position in the linked list. After that we can work our way up either chain of command. As we do so, we print out the current **Rank** and get a pointer to (that is, the array index number of) the next **Rank** at the same time.

Circular Buffers

There is another type of linked list that programmers often use: a list where the last item points to the first one so the whole thing forms a circle. This is called a circular buffer. The most well-known circular buffer in your computer is the keyboard buffer.

What happens there is that while one part of the operating system is putting key codes into the keyboard buffer, another part of the operating system is taking them out. The location in the buffer where the next key code will be placed is called the "tail," and the location where the next key code is to be read from is called the "head."

When keys are typed in, the tail advances. When they are read, the head does. As you write to and read from the keyboard buffer, the head and tail march around (each data location can be either the head or the tail). When the buffer is filled, the tail comes up behind the head, and the buffer-full warning beeps.

You can use circular buffers when some part of your program is writing data and some other part is reading it, but at different rates. Store the location of the head and tail positions, and after you put data into the buffer, advance the tail. When you take data out, advance the head. This way, you can use the same memory space for both reading and writing.

The primary problem with linked lists, however, is that all access to their data is sequential access. To find the last entry in a linked list, for example, you have to start at the very first one and work your way back. That's fine for files tracked through the FAT (where you need every FAT entry before you can read the whole file), but it's a terrible method if you're only looking for a specific record. A better way is to make what's called a *binary tree*.

Binary Trees

Binary trees differ from linked lists in that the data is ordered. We can start with a linked list:

And then make it a *doubly linked list*:

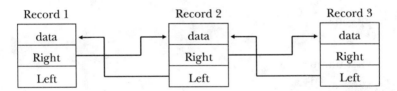

Now there are two pointers in each record; one scans up the chain, the other down. Doubly linked lists have many uses in themselves, but this is still not a binary tree. Instead, let's put in some values for the data fields, -5, 0, and 2:

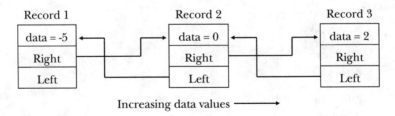

Increasing data values ⟶

Notice that we've constructed a hierarchy based on data values here, arranging them from left to right in increasing order (-5, 0, 2). The record with the data value closest to the median data value becomes the *root* of our binary tree:

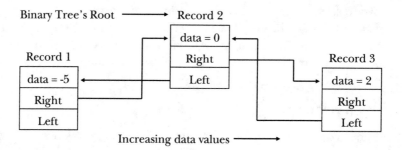

Because it has the data value closest to the middle of all three records, record 2 is the root of our binary tree. If we wanted to find a record with a data value of, say, -5, we'd start at the root, record 2, whose data value is 0. Since -5 is less than 0, we would next search the record to its left (since data values decrease to the left). This record is record 1, with a data value of -5, which means that we've found our target value. This might seem like a small gain here, but imagine having a list like this:

First name = "Denise"
   Age = 23

First name = "Ed"
   Age = 46

First name = "Nick"
   Age = 47

First name = "Dennis"
   Age = 42

First name = "Doug"
   Age = 33

First name = "Margo"
   Age = 27

First name = "John"
   Age = 41

First name = "Cheryl"
   Age = 28

Let's say that it is your job to coordinate this list and find a person with a specified age. To construct a binary tree, you'd pick the person with an age as close to the median as possible (Doug), and put the tree together like this:

Doug (33)

Cheryl (28)   John (41)

Margo (27)   Dennis (42)

Denise (23)   Ed (46)

Nick (47)

Now you can start with Doug and just keep working until you find the age you require. For example, to find the person who is 46 years old, start at Doug, who is 33. Since 46 is greater than 33, continue moving to the right through John and Dennis to Ed, who is the person we're searching for.

We should note that this is an extremely simple binary tree, since, with the exception of Doug, each node only has one way to go — in general, each node can go both ways. Let's put this example into code. We start off by defining a new **Person** Type in the global module, which has two pointers, one to the next older person, and one to the next younger:

```
Type Person
    FirstName As String * 20
    Age As Integer
    NextYoungerPerson As Integer
    NextOlderPerson As Integer
End Type
```

Now we can use that type in a **Form_Load( )** Sub procedure:

```
Sub Form_Load ()

    'Binary Tree example.

→   Static People(10) As Person
:
:   People(1).FirstName = "Denise"
    People(1).Age = 23
    People(1).NextYoungerPerson = 0
    People(1).NextOlderPerson = 6

    People(2).FirstName = "Ed"
    People(2).Age = 46
    People(2).NextYoungerPerson = 4
    People(2).NextOlderPerson = 3

    People(3).FirstName = "Nick"
    People(3).Age = 47
    People(3).NextYoungerPerson = 2
    People(3).NextOlderPerson = 0
```

```
People(4).FirstName = "Dennis"
People(4).Age = 42
People(4).NextYoungerPerson = 7
People(4).NextOlderPerson = 2

People(5).FirstName = "Doug"
People(5).Age = 33
People(5).NextYoungerPerson = 8
People(5).NextOlderPerson = 7

People(6).FirstName = "Margo"
People(6).Age = 27
People(6).NextYoungerPerson = 1
People(6).NextOlderPerson = 8

People(7).FirstName = "John"
People(7).Age = 41
People(7).NextYoungerPerson = 5
People(7).NextOlderPerson = 4

People(8).FirstName = "Cheryl"
People(8).Age = 28
People(8).NextYoungerPerson = 6
People(8).NextOlderPerson = 5
            :
            :
```

Now we can search for the first person who is 46 years old. First, we start off at the root:

```
Sub Form_Load ()

    'Binary Tree example.

    Static People(10) As Person

    People(1).FirstName = "Denise"
    People(1).Age = 23
    People(1).NextYoungerPerson = 0
    People(1).NextOlderPerson = 6

    People(2).FirstName = "Ed"
    People(2).Age = 46
    People(2).NextYoungerPerson = 4
    People(2).NextOlderPerson = 3

    People(3).FirstName = "Nick"
    People(3).Age = 47
```

```
        People(3).NextYoungerPerson = 2
        People(3).NextOlderPerson = 0

        People(4).FirstName = "Dennis"
        People(4).Age = 42
        People(4).NextYoungerPerson = 7
        People(4).NextOlderPerson = 2

        People(5).FirstName = "Doug"
        People(5).Age = 33
        People(5).NextYoungerPerson = 8
        People(5).NextOlderPerson = 7

        People(6).FirstName = "Margo"
        People(6).Age = 27
        People(6).NextYoungerPerson = 1
        People(6).NextOlderPerson = 8

        People(7).FirstName = "John"
        People(7).Age = 41
        People(7).NextYoungerPerson = 5
        People(7).NextOlderPerson = 4

        People(8).FirstName = "Cheryl"
        People(8).Age = 28
        People(8).NextYoungerPerson = 6
        People(8).NextOlderPerson = 5
```

→   ` BinaryTreeRoot% = 5     'Doug has about the median age`

→   ` Print "Searching for a person 46 years old..."`

→   ` CurrentRecord% = BinaryTreeRoot%`
```
            :
            :
```

And check to see if that person is 46 years old:

```
    Sub Form_Load ()

        'Binary Tree example.

        Static People(10) As Person

        People(1).FirstName = "Denise"
        People(1).Age = 23
        People(1).NextYoungerPerson = 0
        People(1).NextOlderPerson = 6
```

```
People(2).FirstName = "Ed"
People(2).Age = 46
People(2).NextYoungerPerson = 4
People(2).NextOlderPerson = 3

People(3).FirstName = "Nick"
People(3).Age = 47
People(3).NextYoungerPerson = 2
People(3).NextOlderPerson = 0

People(4).FirstName = "Dennis"
People(4).Age = 42
People(4).NextYoungerPerson = 7
People(4).NextOlderPerson = 2

People(5).FirstName = "Doug"
People(5).Age = 33
People(5).NextYoungerPerson = 8
People(5).NextOlderPerson = 7

People(6).FirstName = "Margo"
People(6).Age = 27
People(6).NextYoungerPerson = 1
People(6).NextOlderPerson = 8

People(7).FirstName = "John"
People(7).Age = 41
People(7).NextYoungerPerson = 5
People(7).NextOlderPerson = 4

People(8).FirstName = "Cheryl"
People(8).Age = 28
People(8).NextYoungerPerson = 6
People(8).NextOlderPerson = 5

BinaryTreeRoot% = 5     'Doug has about the median age

Print "Searching for a person 46 years old..."

CurrentRecord% = BinaryTreeRoot%

Do
    If People(CurrentRecord%).Age = 46 Then
      Print "That person is: "; People(CurrentRecord%).FirstName
      Exit Do
    End If
      :
      :
```

If not, then we have to compare the current person's age to 46. If it's less, then we want the **NextOlderPerson**; if greater, then we want the **NextYoungerPerson**. That looks like this in **Form_Load( )**:

```
Sub Form_Load ()

    'Binary Tree example.

    Static People(10) As Person

    People(1).FirstName = "Denise"
    People(1).Age = 23
    People(1).NextYoungerPerson = 0
    People(1).NextOlderPerson = 6

    People(2).FirstName = "Ed"
    People(2).Age = 46
    People(2).NextYoungerPerson = 4
    People(2).NextOlderPerson = 3

    People(3).FirstName = "Nick"
    People(3).Age = 47
    People(3).NextYoungerPerson = 2
    People(3).NextOlderPerson = 0

    People(4).FirstName = "Dennis"
    People(4).Age = 42
    People(4).NextYoungerPerson = 7
    People(4).NextOlderPerson = 2

    People(5).FirstName = "Doug"
    People(5).Age = 33
    People(5).NextYoungerPerson = 8
    People(5).NextOlderPerson = 7

    People(6).FirstName = "Margo"
    People(6).Age = 27
    People(6).NextYoungerPerson = 1
    People(6).NextOlderPerson = 8

    People(7).FirstName = "John"
    People(7).Age = 41
    People(7).NextYoungerPerson = 5
    People(7).NextOlderPerson = 4

    People(8).FirstName = "Cheryl"
    People(8).Age = 28
```

```
            People(8).NextYoungerPerson = 6
            People(8).NextOlderPerson = 5

            BinaryTreeRoot% = 5      'Doug has about the median age

            Print "Searching for a person 46 years old..."

            CurrentRecord% = BinaryTreeRoot%

            Do
                If People(CurrentRecord%).Age = 46 Then
                    Print "That person is: "; People(CurrentRecord%).FirstName
                    Exit Do
                End If
      →         If People(CurrentRecord%).Age > 46 Then
      :              CurrentRecord% = People(CurrentRecord%).NextYoungerPerson
      :          Else
                     CurrentRecord% = People(CurrentRecord%).NextOlderPerson
                End If
            Loop While CurrentRecord% <> 0

        End Sub
```

And that's how to search through a binary tree. We just keep going until we find what we're looking for (or we run out of branches). The results of this program appear in Figure 8-2.

With binary trees, we've started ordering our data. That is, we've established the relative position of a record with respect to its two neighbors. But what if we wanted to sort all the data? Sorting data is, of course, a very common thing to do. It's the next, more advanced step in organizing our data. And, because it's so common, we should explore it in some detail. To do that, we'll work through two of the fastest algorithms available, shell sorts and the QuickSort. And we'll put them to work.

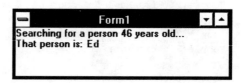

Figure 8-2. Binary Tree Example

Shell Sorts

The standard shell sort is always popular among programmers. It works like this: Say you had a one-dimensional array with these values in it:

8 7 6 5 4 3 2 1

To sort this list into ascending order, divide it into two partitions like this:

8 7 6 5 4 3 2 1

Then compare the first element of the first partition with the first element of the second:

8 7 6 5 4 3 2 1

In this case, 8 is greater than 4, so we switch the elements, and go on to compare the next pair:

4 7 6 5 8 3 2 1

Again, 7 is greater than 3, so we switch and go on:

4 3 6 5 8 7 2 1

We also switch 6 and 2 and then look at the last pair:

4 3 2 5 8 7 6 1

After we switch them too, we get this as the new list:

4 3 2 1 8 7 6 5

While this is somewhat better than before, we're still not done. The next step is to divide each partition itself into two partitions, and repeat the process, comparing 4 with 2 and 8 with 6:

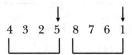

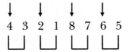

We switch both pairs and go on, comparing 3 with 1 and 7 with 5:

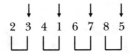

Again, we switch the second set of two pairs, leaving us with this:

2 1 4 3 6 5 8 7

This looks even closer. Now the partition size is down to one element, which means that this is the last time we'll need to sort the list. We need to compare the first, and only, element in each partition with the first, and only, element in the next partition. Here that means that we compare elements 2, 4, 6, and 8 with elements 1, 3, 5, and 7. When we swap them all, we get:

1 2 3 4 5 6 7 8

And that is how the standard shell sort works, at least if there's an even number of items to sort (in which case breaking them up into balanced partitions is easy). The case where we have an odd number of elements is slightly more difficult. For example, if we had a list of nine elements to sort, we would start by breaking them up into two partitions like this (note that there is no last element in the second partition):

9 8 7 6 5 4 3 2 1 x

Now we'd compare as before, switching as necessary, until we try to compare a value in the first partition to a value in the second partition that isn't there:

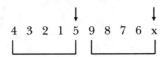

In this case, we just don't perform any comparison (i.e., there is no value in the x position that might have to be placed earlier in the array). Instead, we just continue on to the next smaller partition size. We keep going as before, working until the partition size becomes 1, perform the final switches, and then we're done.

Now let's see this in code. We start off by dimensioning an array and filling it with values (which are as out of ascending order as they can be):

```
Sub Form_Load ()

    Static Array(9) As Integer   ←

    Array(1) = 9
    Array(2) = 8
    Array(3) = 7
    Array(4) = 6
    Array(5) = 5
    Array(6) = 4
    Array(7) = 3
    Array(8) = 2
    Array(9) = 1
        :
        :
```

We can also print those values to the form so they can be compared to the sorted list later:

```
Sub Form_Load ()

    Static Array(9) As Integer

    Array(1) = 9
    Array(2) = 8
    Array(3) = 7
    Array(4) = 6
    Array(5) = 5
    Array(6) = 4
    Array(7) = 3
    Array(8) = 2
    Array(9) = 1

    Print " i" ; Tab(20) ; "Array(i)"     ←
    Print "---" ; Tab(20) ; "--------"
    For i = 1 To 9
        Print i ; Tab(20) ; Array(i)
    Next i
    Print
    Print "Sorting..."
            :
            :
```

Now we have to implement our shell sort. In this type of sorting routine, we loop over partition size (**PartitionSize%** below), so let's set that loop up first:

```
Sub Form_Load ()

    Static Array(9) As Integer

    Array(1) = 9
    Array(2) = 8
    Array(3) = 7
    Array(4) = 6
    Array(5) = 5
    Array(6) = 4
    Array(7) = 3
    Array(8) = 2
    Array(9) = 1

    Print " i" ; Tab(20) ; "Array(i)"
    Print "---" ; Tab(20) ; "--------"
    For i = 1 To 9
        Print i ; Tab(20) ; Array(i)
    Next i
    Print
    Print "Sorting..."

            NumItems% = Ubound(Array, 1)
            PartitionSize% = Int((NumItems% + 1) / 2)

→           Do
                :
                :
→           Loop While PartitionSize% > 0
                :
                :
```

Notice in particular that, since we need the number of items to sort, we can use the Ubound( ) function, which returns the dimensions of an array as in QuickBASIC or other Basics; that is, Ubound( ) returns an array's upper bound, and Lbound( ) returns its lower bound. In the loop, we loop over partition size, cutting it in half each time through:

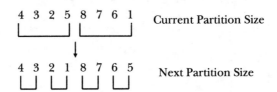

4 3 2 5 8 7 6 1   Current Partition Size

4 3 2 1 8 7 6 5   Next Partition Size

For every partition size, however, the list is broken up into a different number of partitions, and we have to loop over those partitions so we can compare elements in the current partition to the elements of the next one:

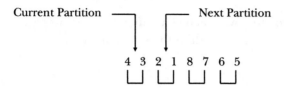

Current Partition ———————— Next Partition

4 3 2 1 8 7 6 5

The loop over partitions looks like this (note that when we're done with each partition, we cut the partition size in half):

```
Sub Form_Load ()

    Static Array(9) As Integer

    Array(1) = 9
    Array(2) = 8
    Array(3) = 7
    Array(4) = 6
    Array(5) = 5
    Array(6) = 4
    Array(7) = 3
    Array(8) = 2
    Array(9) = 1

    Print " i" ; Tab(20) ; "Array(i)"
    Print "---" ; Tab(20) ; "--------"
    For i = 1 To 9
        Print i ; Tab(20) ; Array(i)
    Next i
    Print
    Print "Sorting..."

            NumItems% = Ubound(Array, 1)
            PartitionSize% = Int((NumItems% + 1) / 2)

        Do
→           NumPartitions% = (NumItems% + 1) / PartitionSize%
→           Low% = 1
→           For i = 1 To NumPartitions% - 1
                    :
                    :
→           Next i
```

$\rightarrow$
```
                        PartitionSize% = PartitionSize% \ 2
                Loop While PartitionSize% > 0
                :
                :
```

Finally, we have to loop over each element in the current partition, comparing it to the corresponding element in the next partition:

This is the element-by-element comparison. We'll go from **Array(Low%)** to **Array(High%)** in the current partition, where **Low%** is the array index at the beginning of this partition and **High%** is the index of the element at the end, comparing each element to the corresponding one in the next partition:

```
Sub Form_Load ()

        Static Array(9) As Integer

        Array(1) = 9
        Array(2) = 8
        Array(3) = 7
        Array(4) = 6
        Array(5) = 5
        Array(6) = 4
        Array(7) = 3
        Array(8) = 2
        Array(9) = 1

        Print " i" ; Tab(20) ; "Array(i)"
        Print "---" ; Tab(20) ; "--------"
        For i = 1 To 9
            Print i ; Tab(20) ; Array(i)
        Next i
        Print
        Print "Sorting..."
                NumItems% = Ubound(Array, 1)
                PartitionSize% = Int((NumItems% + 1) / 2)

            Do
                NumPartitions% = (NumItems% + 1) / PartitionSize%
                Low% = 1
                For i = 1 To NumPartitions% - 1
                   High% = Low% + PartitionSize% - 1
```

```
              If High% > NumItems% - PartitionSize% Then High% =
                  NumItems% - PartitionSize%
→             For j = Low% To High%
→                 If Array(j) > Array(j + PartitionSize%) Then
                      :
                      :
→                 End If
              Next j
              Low% = Low% + PartitionSize%
          Next i
          PartitionSize% = PartitionSize% \ 2
      Loop While PartitionSize% > 0
      :
      :
```

If it turns out that the element in the later partition is smaller than the element in the current one, we have to swap them, which we can do this way:

```
Sub Form_Load ()

    Static Array(9) As Integer

    Array(1) = 9
    Array(2) = 8
    Array(3) = 7
    Array(4) = 6
    Array(5) = 5
    Array(6) = 4
    Array(7) = 3
    Array(8) = 2
    Array(9) = 1

    Print " i" ; Tab(20) ; "Array(i)"
    Print "---" ; Tab(20) ; "--------"
    For i = 1 To 9
        Print i ; Tab(20) ; Array(i)
    Next i
    Print
    Print "Sorting..."

            NumItems% = Ubound(Array, 1)
            PartitionSize% = Int((NumItems% + 1) / 2)

            Do
                NumPartitions% = (NumItems% + 1) / PartitionSize%
                Low% = 1
```

```
                    For i = 1 To NumPartitions% - 1
                       High% = Low% + PartitionSize% - 1
                       If High% > NumItems% - PartitionSize% Then High% =
                           NumItems% - PartitionSize%
                       For j = Low% To High%
                          If Array(j) > Array(j + PartitionSize%) Then
→                            Temp% = Array(j)
→                            Array(j) = Array(j + PartitionSize%)
→                            Array(j + PartitionSize%) = Temp%
                          End If
                       Next j
                       Low% = Low% + PartitionSize%
                    Next i
                    PartitionSize% = PartitionSize% \ 2
              Loop While PartitionSize% > 0
                    :
                    :
```

And that's it. We loop over partition sizes, over each partition, and over each element in the current partition, swapping each with its counterpart in the next partition if necessary. At the end, we can print out the newly sorted array. Here's the whole program:

```
Sub Form_Load ()

    Static Array(9) As Integer

    Array(1) = 9
    Array(2) = 8
    Array(3) = 7
    Array(4) = 6
    Array(5) = 5
    Array(6) = 4
    Array(7) = 3
    Array(8) = 2
    Array(9) = 1

    Print " i" ; Tab(20) ; "Array(i)"
    Print "---" ; Tab(20) ; "--------"
    For i = 1 To 9
        Print i ; Tab(20) ; Array(i)
    Next i
    Print
    Print "Sorting..."

            NumItems% = Ubound(Array, 1)
```

```
                PartitionSize% = Int((NumItems% + 1) / 2)

            Do
                NumPartitions% = (NumItems% + 1) / PartitionSize%
                Low% = 1
                For i = 1 To NumPartitions% - 1
                   High% = Low% + PartitionSize% - 1
                   If High% > NumItems% - PartitionSize% Then High% =
                      NumItems% - PartitionSize%
                   For j = Low% To High%
                      If Array(j) > Array(j + PartitionSize%) Then
                         Temp% = Array(j)
                         Array(j) = Array(j + PartitionSize%)
                         Array(j + PartitionSize%) = Temp%
                      End If
                   Next j
                   Low% = Low% + PartitionSize%
                Next i
                PartitionSize% = PartitionSize% \ 2
            Loop While PartitionSize% > 0

        Print
        Print " i" ; Tab(20) ; "Array(i)"
        Print "---" ; Tab(20) ; "--------"
        For i = 1 To 9
            Print i ; Tab(20) ; Array(i)
        Next i
    End Sub
```

The results of this program are shown in Figure 8-3.

We can even do the same thing for two-dimensional arrays. In that case, we simply sort the array on one of its columns. For example, we can adapt the above program to handle a two-dimensional array by adding a column index (**Col%**) to **Array( )**:

```
Sub Form_Load ()

        Static Array(9, 4) As Integer

        Array(1, 1) = 9
        Array(2, 1) = 8
        Array(3, 1) = 7
        Array(4, 1) = 6
        Array(5, 1) = 5
```

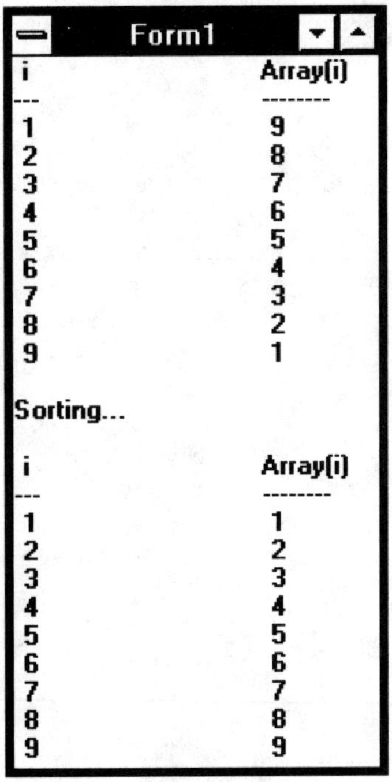

Figure 8-3. Shell Sort Example

```
Array(6, 1) = 4
Array(7, 1) = 3
Array(8, 1) = 2
Array(9, 1) = 1


Print " i" ; Tab(20) ; "Array(i,1)"
Print "---" ; Tab(20) ; "----------"
For i = 1 To 9
    Print i ; Tab(20) ; Array(i, 1)
Next i
Print
Print "Sorting..."

        NumItems% = Ubound(Array, 1)
        PartitionSize% = Int((NumItems% + 1) / 2)
        Col% = 1
        Do
            NumPartitions% = (NumItems% + 1) / PartitionSize%
            Low% = 1
            For i = 1 To NumPartitions% - 1
                High% = Low% + PartitionSize% - 1
```

→

```
            If High% > NumItems% - PartitionSize% Then High% =
                NumItems% - PartitionSize%
            For j = Low% To High%
→           If Array(j, Col%) > Array(j + PartitionSize%,
                    Col%) Then
                Temp% = Array(j, Col%)
                Array(j, Col%) = Array(j + PartitionSize%,
                    Col%)
                Array(j + PartitionSize%, Col%) = Temp%
            End If
            Next j
            Low% = Low% + PartitionSize%
        Next i
        PartitionSize% = PartitionSize% \ 2
    Loop While PartitionSize% > 0

Print
Print " i" ; Tab(20) ; "Array(i,1)"
Print "---" ; Tab(20) ; "----------"
For i = 1 To 9
    Print i ; Tab(20) ; Array(i, 1)
Next i
```

And now we're able to sort two-dimensional arrays on a specified column. That concludes our tour of shell sorts. Let's turn to QuickSorts next.

QuickSorts

Besides shell sorts, another popular sorting algorithm is the QuickSort. That sorting routine works like this. First, we find a key, or test, value to compare values to. The best value here would be the median value of the elements of the array, but, in practice, a random entry is usually chosen. Here, we'll choose a value from the center of the array.

Then we divide the array into two partitions: those less than the test value and those greater. We move upwards in the array until we come to the first value that is greater than the test value, and down the array (starting from the end) until we find a number less than the test value. Then we swap them. We keep going until all the numbers in the first partition are less than the test value, and all the numbers in the second partition are greater.

Next, we do the same thing to each partition: We select a new test value from each partition and break that partition into two *new* partitions. One of those new partitions holds the numbers less than that test value while the other holds those greater. We keep going in that way, splitting partitions continuously until there are just two numbers in a partition, at which point we compare and switch them if necessary.

You may have noticed that each subsequent step is itself a QuickSort. To start, we divide the array into two partitions less than and greater than the test value, take each partition and break *it* into two partitions depending on a new test value, and so on. In this way, QuickSorts lend themselves easily to recursion, and that's the way they're usually coded. And, since Visual Basic supports recursion, the QuickSort we'll develop here is no exception.

If the term *recursion* is new to you, you should know that it just refers to a routine that calls itself. If a programming task can be divided into a number of computationally identical levels, it can be dealt with recursively. Each time the routine calls itself, it deals with a deeper level. After the final level is reached, control returns through each successive level back to the beginning. Let's see how this looks in code.

Since this routine is recursive, we will set up a subprogram called SortQuick( ) to call from the main program (this subprogram will call itself repeatedly; i.e., recursively):

```
Call SortQuick(Array(), SortFrom%, SortTo%)
```

We just pass the array name to sort, the index to start sorting from (**SortFrom%**) and the index to sort to (**SortTo%**); working this way will be useful when we have to sort a particular partition in the array. In SortQuick( ), we first handle the final case; that is, a partition of only two elements:

```
Sub SortQuick (Array() As Integer, SortFrom%, SortTo%)

        If SortFrom% >= SortTo% Then Exit Sub
        If SortFrom% + 1 = SortTo% Then   'Final case
           If Array(SortFrom%) > Array(SortTo%) Then
                Temp% = Array(SortFrom%)
                Array(SortFrom%) = Array(SortTo%)
                Array(SortTo%) = Temp%
        End If
         :
         :
```

In this case, we just compare each element to its neighbor (the only other element in this partition) and swap them if needed. That's all there is to the final case in the QuickSort algorithm.

If the partition size is greater than two, however, we have to sort the values from **Array(SortFrom%)** to **Array(SortTo%)** according to a test value, dividing the elements into two new partitions, and then call SortQuick( ) again on each new partition. Let's see how that works. First, we pick a test value, and then we divide the present partition into two partitions on the basis of it.

We start by moving up from the bottom of the partition, swapping any values that we find are greater than the test value:

```
Sub SortQuick (Array() As Integer, SortFrom%, SortTo%)

            If SortFrom% >= SortTo% Then Exit Sub
            If SortFrom% + 1 = SortTo% Then    'Final case
                If Array(SortFrom%) > Array(SortTo%) Then
                    Temp% = Array(SortFrom%)
                    Array(SortFrom%) = Array(SortTo%)
                    Array(SortTo%) = Temp%
                End If
            Else      'Have to split problem
                AtRandom = (SortFrom% + SortTo%) \ 2
                Test = Array(AtRandom)
                    Temp% = Array(AtRandom)
                    Array(AtRandom) = Array(SortTo%)
                    Array(SortTo%) = Temp%
→               Do
                    'Split into two partitions

→                   For i = SortFrom% To SortTo% - 1
→                           If Array(i) > Test Then Exit For
→                   Next i
                            :
                            :
→                   If i < j Then
                        Temp% = Array(i)
                        Array(i) = Array(j)
                        Array(j) = Temp%
                    End If
→               Loop UNTIL i >= j
                    :
                    :
```

And we also scan from the top of the partition down in the same loop, looking for the first value that's smaller than the test value:

```
Sub SortQuick (Array() As Integer, SortFrom%, SortTo%)

        If SortFrom% >= SortTo% Then Exit Sub
        If SortFrom% + 1 = SortTo% Then   'Final case
            If Array(SortFrom%) > Array(SortTo%) Then
                Temp% = Array(SortFrom%)
                Array(SortFrom%) = Array(SortTo%)
                Array(SortTo%) = Temp%
            End If
        Else      'Have to split problem
            AtRandom = (SortFrom% + SortTo%) \ 2
            Test = Array(AtRandom)
                Temp% = Array(AtRandom)
                Array(AtRandom) = Array(SortTo%)
                Array(SortTo%) = Temp%
        Do
            'Split into two partitions

            For i = SortFrom% To SortTo% - 1
                    If Array(i) > Test Then Exit For
            Next i

            For j = SortTo% To i + 1 Step -1
                    If Array(j) < Test Then Exit For
            Next j

            If i < j Then
                Temp% = Array(i)
                Array(i) = Array(j)
                Array(j) = Temp%
            End If
        Loop UNTIL i >= j
            :
            :
```

We keep going until **i** and **j** meet, at which time we've created our two new partitions. Next we can call SortQuick( ) again for each of the resulting partitions (which may be of unequal size):

```
Sub SortQuick (Array() As Integer, SortFrom%, SortTo%)

        If SortFrom% >= SortTo% Then Exit Sub
        If SortFrom% + 1 = SortTo% Then   'Final case
            If Array(SortFrom%) > Array(SortTo%) Then
```

```
                    Temp% = Array(SortFrom%)
                    Array(SortFrom%) = Array(SortTo%)
                    Array(SortTo%) = Temp%
                End If

            Else     'Have to split problem
                AtRandom = (SortFrom% + SortTo%) \ 2
                Test = Array(AtRandom)
                    Temp% = Array(AtRandom)
                    Array(AtRandom) = Array(SortTo%)
                    Array(SortTo%) = Temp%

                Do
                    For i = SortFrom% To SortTo% - 1
                        If Array(i) > Test Then Exit For
                    Next i

                    For j = SortTo% To i + 1 Step -1
                        If Array(j) < Test Then Exit For
                    Next j

                    If i < j Then
                        Temp% = Array(i)
                        Array(i) = Array(j)
                        Array(j) = Temp%
                    End If

                Loop Until i >= j

                        Temp% = Array(i)
                        Array(i) = Array(SortTo%)
                        Array(SortTo%) = Temp%

→               Call SortQuick(Array(), SortFrom%, i - 1)
→               Call SortQuick(Array(), i + 1, SortTo%)

            End If
    End Sub
```

And that's all there is to it. The sort will continue recursively until we get down to the final case of a partition size of 1, the final swaps will be done if necessary, and then we're finished. Here's the whole thing:

```
Sub Form_Load ()
    Static Array(9) As Integer

    Array(1) = 9
    Array(2) = 8
```

```
        Array(3) = 7
        Array(4) = 6
        Array(5) = 5
        Array(6) = 4
        Array(7) = 3
        Array(8) = 2
        Array(9) = 1

        Print " i" ; Tab(20) ; "Array(i)"
        Print "---" ; Tab(20) ; "--------"
        For i = 1 To 9
            Print i; Tab(20) ; Array(i)
        Next i

        Call SortQuick(Array(), 1, UBound(Array, 1))

        Print
        Print "Sorting..."
        Print
        Print " i" ; Tab(20) ; "Array(i)"
        Print "---" ; Tab(20) ; "--------"
        For i = 1 To 9
            Print i; Tab(20) ; Array(i)
        Next i

End Sub

Sub SortQuick (Array() As Integer, SortFrom%, SortTo%)

        If SortFrom% >= SortTo% Then Exit Sub
        If SortFrom% + 1 = SortTo% Then   'Final case
           If Array(SortFrom%) > Array(SortTo%) Then
               Temp% = Array(SortFrom%)
               Array(SortFrom%) = Array(SortTo%)
               Array(SortTo%) = Temp%
           End If

        Else     'Have to split problem
           AtRandom = (SortFrom% + SortTo%) \ 2
           Test = Array(AtRandom)
               Temp% = Array(AtRandom)
               Array(AtRandom) = Array(SortTo%)
               Array(SortTo%) = Temp%

           Do

               For i = SortFrom% To SortTo% - 1
                   If Array(i) > Test Then Exit For
```

```
            Next i

            For j = SortTo% To i + 1 Step -1
                If Array(j) < Test Then Exit For
            Next j

            If i < j Then
                Temp% = Array(i)
                Array(i) = Array(j)
                Array(j) = Temp%
            End If

        Loop Until i >= j

                Temp% = Array(i)
                Array(i) = Array(SortTo%)
                Array(SortTo%) = Temp%

        Call SortQuick(Array(), SortFrom%, i - 1)
        Call SortQuick(Array(), i + 1, SortTo%)

        End If
  End Sub
```

That's it for sorting. Both the shell sort and the QuickSort are pretty fast. The one you should use will depend on your application. You might want to try them both and use the faster of the two.

Searching Your Data

Now that we've ordered our data, it becomes much easier to search through. If the data is unordered, we'd have no choice but to simply check one value after another until we found a match, as in this example program:

```
Sub Form_Load ()

    'Unordered Search

    Static Array(9) As Integer

    Array(1) = 9
    Array(2) = 7
    Array(3) = 8
    Array(4) = 3
    Array(5) = 5
    Array(6) = 4
```

```
        Array(7) = 6
        Array(8) = 2
        Array(9) = 1

        Print "Searching the unordered list for the value 1."

        For i = 1 To Ubound(Array,1)
                If Array(i) = 1 Then
                        Print "Value of 1 in element";i
                End If
        Next i

    End Sub
```

We just keep scanning up the list of values until we find what we're looking for. On the other hand, we can be more intelligent when searching a sorted list. For example, if our sorted array had these values in it:

1 2 3 4 5 6 7 8 9 10 11 12 13 14 15

and we were searching for the entry with 10 in it, we could start off in the center of the list:

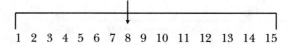

Since 10 is greater than 8, we divide the *upper* half of the array in two and check the mid point again:

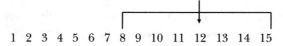

The value we're looking for, 10, is less than 12, so we move *down* and cut the remaining distance in half:

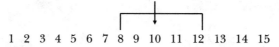

And in this way, we've zeroed in on our number, cutting down the number of values we have to check. Let's see how this looks in a program. First, we set up our array. In this example, let's search an array of 9 elements for the entry with 8 in it:

```
Sub Form_Load()

    'Ordered Search

    Static Array(9) As Integer

    Array(1) = 1
    Array(2) = 2
    Array(3) = 3
    Array(4) = 4
    Array(5) = 5
    Array(6) = 6
    Array(7) = 7
    Array(8) = 8
    Array(9) = 9
```

→   SearchValue% = 8
→   Print "Searching the ordered list for the value 8."
              :

Now we cut the array into two partitions and check the test value which is right between them, at position **TestIndex%**:

```
Sub Form_Load ()

        'Ordered Search

        Static Array(9) As Integer

        Array(1) = 1
        Array(2) = 2
        Array(3) = 3
        Array(4) = 4
        Array(5) = 5
        Array(6) = 6
        Array(7) = 7
        Array(8) = 8
        Array(9) = 9

        SearchValue% = 8
        Print "Searching the ordered list for the value 8."
```

→   Partition% = (Ubound(Array, 1) + 1) \ 2
→   TestIndex% = Partition%
              :
              :

Then we need to start searching. We will keep looping over partition size. If the partition size becomes 0 without success, then the value we're looking for isn't in the array:

```
Sub Form_Load ()

        'Ordered Search

        Static Array(9) As Integer

        Array(1) = 1
        Array(2) = 2
        Array(3) = 3
        Array(4) = 4
        Array(5) = 5
        Array(6) = 6
        Array(7) = 7
        Array(8) = 8
        Array(9) = 9

        SearchValue% = 8
        Print "Searching the ordered list for the value 8."

        Partition% = (Ubound(Array, 1) + 1) \ 2
        TestIndex% = Partition%

→       Do
→           Partition% = Partition% \ 2
                :
            Search this partition
                :
→       Loop While Partition% > 0
        :
        :
```

Let's first check to see if we've found our value, and, if so, we can quit:

```
Sub Form_Load ()

        'Ordered Search

        Static Array(9) As Integer

        Array(1) = 1
        Array(2) = 2
        Array(3) = 3
```

```
        Array(4) = 4
        Array(5) = 5
        Array(6) = 6
        Array(7) = 7
        Array(8) = 8
        Array(9) = 9

        SearchValue% = 8
        Print "Searching the ordered list for the value 8."

        Partition% = (Ubound(Array, 1) + 1) \ 2
        TestIndex% = Partition%

        Do
            Partition% = Partition% \ 2
→           If Array(TestIndex%) = SearchValue% Then
→               Print "Value of"; SearchValue%; "in element"; TestIndex%
→               Exit Do
→           End If
                :
                :
        Loop While Partition% > 0
        :
        :
```

If we haven't found our value, we have to go on to the next iteration of the loop, setting **TestIndex%** to the middle of either the higher or lower partition, and then dividing that partition into two new partitions. If the search value is bigger than the value at our current location in the array, we want to move to the partition at higher values:

```
Sub Form_Load ()

        'Ordered Search

        Static Array(9) As Integer

        Array(1) = 1
        Array(2) = 2
        Array(3) = 3
        Array(4) = 4
        Array(5) = 5
        Array(6) = 6
        Array(7) = 7
        Array(8) = 8
```

```
            Array(9) = 9

            SearchValue% = 8
            Print "Searching the ordered list for the value 8."

            Partition% = (Ubound(Array, 1) + 1) \ 2
            TestIndex% = Partition%

         Do
             Partition% = Partition% \ 2
             If Array(TestIndex%) = SearchValue% Then
                 Print "Value of"; SearchValue%; "in element"; TestIndex%
                 Exit Do
             End If
→            If Array(TestIndex%) < SearchValue% Then
→                TestIndex% = TestIndex% + Partition%
                 :
                 :
         Loop While Partition% > 0
         :
         :
```

But if the search value is smaller, on the other hand, we want to move to the lower partition (which holds lower values):

```
Sub Form_Load ()

        'Ordered Search

        Static Array(9) As Integer

        Array(1) = 1
        Array(2) = 2
        Array(3) = 3
        Array(4) = 4
        Array(5) = 5
        Array(6) = 6
        Array(7) = 7
        Array(8) = 8
        Array(9) = 9

        SearchValue% = 8
        Print "Searching the ordered list for the value 8."
```

```
          Partition% = (Ubound(Array, 1) + 1) \ 2
          TestIndex% = Partition%

          Do
               Partition% = Partition% \ 2
               If Array(TestIndex%) = SearchValue% Then
                    Print "Value of"; SearchValue%; "in element"; TestIndex%
                    Exit Do
               End If
               If Array(TestIndex%) < SearchValue% Then
                    TestIndex% = TestIndex% + Partition%
→              Else
→                   TestIndex% = TestIndex% - Partition%
→              End If
          Loop While Partition% > 0
          :
```

And that's almost all there is. We just keep going until we find what we're looking for, or the partition size becomes 0, in which case it's not there.

If we were unsuccessful, however, there are two last remaining tests that we should apply: We should check the value we're searching for against the very first and last entries in the array. That is, our algorithm demands that all numbers that it checks be *straddled* by two other values, and that's true of every element in the array except for the first and last ones. That means that if we didn't find what we were looking for, we have to check these last two values explicitly:

```
     Sub Form_Load ()

          'Ordered Search

          Static Array(9) As Integer

          Array(1) = 1
          Array(2) = 2
          Array(3) = 3
          Array(4) = 4
          Array(5) = 5
          Array(6) = 6
          Array(7) = 7
```

```
        Array(8) = 8
        Array(9) = 9

        SearchValue% = 8
        Print "Searching the ordered list for the value 8."

        Partition% = (Ubound(Array, 1) + 1) \ 2
        TestIndex% = Partition%

    Do
        Partition% = Partition% \ 2
        If Array(TestIndex%) = SearchValue% Then
            Print "Value of"; SearchValue%; "in element"; TestIndex%
            Exit Do
        End If
        If Array(TestIndex%) < SearchValue% Then
            TestIndex% = TestIndex% + Partition%
        Else
            TestIndex% = TestIndex% - Partition%
        End If
    Loop While Partition% > 0

    'Can only find straddled numbers, so add these tests:

        If Array(1) = SearchValue% Then
            Print "Value of"; SearchValue%; "in element 1"
        End If

        If Array(Ubound(Array, 1)) = SearchValue% Then
            Print "Value of"; SearchValue%; "in element";
                Ubound(Array, 1)
        End If
End Sub
```

And we're done with the ordered search. The result of this program appears in Figure 8-4, and the full program is in Listing 8-1.

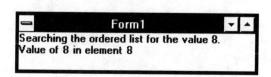

Figure 8-4. Ordered Search Example

Listing 8-1. Ordered Search Example

```
Sub Form_Load ()

    'Ordered Search

    Static Array(9) As Integer

    Array(1) = 1
    Array(2) = 2
    Array(3) = 3
    Array(4) = 4
    Array(5) = 5
    Array(6) = 6
    Array(7) = 7
    Array(8) = 8
    Array(9) = 9

    SearchValue% = 8
    Print "Searching the ordered list for the value 8."

    Partition% = (Ubound(Array, 1) + 1) \ 2
    TestIndex% = Partition%

    Do
        Partition% = Partition% \ 2
        If Array(TestIndex%) = SearchValue% Then
            Print "Value of"; SearchValue%; "in element"; TestIndex%
            Exit Do
        End If
        If Array(TestIndex%) < SearchValue% Then
            TestIndex% = TestIndex% + Partition%
        Else
            TestIndex% = TestIndex% - Partition%
        End If
    Loop While Partition% > 0

    'Can only find straddled numbers, so add these tests:

        If Array(1) = SearchValue% Then
            Print "Value of"; SearchValue%; "in element 1"
        End If

        If Array(Ubound(Array, 1)) = SearchValue% Then
            Print "Value of"; SearchValue%; "in element";
                Ubound(Array, 1)
        End If
    End Sub
```

And That's It

That's it for data handling and sorting. We've seen most of the popular ways of handling numeric data in this chapter. When we're designing code, it's always important to organize our data correctly. As mentioned earlier, that can be half the battle of writing a program. Next, let's see how to debug our programs and handle errors.

Error Handling and Debugging

Errors occur even for the best programmers. In fact, the longer the program, the more complex the code, the more likely errors are to appear. There are several different types of errors: design-time errors, run-time errors, and those that make your programs produce incorrect or unexpected results (bugs). Visual Basic handles the first type, design-time errors, by refusing to run programs until they're fixed, and it usually offers some assistance in the form of help and help messages. The other two types are up to us to fix, and they're what this chapter is about — run-time errors and bugs.

A run-time error is what Visual Basic refers to as a *trappable error*, that is, Visual Basic recognizes that there was an error and allows you to "trap" it, taking some corrective action if it occurs (untrappable errors usually only occur at design-time). Bugs are different, because Visual Basic usually doesn't recognize that there's a problem, but the code still doesn't operate as intended. For example, if you had a function called Counter that was supposed to increment an internal counter and return its current value every time it was called, it might look like this:

```
Function Counter()
    Dim counter_value As Integer

    counter_value = counter_value + 1

    Counter = counter_value
End Function
```

There is a bug here. Counter_value is not declared Static, so every time this function is called, counter_value starts off at 0. The function adds 1 to it and returns that value, so the value returned is 1 every time. A function that simply returns 1 every time it is called does not generate a run-time error, but in the light of its intended purpose, it is a bug.

We'll be able to find trappable errors without difficulty. Because Visual Basic generates them, it knows exactly when they occur, and it allows us to take some action. However, bugs are another story. In their case, we'll have to use Visual Basic's debugging capabilities to find out what went wrong, working our way through the program slowly, possibly even statement by statement. These kinds of skills are necessary tools for programmers, however, especially those who want to produce real applications that are subject to strict testing. And that will be our first topic: how to test the programs we write.

How to Test Programs

When programs run, they usually operate on ranges of data. For example, a program may read the value of an unsigned integer from the user, and that value can range from 0 to 65,535 (i.e., if the value couldn't vary, there would be no point in reading it in). The limits of that value, 0 and 65,535, are called its *bounds.* When you're trying to check your programs for potential problems, it's important that you cover the whole allowed range of such values. That doesn't normally mean checking every value between 0 and 65,535, but it does mean checking values at the bounds of this range, as well as some midrange values, and any other values that are likely to give you problems.

For example, this value may represent the number of students in a class, and, having summed all their test scores, we'd like to divide by it to find the class average. There may be no problem for 15 or 20 students, but what if the user enters a value of 0? Even though it's in the allowed range for unsigned integers, dividing by it will result in an error. Or, what if we stored the students' test scores in another unsigned integer and found that as we went towards higher numbers of students that the division didn't give us the accuracy we want? Checking your program's bounding values like this is vitally important. In general, there will be bounds for every crucial variable, and you should check all combinations of these values when you run your program to see how they interact (this is particularly important when it comes to array indices).

Of course, you should check midrange values as well. It may turn out that some combination of such values gives you unexpected errors as well. The longer you test your program under usual and unusual operating circumstances, the more confidence you'll have in it. As programs get more complex, the testing period normally gets longer and longer, which is why major software companies often send out hundreds of preliminary versions of their software (called beta versions) for testing by programmers (the final software package is usually the gamma version).

In addition, you should attempt to duplicate every run-time problem that may occur to see how your program will react. File operations are great at generating such errors. For example, what if the disk is full and you try to write to it? What if the specified input file doesn't exist? What if the specified file to write is already read-only? What if the diskette has been removed? What if the user asks you to write record -15 in a file? It's hard to generate every conceivable set of problematic circumstances, of course, but the closer you come, the more polished your application will be.

Visual Basic gives us a hand when it comes to certain types of errors, however, and those errors are called trappable errors. Let's take a look at how to handle them first.

Handling Run-Time Errors

You may remember that we already placed some error checking in our Editor program because file handling is such a notorious source of possible errors (as is handling input from the keyboard). For example, if we asked the Editor to read a file on a diskette that's been removed, we would get a message box like the one in Figure 9-1, informing us that there's been a file error. We were able to intercept that kind of error, so let's reexamine how we did it.

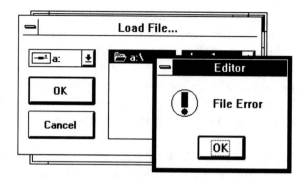

Figure 9-1. The Editor Application's File Error Message

The On Error GoTo Statement

The way we trap trappable errors is with an On Error GoTo statement. For example, here is how we did it in the Editor application:

```
Sub OKButton_Click ()
→       On Error GoTo FileError

        If (Right$(Dir1.Path, 1) = "\") Then        'Get file name
            Filename$ = Dir1.Path + File1.FileName
        Else
            Filename$ = Dir1.Path + "\" + File1.FileName
        End If

        Open Filename$ For Input As # 1             'Open file
        Form1.PadText.Text = Input$(LOF(1), # 1)    'Read file in

        Close # 1                'Close file
        LoadForm.Hide            'Hide dialog box

        Exit Sub

→       FileError:
            MsgBox "File Error", 48, "Editor" 'MsgBox for file error.
            Resume
    End Sub
```

When Visual Basic generates a trappable error after executing a statement like this in a procedure, control jumps to the specified label — in our case, that's FileError. That is exactly what the GoTo statement does: It transfers controls to a new location in the program. The general form for such a procedure is like this:

```
Sub Name ()
    On Error GoTo ErrorLabel
        :
        :

    Exit Sub

ErrorLabel:
    :
    :

End Sub
```

Here, we execute the On Error GoTo statement first, setting up our error handling routine. Note also that we exit the Sub procedure before reaching that routine, so we do not inadvertently execute the error handling code. In this way, the procedure is set up much like a procedure that has subroutines, which are handled with the GoSub statement in Visual Basic just as they are in other forms of Basic; that is, like this:

```
Sub Name ()
        :
    GoSub Label1
        :

    Exit Sub

Label1
    :
    :
    Return
End Sub
```

Note that since the code in an error handling routine (as well as the code in a GoSub subroutine) is in the same Sub or Function procedure, it shares all the variables of the rest of the Sub or Function procedure. That means that we'll have access to variables that may be valuable to us in fixing the error.

We should also note that you can override On Error GoTo statements with later statements of the same kind. This is useful if you've entered a different part of the code, with different potential errors, and want to use a different error handler. However, we haven't done much here. We've only recognized the fact that an error occurred. The next step must be to find out what the error was, and then to take action if possible.

TIP   You can even turn error handling off if you want to. Just execute the statement On Error GoTo 0 in your program.

The Err and Erl Functions

In order to determine what error occurred, we can use the Err function, which returns an error number. These error numbers are predefined in Visual Basic, and the most common ones appear in Table 9-1. Note that it includes such items as array subscripts out of bounds, division by zero, file not found, disk full (a very common file-writing error) and other errors. All of these represent trappable errors that you can catch, and, if you can catch them, there's some possibility of fixing them.

Let's update our Editor program so that it at least can indicate what error occurred. To do that, we can use this statement:

```
Sub OKButton_Click ()
    On Error GoTo FileError

    If (Right$(Dir1.Path, 1) = "\") Then        'Get file name
        Filename$ = Dir1.Path + File1.FileName
    Else
        Filename$ = Dir1.Path + "\" + File1.FileName
    End If

    Open Filename$ For Input As # 1             'Open file
    Form1.PadText.Text = Input$(LOF(1), # 1)    'Read file in

    Close # 1                        'Close file
    LoadForm.Hide                    'Hide dialog box

    Exit Sub

FileError:
→       MsgBox "File Error" + Str$(Err), 48, "Editor"
    Resume
End Sub
```

Error Number	Means
5	Illegal function call
6	Overflow
7	Out of memory
9	Subscript out of range
10	Duplicate definition
11	Division by zero
13	Type mismatch
14	Out of string space
19	No RESUME
20	RESUME without error
28	Out of stack space
51	Internal error
52	Bad file name or number
53	File Not found
54	Bad file mode
55	File already open
57	Device I/O error
58	File already exists
59	Bad record length
61	Disk full
62	Input past end of file
63	Bad record number
64	Bad file name
65	File previously loaded
66	Tried to load file with duplicate procedure definition
67	Too many files
68	Device Unavailable
70	Permission denied
71	Disk Not ready
72	Disk-media error
75	Path/File access error
76	Path Not found
323	Incompatible version created
340	Control array element does not exist

Table 9-1. Common Trappable Errors

Error Number	Means
341	Illegal Control Array index
342	Not enough room to allocate control array
343	Object is not an array
344	Must specify index when using control array
360	Object is already loaded
361	Only forms and control array elements can be loaded or unloaded
362	Controls created at design-time cannot be unloaded
380	Illegal property value
381	Illegal property array index
384	Property cannot be modified when Form Minimized or Maximized
420	Invalid object reference
421	Method not applicable for this object
422	Property not found
423	Property or control not found
424	Object required
425	Illegal object use
427	Object is not the Printer object
428	Object is not a control
429	Object is not a form
430	There is no currently active control
431	There is no currently active form
461	Specified format does not match format of data
480	Unable to create AutoRedraw bitmap
481	Invalid picture

Table 9-1. (continued)

We can do this for both saving and loading files. Now if we select a file from a diskette, remove the diskette and then try to read it, we see that our former error box now displays the message: File Error 68, as shown in Figure 9-2. Checking Table 9-1, we see that this error means: Device Unavailable.

In fact, we can report more information here as well. In particular, we can report the line number that the error occurred in using the Erl function. This

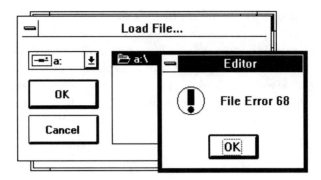

Figure 9-2. Editor Application with Error Number

function returns a number that stands for the line number in the current procedure of the statement that caused the error. To use it, we have to use line numbers (which is no longer standard in Basic). That might look like this:

```
Sub OKButton_Click ()
1    On Error GoTo FileError

2    If (Right$(Dir1.Path, 1) = "\") Then        'Get file name
3        Filename$ = Dir1.Path + File1.FileName
4    Else
5        Filename$ = Dir1.Path + "\" + File1.FileName
6    End If

7    Open Filename$ For Input As # 1             'Open file
8    Form1.PadText.Text = Input$(LOF(1), # 1)    'Read file in

9    Close # 1                 'Close file
10   LoadForm.Hide             'Hide dialog box

11   Exit Sub

FileError:
12   MsgBox "File Error"+Str$(Err)+" in line "+Str$(Erl), 48, "Editor"
13   Resume
End Sub
```

If we cause the same error as before, removing the diskette with the file on it, we see a message informing us that the error occurred in line 7, which is the line in which we try to open the file. On the other hand, that information is of very little use to the user. What does it matter what line number the error occurred on? They would much rather know what the error was. We can of course print out the error number, as above, but that's not necessarily much more help. If the user has no knowledge of Visual Basic, or doesn't have the information in Table 9-1, the simple explanation that error 68 occurred is not going to be well received. However, there is a way to translate that explanation into English from our program with a simple function, and we'll explore that next.

The Error$ Function

The Error$( ) function is a very useful function when handling errors because it can translate the error number we get from Err into English. That means that we can change our procedure to this:

```
Sub OKButton_Click ()
    On Error GoTo FileError

    If (Right$(Dir1.Path, 1) = "\") Then        'Get file name
        Filename$ = Dir1.Path + File1.FileName
    Else
        Filename$ = Dir1.Path + "\" + File1.FileName
    End If

    Open Filename$ For Input As # 1             'Open file
    Form1.PadText.Text = Input$(LOF(1), # 1)    'Read file in

    Close # 1                  'Close file
    LoadForm.Hide              'Hide dialog box

    Exit Sub

FileError:
→   MsgBox Error$(Err), 48, "Editor"
    Resume
End Sub
```

When we run the Editor application with this new error handler (but the same error), we get this message: "Device unavailable," as shown in Figure 9-3. This is a considerable improvement over "File Error 68." In fact, it's like having Table 9-1 built into your program, ready to be used. In general, this is a much better way of handling errors than printing out the error number, which may be meaningless and frustrating to the user. However, even this message leaves something to be desired: What action are we requiring of the user? Does the

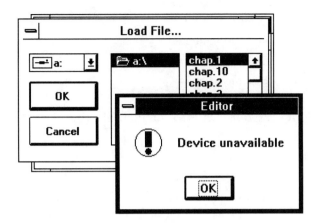

Figure 9-3. Editor Application with English Error Message

user know what device we're talking about? Indicating the next step is still up to us, and we should design our error handler around such contingencies.

Creating Customized Error Handlers

When creating your own error handler, there's some errors that we might anticipate occurring more than others, and we might want to make special provisions for handling them. For example, if we were writing files, we might anticipate error 61, Disk full. If that error occurred, we could place a message in a message box with this message in it: "The disk is full. Please delete some files and click the OK Button." The user could then switch to the Windows File Manager and clear some more disk space (in cases like this, we should also include a Cancel button in case the user wants to cancel the file-writing operation instead). Then, after they clicked the OK button, they could go back and try the operation again, as we'll see soon. Let's see an example of a custom error handler in code. When we load in files, these are some of the errors (and the messages that Error$( ) will give) that we might expect:

7	Out of memory
55	File already open
57	Device I/O error
61	Disk full
67	Too many files

68	Device unavailable
70	Permission denied
71	Disk not ready
72	Disk-media error

We might write our own error handler like this:

```
Sub OKButton_Click ()
        On Error GoTo FileError

        If (Right$(Dir1.Path, 1) = "\") Then          'Get file name
            Filename$ = Dir1.Path + File1.FileName
        Else
            Filename$ = Dir1.Path + "\" + File1.FileName
        End If

        Open Filename$ For Input As # 1               'Open file
        Form1.PadText.Text = Input$(LOF(1), # 1)      'Read file in

        Close # 1                  'Close file
        LoadForm.Hide              'Hide dialog box

        Exit Sub

    FileError:
        Msg$ = Error$(Err)
        Select Case Err     'Display our own message?
            Case 7
                Msg$ = "File is too big to open."
            Case 57, 68, 71, 72
                Msg$ = "Please check the disk and try again."
            Case 67
                Msg$ = "Too many files open. Close some and try again."
        End Select
→       MsgBox Msg$, 48, "Editor"
        Resume
    End Sub
```

Now if we produce the same error as before, we'll see the message shown in Figure 9-4: "Please check the disk and try again." In general, the more information you can provide the user, the better. (Of course, it's usually better to handle the error internally if at all possible.) Often, we'll want the user to take some action, and then to click the OK button. When they do, we should retry the operation, such as trying to read in the file again. Let's see how to do that next.

Figure 9-4. Customized Error Message

NOTE Two very useful places to add error handling to our Editor application are when the user is about to write over an already existing file ("Overwrite existing file NOVEL.TXT?"), and when the file doesn't exist and we're about to create it ("File doesn't exist — create it?").

The Resume Statement

Note the line at the end of our error handler:

```
Sub OKButton_Click ()
    On Error GoTo FileError

    If (Right$(Dir1.Path, 1) = "\") Then         'Get file name
        Filename$ = Dir1.Path + File1.FileName
    Else
        Filename$ = Dir1.Path + "\" + File1.FileName
    End If

    Open Filename$ For Input As # 1              'Open file
    Form1.PadText.Text = Input$(LOF(1), # 1)     'Read file in

    Close # 1                      'Close file
    LoadForm.Hide                  'Hide dialog box

    Exit Sub

FileError:
    Msg$ = Error$(Err)
    Select Case Err      'Display our own message?
        Case 7
            Msg$ = "File is too big to open."
```

```
                  Case 57, 68, 71, 72
                      Msg$ = "Please check the disk and try again."
                  Case 67
                      Msg$ = "Too many files open. Close some and try again."
              End Select
              MsgBox Msg$, 48, "Editor"
  →          Resume
          End Sub
```

This simple statement, Resume, will let us retry the operation that caused the error after the user took some corrective action. When Visual Basic encounters a Resume statement in an error handler — i.e., after an On Error GoTo type of routine has been set up and entered (the error trap is said to be active at this point) — it leaves the error handler and returns to the statement that caused the error. In other words, Resume allows us to retry on operation, like this:

```
Sub OKButton_Click ()
    On Error GoTo FileError

    If (Right$(Dir1.Path, 1) = "\") Then        'Get file name
        Filename$ = Dir1.Path + File1.FileName
    Else
        Filename$ = Dir1.Path + "\" + File1.FileName
    End If

    Open Filename$ For Input As # 1             'Open file
    Form1.PadText.Text = Input$(LOF(1), # 1)    'Read file in

    Close # 1                       'Close file
    LoadForm.Hide                   'Hide dialog box

    Exit Sub

FileError:
    Msg$ = Error$(Err)
    Select Case Err     'Display our own message?
        Case 7
            Msg$ = "File is too big to open."
        Case 57, 68, 71, 72
            Msg$ = "Please check the disk and try again."
        Case 67
            Msg$ = "Too many files open. Close some and try again."
    End Select
    MsgBox Msg$, 48, "Editor"
    Resume
End Sub
```

If we had a problem trying to open the file, we display an error message, let the user take some corrective action, and then try opening the file again. Note, however, that this is a potential problem. If the user decides not to open the file after all, we should provide some way of exiting this Sub procedure. We can do that by using a message box that has two buttons instead of one; that is, a box with both OK and Cancel buttons. We can also read the response in the same statement with the MsgBox( ) function (i.e., you might recall that MsgBox has two forms: as a statement if you expect no reply, and as a function if you want input from the user):

```
Response% = MsgBox(Msg$, 49, "Editor")
```

We're passing a message box type parameter of 48 (display exclamation point symbol) + 1 (include both OK and Cancel buttons) = 49, and placing the user's response in the variable **Response%**. If they select the OK button, this response will equal 1. If they select the Cancel button, it will equal 2. We can modify our code to retry the problematic operation if the user selected the OK button like this:

```
Sub OKButton_Click ()
    On Error GoTo FileError

    If (Right$(Dir1.Path, 1) = "\") Then         'Get file name
        Filename$ = Dir1.Path + File1.FileName
    Else
        Filename$ = Dir1.Path + "\" + File1.FileName
    End If

    Open Filename$ For Input As # 1              'Open file
    Form1.PadText.Text = Input$(LOF(1), # 1)     'Read file in

    Close # 1                      'Close file
    LoadForm.Hide                  'Hide dialog box

    Exit Sub

FileError:
    Msg$ = Error$(Err)
    Select Case Err      'Display our own message?
        Case 7
            Msg$ = "File is too big to open."
        Case 57, 68, 71, 72
            Msg$ = "Please check the disk and try again."
        Case 67
            Msg$ = "Too many files open. Close some and try again."
    End Select
```

```
→         Response% = MsgBox(Msg$, 49, "Editor")
→         If Response% = 1 Then Resume
       End Sub
```

In this case, if the user chose OK, we move back to the same line that caused the error (probably the Open statement), and try it again. On the other hand, if the user chose the Cancel button, we want to exit the Sub procedure entirely. To do that, however, it's not enough to rely on the End Sub statement at the end of the procedure, as we're doing above. If Visual Basic is in an error handler and reaches the end of the procedure without finding a Resume, it stops everything and helpfully points out that you have no Resume statement in your error handler. (It even does this in complied code, placing a special "No Resume" window on the screen.)

However, we really don't want to use Resume if the user chose Cancel because there are some errors that they can't fix at this level. For example, if the error was that the file was too big to fit into memory, they'll have to leave this procedure (OKButton_Click( )), select a new file, and then select the OK button again. To leave this procedure without messages about our lack of a Resume statement, we need to use Exit Sub, like this:

```
Sub OKButton_Click ()
    On Error GoTo FileError

    If (Right$(Dir1.Path, 1) = "\") Then       'Get file name
        Filename$ = Dir1.Path + File1.FileName
    Else
        Filename$ = Dir1.Path + "\" + File1.FileName
    End If

    Open Filename$ For Input As # 1            'Open file
    Form1.PadText.Text = Input$(LOF(1), # 1)   'Read file in

    Close # 1                  'Close file
    LoadForm.Hide              'Hide dialog box

    Exit Sub

FileError:
    Msg$ = Error$(Err)
    Select Case Err      'Display our own message?
        Case 7
            Msg$ = "File is too big to open."
```

```
                  Case 57, 68, 71, 72
                      Msg$ = "Please check the disk and try again."
                  Case 67
                      Msg$ = "Too many files open. Close some and try again."
          End Select
              Response% = MsgBox(Msg$, 49, "Editor")
              If Response% = 1 Then
                  Resume
   →          Else
   →              Exit Sub
   →          End If
          End Sub
```

This avoids the "No Resume" messages from Visual Basic and fixes the problem. In fact, there are other ways of handling Resume statements as well. Visual Basic supports two variations of Resume: Resume Next and Resume Line #.

Resume Next and Resume Line

Sometimes, you don't want to keep retrying the operation that caused the error. We've seen that one alternate method is to simply leave the procedure entirely and let the user select some other action. Two other methods are Resume Next and Resume Line #. The Resume Next statement causes Visual Basic to resume with the statement following the one that caused the error. In effect, we are simply skipping the statement that produced the problem. This can be useful, but it's usually not good simply to skip a line and then continue executing the rest of the code. For example, if we used Resume Next instead of Resume, and the Open statement had caused the error, we'd continue with the next statement after that, which tries to read from the file that we haven't been able to open:

```
Sub OKButton_Click ()
    On Error GoTo FileError

    If (Right$(Dir1.Path, 1) = "\") Then        'Get file name
        Filename$ = Dir1.Path + File1.FileName
    Else
        Filename$ = Dir1.Path + "\" + File1.FileName
    End If

    Open Filename$ For Input As # 1             'Open file
```

```
        Form1.PadText.Text = Input$(LOF(1), # 1)      'Read file in
        Close # 1                       'Close file
        LoadForm.Hide                   'Hide dialog box

        Exit Sub

    FileError:
        Msg$ = Error$(Err)
        Select Case Err      'Display our own message?
            Case 7
                Msg$ = "File is too big to open."
            Case 57, 68, 71, 72
                Msg$ = "Please check the disk and try again."
            Case 67
                Msg$ = "Too many files open. Close some and try again."
        End Select
        MsgBox Msg$, 48, "Editor"
        Resume Next
    End Sub
```

However, there are times when Resume Next is exactly what we need. Let's see an example of this in code. One common method in Visual Basic of determining whether or not a file exists on disk is to create a deliberate, trappable error. You may recall that in almost all Open modes (e.g., For Random, For Binary, etc.), the file is automatically created if it doesn't already exist. On the other hand, if you open a file For Input, Visual Basic generates a trappable error if the file doesn't exist (i.e., it doesn't make sense to create the file from scratch if we're about to read from it). We can use that error to indicate whether or not the file exists. Let's write a function called Exist( ), which takes a file name as its argument and returns True if the file exists, and False otherwise. In other words, we might use it like this:

```
Sub Form_Load ()
    If Exist("C:\AUTOEXEC.BAT") Then Print "Boot batch file
        exists."
End Sub
```

To add this function at the form level, click on general in the Object box of the code window, click on New Procedure... in the Code menu, click the Function option button, and give it a name of Exist. This template appears:

```
Function Exist ()

End Function
```

Give this function an argument of FileName As String, and set up the error handler like this:

```
Function Exist (FileName As String)
    On Error GoTo DoesNotExist
        :
        :

    Exit Function

DoesNotExist:
        :
        :

End Function
```

If there's no error, we should return a value of True, so we set Exist to True (-1), and try to open the file:

```
Function Exist (FileName As String)
    On Error GoTo DoesNotExist
    Exist = -1                  'Set to True
    Open (FileName) For Input As #200   'Unlikely to conflict
        :
        :

    Exit Function

DoesNotExist:
        :
        :

End Function
```

Here, we open the file as #200 because that file number is unlikely to conflict with other file numbers used elsewhere in the program. If the file does not exist, we'll go to the location DoesNotExist, where we want to set Exist to False (0). Then we want to use Resume Next, not Resume (which would cause us to try to open the file again):

TIP Although it is usually safe to use a number like 200 for a file number, you can also use the FreeFile function, which returns the number of the next free file.

```
Function Exist (FileName As String)
    On Error GoTo DoesNotExist
    Exist = -1                'Set to True
    Open (FileName) For Input As #200    'Unlikely to conflict
      :
      :

    Exit Function

DoesNotExist:
    Exist = 0                 'Set to False
    Resume Next
End Function
```

→ (arrows pointing to `Exist = 0` and `Resume Next`)

TIP   Here, we're assuming that the error was caused because the file was not found. In a real application, however, we might not be able to open the file for a variety of reasons (disk does not respond, device I/O error, etc.). To make sure that the file was simply not found, you might add a line in the error handler to make sure that Err = 53, which is the error generated when a file is not found (as shown in Table 9-1).

At this point, Exist holds the correct value, True or False. All that remains is to close the file and exit the function, which we can do like this:

```
Function Exist (FileName As String)
    On Error GoTo DoesNotExist
    Exist = -1                'Set to True
    Open (FileName) For Input As #200    'Unlikely to conflict
    Close #200
    Exit Function

DoesNotExist:
    Exist = 0                 'Set to False
    Resume Next
End Function
```

→ (arrow pointing to `Close #200`)

And that's it. Exist( ) is ready to go, giving us a good use for Resume Next. However, it's usually better to move to an entirely different part of the code and take some alternate action (and let the user know that you're doing so). That's what the Resume Line # statement allows us to do: With it, we can specify the line number to resume execution at. For example, we might decide that our Editor application should always try to open and load a default file named File.Txt when we start the application. To do that, we can put this code in the Form_Load( ) Sub procedure:

```
Sub Form_Load ()
    Open "File.Txt" For Input As # 1            'Open file
    Form1.PadText.Text = Input$(LOF(1), # 1)    'Read file in
    Close # 1                    'Close file
End Sub
```

On the other hand, if there was an error, we might want to pop the Load File... dialog box on the screen. First, we set up our error handler:

```
       Sub Form_Load ()
→          On Error GoTo FileError

           Open "File.Txt" For Input As # 1            'Open file
           Form1.PadText.Text = Input$(LOF(1), # 1)    'Read file in
           Close # 1                    'Close file
           Exit Sub

→      FileError:
             :
             :

       End Sub
```

Then, we can resume to another part of the procedure entirely with a Resume Line # statement like this, where we pop the Load File... dialog box up:

```
       Sub Form_Load ()
           On Error GoTo FileError

           Open "File.Txt" For Input As # 1            'Open file
           Form1.PadText.Text = Input$(LOF(1), # 1)    'Read file in
           Close # 1                    'Close file
           Exit Sub

→      10  LoadForm.Show
→          Exit Sub

       FileError:
→          Resume 10
       End Sub
```

And that's almost it for Resume, Resume Next, and Resume Line #. There's only one more point to consider. Let's say that **Proc1** calls **Proc2**:

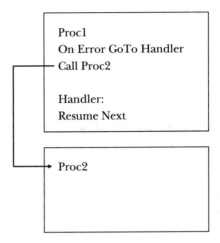

Next, let's assume that an error occurs while we're in **Proc2**, but that it has no error handler. Instead, Visual Basic works its way back up the calling ladder, searching for an error handler. In this case, that's **Proc1**:

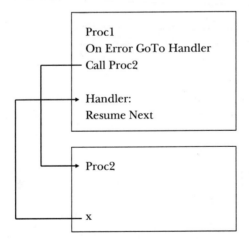

In other words, **Proc1** is handling **Proc2**'s error this way. If you leave an error handler out of **Proc2**, you should be aware of this point. That is, statements like Resume Next in **Proc1**'s error handler may cause unexpected or even disastrous results.

That's it for our coverage of trappable errors in Visual Basic. As you can see, we can do a lot with the On Error GoTo statement, especially when coupled with the Resume statement. However, there's more to finding and eliminating errors than this. Now it's time to turn to debugging.

Debugging

As we type our program into Visual Basic, we may have errors in syntax. That is, we may type something like this:

```
Circle (ScaleWidth/2, ScaleHeight/2)
```

When we try to move on to the next line, Visual Basic puts a warning box on the screen, indicating that something more is expected. In this case, we need to indicate the circle's radius (at least). In this way, Visual Basic catches syntax errors at design-time. On the other hand, we may end up with errors in run-time that are impossible to avoid at design-time, out of memory or disk full errors, for example, trappable errors, in other words. We've just seen that if we can anticipate such errors, we can trap and deal with them.

The kinds of errors that we're going to turn to next are usually harder to find: logic errors, or, in a word, bugs. Here, an error may be buried deep in a long chain of complex statements, pages and pages of code, in fact. Fortunately, Visual Basic provides us with some debugging tools that we can use to locate and even fix errors with.

TIP   In fact, even text boxes can make excellent debugging tools if you use them to print out intermediate results in your programs. To use them, simply add a few extra text boxes to your application, and print out crucial values in them as your program is running. For example, you might want to see what's happening to a variable that's supposed to be counting keystrokes: Is it incremented every time you press a key? Or you might want to make sure you're reading mouse cursor coordinates correctly in a MouseDown( ) event, and you can display them in text boxes as well. In general, temporary text boxes can provide a window into what's happening behind the scenes in your program, and that's what debugging is all about.

For the purposes of exploring debugging, let's set ourselves the task of alphabetizing 10 or so names, like these:

John

Tim

Edward

Samuel

Frank

Todd

George

Ralph

Leonard

Thomas

We can start by setting up an array to hold all the names in the **Form_Click( )** Sub procedure:

```
Sub Form_Click ()
    Static Names(10) As String

    Names(1)  = "John"
    Names(2)  = "Tim"
    Names(3)  = "Edward"
    Names(4)  = "Samuel"
    Names(5)  = "Frank"
    Names(6)  = "Todd"
    Names(7)  = "George"
    Names(8)  = "Ralph"
    Names(9)  = "Leonard"
    Names(10) = "Thomas"
    :
```

Then we arrange them in alphabetical order with these Basic instructions (this part of the code has three very common bugs in it):

```
Sub Form_Click ()
    Static Names(10) As String

    Names(1)  = "John"
    Names(2)  = "Tim"
    Names(3)  = "Edward"
    Names(4)  = "Samuel"
```

```
        Names(5) = "Frank"
        Names(6) = "Todd"
        Names(7) = "George"
        Names(8) = "Ralph"
        Names(9) = "Leonard"
        Names(10) = "Thomas"


→       For i = i To 10
:           For j = i To 10
:               If Names(i) > Names(j) Then
                        Temp$ = Names(i)
                        Names(j) = Names(j)
                        Names(j) = Tmp$
                    End If
            Next j
        Next i
        :
```

Note here that we're using the > logical operator with which to compare strings. This is perfectly legal in Visual Basic, and it allows us to determine the alphabetical order of such strings. Finally, we can print out the result, name by name:

```
Sub Form_Click ()
    Static Names(10) As String

    Names(1) = "John"
    Names(2) = "Tim"
    Names(3) = "Edward"
    Names(4) = "Samuel"
    Names(5) = "Frank"
    Names(6) = "Todd"
    Names(7) = "George"
    Names(8) = "Ralph"
    Names(9) = "Leonard"
    Names(10) = "Thomas"

    For i = i To 10
        For j = i To 10
            If Names(i) > Names(j) Then
                    Temp$ = Names(i)
                    Names(j) = Names(j)
                    Names(j) = Tmp$
                End If
        Next j
    Next i
```

```
→        For k = 1 To 10
→                Print Names(k)
→        Next k
     End Sub
```

Unfortunately, this is the result of the program when we execute the **Form_Click( )** procedure by clicking on the form:

John
Tim

Todd

This looks a little incomplete. It's time to debug. In fact, we can start debugging without even stopping the program. To do that, select the View Code item in Visual Basic's Code menu. The **Form_Click( )** Sub procedure pops up as shown in Figure 9-5.

Visual Basic gives us the chance to scan the code for possible errors while the program is running. When we do that, we might spot one error right away just by reading the code. In particular, when we switch elements around in the

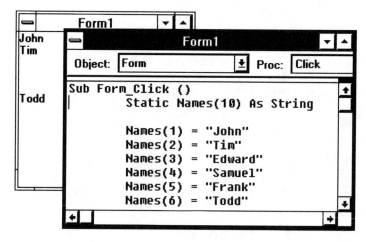

Figure 9-5. Editing Code While Running a Program

array, we load them temporarily into a variable named **Temp$**, but, when we load them back into the array, we use a (misspelled) variable named **Tmp$**:

```
Sub Form_Click ()
    Static Names(10) As String

    Names(1)  = "John"
    Names(2)  = "Tim"
    Names(3)  = "Edward"
    Names(4)  = "Samuel"
    Names(5)  = "Frank"
    Names(6)  = "Todd"
    Names(7)  = "George"
    Names(8)  = "Ralph"
    Names(9)  = "Leonard"
    Names(10) = "Thomas"

    For i = i To 10
            For j = i To 10
                    If Names(i) > Names(j) Then
→                           Temp$ = Names(i)
                            Names(j) = Names(j)
→                           Names(j) = Tmp$
                    End If
            Next j
    Next i

    For k = 1 To 10
            Print Names(k)
    Next k
End Sub
```

This is probably the most common of Visual Basic logic errors — misspelling a variable's name. Visual Basic does not complain about such errors because it assumes that you're implicitly declaring a new variable, **Tmp$**, and it sets that new variable to the empty string, " ".

We can actually fix this problem without ending the program. Just open Visual Basic's Run menu, where you'll see three choices highlighted: Break, End, and Restart. Select Break, temporarily stopping the program. Now we can change the code (to a certain extent) and then continue with the program execution (Visual Basic usually allows us to make changes up to the level of declaring new variables). Here, we just edit the code to change **Tmp$** to **Temp$**, as shown in Figure 9-6.

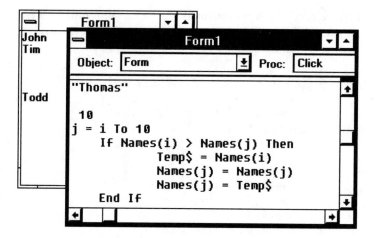

Figure 9-6. Editing Code in a Running Application

Now the program looks like this:

```
Sub Form_Click ()
    Static Names(10) As String

    Names(1) = "John"
    Names(2) = "Tim"
    Names(3) = "Edward"
    Names(4) = "Samuel"
    Names(5) = "Frank"
    Names(6) = "Todd"
    Names(7) = "George"
    Names(8) = "Ralph"
    Names(9) = "Leonard"
    Names(10) = "Thomas"

    For i = i To 10
        For j = i To 10
                If Names(i) > Names(j) Then
                        Temp$ = Names(i)
                        Names(j) = Names(j)
                        Names(j) = Temp$
                End If
        Next j
    Next i

    For k = 1 To 10
            Print Names(k)
    Next k
End Sub
```

We can let the program continue now by selecting the Continue item in the Run menu. After we do, we can click on the form to see if we've made a difference. This is the list that appears:

John

Tim

Tim

Tim

Tim

Todd

Todd

Todd

Todd

Todd

There's been a change, but the result is clearly not yet right. The obvious problem in our program is that the entries in the **Names( )** array are being filled incorrectly. To check what's happening, we should watch the array elements as they're filled. And we can do that by setting *breakpoint.* A breakpoint halts program execution when it is reached. For example, we can set a breakpoint by moving the cursor on the screen down to the line that reads "If Names(i) > Names(j) Then":

```
Sub Form_Click ()
    Static Names(10) As String

    Names(1)  = "John"
    Names(2)  = "Tim"
    Names(3)  = "Edward"
    Names(4)  = "Samuel"
    Names(5)  = "Frank"
    Names(6)  = "Todd"
    Names(7)  = "George"
    Names(8)  = "Ralph"
    Names(9)  = "Leonard"
    Names(10) = "Thomas"

    For i = i To 10
        For j = i To 10
                If Names(i) > Names(j) Then     ←
                    Temp$ = Names(i)
                    Names(j) = Names(j)
```

```
                          Names(j) = Temp$
                    End If
          Next j
      Next i
      For k = 1 To 10
              Print Names(k)
      Next k
  End Sub
```

Now we press <F9> or select Toggle Breakpoint in the Run menu. The statement we've selected appears in bold print to indicate that a breakpoint has
been set, as shown in Figure 9-7.

Next, we run the program by selecting Start in the Run menu. Program execution continues until we reach the breakpoint, and then it stops; the breakpoint line, "If Names(i) > Names(j) Then," is outlined with a dotted border, as
in Figure 9-8. We can check the values of Names(i) and Names(j) in Visual
Basic's *immediate window.*

The immediate window lets us check the values of a program while we're in a
break state (i.e., which happens when you select Break in the Run menu, or
the program reaches a breakpoint). To check the value of **Names(i)**, we only
need to type ?Names(i) in the immediate window and press <Enter>. When we

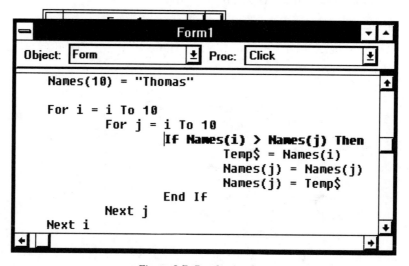

Figure 9-7. Breakpoint Set

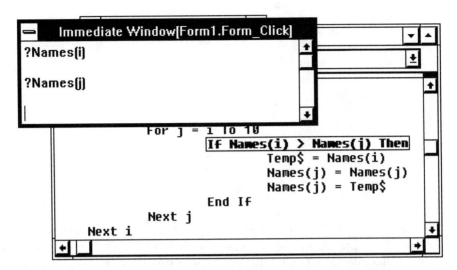

Figure 9-8. The Immediate Window

check the values of **Names(i)** and **Names(j)**, we see that there's nothing in them, as shown in Figure 9-8.

In other words, the line, "If **Names(i)** > **Names(j)** Then" is comparing nothing; the values in **Names(i)** and **Names(j)** are not valid. At this point in the program, the beginning, both **i** and **j** are supposed to point at the first element in the array. That is, both **i** and **j** should be 1. We can check the value of **i** simply by executing ?i in the immediate window. When we do, we see that **i** = 0, which is a problem. This line, below, in the code must be changed to For **i** = 1 To 10 because we need to initialize **i** before using it.

```
Static Names(10) As String

Names(1)  = "John"
Names(2)  = "Tim"
Names(3)  = "Edward"
Names(4)  = "Samuel"
Names(5)  = "Frank"
Names(6)  = "Todd"
Names(7)  = "George"
Names(8)  = "Ralph"
Names(9)  = "Leonard"
Names(10) = "Thomas"
```

```
→    For i = i To 10
        For j = i To 10
              If Names(i) > Names(j) Then
                       Temp$ = Names(i)
                       Names(j) = Names(j)
                       Names(j) = Temp$
              End If
        Next j
     Next i

     For k = 1 To 10
           Print Names(k)
     Next k
```

However, when we make the change and run the program (note that you can use F9 to toggle off the breakpoint we set, or you can remove all breakpoints by selecting the Clear All Breakpoints in the Run menu), we still see:

John

Tim

Tim

Tim

Tim

Todd

Todd

Todd

Todd

Todd

Obviously there is still a problem. Let's examine the part of the program where the actual elements are switched, the only other part of the program. We can put a breakpoint in at the end of the element switching section like this:

```
Static Names(10) As String

Names(1) = "John"
Names(2) = "Tim"
Names(3) = "Edward"
Names(4) = "Samuel"
Names(5) = "Frank"
Names(6) = "Todd"
```

```
Names(7) = "George"
Names(8) = "Ralph"
Names(9) = "Leonard"
Names(10) = "Thomas"

For i = i To 10
    For j = i To 10
            If Names(i) > Names(j) Then
                    Temp$ = Names(i)
                    Names(j) = Names(j)
                    Names(j) = Temp$        ←
            End If
        Next j
Next i

For k = 1 To 10
        Print Names(k)
Next k
```

Now when we execute the program, we'll stop at the breakpoint, where we'll be able to determine whether the elements really were switched. In fact, we don't need to evaluate elements in the immediate window with the ? command at all. We can actually print directly to the immediate window from the program. To do that, we use the **Print** method of the **Debug** object, which is the object responsible for maintaining the immediate window:

```
Static Names(10) As String

Names(1) = "John"
Names(2) = "Tim"
Names(3) = "Edward"
Names(4) = "Samuel"
Names(5) = "Frank"
Names(6) = "Todd"
Names(7) = "George"
Names(8) = "Ralph"
Names(9) = "Leonard"
Names(10) = "Thomas"

For i = i To 10
    For j = i To 10
            If Names(i) > Names(j) Then
                    Temp$ = Names(i)
                    Names(j) = Names(j)
                    Debug.Print Names(i), Names(j)   ←
                    Names(j) = Temp$
```

```
                End If
    Next j
Next i

For k = 1 To 10
        Print Names(k)
Next k
```

Now we run the program. Execution halts at the breakpoint, (i.e., the line that reads: **Names(j) = Temp$**), and we examine **Names(i)** and **Names(j)** in the immediate window, as shown in Figure 9-9. One is **John**, and the other is **Edward**.

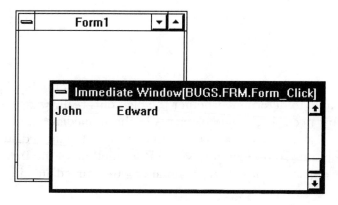

Figure 9-9. Immediate Window with Names(i) and Names(j)

The exchange of array elements is supposed to go like this: We take the value in **Names(i)** and place it in **Temp$**. Then we copy the element in **Names(j)** and place it into **Names(i)**. The final step is to move **Temp$** into **Names(j)**. At this breakpoint, all but the final step has been taken: We are about to move the value in **Temp$** into **Names(j)**.

In other words, we'd expect **Names(i)** and **Names(j)** to hold the same value values, but they do not. **Names(i)** holds "John" and **Names(j)** holds "Edward." Something is wrong. If we look back one line in our code, we see this line:

```
Static Names(10) As String

    Names(1) = "John"
    Names(2) = "Tim"
    Names(3) = "Edward"
```

```
      Names(4)  =  "Samuel"
      Names(5)  =  "Frank"
      Names(6)  =  "Todd"
      Names(7)  =  "George"
      Names(8)  =  "Ralph"
      Names(9)  =  "Leonard"
      Names(10) =  "Thomas"

      For i = 1 To 10
         For j = i To 10
                 If Names(i) > Names(j) Then
                         Temp$ = Names(i)
→                       Names(j) = Names(j)
                         Names(j) = Temp$
                 End If
         Next j
      Next i

      For k = 1 To 10
              Print Names(k)
      Next k
```

It is apparent that this line should be **Names(i) = Names(j)**. We make the change, yielding the debugged program:

```
Static Names(10) As String

Names(1)  = "John"
Names(2)  = "Tim"
Names(3)  = "Edward"
Names(4)  = "Samuel"
Names(5)  = "Frank"
Names(6)  = "Todd"
Names(7)  = "George"
Names(8)  = "Ralph"
Names(9)  = "Leonard"
Names(10) = "Thomas"

For i = 1 To 10
    For j = i To 10
            If Names(i) > Names(j) Then
                    Temp$ = Names(i)
                    Names(i) = Names(j)
                    Names(j) = Temp$
            End If
    Next j
Next i
```

```
For k = 1 To 10
        Print Names(k)
Next k
```

And this is the final result when we run it:

Edward

Frank

George

John

Leonard

Ralph

Samuel

Thomas

Tim

Todd

The program has been debugged. As you can see, we have some powerful debugging tools available to us in Visual Basic, including the immediate window and breakpoints. In fact, these tools have more capabilities still. For example, we can execute a program line by line if we want to, and even change the values of variables while the program is running. Let's see how this works with an example.

Debugging an Investment Calculator

For instance, we might decide to write a small investment calculator to tell us what an investment would be worth in a certain number of years. That is, we might invest $1,000.00 at 7% for 12 years; if we did, that investment would be worth (if it was compounded annually):

$$(\$1,000.00) \times (1.07)^{12} = \$2,252.19$$

Let's put this calculator together. Start Visual Basic and place three text boxes on the form to hold the three values: **Investment** ($1,000.00 above), **Interest-Rate** (7%), and **Years** (12). The calculation that we want to perform is:

Result = **Investment** $\times$ (1 + **InterestRate** / 100)$^{\textbf{Years}}$

Label the boxes as shown in Figure 9-10, and give them the **CtlNames** (from the top) of **InvestmentText, InterestRateText,** and **YearsText.** Next, place a button with the caption Yields and **CtlName YieldsButton** under them, and a label at the bottom (set its **BorderStyle** to Fixed Single so it looks like the text boxes), with the **CtlName ResultLabel,** as shown in Figure 9-11.

Our investment calculator template is set. All that remains is the code. To use the calculator, the user places the investment amount in the top text box, the interest rate in the next box, and the number of years that the investment will last in the third text box. Then they click the Yields button to see the result in the bottom box. That means that all the action will take place in **YieldsButton_Click ( )**; click on that button to bring up the code window:

```
Sub YieldsButton_Click()

End Sub
```

We can start by converting the text in the text boxes into numeric values like this:

```
Sub YieldsButton_Click()
    Investment = Val(InvestmentText.Text)
    InterstRate = Val(InterestRateText.Text)
    Years = Val(YearsText.Text)
        :

  End Sub
```

Next, we can perform the calculation:

```
    Sub YieldsButton_Click()
        Investment = Val(InvestmentText.Text)
        InterstRate = Val(InterestRateText.Text)
        Years = Val(YearsText.Text)
→       Result = Investments * (1 + InterestRate / 100) ^ Years
            :

        End Sub
```

Finally, we display the result like this:

```
    Sub YieldsButton_Click()
        Investment = Val(InvestmentText.Text)
        InterstRate = Val(InterestRateText.Text)
```

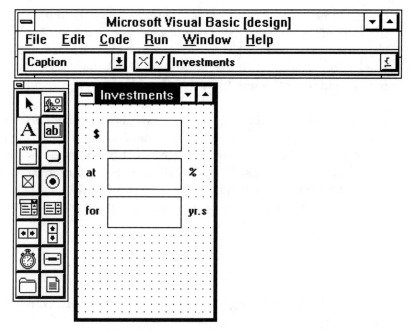

Figure 9-10. Investment Calculator Template

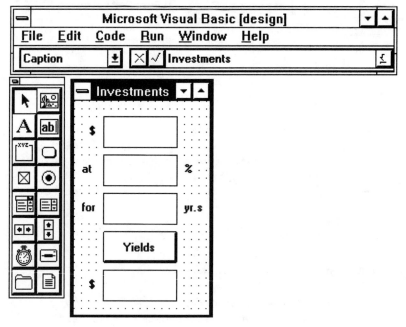

Figure 9-11. Completed Investment Calculator Template

```
         Years = Val(YearsText.Text)
         Result = Investments * (1 + InterestRate / 100) ^ Years
  →      ResultLabel.Caption = Format$(Result, "###,###,##0.00")
    End Sub
```

Let's give it a try. For example, we can try the above calculation, $1,000.00 at 7% for 12 years. However, the result is $0.00, as shown in Figure 9-12. Obviously, there's a problem. It's time to debug.

We can start by placing a breakpoint (i.e., by using F9 or Toggle Breakpoint in the Run menu) in the first line of the **YieldsButton_Click ( )** procedure:

```
    Sub YieldsButton_Click()
  →      Investment = Val(InvestmentText.Text)
         InterstRate = Val(InterestRateText.Text)
         Years = Val(YearsText.Text)
         Result = Investments * (1 + InterestRate / 100) ^ Years
         ResultLabel.Caption = Format$(Result, "###,###,##0.00")
    End Sub
```

When we reach this point, the program will automatically break. Start the program again, place the same values in the text boxes, and click the Yields button. When you do, the program reaches the breakpoint and stops. Now we can single step through each line of the code, one line at a time, using the F8 key or by selecting the Single Step item in the Run menu. Press <F8> once to execute the first line. The box around the first line (as is usual for a breakpoint) moves to the second line, indicating where we are, as shown in Figure

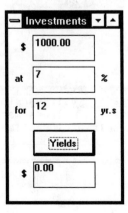

Figure 9-12. Investment Calculator, First Attempt

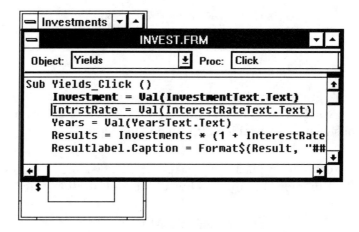

Figure 9-13. Single Stepping in the Investment Calculator

9-13. Note also that the text of the first line stays bold, indicating that there is still a breakpoint there.

After executing the first line, we can check the value of Investment in the immediate window with a ? command as shown in Figure 9-14, where we see that **Investment** holds 1000.00, as it should.

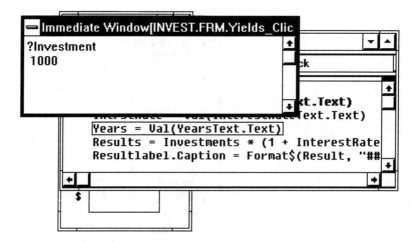

Figure 9-14. The Immediate Window with Investment's Value

The next step is to set the interest rate. We execute the next line by pressing <F8> again:

```
Sub YieldsButton_Click()
    Investment = Val(InvestmentText.Text)
→    InterstRate = Val(InterestRateText.Text)
    Years = Val(YearsText.Text)
    Result = Investments * (1 + InterestRate / 100) ^ Years
    ResultLabel.Caption = Format$(Result, "###,###,##0.00")
End Sub
```

We then check the value of **InterestRate** in the immediate window by typing ?InterestRate. This value should be 7, but the result, as shown in Figure 9-15, is 0. This is clearly a bug. By checking the code, we can see that **InterestRate** is misspelled in the second line (i.e., "InterstRate"). Fixing that yields this code:

```
Sub YieldsButton_Click()
    Investment = Val(InvestmentText.Text)
→    InterestRate = Val(InterestRateText.Text)
    Years = Val(YearsText.Text)
    Result = Investments * (1 + InterestRate / 100) ^ Years
    ResultLabel.Caption = Format$(Result, "###,###,##0.00")
End Sub
```

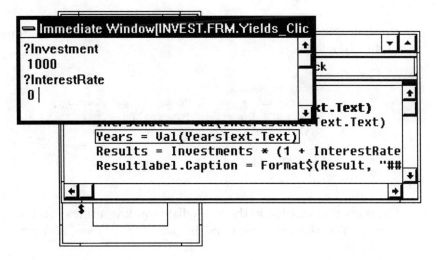

Figure 9-15. The Immediate Window Showing InterestRate

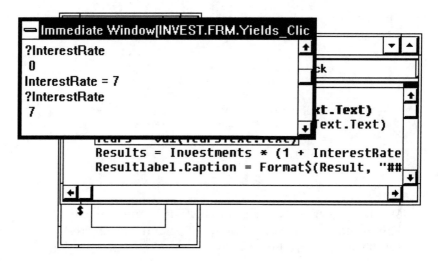

Figure 9-16. Working Investment Calculator

We can also fix the problem without stopping the program, by placing a value directly into **InterestRate**. That is, Visual Basic allows us to load values into our variables even when the program is running. In particular, we want to load a value of 7 into **InterestRate**. To do that, simply type the line InterestRate = 7 into the immediate window. We can then check the new value of **InterestRate** by typing ?InterestRate. As shown in Figure 9-16, **InterestRate** does indeed hold 7 now.

Pressing <F8> once again executes the third line in the code, setting the value of the variable **Years**:

```
     Sub YieldsButton_Click()
         Investment = Val(InvestmentText.Text)
         InterestRate = Val(InterestRateText.Text)
→        Years = Val(YearsText.Text)
         Result = Investments * (1 + InterestRate / 100) ^ Years
         ResultLabel.Caption = Format$(Result, "###,###,##0.00")
     End Sub
```

Checking that variable in the immediate window verifies that it does hold 12, as it should. The next line does the actual calculation, and pressing <F8> a fourth time executes it:

```
      Sub YieldsButton_Click()
          Investment = Val(InvestmentText.Text)
          InterestRate = Val(InterestRateText.Text)
          Years = Val(YearsText.Text)
→         Result = Investments * (1 + InterestRate / 100) ^ Years
          ResultLabel.Caption = Format$(Result, "###,###,##0.00")
      End Sub
```

This line assigns the results of the calculation to a variable named **Result**. We can check the value of **Result** in the immediate box. When we do, however, we find that it's 0. Once again, we check the code, finding that we're using a variable named **Investments**, not **Investment**, in the fourth line. Since we've already executed that line, however, we can't execute it again without reentering the **YieldsButton_Click( )** procedure. Even so, we have isolated that problem, so we can fix the code. Change that line so that it uses the variable **Investment** instead of **Investments**:

```
      Sub YieldsButton_Click()
          Investment = Val(InvestmentText.Text)
          InterestRate = Val(InterestRateText.Text)
          Years = Val(YearsText.Text)
→         Result = Investment * (1 + InterestRate / 100) ^ Years
          ResultLabel.Caption = Format$(Result, "###,###,##0.00")
      End Sub
```

Now we can rerun the program using the same values. When we do, we see that indeed:

$$(\$1{,}000.00) * (1.07)^{12} = \$2{,}252.19$$

And the program is debugged. As you can see, single stepping like this can be a powerful debugging tool, giving us a picture of what our program is doing line by line. In general, then, we've gotten a good idea of the debugging capabilities of Visual Basic, which are considerable. If we suspect errors in a program's logic, we can set breakpoints inside it, stopping it at strategic locations and checking what's happening. In addition, we can print values to the Debug object, and we'll see them appear in the immediate window when our program runs in the Visual Basic environment. To further locate the problem, we can even work through the code line by line if we must.

There is, however, one problem that we should mention before finishing with debugging and moving on to the next chapter. Because Visual Basic programs are event driven, there is one consideration that we must take into account. If you place a breakpoint in a MouseDown or KeyPress event procedure and then release the mouse button or key while the program is in a break state, you may never get a MouseUp or KeyUp event when you continue. In other words, keep in mind that Visual Basic programs respond to the computer environment, and if you change that environment while debugging, it may result in unexpected consequences.

That's it for our coverage of debugging and error handling. Let's move on to our next topic now: communicating (or "interfacing") between Windows applications.

Interfacing to Other Windows Applications

What Is DDE?

One of the benefits of the Windows operating environment is that it's multi-tasking; that is, it can run several different applications at once, making it substantially different from DOS. This capability of Windows raises some interesting possibilities for program interaction. For example, what if two programs were able to communicate in some way, passing data and instructions back and forth? In this way, each could handle the tasks that it was best at: A spreadsheet could manipulate data in cells; a word processor could format data into documents; and the power of both would be increased by being able to work together. In fact, all this is possible under Windows, and it's referred to as *Dynamic Data Exchange*, or DDE.

Using DDE, we can coordinate the transfer of data between a number of Windows applications. For example, Word for Windows can talk with Excel for Windows, allowing the user to design something of an integrated program environment. However, DDE is also available to us in Visual Basic, and the possibilities are richer here because we can design our own programs from scratch. For example, you might be interested in modeling some complex financial or scientific model that's beyond a spreadsheet's capabilities, even though the spreadsheet is useful for entering and examining data points with.

Using DDE, we can actually connect the spreadsheet's individual cells — or a range of those cells — to a Visual Basic form or control, where we can manipulate that data as we wish.

In this chapter, we'll see DDE at work and explore its possibilities. We'll use two popular Windows software packages to see how it works, Word for Windows and Excel for Windows, setting up conversations with both of them. This doesn't mean you have to have these packages, of course. Many applications support Windows DDE (in fact, we'll write Visual Basic programs ourself that will be able to communicate). We'll start by establishing a DDE link between our program and these packages at design-time, and then move on to establishing such links when our programs run through the use of built-in Visual Basic properties. Next, we'll see how to let the user set up his own DDE links between the controls in our programs and other applications (i.e., DDE links that we didn't design into the program originally), as well as how to start the application that we're supposed to be communicating with if it isn't already running. Finally, we'll see some advanced DDE topics, such as how to send actual commands to other applications (e.g., closing or saving Excel spreadsheets), and how to handle DDE errors. With all this coming, then, let's start at once by examining what makes DDE tick.

How DDE Works

There are two ways of opening a link between programs, as a *hot* link or as a *cold* link. For example, in a hot link, data would be updated in our Visual Basic program whenever it's changed in a spreadsheet. This kind of communication is impressive. Imagine entering a value in a spreadsheet cell and seeing it appear simultaneously in some text box in a program you've written. A cold link functions in much the same way, except that we have more control over when the exchanged data is updated; that is, in a cold link, data updates are made only on request, not whenever the data itself changes.

In addition, there are two different types of links themselves, *client* links and *server* links, depending on which role our application is taking: either that of a DDE client, or that of a DDE server. In general, data flows from a DDE server to the DDE client like this (although it is actually possible for the DDE client to send data back as well):

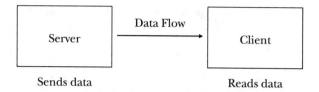

If we want to read data, we'll set ourselves up as a client (establishing a client link). If we want to supply data, we'll set ourselves up as a server (and establish a server link). For example, if we wanted to read some cells in an Excel spreadsheet, we would be the client and Excel the server.

In Visual Basic, three types of controls can act as clients; that is, they can get DDE data such as picture boxes, text boxes, and labels. In other words, we'll be able to read text and place it into text boxes or labels, and read pictures and place them in picture boxes. Only forms can act as servers; that is, they can send DDE data. However, the controls on the form can be the sources of that data. For example, if Form1 is the server, then a control like Text1 can be the actual source of the data, depending on what the client asks for (it will supply the actual name of the control it wants to read from).

We should also note that DDE works through the clipboard. That is, the data and DDE requests are passed back and forth in the clipboard object. This will be valuable to you if you're going to do a lot of DDE programming because you only need to see what's in the clipboard (by clicking on the clipboard icon in the Windows' Program Manager's Main window) to see what's actually being passed back and forth. With all this preparation, then, let's get started with some design-time DDE links.

Design-Time Client Links

Establishing DDE links at design-time is very easy in Visual Basic. For example, let's say that we had a document in Word for Windows named **Document1** (Word's default document name). We might want to establish a link between the text in that document and a text box, **Text1**, in a program we're designing. If we do establish such a link, it will remain as part of the program when it runs. We should note, however, that we can only establish hot links at

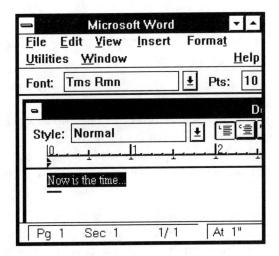

Figure 10-1. Selecting Text in WinWord

design-time, not cold links (i.e., data is transferred to the client immediately after being changed in the server).

In this case, we want the text box to mirror what's in the Word document, so Word will be the server and **Text1** the client. To establish this link, start Visual Basic and Word for Windows, WinWord, if you have it. Select all the text in **Document1**, as shown in Figure 10-1, and then copy it using the Copy item in WinWord's Edit menu. This transfers the text to the clipboard (as you can see in the clipboard itself), and establishes WinWord as the source of the data, that is, as the server.

The next step is to set up the link itself with **Text1**. To do that, select **Text1** in Visual Basic and select the Paste Link item in Visual Basic's Edit menu. This item will be active only if there is data in the clipboard which conforms to the DDE link standards (as we'll see later). After you select Paste Link, the link is formed, and immediately the text in Document1 appears in Text1, as shown in Figure 10-2. You'll find that editing the text in Document1 produces similar changes in **Text1**. Congratulations — you've just set up your first DDE link (in this case, a design-time client link). If you go on and write a program using **Text1**, the link will be preserved, and when the program starts, it will attempt to reestablish that link.

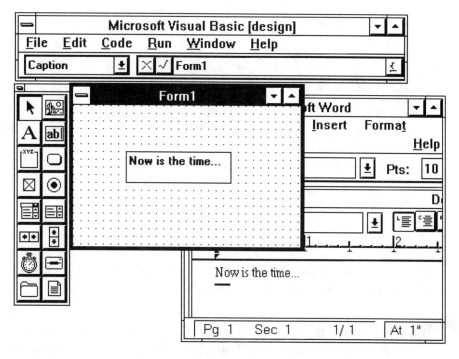

Figure 10-2. A Design-Time DDE Client Link

NOTE If you run a program with a design-time link in the Visual Basic environment, Visual Basic has to cut the link temporarily when it switches from design- to run-time. Most applications, such as WinWord or Excel, attempt to reestablish the link, but not all.

TIP If you only want to link to a certain part of the text in a WinWord document, you can do that by only selecting and then copying that part of the text. From then on, only that range of text, and changes to that range of text, will appear in **Text1**.

Since we're dealing with Visual Basic, you might expect that information about this link — whether it's hot or cold, what we're linking to and so on — might be stored in Visual Basic properties. And, in fact, this information is indeed stored in a special set of **Text1**'s properties: its **Link** properties: **LinkMode**, **LinkTopic**, **LinkItem**, and **LinkTimeout**. Since Visual Basic has already set these properties up for us automatically, it will be easy to see what they hold.

DDE's LinkMode

Select **Text1** and find the link properties in the properties bar. These properties are available even if you're not linked to anything (e.g., if you don't have WinWord). Next, find the **LinkMode** property; you'll find that this property has a value of Hot, which corresponds to a **LinkMode** setting of 1. A LinkMode setting of 2 is a Cold link, and a setting of 0 means that there is no DDE link (the default).

In other words, this control (**Text1**) has a hot DDE client link with some external data source (recall that individual controls cannot function as DDE servers, only forms can do that). To find out what the other end of the link is, look at the **LinkTopic** property next.

NOTE   The reason we cannot set up cold links at design-time is that some code is needed to maintain a cold link. In particular, we'll need the **LinkRequest** method in the code to request a data update.

DDE's LinkTopic

Find the **LinkTopic** property in the properties bar. You'll find that it's set to WinWord¦Document1. This is the normal form for a LinkTopic to take: Application¦File. In other words, we've already found that there is a hot link with another application. Now we can find what the actual link is to. It's not enough to know the name of the application. We also have to know the name of the file that holds the data item we're linked to. The process is a little like tracking down someone we want to talk to who's staying in a hotel somewhere: We not only need to know what town they're in but the name of the hotel as well.

There are specific DDE application names given to Windows programs that support DDE. For example, the two we're dealing with here, Excel and Word for Windows, have the DDE names Excel and WinWord, which is why **LinkTopic** is set to WinWord¦Document1. **Document1**, of course, is the name of the file that the data we want is in. If we saved it, as, say, Doc1.Doc (.Doc is WinWord's normal extension), then the **LinkTopic** could be WinWord¦Doc1.Doc or even WinWord¦C:\Winword\Doc1.Doc. (If you have questions about an application's DDE name or the way it names files, check the documentation that came with it, which usually addresses such problems.)

Now we've narrowed down the link to an application and a file; however, we need more than that. We'll need the name(s) of the data item(s) we're interested in. That is, we may have the name of the town in which our friend's hotel is and the name of the hotel, but we still need a room number. That kind of information is stored in **LinkItem**.

DDE's LinkItem

If you check the **LinkItem** property next, you'll find that it's set to DDE_LINK, which is a generic name for a link item, meaning that the server application determines what particular data item we're linked to (i.e., the text we selected). If we were dealing with an application that had many discrete data items, like the cells in a spreadsheet, **LinkItem** would hold the name of the cell(s) we're linked to. For example, in Microsoft Excel, if you wanted to link to row 1, column 1 in the spreadsheet, you'd set **LinkItem** to R1C1 (as we'll see how to do later), which is the way Excel names its cells for DDE purposes. Usually, then, **LinkTopic** holds both the name of the application and the file which holds the data item we're interested in, and **LinkItem** holds the name of that item if it has a name, or DDE_LINK otherwise (the second such link would be named DDE_LINK2, and so on).

The last client **Link** property we can set at design-time is **LinkTimeout**, which indicates the time we'll allow for the DDE link to be established.

DDE's LinkTimeout

The **LinkTimeout** property is measured in tenths of a second, and the default value is 50, corresponding to five seconds. In other words, if we put a link into our program at design-time, the program attempts to establish that link as soon as it is run. If it can't do so before the timeout period, however, it quits, placing an error message box on the screen, and asking you if it should start the application that makes up the other end of the link. If you answer yes, the program will attempt to run the other application and set up the link.

If you check **Text1**'s **LinkTimeout** value, you'll find that it's set to 50, which corresponds to the default value of five seconds. This is usually more than adequate, but you should keep in mind that this means five real-time seconds, so you might want to extend this on slower computers if tests show that your program's DDE attempt is timing out before the DDE link is established.

As you can see, then, it's not at all difficult to establish a client link at run-time (i.e., where we read data from another application). Let's move on, then, and see if we can't do the same for establishing a server link (i.e., where we provide data to another application).

Design-Time Server Links

Start Visual Basic over again, or select New Project in the File menu, and start Microsoft Excel also if you have it. This time we'll go the other way: Our application will be the server, and the other application, say Microsoft Excel, will be the client. To set up this link at design-time, place a text box, **Text1**, on the default form (**Form1**), and make sure it's selected. Next, select the copy command in Visual Basic's Edit menu, placing the string in **Text1** (which is simply "Text1" at the moment) into the clipboard. Next, move to Excel and select one of the cells in the spreadsheet, say the top left hand cell, R1C1. Now, move to Excel's Edit menu and open it; the Paste Link item should be enabled. When you select it, a link is established between **Text1** and cell R1C1, and the string in **Text1** (i.e., "Text1") appears in R1C1, as shown in Figure 10-3.

That's it. The server link is established as a hot link. Now whatever we type in **Text1** appears in R1C1 as well. However, we should note that this is not a server link between **Text1** and R1C1; if we check the Link properties of **Text1**, we'll find that **LinkMode** = 0 (no link). Instead, only forms can have server links, so the link has been established between **Form1** and R1C1. If you check **Form1**'s **LinkMode** property, you'll see that it's set to Server (**LinkMode** = 1; the only other possibility is None: **LinkMode** = 0). In addition, **Form1**'s **LinkTopic** property is set to **Form1** because that's the current name of our application, and therefore its DDE name as well.

When other applications try to establish a link with our new server application, they should try to contact **Form1** (i.e., instead of WinWord or Excel) because that's our default application name. In addition, the controls on **Form1**, like **Text1**, can be the source of the data that they read. That is, from Excel's point of view, it now has a link to Form1 ¦ Text1. That's it: The server link is in place. If you create a program using this form, the link will be preserved, and any-

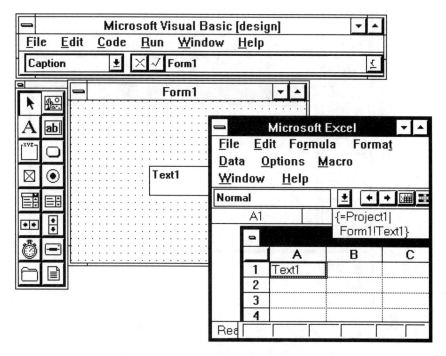

Figure 10-3. A Design-Time DDE Server Link

thing you type in **Text1** (in the server application **Form1**) will instantly be communicated to R1C1 (in the client application Excel).

At this point, then, we've set up both client and server links at design-time, and they will be preserved when our programs run. However, we can do the same thing at run-time, and, even more, we can set up and maintain cold links as well. Let's look into this next.

Run-Time Client Links

Let's put together a program that can read data (i.e., a client application) from an Excel spreadsheet by setting up a hot link at run-time. Start a new project in Visual Basic, adding a text box, **Text1**, and a check box by double-clicking on the check box tool. A check box appears in the center of the form. This button acts just as any command button might, except that when clicked, it stays clicked (as indicated with an x) until you click it again (when the x

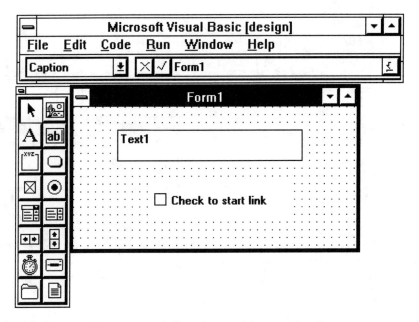

Figure 10-4. Run-Time Client Application Template

disappears). Change the caption of this check box, **Check1**, to "Check to start link" as shown in Figure 10-4.

When the user clicks this check box, a Click event is generated, and we can set up the link from an Excel spreadsheet to **Text1** at that time (the spreadsheet will be the server and we'll be the client; that is, data will be sent from Excel to **Text1**). Click on the check box now to bring up the **Check1_Click( )** template:

```
Sub Check1_Click ()

End Sub
```

Here, we'll set the appropriate link properties. To start, we set **Text1**'s **LinkMode** to NONE:

```
Sub Check1_Click ()
    Text1.LinkMode = NONE
        :
End Sub
```

DDE constants like NONE (and the one we're about to use: HOT) are defined in CONSTANT.TXT, so we have to make sure that we've loaded that file into the global module as well. Setting the **LinkMode** property in Visual Basic is the important thing to establish or break DDE links. By setting **Text1**'s **LinkMode** property to NONE (which equals 0), we break any links that it has now.

Next, we can set **Text1**'s **LinkTopic** property. This property has the format: "Application│File"; let's say that we had a spreadsheet open in Excel named **Sheet1** (the default name for a spreadsheet). In that case, we can set **LinkTopic** like this:

```
Sub Check1_Click ()
    Text1.LinkMode = NONE
    Text1.LinkTopic = "Excel│Sheet1"
        :

End Sub
```

The next step is setting the **LinkItem**. For example, we could link to Row 1, Column 1 (R1C1) of the spreadsheet like this:

```
Sub Check1_Click ()
    Text1.LinkMode = NONE
    Text1.LinkTopic = "Excel│Sheet1"
    Text1.LinkItem = "R1C1"
        :

End Sub
```

Now we're set. All that's needed to initiate a DDE link are the two properties, **LinkTopic** and **LinkItem**. To start the link, we simply set **LinkMode** to HOT, and we're done:

```
Sub Check1_Click ()
    Text1.LinkMode = NONE
    Text1.LinkTopic = "Excel│Sheet1"
    Text1.LinkItem = "R1C1"
    Text1.LinkMode = HOT
End Sub
```

At this point — as soon as **LinkMode** becomes HOT — Visual Basic attempts to form the link with the target application by sending out the **LinkTopic** and **LinkItem** and waiting to see if an application answers. If the correct applica-

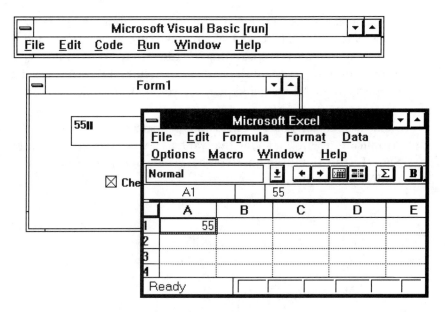

Figure 10-5. Run-Time Client Link

tion does answer, the link is established. In this case, Excel should answer, linking **Text1** to R1C1 as shown in Figure 10-5. Now everything we type in R1C1 also appears in **Text1**, so it's accessible to our program as Val(**Text1.Text**); that is, we're now able to read data directly from Excel and manipulate it if we wish.

Now that the link is established, we can also change the **LinkItem** (in this case, the cell in the spreadsheet) at run-time without breaking it. Let's examine that process next.

Changing the LinkItem at Run-Time

Let's put a counter into our program that will let us keep track of how many times the check box has been clicked. We can call this variable **First** (so that it indicates whether we're in **Check1_Click ( )** for the first time), and declare it Static like this:

```
      Sub Check1_Click ()
 →        Static First As Integer
          Text1.LinkMode = NONE
```

```
        Text1.LinkTopic = "Excel¦Sheet1"
        Text1.LinkItem = "R1C1"
        Text1.LinkMode = HOT
    End Sub
```

When the program starts, **First** will be set to 0; we can increment the value in **First** by adding 1. If **First** = 1 after that operation, then the check box was clicked for the first time, and we want to establish the link:

```
    Sub Check1_Click ()
→       Static First As Integer
→       First = First + 1
→       If First = 1 Then
        Text1.LinkMode = NONE
        Text1.LinkTopic = "Excel¦Sheet1"
        Text1.LinkItem = "R1C1"
        Text1.LinkMode = HOT
→       Else
            :

    End Sub
```

We can change the **LinkItem** the next time that the check box is clicked. For example, we can change it to R2C1 (Row 2, Column 1) in the spreadsheet like this:

```
    Sub Check1_Click ()
        Static First As Integer
        First = First + 1
        If First = 1 Then
            Text1.LinkMode = NONE
            Text1.LinkTopic = "Excel¦Sheet1"
            Text1.LinkItem = "R1C1"
            Text1.LinkMode = HOT
        Else
→           Text1.LinkItem = "R2C1"
→       End If
    End Sub
```

In this way, you don't have to break the link with the external application before switching your attention to other data items. That's it. Now we've seen how to establish a run-time hot link (where data is automatically updated each time it's changed in the server). Let's look at the other option now: run-time cold links.

Cold Run-Time Client Links

A cold link differs from a hot link in one respect. In a hot link, data is automatically updated in the client (in our case, it goes into the control **Text1**) whenever it changes in the server (Excel in our example). However, our program may not be ready for new data so quickly. For example, if we're carrying out some complex calculation with a number of links, it might be inadvisable to have the data in some of those links fluctuate before the whole calculation is done because it could lead to misleading results. Instead, we can create a cold link. With cold links, data is *not* sent to the client as soon as it changes in the server. Instead, the client must specifically request updates when it wants new data.

We do this with the **LinkRequest** method. After a cold link to some control has been set up, it takes a **LinkRequest** statement to update the data in it. Since **LinkRequest** is a method, it is associated with the control you want to update, like this: **Text1.LinkRequest**. To set up our cold link, we start off as before in our check box Sub procedure:

```
Sub Check1_Click ()
    Text1.LinkMode = NONE
    Text1.LinkTopic = "Excel|Sheet1"
    Text1.LinkItem = "R1C1"
        :

End Sub
```

However, when we define the **LinkMode**, we use COLD instead of HOT:

```
      Sub Check1_Click ()
          Text1.LinkMode = NONE
          Text1.LinkTopic = "Excel|Sheet1"
          Text1.LinkItem = "R1C1"
→         Text1.LinkMode = COLD
      End Sub
```

NOTE   The constant COLD has a value of 2, HOT equals 1, and NONE equals 0.

This sets up our cold link. When the link is established, nothing visible occurs, because we have not specifically asked for an update. We can do that, however, whenever the form is clicked. Open the **Form_Click( )** Sub procedure like this:

```
Sub Form_Click ()

End Sub
```

Now all we have to do is to execute **Text1.LinkRequest** this way:

```
Sub Form_Click ()
    Text1.LinkRequest
End Sub
```

When the program runs, the cold link is set up with Excel R1C1, **Sheet1**. The next step is to get some data, and you can do that simply by clicking the form. At that point, **Text1.LinkRequest** is executed, and the data now in R1C1 appears in **Text1** as well.

You might notice the two stubby upright bars in **Text1** that appear after we've established a link (for example, look in Figure 10-5), and you might wonder why they're there. Those bars are sent as delimiters when we interact with Excel, and they're meant to separate the data from different cells in the spreadsheet. Does this mean that we can send the data from more than one cell to **Text1**? The answer is yes. In particular, we can specify a *range* of cells to read. For example, if we wanted the data from the first two cells of column 1 in spreadsheet **Sheet1**, we would specify the appropriate range like this: R1C1:R2C1 (i.e., from Row 1, Column 1 to Row 2, Column 1). In code that looks like this:

```
       Sub Check1_Click ()
           Text1.LinkMode = NONE
           Text1.LinkTopic = "Excel¦Sheet1"
    →      Text1.LinkItem = "R1C1:R2C1"
           Text1.LinkMode = HOT
       End Sub
```

The result of this program appears in Figure 10-6, showing that both of the values we want — R1C1 and R2C1 — appear in **Text1**, separated by the cell delimiter. In this way, we can pack a whole range of Excel cells into a single control if we want to.

So far, then, we've examined how to set up hot run-time client links and cold run-time client links. Let's explore the process of setting up run-time server links next.

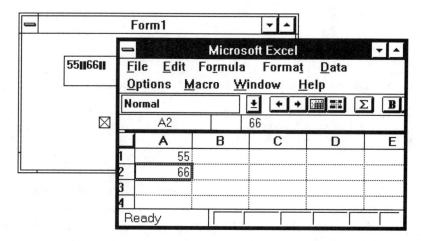

Figure 10-6. Client Link to a Range of Excel Cells

Run-Time Server Links

Now we'll get a chance to see how setting up a server application works. As it turns out, Visual Basic handles most of the details for us here. All we have to do is to set the correct **Link** properties, and Visual Basic will handle the actual transfer of data.

For an added twist, let's send pictures this time instead of text since DDE links can be established for bitmaps as well as for text (and you won't need Excel or WinWord for this example). To start, open the Windows Paintbrush program and draw some figure with the drawing tools. Next, choose the Selection tool from Paintbrush's toolbox (the upper-left tool in the toolbox), and stretch a dotted rectangle around the figure you've drawn, selecting it. This is the figure we'll transfer between applications in our client-server link.

The first step is to move the figure into a picture box, so select the Copy item in Paintbrush's Edit menu, placing a copy of the figure in the clipboard. Now we have to display that figure in a Visual Basic application, so start a new project in Visual Basic and double-click on the picture box tool, creating a picture box on the form. To paste the figure now in the clipboard into that picture box, simply make sure the picture box is selected and choose the Paste item in Visual Basic's Edit menu. The figure should appear in the picture box, something like Figure 10-7 (in addition, you should set the picture box's **AutoRedraw** property to True).

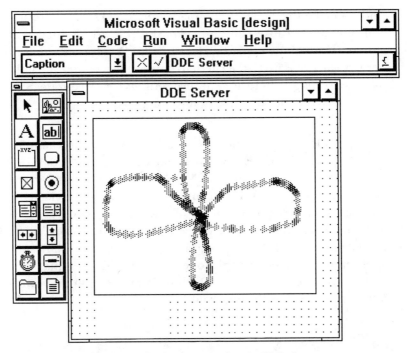

Figure 10-7. Server Application Template

Since this application already has the figure in a picture box, **Picture1**, this will become our server application. As you may recall, only forms can be servers, not individual controls, so click on the form itself to bring up the **Form_Click( )** template:

```
Sub Form_Click()

End Sub
```

The first thing we can do to make this application into a server is to set the form's **LinkMode** property to SERVER:

```
Sub Form_Click()
    LinkMode = SERVER          'Default = NONE
        :

End Sub
```

And, to make this meaningful, load CONSTANT.TXT into the server's general module, because constants like SERVER are defined there. Note that, although **LinkMode** could be HOT or COLD before, there is no such option here, because it is up to the client to determine whether the link is hot or cold. As far as forms go, there are only two settings for **LinkMode**: SERVER (i.e., the form is a server) or NONE (i.e., it is not a server).

Having made this application a server, let's give it a name as well. For example, we could call it Server.Exe when we create the .Exe file. To do that, save the general module (which has CONSTANT.TXT in it) as Server.Bas, the form we're designing as Server.Frm, and the project itself as Server.Mak. By doing this, we set the program's DDE application name as well. It is now Server. That is, the name given to the .Exe file when you create it using Visual Basic's Make Exe File... window is the application's DDE name as well. Besides a name, this application also needs a **Topic** to respond to DDE attempts. The default **Topic** is the name of the form itself, which is **Form1** here, but we can change that by setting the **LinkTopic** property like this:

```
        Sub Form_Click()
  →         LinkTopic = "Figure"     'Default = form name
            LinkMode = SERVER        'Default = NONE
        End Sub
```

If applications want to use our Server application as a server, they'll have to look for an application with the link topic of "Server | Figure." In fact, let's put together a client application, also in Visual Basic, that will read the figure in Server's **Picture1** control. Now that we've set up the current application as a server, the controls on it are suitable items for a DDE conversation. In other words, if "Server | Figure" is the DDE topic that this server will support, then "Picture1" is the DDE item. The last step in creating the server is making and running the .Exe file; to do that, simply select Make Exe File... in the File menu, and then switch to the Windows Program Manager and run Server. The Server window appears with the figure in its **Picture1** control. Now we're all set to use that application as a server for the client application that we can write next.

NOTE   It's worth emphasizing again that there are no hot or cold servers. The selection of hot or cold links is up to the client (although the server may elect not to grant such a link).

We've already seen how to write client applications that establish links in code (as opposed to at design-time). To do that, we can start a new project in Visual Basic and create a picture box (set the picture box's **AutoRedraw** property to True), named **Picture1**, about the same size as the picture box in the server application. Next, bring up the **Form_Load** Sub procedure like this:

TIP You can set **Picture1**'s **AutoSize** property to True in the client application in order to account for any difference in sizes between the picture boxes in the client and server applications. For example, if the server picture is smaller, the client picture box will shrink to fit it when it's transferred over.

```
Sub Form_Click ()

End Sub
```

This is where we'll add the code to create the link. When you click the form, the picture will be transferred from the server to our client application. First, we turn off any current links to the client application's Picture1 like this:

```
Sub Form_Click ()
    Picture1.LinkMode = NONE
        :

End Sub
```

Next, we have to specify the **LinkTopic**. The name of the application we're trying to link to is Server, and the **LinkTopic** property is set to Figure (instead of the default, which is the name of the form acting as a server), so we set **LinkTopic** like this:

```
    Sub Form_Click ()
        Picture1.LinkMode = NONE
→       Picture1.LinkTopic = "Server|Figure"
            :

    End Sub
```

Now we're ready for the **LinkItem**. In Visual Basic, that's the name of the actual control; that is, any of the controls on a form can be **LinkItems**. In this case, that's **Picture1**, which is the name of the picture in the server application that holds the figure we want, and that means we can set **LinkItem** like this in our client application:

```
        Sub Form_Click ()
            Picture1.LinkMode = NONE
            Picture1.LinkTopic = "Server|Figure"
  →         Picture1.LinkItem = "Picture1"
                   :

        End Sub
```

Finally, we initiate the hot link:

```
    Sub Form_Click ()
            Picture1.LinkMode = NONE
            Picture1.LinkTopic = "Server|Figure"
            Picture1.LinkItem = "Picture1"
  →         Picture1.LinkMode = HOT
        End Sub
```

Now the code is set. Run this application in Visual Basic and a window appears (our client application) that looks much like the server application, except that the figure is only in the server's picture box. Next, click the client application's window to execute the above code and establish the link. When you do, the picture is copied from the picture box in the server to the picture box in the client, as shown in Figure 10-8. In this way, it's just as easy to link pictures as it is to link text.

Or it's almost as easy. In fact, the initial link is as easy to make, but maintaining that link is a little more difficult when we're working with picture boxes instead of text. The reason for this is that changes in text boxes are usually very small scale when compared to changes in figures and pictures. When you start changing a picture, you may change hundreds or thousands of pixels at a time. In a hot link, data is transferred from server to client any time there's any change in the data, which would mean that the server would have to send the whole picture to the client any time you change even a pixel. Needless to say, this can be disastrous if you do any kind of graphics. The way Visual Basic handles this is by only sending updates to pictures when the server specifically requests that updates be sent (as opposed to text box or label changes, which are sent instantaneously in hot links, or when the client requests updates in cold links). And the server does that with the **LinkSend** method.

Maintaining a Picture Box Link

Let's say that we modify our server application so that the first time you click it, it sets itself up as a server; however, if you click it again, let's have it draw

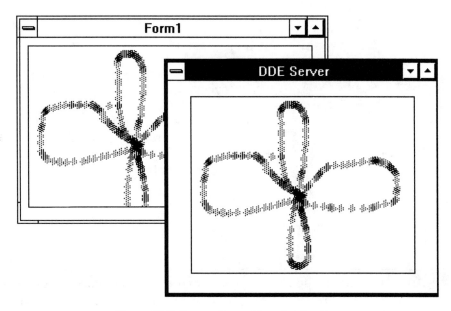

Figure 10-8. Custom Server-Client Applications

some additional graphics figures in the picture box, **Picture1**. For example, we might draw randomly sized rectangles. To do that, we modify the server application's **Form_Click( )** Sub procedure so that it knows when it's been clicked more than once:

```
      Sub Form_Click()
→         Static First
→         First = First + 1
→         If First = 1 Then
              LinkTopic = "Figure"      'Default = form name
              LinkMode = SERVER         'Default = NONE
→         Else
            :

→         End If
          End Sub
```

We can determine the coordinates (**x1, y1**) and (**x2, y2**) of the randomly sized rectangles using the size of the picture box — that is, **Picture1.ScaleWidth** and **Picture1.ScaleHeight** — and the Visual Basic Rnd function, which returns a random floating point number from 0 to 1:

```
Sub Form_Click()
    Static First
    First = First + 1
    If First = 1 Then
        LinkTopic = "Figure"     'Default = form name
        LinkMode = SERVER        'Default = NONE
    Else
→       x1 = Picture1.ScaleWidth * Rnd
→       y1 = Picture1.ScaleHeight * Rnd
→       x2 = Picture1.ScaleWidth * Rnd
→       y2 = Picture1.ScaleHeight * Rnd
                  :

    End If
End Sub
```

TIP   The Rnd function always generates the same sequence of random numbers when you restart the application that uses it; that is, if Rnd generated .010231, .782625, and .347276 as the first numbers when you started this application, it will generate them again, in the same order, the next time you start it also. You can change that by using the Randomize statement before executing Rnd. This statement resets Rnd so that it generates a sequence of numbers that doesn't repeat itself each time you start over.

Finally, we just draw the box itself, using **Picture1**'s **Line** method (and specifying the **B** argument for a box):

```
Sub Form_Click()
    Static First
    First = First + 1
    If First = 1 Then
        LinkTopic = "Figure"     'Default = form name
        LinkMode = SERVER        'Default = NONE
    Else
        x1 = Picture1.ScaleWidth * Rnd
        y1 = Picture1.ScaleHeight * Rnd
        x2 = Picture1.ScaleWidth * Rnd
        y2 = Picture1.ScaleHeight * Rnd
→       Picture1.Line (x1, y1)-(x2, y2), , B
    End If
End Sub
```

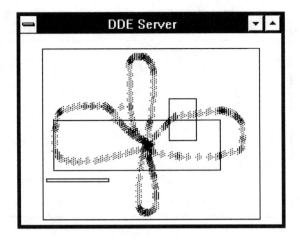

Figure 10-9. Server Application with Random Rectangles

The result is something like that shown in Figure 10-9. The first time you click the Server window when it's running, it sets itself up as a DDE server. Every time you click it thereafter, it draws a random rectangle in the picture box, overlapping the figure that's already there.

Now when we run Server, click it once to make it respond as a DDE server, run the client to get the figure into the client's picture box, and then start generating random rectangles. You'll see that the rectangles do not appear in the client application's picture box, but only in the server's picture box.

We can fix this, however, with the **LinkSend** method. Close the server application, and exit the client application in Visual Basic as well. Next bring up Server in Visual Basic once more and add a command button, **Command1**, with the caption "Send figure" as shown in Figure 10-9. Click once on the command button to bring up this template:

```
Sub Command1_Click ()

End Sub
```

Here's where we can use the LinkSend method to send an updated version of the picture to our clients. We do that like this (note that since **LinkSend** is a method, it is associated with the control **Picture1**):

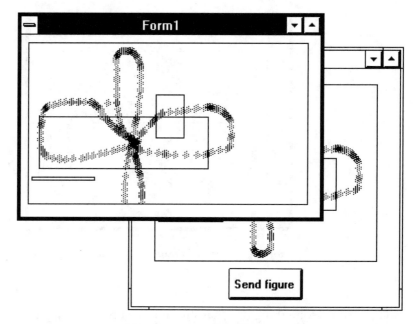

Figure 10-10. Server-Client Graphics Link with Update

```
Sub Command1_Click ()
    Picture1.LinkSend
End Sub
```

Now we're all set: Make the Exe file Server.Exe and run it. Once again, the server application appears on the screen. Next, click it once to make it active as a server. Now bring up the client application in Visual Basic again and run it. Click it once to establish the link and send over the original version of the figure in the server's picture box.

Next, we can generate some random rectangles. Click the server's window a few times to generate them as shown in Figure 10-9. Again, they do not appear in the client window. However, we can change that by clicking the "Send figure" button. Click it, and you'll see the whole figure transferred, rectangles and all, to the picture box in the client application, similar to Figure 10-10. And that's how to maintain a graphics DDE link.

Now we're pretty familiar with the idea of clients and servers, and how to set them up in our programs. However, it may surprise you to learn that there are actually times that a client can act as a server and send data itself. Now that we've set up our own server application, let's check into this.

Sending Data Back to a DDE Server

Usually, of course, data goes from a DDE server to the client, automatically if there is a hot link between then, or on request if the link is cold. However, we can reverse the direction of data flow in a link if we want to with the **LinkPoke** method. In other words, for each link we've set up between applications, we can actually send data two ways if required, but to send data from the client to the server, we have to take specific steps (i.e., there is no such thing as a two way hot DDE link).

Let's see this in action. Currently, this is the way the **Form_Click( )** Sub procedure looks in our client application:

```
Sub Form_Click ()
    Picture1.LinkMode = NONE
    Picture1.LinkTopic = "Server|Figure"
    Picture1.LinkItem = "Picture1"
    Picture1.LinkMode = HOT
End Sub
```

We can change this so that the first time the client form is clicked, it establishes the link:

```
Sub Form_Click ()
    Static First
    First = First + 1
    If First = 1 Then
        Picture1.LinkMode = NONE
        Picture1.LinkTopic = "Server|Figure"
        Picture1.LinkItem = "Picture1"
        Picture1.LinkMode = HOT
    Else
        :

    End If
End Sub
```

When the link is established like this with the server, the figure is transferred to the client's picture box. The next time the client is clicked, however, let's draw a circle in that picture box, changing the figure we got from the server:

```
Sub Form_Click ()
    Static First
    First = First + 1
```

```
        If First = 1 Then
            Picture1.LinkMode = NONE
            Picture1.LinkTopic = "Server|Figure"
            Picture1.LinkItem = "Picture1"
            Picture1.LinkMode = HOT
        Else
→           x = Picture1.ScaleWidth/2
→           y = Picture1.ScaleHeight/2
→           r = Picture1.Width/4
→           Picture1.Circle (x, y), r
                :
        End If
    End Sub
```

At this point, the circle appears in the client and not in the server; however, we can reverse the direction of a DDE link temporarily with the **LinkPoke** method:

```
    Sub Form_Click ()
        Static First
        First = First + 1
        If First = 1 Then
            Picture1.LinkMode = NONE
            Picture1.LinkTopic = "Server|Figure"
            Picture1.LinkItem = "Picture1"
            Picture1.LinkMode = HOT
        Else
            x = Picture1.ScaleWidth/2
            y = Picture1.ScaleHeight/2
            r = Picture1.Width/4
            Picture1.Circle (x, y), r
→           Picture1.LinkPoke
        End If
    End Sub
```

This statement reverses the roles of client and server temporarily, so the picture in the client's picture box is sent to the server, as shown in Figure 10-11. Our attempt to send data back to the server is a success.

It turns out that this method can be very useful not just for sending data to the server but for sending commands as well. In fact, there is an additional way to do this with DDE: We can send commands explicitly.

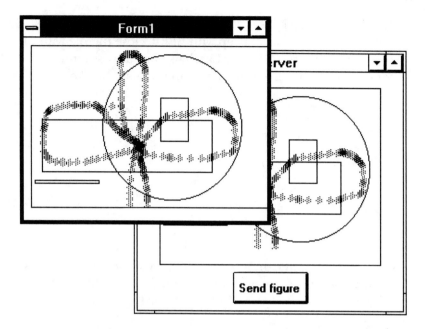

Figure 10-11. Poking Data Back to the Server

Sending Commands through DDE

Some applications let you send commands to them through a DDE channel. For example, Excel will accept any of its legal macro commands like OPEN( ), AVERAGE, CLOSE( ), and so on (see the Excel Function Reference for additional commands) through DDE. To see how this works, set up a hot link with Excel:

```
Sub Check1_Click ()
 Text1.LinkMode = NONE
 Text1.LinkTopic = "Excel|Sheet1"
 Text1.LinkItem = "R1C1"
 Text1.LinkMode = HOT
    :

End Sub
```

This connects Excel to a text box named **Text1**. To actually send the commands, we need to use the **LinkExecute** method. For example, we can open a file named C:\Excel\Sheet1.Xls like this: OPEN(" "C:\EXCEL\SHEET1.XLS" "). Next, we can have Excel beep with BEEP, close the file with FILE.CLOSE( ), and then quit with QUIT( ). Excel also lets us pass a number of such macro commands at once if we enclose them in square brackets this way:

```
Sub Check1_Click ()
 Text1.LinkMode = NONE
 Text1.LinkTopic = "Excel¦Sheet1"
 Text1.LinkItem = "R1C1"
 Text1.LinkMode = HOT
 Text1.LinkExecute
 "[OPEN(""C:\EXCEL\SHEET1.XLS"")][BEEP][FILE.CLOSE()][QUIT()]"
End Sub
```

Give this a try. After the link is set up, Excel opens Sheet1.Xls, beeps, closes the file and quits. Not all Windows applications that support DDE can take commands this way (for example, WinWord cannot), but some, like Excel can.

However, this raises one of the conventional problems of DDE: What if the other application is not running? As things stand now, we would get a Visual Basic error message in a message box indicating that the other application is not running, and asking us whether we'd like to start it. It turns out that this is a trappable error, and that often we can take care of errors like this ourselves.

Handling DDE Errors

The trappable DDE errors appear in Table 10-1. We can make use of these errors in the same way as we did in the last chapter. For example, if the other application isn't running, we'll get a No Foreign Application error, number 282, and we can make use of that in our programs.

For example, if Excel is not running, we can start it. To begin, we can set up an error handler:

```
Sub Check1_Click ()
 On Error GoTo ErrorHandler    ←
 Text1.LinkMode = NONE
 Text1.LinkTopic = "Excel¦Sheet1"
 Text1.LinkItem = "R1C1"
 Text1.LinkMode = HOT
```

Error	Means
280	The DDE channel has not been fully closed, waiting for a response
281	No More DDE channels
282	No foreign application responded to a DDE initiate
283	Multiple applications responded to a DDE initiate
284	DDE channel locked
285	Received Negative DDE Acknowledgement from foreign application
286	Timeout occurred while waiting for DDE response
287	User Hit DDE Attention Key
288	Destination is busy
289	No Data for DDE data message
290	Data in wrong format
291	Foreign application terminated
292	An invalid DDE channel has been referenced
293	A DDE Method was invoked with no channel open
294	Invalid DDE Link format
295	The message queue was filled and a DDE message was lost
296	A PasteLink has been executed on a channel with an existing PasteLink

Table 10-1. DDE Errors

```
Text1.LinkExecute
"[OPEN(""C:\EXCEL\SHEET1.XLS"")][BEEP][FILE.CLOSE()][QUIT()]"
ErrorHandler:
    :

End Sub
```

Next, we check to make sure that the error was number 282, in which case we can start Excel using Visual Basic's Shell function, which will start a Windows application like this:

```
Sub Check1_Click ()
 On Error GoTo ErrorHandler
 Text1.LinkMode = NONE
```

```
Text1.LinkTopic = "Excel¦Sheet1"
Text1.LinkItem = "R1C1"
Text1.LinkMode = HOT
Text1.LinkExecute
"[OPEN(""C:\EXCEL\SHEET1.XLS"")][BEEP][FILE.CLOSE()][QUIT()]"
ErrorHandler:
If Err = 282 Then    'No foreign application error.
→    temp = Shell("C:\Excel\Excel.Exe")
       :

End Sub
```

After Excel is started, we can execute a Resume statement so that Visual Basic goes back and tries to reestablish the link:

```
Sub Check1_Click ()
 On Error GoTo ErrorHandler
 Text1.LinkMode = NONE
 Text1.LinkTopic = "Excel¦Sheet1"
 Text1.LinkItem = "R1C1"
 Text1.LinkMode = HOT
 Text1.LinkExecute
 "[OPEN(""C:\EXCEL\SHEET1.XLS"")][BEEP][FILE.CLOSE()][QUIT()]"
 ErrorHandler:
 If Err = 282 Then    'No foreign application error.
     temp = Shell("C:\Excel\Excel.Exe")
→       Resume
 Else
     :

End Sub
```

If, on the other hand, this was not the error that we can handle, we place a message box on the screen ourselves indicating which error occurred:

```
Sub Check1_Click ()
 On Error GoTo ErrorHandler
 Text1.LinkMode = NONE
 Text1.LinkTopic = "Excel¦Sheet1"
 Text1.LinkItem = "R1C1"
 Text1.LinkMode = HOT
 Text1.LinkExecute
 "[OPEN(""C:\EXCEL\SHEET1.XLS"")][BEEP][FILE.CLOSE()][QUIT()]"
 ErrorHandler:
```

```
        If Err = 282 Then    'No foreign application error.
            temp = Shell("C:\Excel\Excel.Exe")
            Resume
        Else
→           MsgBox "Error number" + Str$(Err)
→           Exit Sub
        End If
    End Sub
```

That's it, then. If Excel is not currently running, we intercept the error and start it ourselves so that we can set up the link. This is an extraordinarily powerful DDE technique. We're no longer dependent on linking only to Windows applications that are already running. Instead, we can start the other Windows application if we wish, and this is a valuable use for DDE errors. (In fact, if the other application accepts commands with LinkExecute as Excel does, we can also terminate it as well.)

However, because there are two applications involved here, we should note that DDE errors don't only occur when we're handling events in one of them. For example, if the link is hot and the server application sends data in the wrong format, a DDE error is generated even if nothing is happening in the client. Nonetheless, the client should have some way of noticing that such errors are occurring and be able to either fix or report the problem. For this reason, when there's a DDE error, a *LinkError* event is generated.

This kind of event is associated with the objects that can support DDE: forms, picture boxes, text boxes, and labels. For instance, two common DDE errors are running out of memory (Err = 7) and attempting to send data in the wrong format (Err = 290). If we were using a text box, **Text1**, then you'll find this template for the associated LinkError event in the code window:

```
Sub Text1_LinkError (LinkError As Integer)

End Sub
```

Note that an argument is passed to this Sub procedure: LinkError. We can test that argument, checking to see what kind of error occurred like this:

```
Sub Text1_LinkError (LinkError As Integer)

    If LinkError = 7 Then    'Out of memory
        MsgBox "Out of memory for DDE"
```

```
        End If

        If LinkError = 290 Then 'Wrong format for data
            MsgBox "DDE data in wrong format"
        End If

    End Sub
```

Note that if our application was a server and not a client, we'd have to intercept DDE errors like this in the **Form_LinkError( )** Sub procedure since only forms can act as servers.

The LinkOpen and LinkClose Events

LinkError is one of three DDE events that exist: The other two are LinkOpen and LinkClose. As you might imagine, the LinkOpen event occurs when a link is established with the current application as a participant, and LinkClose occurs when such a link is terminated. Both kinds of events occur for server or client applications (i.e., forms can have LinkOpen and LinkClose events in server applications, as well as in picture boxes, text boxes and labels in client applications).

The LinkOpen event also offers us an important option: We can refuse the link if we want to. For example, if we have a form that can act as a server (i.e., its **LinkMode** is set to Server), then other applications may try to establish conversations with it, depending on its **LinkTopic** and **LinkMode**. If you look through the code window, you'll find this Sub procedure template:

```
    Sub Form_LinkOpen (Cancel As Integer)

    End Sub
```

Notice in particular that an argument is passed to this procedure: Cancel. If we set this argument to True (-1) in our procedure, then the link will be refused. If we leave it False (0), then the link will be accepted. In this way, we can restrict the number of such links we allow, or refuse links until our data is ready. In a similar way, we can use the LinkClose event to indicate when a link is broken (note that it takes no arguments):

```
    Sub Form_LinkClose()

    End Sub
```

This is fine as far as it goes, but we're operating in the dark here: Who's trying to establish or break DDE links with us (how is that information encoded)? And what controls is Visual Basic connecting the foreign application to? To find the answers to these and other questions, we can turn to some advanced DDE topics next.

Pasting Links in Code

Let's say that we had a window with two text boxes, and that we wanted to let the user connect them, as clients, to an application of their choice. In other words, we don't know ahead of time what application they want to link to. We've seen that this can be done at design-time in Visual Basic by copying an item in another application and then using Paste Link in Visual Basic. However, the user usually isn't present at design-time, so that capability isn't useful here. Instead, we can provide a Paste Link option in our programs that can be used at run-time. This way, the user will be able to paste links to the controls of their choosing (i.e., we won't be able to program the target control name into our code while writing the program).

Let's see how this works. Start up Visual Basic and place two text boxes, **Text1** and **Text2**, on the default form. Then add an Edit menu with one item in it: Paste Link, with the **CtlName PasteItem**, as in Figure 10-12. Next, click on Paste Link in the menu to open the associated procedure:

```
Sub PasteItem ()

End Sub
```

When the user selects this menu choice, they want to paste a link into our application from another application. To do that, they must first have copied an item in that other application, which now resides in the clipboard. Our task now is to decipher the information there and connect it to the correct control in our application.

In general, applications provide link information in the clipboard like this: Application¦Topic!Item. This is stored in the part of the clipboard reserved for DDE link information, and, when the user tries to paste a link in our application, we assume that it is waiting for us there. We can retrieve this text using the clipboard's **GetText( )** method, specifying that we want DDE link information with CF_LINK:

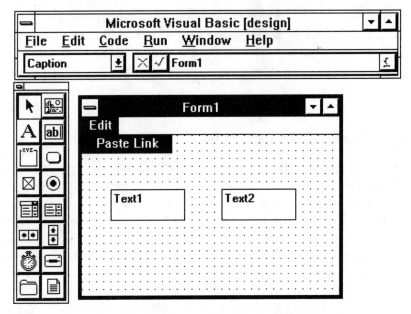

Figure 10-12. Paste Link Application Template

```
Sub PasteItem ()
    DDEData$ = Clipboard.GetText(CF_LINK)
        :
End Sub
```

The constant CF_LINK, which indicates that we want DDE format data from the clipboard, is defined in CONSTANT.TXT, so we should include that in our application's global module. Next, we have to decipher the name of the DDE topic and item from the string we received, DDEData$.

We can do that with some Visual Basic string manipulations. After we get the **LinkTopic** and **LinkItem**, we'll be able to connect them to the control that the user has selected. In other words, let's say that the user selected a cell in an Excel spreadsheet, and copied it, placing it into the clipboard. Next, they might select a text box in our application (i.e., giving it the focus), open our Edit menu, and paste the link. That means that we have to determine which of the two text boxes is active (i.e., has the focus) now. We can do that by using the **ActiveControl** property of the Screen object. That is, if the user selects **Text1**, then **Screen.ActiveControl** will equal **Text1**.

First, we set the control's **LinkMode** to NONE:

```
Sub PasteItem ()
    DDEData$ = Clipboard.GetText(CF_LINK)
    Screen.ActiveControl.LinkMode = NONE
        :

End Sub
```

Next, we can cut the **LinkTopic** out of the string DDEData$ this way (that string looks like this now: "ApplicationGTopic!Item"):

```
        Sub PasteItem ()
            DDEData$ = Clipboard.GetText(CF_LINK)
            Screen.ActiveControl.LinkMode = NONE
→           Screen.ActiveControl.LinkTopic = Left$(DDEData$,
                InStr(DDEData$, "!")-1)
                :

        End Sub
```

After that, we can cut the **LinkItem** from DDEData$ like this:

```
        Sub PasteItem ()
            DDEData$ = Clipboard.GetText(CF_LINK)
            Screen.ActiveControl.LinkMode = NONE
            Screen.ActiveControl.LinkTopic = Left$(DDEData$, InStr(DDEData$,
                "!")-1)
→           Screen.ActiveControl.LinkItem = Right$(DDEData$,

                Len(DDEData$) - InStr(DDEData$, "!"))
                :

        End Sub
```

The last step is to set the active control's **LinkMode** to HOT, and we're done:

```
        Sub PasteItem ()
            DDEData$ = Clipboard.GetText(CF_LINK)
            Screen.ActiveControl.LinkMode = NONE
            Screen.ActiveControl.LinkTopic = Left$(DDEData$, InStr(DDEData$,
                "!")-1)
            Screen.ActiveControl.LinkItem = Right$(DDEData$,
                Len(DDEData$) - InStr(DDEData$, "!"))
→           Screen.ActiveControl.LinkMode = HOT
        End Sub
```

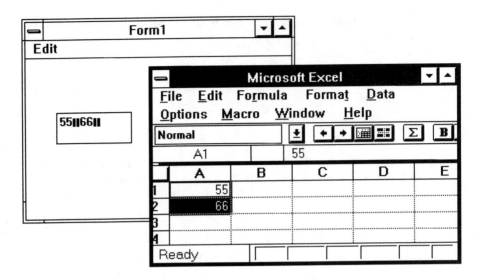

Figure 10-13. Run-Time Paste Link Operation

At this point, the link is established with the other application. For example, we can select two cells, R1C1 and R2C1, in an Excel spreadsheet and copy them using the Excel Copy menu. This places the string "Excel|Sheet1!R1C1:R2C1" in the clipboard. If **Text1** is the active control when the user selects the Paste item in our Edit menu, we can then use that data and set **Text1**'s **LinkTopic** to "Excel|Sheet1" and its **LinkItem** to "R1C1:R2C1." Next we establish the link, as shown in Figure 10-13. In this way, we allow the user to select what links they want to set up with which of our controls they choose.

That's one side of the story. So far, we've enabled the user to form client links with specific controls. However, we can also set up our application as a server by placing a Copy command in our Edit menu. In other words, we'll let the user set up a server link the same way as we did in the beginning of the chapter — by simply using the Copy command. Here, however, we'll use our own application's Copy command, not Visual Basic's. Later, they can use Paste Link in another application, forming the link with any application that supports DDE. Let's look into this next.

Customized Server Applications

Our goal here is to add a Copy item to our application's Edit menu so that the user can set up a link — which they can then paste into another application.

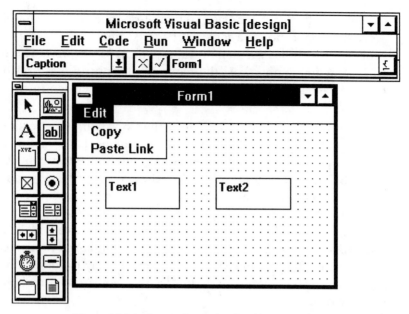

Figure 10-14. Custom Server Application with Copy Item

To start, add a Copy item to the Edit menu, as shown in Figure 10-14, giving it the **CtlName CopyItem**.

Next, open the **CopyItem_Click ( )** Sub procedure:

```
Sub CopyItem_Click ()

End Sub
```

We're going to load DDE data into the clipboard, so we begin by clearing it of any data that might be in there now, like this (using the Clipboard object's **Clear** method):

```
Sub CopyItem_Click ()
    Clipboard.Clear
        :

End Sub
```

Now we can assemble the string we want to send to the clipboard. In general, as we've seen, DDE strings look like this: "Application | Topic!Item." Let's give this project the name Custom.Mak (and save the form as Custom.Frm, the global module as Custom.Bas), so that our application name will be Custom. Since this application is a server, the topic comes from the form's **LinkTopic** property, which has the default value "Form1" right now. The real problem here is the item name (i.e., the name of the control that provides the data) because names like **Text1** and **Text2** are not stored when the program runs.

In other words, when the user selects the Copy item, they've already selected one of the controls in our application, making it the active control. The problem now is locating that item's CtlName so we can copy it because the actual **CtlNames** are not present when the program runs. Visual Basic handles this problem by providing a **Tag** property for each object. The **Tag** property is made up of a string that is preserved even when the program runs, and a common use for the **Tag** property is exactly the one we'll make of it: to store the **CtlNames** like **Text1** and **Text2**. Click on **Text1** now, locate the **Tag** property in the properties window, and set it to "Text1." Then do the same for **Text2**, setting its **Tag** property to "Text2." Now we can make up our DDE string like this:

```
Sub CopyItem_Click ()
    Clipboard.Clear
    DDEData$ = "Custom¦Form1!" + Screen.ActiveControl.Tag
       :

End Sub
```

After that, we can place it into the clipboard using the **Clipboard.SetText** method, indicating that it is a DDE string with the CF_LINK option:

```
Sub CopyItem_Click ()
    Clipboard.Clear
    DDEData$ = "Custom¦Form1!" + Screen.ActiveControl.Tag
    ClipBoard.SetText DDEData$, CF_LINK
       :

End Sub
```

Technically, we're ready to go at this point; however, it's customary for applications to store the data currently in the control in the clipboard at the same time so that the client application can read it immediately. For example, if the control selected was a text box or label, we want to place the text in it into the clipboard; if it was a picture, we want to place that into the clipboard.

We can actually check the type of the active control with the TypeOf keyword in an If statement. For example, we can check whether or not the active control is a text box like this:

```
If TypeOf Screen.ActiveControl Is TextBox Then...
```

Note that we must use Is instead of an equals sign (=) in an If TypeOf statement like this. We can make use of this statement like this:

```
Sub CopyItem_Click ()
    Clipboard.Clear
    DDEData$ = "Custom|Form1!" + Screen.ActiveControl.Tag
    ClipBoard.SetText DDEData$, CF_LINK

→   If TypeOf Screen.ActiveControl Is TextBox Then
        Clipboard.SetText Screen.ActiveControl.Text
    End If
        :

End Sub
```

Here we send the text in the active text box into the clipboard (note that it remains separate from the **DDEData$** string we placed in the clipboard earlier because we specified that that was a DDE string with CF_LINK). In addition, we can check for other types of controls. The control type returned by TypeOf can also include Label or PictureBox. We can test if the control is a label and, if so, send the caption to the clipboard like this:

```
Sub CopyItem_Click ()
    Clipboard.Clear
    DDEData$ = "Custom|Form1!" + Screen.ActiveControl.Tag
    ClipBoard.SetText DDEData$, CF_LINK

    If TypeOf Screen.ActiveControl Is TextBox Then
        Clipboard.SetText Screen.ActiveControl.Text
    End If

→   If TypeOf Screen.ActiveControl Is Label Then
        Clipboard.SetText Screen.ActiveControl.Caption
    End If
        :

End Sub
```

We can also check whether the active control is a picture box, and, if it is, send the picture like this (using the **Clipboard** object's **SetData** method):

```
Sub CopyItem_Click ()
    Clipboard.Clear
    DDEData$ = "Custom¦Form1!" + Screen.ActiveControl.Tag
    ClipBoard.SetText DDEData$, CF_LINK

    If TypeOf Screen.ActiveControl Is TextBox Then
        Clipboard.SetText Screen.ActiveControl.Text
    End If

    If TypeOf Screen.ActiveControl Is Label Then
        Clipboard.SetText Screen.ActiveControl.Caption
    End If

    If TypeOf Screen.ActiveControl Is PictureBox Then
        Clipboard.SetData Screen.ActiveControl.Picture
    End If

End Sub
```

Our new application, complete with Copy and Paste Link, is ready. For example, you can use it to establish a server link with Excel. We might copy the text in **Text2** with the Copy item, and then move over to Excel, choosing its Paste Link option. That establishes us as a DDE server, as shown in Figure 10-15.

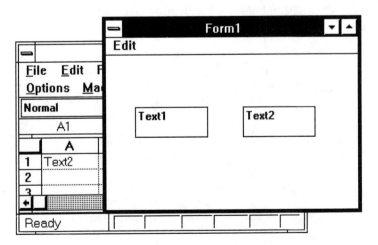

Figure 10-15. Custom Server Application in Action

That's it for DDE — and that's it for our book. We've gone far with Visual Basic. From our most elementary forms up through buttons, menus, dialog boxes, and file handling. From there, we continued with graphics and the mouse, adding more power to our Windows applications. Finally, we saw how to handle errors, some advanced data handling techniques, and now even dynamic data exchange. Now all that remains is putting all this power to work (happy programming).

Index

About the Author

Steven Holzner, 33, is the author of 14 books on personal computing and a former contributing editor to *PC Magazine*. He earned his B.S. at MIT and his Ph.D. at Cornell University. He has travelled to over 30 countries and has lived for a year each in Hong Kong and Hawaii. Steven spends as many summers as he can in the Austrian Alps.

Steven is bicoastal, dividing his time between California and New York, where he teaches physics at Cornell University and is part owner of a 100-acre estate. He's currently at work on a novel and, by his own admission, still hasn't learned how to tie a tie properly.

The New Peter Norton Microcomputer Libraries from Brady Publishing

All of the volumes in the Peter Norton Libraries, written in collaboration with The Peter Norton Computing Group, provide clear, in-depth discussions of the latest developments in computer hardware, operating systems, and programming. Fully tested and rigorously reviewed, these libraries deserve a special place on your bookshelf. These libraries are comprised of two series:

The Peter Norton Hardware Library gives you an insider's grasp of your computer and the way it works. Included are such bestselling classics as *Inside the IBM PC, Inside the Apple Macintosh*, and *The Hard Disk Companion*.

The Peter Norton Programming Library offers books and book/disk utilities for readers at all levels of expertise—beginning to intermediate to advanced. They focuses on creating programs that work right away and offers the best tips and techniques in the industry. This library includes *Advanced BASIC, Advanced Assembly Language, QBasic Programing*, and more.

For a direct, no-nonsense approach to performance computing, look to Brady Publishing's Peter Norton Libraries.

Visual Basic
Disk Offer

A companion disk is available for this book. The companion disk contains:

- All of the programs described in the book
- A battleship game for Windows
- A graphics sprite animation example
- A color editor for designing custom Windows colors

To order your disk, simply fill out coupon below and mail it to MICROSERVICES, 200 Old Tappan Road, Old Tappan, NJ 07675.

Visual Basic

I am ordering the companion disk for this book and have enclosed my check for $15.00 payable to Simon & Schuster, Inc.

Please send a   ☐ 3.5-inch disk   ISBN: 0-13-489287-9

☐ 5.25-inch disk   ISBN: 0-13-952755-9

Name_____

Address_____

City _____ State _____ Zip _____

Phone Number (   ) _____

Please mail this request to MICROSERVICES, 200 Old Tappan Road, Old Tappan, NJ 07675. For more information call (201) 767-5054.